MIND
IN
MOTION

MIND
IN
MOTION

How Action Shapes Thought

BARBARA TVERSKY

BASIC
BOOKS
NEW YORK

Basic Books
Hachette Book Group
1290 Avenue of the Americas, New York, NY 10104
www.basicbooks.com

Printed in the United States of America
First Edition: May 2019

Published by Basic Books, an imprint of Perseus Books, LLC, a subsidiary of
Hachette Book Group, Inc. The Basic Books name and logo is a trademark of
the Hachette Book Group.

The Hachette Speakers Bureau provides a wide range of authors for speaking
events. To find out more, go to www.hachettespeakersbureau.com or call
(866) 376-6591.

The publisher is not responsible for websites (or their content) that are not
owned by the publisher.

Print book interior design by Linda Mark.

Library of Congress Cataloging-in-Publication Data

Names: Tversky, Barbara Gans, author.
Title: Mind in motion: how action shapes thought / Barbara Tversky.
Description: New York: Basic Books, [2019] | Includes bibliographical
  references and index.
Identifiers: LCCN 2019007927| ISBN 9780465093069 (hardcover) |
  ISBN 9780465093076 (ebook)
Subjects: LCSH: Thought and thinking. | Intellect. | Space. | Cognition.
Classification: LCC BF441 .T94 2019 | DDC 153.4—dc23
LC record available at https://lccn.loc.gov/2019007927

ISBNs: 978-0-465-09306-9 (hardcover); 978-0-465-09307-6 (ebook)

LSC-C

10 9 8 7 6 5 4 3 2 1

To Amos, whose mind was always in motion.

Contents

PROLOGUE

Moving in Space: The Foundation of Thought 1

PART I: THE WORLD IN THE MIND

CHAPTER ONE

The Space of the Body: Space Is for Action 9

CHAPTER TWO

The Bubble Around the Body: People, Places, and Things 33

CHAPTER THREE

Here and Now and There and Then: The Spaces Around Us 59

CHAPTER FOUR

Transforming Thought 85

PART II: THE MIND IN THE WORLD

CHAPTER FIVE

The Body Speaks a Different Language 109

CHAPTER SIX

Points, Lines, and Perspective: Space in Talk and Thought 141

CHAPTER SEVEN

Boxes, Lines, and Trees: Talk and Thought About Almost Everything Else 155

CHAPTER EIGHT

Spaces We Create: Maps, Diagrams, Sketches, Explanations, Comics 189

CHAPTER NINE

Conversations with a Page: Design, Science, and Art 257

CHAPTER TEN

The World Is a Diagram 277

The Nine Laws of Cognition 289
Figure Credits 291
Bibliographic Notes 295
Index 359

Moving in Space:
The Foundation of Thought

> *A creature didn't think in order to move; it just*
> *moved, and by moving it discovered the world*
> *that then formed the content of its thoughts.*
>
> —Larissa MacFarquhar, "The mind-expanding ideas
> of Andy Clark," *The New Yorker*

Everything is always in motion. Physicists tell us that if the quivering molecules in your desk moved in sync, the desk would leap from the floor. Even sedentary plants grow and sway and turn toward the sun and open and close. They have to; they would die if they didn't move. Space places two fundamental constraints on movement, constraints that are reflected in thought: proximity—near places are easier to get to than far ones; and gravity—going up is more effortful than going down.

Thought, too, is constantly moving, and sometimes hard to catch. Ideas leapfrog over ideas. But there it is: idea. I've frozen it, reified it into something static, the only way to catch it. From the never-ceasing flux around us, we carve entities out of space and out of time: people, places, things, events. We freeze them, turn them into words and concepts. We change those moving things into static things so that we can act on them with our minds.

Constant motion in space is a given, the background for everything that has happened and that will happen. No wonder it is the foundation of thought. Action in space came long before language, as did thought based on action in space.

1

Our actions in space change space, change ourselves, and change others. Our actions create things we put in space that change us and others. They change our thought and the thought of others. The things we create (like these words) stay there, in space, changing the thought of people we will never know and can't even imagine.

We don't just freeze the stuff in space and time. We study its form and look for its structure: in our bodies, in our actions and reactions, in the world, in the events that happen in the world, in the language we speak. We find the parts and how they connect to form a whole. The parts and how they fit together tell us what the things can do and what can be done with them. We look for patterns, lines, circles, shapes, branching. We create structure, too, in actions, in talk, in communities, in science, in art—painting, sculpture, film, dance, poetry, drama, opera, journalism, fiction, music. Structure is what holds the pieces together; without structure, things fall apart. And sometimes we do just that, deconstruct and even destroy, to see what happens, to shake things up, to find new structures. Pick Up Sticks. Rearrange the furniture. Reorganize the company. Select musical notes from a random number table. Read *Hopscotch* in any order. Revolt. Spew chaos on the world.

Prose is linear, one word after another. Narratives have a linear structure driven by time, theories have a linear structure directed by logic. In theory, that is. The structure of Perec's *Life: A User's Manual* is place, an apartment building and a puzzle, not time. The linearity of prose doesn't harness readers, they can jump back and forth. Speaking is linear, one word after another, but that doesn't stop speakers from interrupting themselves with tangential thoughts nor does it stop listeners from doing the same. Then there are our own thoughts, frequently articulated in inner speech; they hardly walk a straight line and sometimes fly out in too many directions at once. Music is linear in time but spatial over the instruments, which can come in at different times and play different notes at different paces and places. Painting has composition, not linear, but center and periphery. Until Pollack and Rothko. Structure is complicated. It gets done, undone, and redone.

Pleas, plays, sermons, campaign speeches. Like music, they zig and zag between the earthly and the lofty, the logical and the emotional, stories that become parables with messages; they zig and zag emotionally, pensive, spirited, ominous, wistful, joyful. They change pace, slow and ponderous, fast and light. Narrative does that, too.

Formal gardens are arranged in perfectly symmetric patterns, with distinct straight paths among the beds of flowers and pruned trees; everything is clear and certain; don't dare go off the paths. Chinese gardens are different. The paths curve and twist this way and that, up and down, always new vistas around the bend pulling you onward; little is clear, nothing certain; you get lost, and then found.

Writing a book makes you, or me, think of structure. There is structure to this book, but you don't have to stay on the paths, you are free to explore it like a Chinese garden rather than a formal one. The book means to show how we think about space and how we use space to think. These are the two parts of the book. The premise is audacious: spatial thinking, rooted in perception of space and action in it, is the foundation for all thought. The foundation, not the entire edifice. Try describing the faces of friends, places you love, events that were meaningful. The memories and images may be vivid, but words flail and fail to capture them. Think about rearranging the furniture in your living room or how to fold a sweater or how many windows were in your childhood home or where the X key is on the keyboard. You might feel your eyes moving or your body squirming. Words alone won't do it.

This focus, on space, action, and thought, means that there are large swaths of excellent work I couldn't include, to my regret. This book is meant to interest many different communities, the diverse communities that I've had the good fortune to work with: psychologists, computer scientists, linguists, neuroscientists, biologists, chemists, designers, engineers, artists, art educators, museum educators, science educators, and others who, for one reason or another, are interested in spatial thinking. As for a stroll in a Chinese garden, some of you may want to walk from end to end, others may go hither and thither, visiting some sights and skipping others. You don't have to look at every tree and flower.

Below, a guide for special interests.

For the fundamentals, how perception and action mold thinking about the spaces we inhabit: Chapters One (space of the body), Two (space around the body), Three (space of navigation).

For varieties and transformations of spatial thinking and spatial ability, Chapter Four.

For ways gesture reflects and affects thought, Chapter Five.

For talk and thought about space and just about everything else: Chapters Five, Six, and Seven.

For designing and using cognitive tools, maps, diagrams, notation, charts, graphs, visualizations, explanations, comics, sketches, design, and art, Chapters Eight, Nine, and Ten.

An artist I know and admire, Gideon Rubin, says he always leaves his paintings unfinished. That way, the viewers finish them. His art is based in old nostalgic photographs, the kind you might find in your grandparents' albums, sweet photos of children and youths in happy settings, looking at the camera. He paints over the faces so you find yourself looking at, indeed feeling, the postures of the body and you realize how much you learn from the bodies and the clothing and the background. You look at the background and the clothing and you realize that you usually miss that because you're looking at the faces. You can fill in the empty faces, with your grandmother's or your cousin's, and you realize that you forgot what people looked like when they were young. And many viewers fill in so intently that they are sure they saw a face.

In science, history, politics, perhaps even more than in art, nothing is ever finished.

That said, this book is finished. Or rather, I have to let it go.

Research is nearly impossible to do without funding, and I have been fortunate for support from NSF, ONR, NIMH, AFOSR, and the John Templeton Foundation. I have been blessed by the many students, friends, and colleagues whose thinking I have drawn on, directly or indirectly, over many years. Most of you are unaware of this book and haven't seen it. I apologize to those I've forgotten, to those I've misrepresented or failed to represent. There was so much more I wanted to include. I've reduced you to an alphabetic list, which pains me; each of you gave me something unique and each of you is insightful, inimitable, and irreplaceable. Maneesh Agrawala, Gemma Anderson, Mireille Betrancourt, Gordon Bower, Jonathan Bresman, Jerry Bruner, David Bryant, Stu Card, Daniel Casasanto, Roberto Casati, Juliet Chou, Eve Clark, Herb Clark, Tony Cohn, Michel Denis, Susan Epstein, Yvonne Eriksson, Steve Feiner, Felice Frankel, Nancy Franklin, Christian Freksa, Randy Gallistel, Rochel Gelman, Dedre Gentner, John Gero, Valeria Giardino, Susan Goldin-Meadow, Pat Hanrahan, Eric Henney, Bridgette Martin Hard, Julie Heiser, Kathy Hemenway, Azadeh Jamalian, Danny Kahneman, Andrea Kantrowitz, T. J. Kelleher, David Kirsh, Stephen Kosslyn, Pim Levelt, Steve Levinson, Elizabeth Marsh, Katinka Matson, Rebecca McGinnis, Julie Morrison, Morris Moscovitch, Lynn Nadel, Jane Nisselson, Steven Pinker, Dan Schacter, Roger Shepard, Ben Shneiderman, Ed Smith, Masaki Suwa, Holly Taylor, Herb Terrace, Anthony Wagner, Mark Wing-Davey, Jeff Zacks.

For not enough years, there was Amos, and his voice stays with me. The kids, too, my second biggest fans, I can hear all of them echoing him, shouting, "Go, Mom," the way I shouted at them watching their soccer games.

PART I

THE WORLD IN THE MIND

CHAPTER ONE

The Space of the Body:
Space Is for Action

In which we show that we have an insider's view of the body, one
shaped by our actions and sensations, unlike our outsider view of other
things in our world that is shaped by appearance. Mirror neurons map
others' bodies onto our own, allowing us to understand other bodies
through our own and to coordinate our actions with theirs.

WE BEGIN IN OUR SKIN, THAT THIN, FLEXIBLE MEMBRANE THAT
encloses our bodies and separates us from everything else. A highly
significant boundary. All our actions take place in the space outside
our skin, and our lives depend on those actions. As any mother will
happily tell you, that activity begins before birth. Who knows why
those curious creatures growing inside us keep "kicking"—perhaps
to find a more comfortable position? Or why they seem so active at
importune times—one of them kept popping my dress up and down
during my PhD orals.

Mercifully, bodies do far more than kick. They eventually perform
an astounding assortment of activities. The harmonious coordination underlying those diverse behaviors depends on the continuous
integration of a variable stream of information from many senses
with the articulated actions of dozens of muscles (apologies for beginning with such a mouthful!). Although our skin encloses and separates our bodies from the surrounding world, accomplishing those
activities entails countless interactions with the world. We cannot

truly be separated from the world around us. It is those interactions that underlie our conceptions of our bodies.

Viewed from the outside, bodies are like other familiar objects: tables, chairs, apples, trees, dogs, or cars. We become adept at rapidly recognizing those common objects, primarily from their outlines, their contours, in their prototypical orientations. The contours of objects are, in turn, shaped by the configuration of their parts, legs and bodies for dogs and tables, trunks and canopies for trees. That skill, recognizing objects, takes up residency in a slew of places in the brain. Faces in one array, bodies in another, scenes in yet another. Those regions are active—light up—when we view those kinds of things and not when we view things from other categories.

For objects (and faces), some views are better than others. An upside-down table or tree is harder to recognize than a right-side-up version; the backside of a dog or the top view of a bicycle is harder to recognize than side views of either. A good view is one that shows the distinctive features of the object. A prototypical dog has four legs (like a prototypical table), an elongated horizontal tube for a body, and a symmetric head with eyes, snout, and a mouth as well as ears protruding from either side. The best view of a dog would show those features. Exactly those views, the ones that present more of the characteristic features in the proper configuration, are the ones we are fastest to recognize and the ones we judge as better representations of the object. For many objects, like dogs or tables, the best views are of course upright, and three-quarters view or profile. In many cases, the contours or silhouettes of good views are sufficient for rapid recognition.

BODIES AND THEIR PARTS

Just as for objects, contours of canonical orientations are especially effective for recognizing bodies—when we view them from the outside. But, singularly, for bodies we also have an insider perspective. That intimate insider perspective comes with many extras. We know what bodies can do and what bodies feel like from the inside. We can't have that knowledge for chairs or even bugs (Kafka aside) or dogs or chimpanzees. We know what it feels like to stand tall or sit slumped, to climb stairs and trees, to jump and hop, to fasten buttons and tie shoes, to signal thumbs up or OK, to cry and laugh. We know not only what it feels like to act in those ways but, even more significantly, also what it *means* to act in those ways, stretching or slumping, crying or laughing. Importantly, we can map other bodies and their actions onto our own, suggesting that we understand other bodies not only by recognizing them but also by internalizing them.

Before that, we map our bodies onto our brains, onto the homunculus, the "little man," sprawled ear-to-ear across the top shell, the cortex, of our brains. (See Figure 1.1.) The cortex is a thick, crenellated layer splayed over the parts of the brain that are evolutionarily older. From the outside, the brain looks like a giant walnut. And like a walnut, the brain is divided front to back into two not quite symmetric halves, or hemispheres, right and left. For the most part, the right hemisphere controls and has inputs from the left side of the body. The reverse holds for the left hemisphere. Each hemisphere is divided into plateaus called lobes that are separated by valleys, or sulci (singular, *sulcus*). It's hard not to talk about the cortex geographically, and undoubtedly there are analogies in the formation of plateaus and layers and valleys on the earth and in the brain. Those wrinkles create more surface, important for the land and important for the brain. The inputs from the various sensory systems are partly channeled to separate lobes of the cortex, for example, vision to the occipital lobe at back of the head and sound to the temporal lobes above the ears. Yet each lobe is wondrously complex, with many regions, many layers, many connections, many kinds of cells, and many functions. Remarkably, even single neurons can be specialized, for a specific view of a face or for tracking an object that moves behind a screen. And there are billions of them in the human brain. A recent estimate is eighty-six billion.

There are actually two pairs of homunculi splayed along the central sulcus; one pair maps the sensations from the body, the other pair maps motor output to the body. The pair on the left side of the

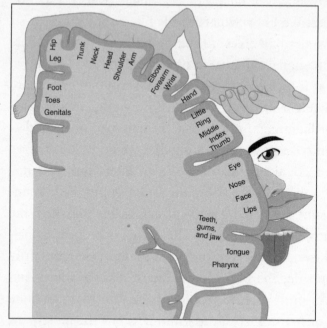

FIGURE 1.1.
Sensory homunculus.

brain maps the right side of the body and the pair on the right side of the brain maps the left side of the body. The sensory and motor homunculi face each other. The motor homunculus is, perhaps significantly, positioned more forward (technical terms: *anterior* or *frontal*), toward the eyes and nose. It controls the output, telling the muscles how to move. The sensory homunculus is positioned toward the back of the head (technical terms: *posterior* or *dorsal,* from Latin for "tail"). It brings the input from the many kinds of sensations our bodies respond to, position, pain, pressure, temperature, and more. The homunculi are strange little people, with oversized heads, huge tongues, enormous hands, and skinny torsos and limbs.

You can't help but see that these cortical proportions are far from the proportions of the body. Rather than representing the sizes of the body parts, the sizes of the cortical representations of the various body parts are proportional to the quantities of neurons ascending to them or descending from them. That is, the head and hands have more cortical neurons relative to their body size, and the torso and limbs have fewer cortical neurons relative to their body size. More neural connections mean more sensory sensitivity on the sensory side and more action articulation on the action side. The disproportionate sizes of cortical real estate make perfect sense once we think about the multitude of articulated actions that the face, tongue, and hands must perform and the sensory feedback needed to modulate their actions. Our tongues are involved in the intricate coordinated actions necessary for eating, sucking, and swallowing, for speaking, groaning, and singing, and for many other activities that I will leave to your imagination. Our mouths smile and frown and scowl, they blow bubbles and whistle and kiss. Hands type and play the piano, throw balls and catch them, weave and knit, tickle babies and pat puppies. Our toes, on the other hand, are sadly underused, incompetent, and unnoticed—until we stub them. That functional significance trounces size is deep inside us, or rather, right there at the top of the head.

Significance trounces size not only in the brain but also in talk and thought. We saw this in research in our laboratory. We first collected the body parts most frequently named across languages. Zipf's Law tells us that the more a term gets used, the shorter it gets; *co-op*, *TV*, and *NBA* are examples. The presumption is that if a body part is named across languages, it's probably important irrespective of culture. The top seven were head, hands, feet, arms, legs, front, back. All the names are short, and, in fact, all are important even compared to other useful parts, like elbow or forearm. We asked a large group of students to rank those parts by significance and another group by size. As expected, similar to the homunculus in the brain, significance and size didn't always line up. Significance reflected size of cortical territory, not body size: head and hands were rated as highly significant but aren't particularly large, and backs and legs are large but were rated lower in significance.

Next, we asked which body parts were faster for people to recognize, the large ones or the significant ones? We tried it two ways. In one study, people saw pairs of pictures of bodies, each in a different pose, each with a part highlighted. You might be thinking that people would naturally find large parts faster. To make all parts equal irrespective of size, we highlighted with a dot in the middle of the part. In the other study, people first saw a name of a body part and then a picture of a body with a part highlighted. In both studies, half the pairs had the same part highlighted and half had different parts highlighted. Participants were asked to indicate "same" or "different" as fast as possible. An easy task; there were very few errors. Our interest was in the time to respond: Would people respond faster for significant parts or for large ones? You've probably already guessed what happened. Significant parts were faster.

The triumph of significance over size was even stronger for name-body comparisons than for body-body comparisons. Names are a string of letters; they lack the concrete features of pictures like size and shape. Names, then, are more abstract than depictions. Similarly, associations to names of objects are more abstract than associations to depictions of objects. Names of things evoke abstract features like function and significance, whereas pictures of things evoke concrete perceptible features.

First General Fact Worth Remembering: Associations to names are more abstract than associations to pictures.

Remember that all the parts used in our studies were significant compared to familiar but less significant parts like shoulder or ankle. Notably, the word for each part—*head, hands, feet, arms, legs, front,* and *back*—has numerous extended uses, uses so common that we're unaware of their bodily origins. Here are just a few: head of the nation, lost his head; right-hand person, on the one hand, hands down; foot of the mountains, all feet; arm of a chair, arm of the government; the idea doesn't have legs, shake a leg, break a leg; up front, front organization; not enough backing, behind the back. Notice that some of these figurative meanings play on the appearance of the parts, elongated as in *the arms and legs of a chair;* others play on the functions of the parts, such as *the head of the nation* and *the idea has no legs.* Of course, many other body parts have figurative extensions: someone might be the butt of a joke or have their fingers into everything. Then there are all the places claiming to be the navel of the world—visiting all of them could keep you traveling for months—the navel, that odd dot on our bellies, a remnant of the lifeline that once connected us to our mothers. Once you start noticing figurative uses, you see and hear them everywhere.

Like our knowledge of space, we know about our bodies from a multitude of senses. We can see our own bodies as well as those of others. We can hear our footsteps and our hands clapping and our joints clicking and our mouths speaking. We sense temperature and texture and pressure and pleasure and pain and the positions of our limbs both from the surface of our skin and from proprioception, those sensations of our bodies from the inside. We know where our arms and legs are without looking, we can feel when we are off balance or about to be. It's mind-boggling to think of how much delicate and precise coordination of so many sensory systems is needed just to stand and walk, not to mention shoot a basket or do a cartwheel. We weren't born doing those things.

Babies have so much to learn. And they learn so fast: their brains create millions of synapses, connections between neurons, per second. But their brains also prune synapses. Otherwise, our brains would become tangled messes, everything connected to everything else, a multitude of possibilities but no focused action, no way to strengthen important connections and weaken irrelevant ones, no way to choose among all those possibilities and organize resources to act. Among other things, pruning allows us to quickly recognize objects in the world and to quickly catch falling teacups but not burning matches. But that process has costs: we can mistake a coyote for a dog and a heavy rock for a rubber ball.

This brings us to our **First Law of Cognition: There are no benefits without costs.** Searching through many possibilities to find the best can be time consuming and exhausting. Typically, we simply don't have enough time or energy to search and consider all the possibilities. Is it a friend or a stranger? Is it a dog or a coyote? We need to quickly extend our hands when a ball is tossed to us but quickly duck when a rock is hurled at us. Life, if nothing else, is a series of trade-offs. The trade-off here is between considering possibilities and acting effectively and efficiently. Like all laws in psychology,

this one is an oversimplification, and the small print has the usual caveats. Nevertheless, this law is so fundamental that we will return to
it again and again.

INTEGRATING BODIES: ACTION AND SENSATION

With this in mind, watching five-month-old babies is all the more
mystifying. On their backs, as they are now supposed to be placed,
they can suddenly catch sight of their hand and are captivated. They
stare intently at their hand as though it were the most interesting
thing in the world. They don't seem to understand that what they are
regarding so attentively is their own hand. They might move their
hand quite unintentionally and then watch the movement without
realizing that they've caused it. If you put your finger or a rattle in
their hand, they'll grasp it; grasping is reflexive. But if the hand and
the rattle disappear from sight, they won't track them. Gradually,
sight and sensation and action get integrated, starting at the top of
the body, hands first. Weeks later, after they've accomplished reaching and grasping with their hands, they might accidentally catch
their foot. Flexible little things with stubby legs, they might then
bring their foot to their mouth. Putting whatever's in the hand into
the mouth is also quite automatic, but at first they don't seem to realize that it's their own foot.

Babies start disconnected. They don't link what they see with
what they do and what they feel. And they don't link the parts of
their body with each other. We take the connections between what
we see and what we feel for granted, but human babies don't enter
the world with those connections; the connections are learned, slowly
over many months. Ultimately, what unites the senses foremost is action. That is, the output—action—informs and integrates the input—
sensation—through a feedback loop. Unifying the senses depends on
acting: doing and seeing and feeling, sensing the feedback from the
doing at the same time.

It's not just babies who calibrate perception through action. We
adults do it too. Experiments in which people don prismatic glasses

that distort the world by turning it upside down or sliding it sideways show this dramatically. The first known experiments showing adaptation to distorting lenses were performed in the late nineteenth century by George Stratton, then a graduate student and later the founder of the Berkeley Psychology Department. Stratton fashioned lenses that distorted vision in several ways and tried them himself, wearing them for weeks. At first, Stratton was dizzy, nauseated, and clumsy, but gradually he adapted. After a week, the upside-down world seemed normal and so was his behavior. In fact, when he removed the lenses, he got dizzy and stumbled again. Since then, experiments with prismatic lenses that turn the world every which way have been repeated many times. You can try the lenses in many science museums or buy them on the Web. A charismatic introductory psychology teacher at Stanford used to bring a star football player to class and hand him distorting lenses. Then the instructor would toss the player a football, and of course the star player fumbled, much to everyone's delight. A rather convincing demonstration! That disrupted behavior, the errors in reaching or walking, is the measure of adaptation to the prismatic world.

The surprising finding is this: seeing in the absence of acting doesn't change perception. If people are wheeled about in a chair and handed what they need—if they don't walk or reach for objects—they do not adapt to the prismatic lenses. Then, when the lenses are removed, the behavior of passive sitters is normal. No fumbling. No dizziness.

Because acting changes perception, it should not be surprising that acting changes the brain. This has been shown many times in many ways, in monkeys as well as in humans. Here's the basic paradigm: give an animal or a person extensive experience using a tool. Then check areas of the brain that underlie perception of the body to see if they now extend outside the body to include the tool. Monkeys, for example, can quickly learn to use a hand rake to pull out-of-reach objects, especially treats, to themselves. After they become adept at using a rake, the brain regions that keep track of the area around the hand as it moves expand to include the rake as well as the hand.

These findings were so exciting that they have been replicated many times in many variations in many species. The general finding is that extensive practice using tools enlarges both our conscious body image and our largely unconscious body schema.

That extensive tool use enlarges our body images to include the tools provides evidence for the claim that many of us jokingly make, that our cell phones or computers are parts of our bodies. But it also makes you wish that the people who turn and whack you with their backpacks had had enough experience with backpacks that their backpacks had become part of their body schemas. Too bad we don't use our backpacks the ways we use the tools in our hands.

The evidence on action is sufficient to declare the **Second Law of Cognition: Action molds perception.** There are those who go farther and declare that perception is for action. Yes, perception serves action, but perception serves so much more. There are the pure pleasures of seeing and hugging people we love, listening to music we enjoy, viewing art that elevates us. There are the meanings we attach to what we feel and see and hear, the sight of a forgotten toy or the sound of a grandparent's voice or the taste, for Proust, of a madeleine. Suffice it to say that action molds perception.

Earlier I observed that our skin surrounds and encloses our bodies, separating our bodies from the rest of the world. It turns out that it's not quite that simple (never forget my caveats and my caveats about caveats). It turns out that we can rather easily be tricked into thinking that a rubber hand—yuck—is our own.

In a paradigmatic experiment, participants were seated at a table, with their left arm under the table, out of view. On the table was a very humanlike rubber hand positioned like the participant's real arm. Participants watched as the experimenter gently stroked the rubber arm with a fine paintbrush. In synchrony, the experimenter stroked the participant's real but not visible arm with an equivalent brush, matching the rhythm. Amazingly, most participants began to think that the arm they could see, the rubber arm, was their own. They reported that what they saw was what they felt. Action, per se, is not involved in creating this illusion, but proprioceptive feedback seems to be crucial. Both hands, the participant's real hand and the rubber hand, are immobile. What seems to underlie the illusion is sensory integration, the integration of simultaneously seeing and feeling.

If people perceive the rubber arm as their own arm, then if they watch a threat to the rubber arm, they should get alarmed. This happened in subsequent experiments. First, as before, participants experienced enough synchronous stroking of their hidden real arm and the visible rubber arm to claim ownership of the rubber arm. Then the experimenters threatened the rubber arm by initiating an attack on the arm with a sharp needle. At the same time, they measured activation in areas of the brain known to respond to anticipated pain, empathetic pain, and anxiety. The more participants reported ownership of the rubber hand, the greater the activation in the brain regions underlying anticipated pain (left insula, left anterior cingulate cortex) during the threatened, but aborted, attack with a sharp needle.

The rubber hand phenomenon provides yet another explanation of why people's body schemas enlarge to include tools but don't seem to enlarge to include their backpacks. Ownership of a rubber hand depends on simultaneous seeing and sensing, seeing the rubber hand stroked and sensing simultaneous stroking on the real hand. We can't see our backpacks and whatever sensations we have are pressure or weight on our backs and shoulders, which give no clue to the width of the backpack generating the pressure.

UNDERSTANDING OTHERS' BODIES

Now to the bodies of others. It turns out that our perception and understanding of the bodies of others are deeply connected to the actions and sensations of our own bodies. What's more, the connection of our bodies to those of others is mediated by the very structure of the brain and the nervous system. Let's begin again with babies, let's say, one-year-olds. Babies that young have begun to understand the goals and intentions of the actions of others, at least for simple actions like reaching. You might wonder how we know what babies are thinking.

After all, they can't tell us (not that what we say we are thinking is necessarily reliable). We know what babies are thinking the same way we often know what adults are thinking: from what they are looking at. Sometimes actions can be more revealing than words.

The most common way researchers infer the thoughts of babies is through a paradigm known as habituation of looking. Two ideas underlie this paradigm: people, even, or especially, babies, look at what they're thinking about; and second, stuff that's new grabs attention and thought. In a typical task, researchers show infants a stimulus or an event, in this case, a video of someone reaching for an object. At the same time, they monitor how much the infants are looking at the event. They show the event again, and monitor again. The researchers show the stimulus or the event over and over until the baby loses interest and looks away, that is, until the infant *habituates* to the event. After the infant habituates, the researchers show a new event that alters the previous one in one of two ways. They change the goal of the action by switching the object of reaching or they switch the means of attaining the goal by changing the manner of reaching. The question of interest is whether infants will look more at the event where the goal of reaching was changed or the event where the means of attaining the goal was changed.

If the infant understands that it's the goal that matters, not the means to the goal, the infant should look more when the goal changes than when the means changes. At ten months, infants were indifferent to the changes; they looked equally at both. Both events were new, and the infants didn't regard a change of goal as more interesting than a change of manner of attaining the goal. That changed in only two months. Twelve-month-old infants looked more when the goal changed than when the means to the goal changed. A leap of understanding of goal-directed behavior in two months.

More support for the notion that one-year-olds understand action-goal couplings comes from tracking their eye movements as they watch someone reaching. Remarkably, the eye movements of one-year-old infants jump to the goal of the action before the hand even reaches the goal, suggesting that they anticipate the goal.

Perhaps even more impressive is what happens even earlier, at three months. At that tender age, if infants have performed similar actions, they are more likely to understand the goals of others' actions. At three months, infants don't have good motor control, they cannot yet reach and grasp reliably, and their hands flail about. The clever experimenters put mittens with Velcro on the baby's hands and a toy in front of the infant. Eventually, with enough flailing, the Velcroed hand would catch the toy. The infants who had had practice "grasping" objects in this way anticipated the viewed reaching and grasping actions of others more reliably than infants without practice grasping.

This is remarkable evidence that infants can understand the intentions behind the actions of others. Not all intentions and actions, of course, but reaching for an object is an important and common one, and there are undoubtedly others. Understanding others' intentions comes about in part because of experience enacting similar actions with similar intentions. Moreover, as we shall see next, it has become clear that the very structure of the brain is primed for understanding observed action, through the mirror neuron system.

MIRROR NEURONS

In the late 1980s, a group of neuroscientists in Parma, Italy, led by Giacomo Rizzolatti made a surprising discovery. They implanted tiny electrodes in individual neurons in premotor cortex (inferior frontal gyrus and inferior parietal lobe) of macaque monkeys that allowed them to record activity in single neurons in animals who were moving about as they normally do. They found single neurons that fired when the monkey performed a specific action, like grasping or throwing. What was remarkable was that the exact same neuron fired when the animal saw someone else, in this case, a human, perform the same action. They called these remarkable neurons *mirror neurons*. Mirror neurons unite doing and seeing for specific actions. This extraordinary discovery means that action and perception are joined automatically by specific individual neurons without any mediation whatsoever. Different actions are encoded by different neurons: for monkeys, grasping, throwing, tearing. You can watch the action and listen to the simultaneous firing of these neurons online. More generally, the finding suggests that action mirroring, sometimes called motor resonance, underlies action understanding. Seeing is mapped to doing and doing is mapped to seeing. I understand what I see you doing because an echo of the doing resonates in my own action system. Of course, it's just an echo; I'm not actually doing what I'm seeing, which is a good thing. Otherwise, we'd be caught in an unending cycle of imitation. Mirror neurons underlie the understanding part of imitation, but not the doing part.

Naturally, these findings, now replicated many times, have generated enormous excitement. Overinterpretation of tantalizing findings like these is inevitable. Might mirror neurons underlie imitation, learning, and memory? The research group in Parma has gone to great effort to explain that seeing is not imitating and that understanding is not doing. If it were that simple, we'd all be expert pianists or basketball players or acrobats. Motor resonance, however, is real: that is, seeing action causes associated motor regions of the brain and even associated muscles to activate.

It's problematic to perform these experiments in humans. We don't simply implant electrodes in individual neurons in other humans. There are cases, however, when recording from single cells in the alert human brain is crucial for people's health and well-being, for example, for people with intractable epilepsy. Epilepsy can often be controlled by destroying the brain tissue that seems to initiate seizures, but neurosurgeons first make sure the brain locations are not involved with core functions like speech. The way to find out is by implanting electrodes in the suspect areas, and sometimes in other areas, where the electrodes would cause no damage. Studies recording from single cells in those patients have found evidence for mirror neurons in multiple parts of the human brain, for example, individual neurons that responded when people observed or performed actions and also when people viewed or expressed facial emotions.

The actions of bodies are qualitatively different from the actions of other objects. A crucial difference: bodies are self-propelled, which means bodies can perform gravity-defying actions, like jumping up in the air all by themselves, feats that baseballs and leaves cannot perform. Even small children do a decent job telling whether a path of motion is from an animate being or an inanimate object. Of course, animacy is far more than paths of motion, and even small children understand that. Yet, it is significant we and small children can make a good guess as to whether something moving is animate or not simply from an easily perceivable path of motion. It is sometimes surprising how much deep essential qualities like animacy are apparent from superficial perceptual features. Earlier we saw that objects can be recognized by their contours. Other examples to come.

MOTOR RESONANCE

Just as infants understand viewed actions better if they have performed the same actions, not surprisingly, so for adults. Our experience performing specific actions modulates our perception of the same actions performed by others. In an experiment that has generated smiles, excitement, and even some controversy, experts in capoeira, experts in ballet, and nonexperts viewed videos of standard movements in capoeira and ballet while in a scanner that measured their brain activity. Brain activity in a network involved in the mirror system (premotor cortex, intraparietal sulcus, right superior parietal lobe, and left posterior superior temporal sulcus) showed more activation when observers watched the movements for which they were experts.

The broader implication is by now a familiar one: we understand actions that we view by simulating the actions in our bodies, by embodying the perception. Many names for more or less the same phenomenon: motor simulation, motor resonance, embodiment. There are even more.

Motor simulation has implications beyond understanding action. It affects our predictions and expectations about action, for example, whether a basketball will make the basket. In one study, professional basketball players, sports reporters, and professional basketball coaches were asked to predict whether free throws would make the basket. Coaches and sports reporters have extensive outsider, that is, visual, experience watching basketball, and from many different points of view. Basketball players have that visual experience, but they also have the insider view. They know what it feels like to shoot a basket, and most likely they have developed good intuitions about which shots they take themselves will make the basket. Professional basketball players are so practiced at shooting baskets that they have often been called shooting machines.

You've guessed the results. All three groups, coaches, reporters, and players, were impressively good at predicting which balls would land in the basket. That said, the players were far better. Their extensive insider knowledge enabled professional basketball players to predict shots better than coaches or sports reporters. The experimenters stopped the videos at varying intervals from the beginning of the shot until the ball was very close to the basket. What was especially impressive is that the players' predictions were superior even before the ball left the player's hands! This suggests that the players had insider motor understanding of the body kinematics underlying basketball shots, and that this understanding allowed them to better predict the outcomes of the actions. Players have more motor experience than coaches and sports reporters and that motor experience enables better predictions. Along with other evidence and more to come, it suggests that we map body action that we see onto our own body's action system. Perception of action acquires meaning through motor understanding. Experts with more articulated motion systems perceive more meaning in what they see.

Back in the 1970s, a Swedish psychologist, Gunnar Johansson, dressed people in black and attached small lights to their major parts and joints, head, shoulder, elbow, wrist, hips, and so forth. He then filmed them as they performed a common set of human actions, walking, running, and dancing. This paradigm, using point-light videos, has been adopted, adapted, and simulated many times since. You can find many captivating examples online. A static image of any of the point-light bodies is unidentifiable; it looks like a random collection of dots. But once the set of dots is set in motion, you can immediately see that it's a human body, you know if it's walking or running or dancing, you know if it's a man or a woman (by the ratio of the shoulders to the hips), you can tell if it's happy or sad, energetic or tired, heavy or light.

More recently, a group of researchers used that paradigm to ask how well we can recognize individuals from point-light videos. They brought pairs of friends into their laboratory, dressed them in black, attached lights to their heads and joints, and filmed them dancing, running, boxing, walking, playing Ping-Pong, and more, altogether ten different activities. Some months later, all participants were invited back to the lab to view all the videos. For each video, they were asked to identify the specific person moving. Perhaps not surprisingly, people were pretty good at recognizing their friends from their friends' movements but poor at recognizing strangers. It was far easier to recognize individuals from the videos depicting more vigorous activities like dancing, jumping, playing Ping-Pong, and jumping than from the videos showing walking and running. The next finding is truly surprising. Participants were best at recognizing themselves! Most of us, and certainly the participants in this experiment, don't spend a lot of time looking at our movements in the mirror unless we are dancers or models or yoga practitioners. How is it that we are best at recognizing ourselves, people we never or rarely see playing Ping-Pong or jumping, better than we are at recognizing our friends, whom we've presumably had extensive experience watching in motion? As before, the mirror system, motor resonance, seems to underlie that impressive ability. The theory goes like this. As participants watched the videos of people in action, their mirror systems resonated to the actions they were seeing as if they were trying the movements on for size. When they watched videos of themselves in action, the movements fit perfectly, they felt right, felt natural, felt like themselves.

COORDINATING BODIES

Birds flock, fish school, troops march. Bees gather nectar, ants build nests; basketball players coordinate on the court; boxers, on the mat; improvisors, on the stage. Commuters race every which way through Grand Central. For the most part, there are no collisions and there's no one directing the traffic. There are so many ways that organisms rapidly coordinate their behavior with each other and so many reasons for the coordination. The mere presence of others affects our behavior, without any need to coordinate. You're sitting alone in a waiting room or on a seat in a train or in line to buy a ticket. A total stranger arrives and does the same, sits down across the aisle or stands behind you in line. Unless you are completely distracted, say, by the smartphone at your fingertips or near your ear, you can't help but be aware of the presence of the other, and that presence affects your behavior.

In situations like those, standing in line, sitting in a waiting room or on a train, you and the stranger are performing the same action at the same time in the same space. Providing that there is plenty of room for each of you, your actions do not have to be coordinated. If the train or waiting room is crowded, you might have to coordinate, making room for each other and each other's belongings. Walking down nearly empty streets doesn't require much coordination with others; nor does clapping at the end of a performance. Yet, remarkably, pedestrians tend to synchronize their walking and audiences their clapping.

Presumably, like birds flying in flocks, the synchronization of the group organizes and eases the actions of the individuals. Since my walking or clapping is in sync with others', I can attend less to mine. In the human case, perfect strangers fall into rhythm. Rhythm is deeply embedded in our bodies, in our hearts, our breathing, our brains, our actions—walking, talking, thinking, dancing, sleeping, waking—our days and nights. Our rhythms organize and synchronize our bodies and come to organize and synchronize our bodies with the bodies of others.

The games we play with babies practice those skills, although that's probably not why we play them. The baby says "ahh." We say "ahh." The baby says "ahh." We take turns doing the same thing. Later we change our responses slightly, they say "ahh," we say, "ahh ahh." We roll a ball to baby, baby rolls it back to us. We clap together or in alternation. Our play is unintentionally training the elements of joint action: synchronization, turn-taking, imitation, entrainment, joint attention, joint understanding. And we—and they—just thought we were having fun. We were. There is something so satisfying about doing something together, in sync.

In humans, coordination quickly turns into cooperation. As early as fourteen months, when a child sees an adult trying to get an object out of reach but close to the child, the child will hand the object to the adult. Both the social understanding and the social behavior are remarkable, all the more so because they don't require language or any explicit coordination. Other primates, monkeys and great apes, can be induced to work together to achieve a joint goal. The standard laboratory task is jointly pulling on separate ropes to bring some nuts or bananas in reach. Elephants cooperate, as do dolphins, both often with humans, just like dogs. Indeed, research in Tomasello's lab has shown that cooperation is the origin of moral behavior; we need to work together, but then we must, or rather should, split the rewards. When small children are given more than their share, they share their share with the others.

At the other end of the continuum of joint action are tasks that require continuous and continuously changing coordination. To study this kind of coordination, we brought pairs of students who had never met each other into a lab room. On a table was a stack of parts of a TV cart and a photo of the completed cart. The pairs were asked to assemble the TV cart using the photo as a guide. We'd done many experiments on TV cart assembly by then, so we knew that students could do this individually, even without instructions. We even began to think this simple experiment was an important part of their undergraduate education.

Sure enough, the pairs were successful at assembling the TV cart. They did it correctly and efficiently, if each pair differently. Unlike walking or clapping, assembling the TV cart required partners to work together while performing different actions that were the components of each assembly step. The pairs spontaneously assumed different roles, usually implicitly, without even speaking. One would take the role of the *heavy lifter* and the other, the role of the *attacher*. The heavy lifter would hold a large part steady so that the attacher could connect another part to it. Each step in the assembly was more efficient with both partners, and to accomplish each step, the partners had to perform complementary actions. What was fascinating is that so much of the coordination happened without explicit negotiation, without words, even though the assembly actions were asymmetric and had to be done together. What's more, each partner knew what the other needed to do, often anticipating the partner's next action. The heavy lifter might see that the attacher would soon need a specific part and hand it to the attacher. When the attacher had the next part in hand, the heavy lifter would position the base so the attacher could easily attach the part. And so on. A kind of dance.

It seems amazing that this intricate set of interactive actions can happen almost wordlessly, without explicit organization. But on deeper reflection, perhaps it should not be so surprising. An orchestra needs a conductor, but a string quartet does not. Jazz improv can be beautifully coordinated as can comedy improv, without scores or scripts or a leader. At the core of joint action is joint understanding, shared knowledge of the goals and subgoals of the task and the procedures needed to accomplish it. For the TV cart, the procedures are a sequence of actions on parts, placing each part in turn in the correct configuration and attaching it with the appropriate means of attachment. The joint understanding of the goals of the task resides in each partner's mind. In fact, people have numerous event schemas in their minds, representations of the sequences of actions on objects needed to accomplish a range of ordinary tasks, like making a bed or doing the dishes or assembling a piece of furniture. These representations allow people to interpret ongoing action, to predict what happens next in ongoing action, and to generate step-by-step instructions to accomplish the tasks.

Peering inside the brain can reveal some of the processes that track joint action. Both electroencephalogram (EEG) and functional MRI (fMRI) research shows that participants keep their joint task active in the brain as well as in the mind. Surprisingly, partners keep each other's task in mind even when doing so interferes with their own performance, slows them down, and makes them more prone to error.

Although the representation of the task resides in each partner's mind, the set of procedures to carry out the task relies on objects and partners in the world. Participants have to keep in mind the overall goal and procedures and use that to guide their own actions. To prepare their own actions, people need to monitor each other's actions as they proceed step-by-step. This means that to collaborate, partners must share and maintain joint attention in real time. For this kind of ongoing collaborative task, joint attention doesn't necessarily mean joint gaze. Think of a duet between a pianist and a violinist; their eyes are looking at different scores and their hands are playing different instruments. Their joint attention is on the music they are creating together. Rhythm, the most fundamental requirement for minimal joint action, is also the foundation for maximal joint action.

Conversation, too, requires complementary coordination and on many levels. Importantly, conversation partners collaborate on creating meaning, and much of that collaboration is direct, deliberate, and even deliberated. In actuality, conversation partners do not just coordinate the content and the timing of the conversation, they also coordinate aspects of their behavior that do not at first seem relevant to the conversation. They coordinate their actions, leaning forward to take the stage or backward to yield the stage, crossing or uncrossing their legs. They mimic each other, a phenomenon known as *entrainment*. They adopt each other's words and phrases, even accents. They copy each other's facial expressions, eye gaze, and body movements. These seemingly irrelevant behaviors turn out not to be irrelevant; they serve as "social glue," showing and promoting mutual understanding, thereby enhancing communication and cooperation. If we use the same words, if we make complementary actions, we are understanding each other. And we like each other more.

Thinking more broadly, interactions are important in and of themselves, but they are also opportunities for learning actions and behaviors. Being primed to mimic others' actions can surely help us to learn. We observe others' actions to coordinate with our own actions, to plan our own actions, but also to learn new actions. Remember that last time you were in an unfamiliar situation, an airport or government office or museum or foreign country. Even at a crosswalk. You probably watched what others were doing. Watching what others do might be the most efficient way to figure out what you need to do. Small children study their older siblings, imitating even incidental irrelevant actions.

AFTERTHOUGHT: MINDS IN OTHER MINDS, BODIES IN OTHER BODIES

We began this chapter, indeed the book, with us, perhaps naturally, with our bodies swathed in skin, separating us from everything else in the world. Yet from the beginning of life we move and act in space, interacting with our surroundings, with space itself, and with the things we encounter in space. Those actions yield sensations, both from within the body and from outside the body. The actions and sensations of our bodies form our conceptions of our bodies.

The world is never static. We are constantly acting in that world and adapting to it. The parts of our bodies that are most important for our interactions in the world are, not accidentally, the ones most salient in our brains and in our minds. How we interact with the things in the world alters the ways we perceive the world. The bodies of others are undoubtedly the most important things we encounter and interact with throughout our lives. We understand others' bodies and their actions through our own bodies, beginning with the mirror system: viewing actions of others' resonates in the areas of our brains that create our own actions. Coordinating our actions with others depends on understanding others' actions but also on shared understanding of what we are engaged in, on rhythm, on joint attention, on the task at hand, and on what surrounds us in the world. The mirror system mediates and reflects just about every kind of action: of our hands, our legs, our posture, our faces. The mimicking is internal, but it can leak out into actual behavior. We imitate each other's body movements and facial expressions. Mirroring means that the bodies of others get internalized in our minds and our bodies get internalized in theirs.

That spiritual metaphor that we are each parts of others' minds and they of ours has become a reality. Fascinating new research has refuted what we all learned in elementary biology, that the DNA in every cell in our bodies is identical. Geneticists have found evidence for patchy microchimerism, that is, colonies of different DNA in different places in our bodies. If we carry different DNA, who are we? The research is just beginning, but it is already known that the DNA of babies can colonize in the mothers who carried them, that DNA from transplanted organs can colonize in other parts of the body, that many of us had a fraternal twin who disappeared in utero and that we may be carrying the twin's DNA. Others aren't just in our minds. We really are parts of others and they of us, even within our own skin.

CHAPTER TWO

The Bubble Around the Body: People, Places, and Things

In which we learn how people recognize, categorize, and understand the people, places, and things around us. We note that many everyday categories such as chairs and dogs are bins of common features that differentiate them from the feature bins of even nearby categories, such as carpets and snakes. But not always, and then we need to think harder, about dimensions and the features shared across categories.

> *We live not only in a world of thoughts, but also in a world of things.*
> —VLADIMIR NABOKOV

SURROUNDING OUR BODIES ARE THE PEOPLE, PLACES, AND THINGS in reach of eye or hand. These are the immediate influences on our perception, on our behavior, and on our thought. In a fraction of a second, before we can find the words to say it, we know where we are, at home, in the supermarket, at the park. We know what's around us, chairs and tables or shopping carts and packages of food or trees and swing sets. We know who's around us, what they are doing, making dinner, shopping, swinging. We know what kind of people they are, we can sense their feelings and their health from their faces and bodies, we can judge their social and economic status from their clothing and behavior, we can make good guesses as to their ages, gender, even political leanings. We people wear so much of our insides on our outsides. We take in our surroundings automatically and instantly. Unless we are blindfolded and our ears are covered, we can't *not* pick it up. This isn't to say that we are always correct, but it is remarkable how often we are.

We didn't enter the world with this impressive ability. Newborns need to learn to see the very elements of objects, edges and corners, and to connect them to form the shapes that are used to recognize people and things. They need to learn to discern and recognize faces and objects and scenes. Babies learn that wordlessly in the first few months of life, simply by looking. It happens so fast that parents miss it unless they know what to look for. Much of that learning happens while the brain is maturing. People who were born blind and gain sight as adults can't make heads or tails out of what they see, a surprising and often wrenchingly disappointing outcome. Fortunately, blindness from birth has become far less frequent, and with training and experience, some visual competence can be acquired if sight is restored later in life.

Who, what, and *where* are so fundamental that the brain has specialized regions for recognizing them, in fact, usually multiple regions for each: faces, bodies, objects, scenes. The retina captures information as it is arrayed in the world, if upside down. The upside-down part is the easy part for the brain. Making sense of what's on the retina is far harder. That information is essentially an array of raw pixels, devoid of meaning. It has to be segmented into figures and background. That entails finding edges and connecting them. Both figures and ground need to be interpreted, given meaning. That happens by routing information from the retina, and for that matter, from all the senses, to different parts of the brain. The different locations perform different computations on the information from the senses, computations specialized for creating the different meanings relevant to our lives, computations specialized for faces, places, and things of all sorts.

When and *why* are far harder. They can't be easily computed from sensory input the ways that color and shape and even faces and objects and scenes can be. Except for a handful of hyperorganized individuals who remember the exact dates and details of many events of their lives, the brain doesn't put a date stamp on events. And even in those perhaps enviable individuals, memory is constructed, the time stamp is added symbolically, in words and numbers from the conventional Gregorian calendar. No brain area codes that. *Why* is even more complicated, so many events have so many possible explanations, providing endless work for scientists, political analysts, and advice columnists. And disagreements between couples and countries. Because the mechanisms we use to construct *when* and especially *why* are imperfect and biased, so are our judgments and explanations.

THINGS

Of all those crucial entities in the world, and components of knowledge, things are the simplest. Yet, there are so many things, how to make sense of them? One way to make sense of things is to group them into categories, but which categories? First, consider this set of categories from the literary philosopher Jorge Borges:

> The following is a taxonomy of the animal kingdom. It has been attributed to an ancient Chinese encyclopedia entitled the *Celestial Emporium of Benevolent Knowledge:* On those remote pages it is written that animals are divided into (a) those that belong to the Emperor, (b) embalmed ones, (c) those that are trained, (d) suckling pigs, (e) mermaids, (f) fabulous ones, (g) stray dogs, (h) those that are included in this classification, (i) those that tremble as if they were mad, (j) innumerable ones, (k) those drawn with a very fine camel's hair brush, (l) others, (m) those that have just broken a flower vase, (n) those that resemble flies from a distance.

Poetic categories they are, but useful they are not. Good categories sort most things into separate bins, not partially overlapping ones. Good categories should be easy to identify. Good categories should be informative, they should tell us what they're good for. Good categories should reduce the enormous numbers of different things to a manageable number. The key to recognizing and categorizing things, objects, is *shape:* objects have shapes and the visual system is biased toward finding them. It homes in on edges and connects the dots when objects occlude other objects.

Around the first year of life, parents and babies begin to play a naming game, pointing, showing, labeling everything that catches the baby's attention. Babies and children acquire words at an amazing speed. One estimate is that seventeen-year-olds know eighty thousand words. For convenience, let's say babies begin learning words around their first birthday (of course they begin much earlier, before they can talk). That would mean five thousand words a year, or fourteen a day, and undoubtedly many more of them earlier in life than later. This pace is much faster than the naming game; kids are picking up words for things without being taught. This astounding pace of acquisition is just for the labels of things. To add to the wonder, we have labels for only a fraction of what we, babies, children, learn and know, people, places, things, emotions, and more.

HIERARCHICAL ORGANIZATION
Basic level

Toddlers learn to call the things around them apples and bananas, cars and buses, shirts and shoes. They don't begin with labels like *Gala apple* or *fruit, Prius* or *vehicle, knit shirt* or *clothing*. Even adults prefer those simple labels. Calling ordinary things with more abstract or more specific labels sounds odd in ordinary situations. If I offer you a ride because I've brought my Tesla X, I'm showing off. If I tell you I've brought my vehicle, I'm being silly. If I ask you to put the animal out instead of the dog, I'm implying the dog is wild and beastly rather than docile and friendly. Languages have those more abstract and more specific labels for good reasons, but for everyday use, the middle level, the level of *apple, car,* and *shirt,* is preferred. Interestingly, these labels are typically shorter and more frequent than more general or more specific labels (Zipf's law again: more frequent words are shorter). The default and neutral way of referring to things, the level first used by children, the level of *apple* and *car,* has been called the *basic* level. The more general level, the level of *vehicle, fruit,* and *animal,* has been called the *superordinate* level, and the more specific level, *Tesla, Gala apple,* and *cocker span-iel,* has been called the *subordinate* level.

The basic level is special for many reasons. Objects at the basic level like apples and tables and hammers and belts generally have the same shapes, so it is easy to identify them. So do their subcategories, Gala and Delicious apples, leather and cloth belts, dining tables and coffee tables. Features other than shape, like color or material or size, distinguish one subordinate category member from another. Unless there's good reason, there's no need to make people attend to the fine discriminations and plethora of names that labeling at the subordinate level entails. Jumping up a level, to superordinate categories, we see that different kinds of *fruit, furniture, tools,* and *clothing* do not share shapes. On the contrary, they come in a variety of shapes. Bananas have different shapes from apples and watermelons, airplanes from cars and trucks, shirts from pants and belts. A composite shape of a couple of apples or hammers is identifiable, but a composite of fruit or vehicles creates a blob. The basic level is privileged for behavior as well as perception. We behave the same way toward apples and bicycles and sweaters, but we behave differently to melons than to apples, to cars than to bicycles, to hats than to sweaters. What *fruit* and *vehicles* and *tools* share are not specific shape or action but something more general, function or use. *Fruit* are for eating, *vehicles,* for transporting, *tools,* for building or repairing. Those properties aren't visible like peels and pulp, wheels and doors, handles and heads. As a consequence, learning those more general categories based on common function takes longer. True understanding of superordinate categories like *tool* and *vehicle* usually doesn't come in reliably until the early school years.

Basic-level categories like *table* and *apple* and *shirt* are Goldilocks categories, not too abstract, not too concrete. They're in the middle, right between more general categories that are organized around function, such as *furniture, tool,* and *fruit,* and specific ones organized by a variety of features, such as *kitchen table, Phillips head screwdriver,* and *Jonathan apple.* Of course, sometimes those general ways of referring are enough: I need furniture for my apartment or fruit for my salad or tools for my garage; sometimes the more specific terms are necessary: only a Phillips head screwdriver works for that screw, only a dress shirt for the reception, only Pippin apples for the pie. Basic-level labels are multipurpose names.

Basic-level categories are not just easy to identify but also provide a wealth of information. What something looks like. What it's composed of. How it functions in our lives. How we behave toward it. That's an apple: it's fruit, it's round, red or green, grows on a tree, has a peel, pulp, and seeds, is edible, sweet, hard, and juicy. It doesn't matter if it's a Gala apple or a Fuji. That's a shirt: it's clothing, it covers the upper body, it has holes for the head and the arms and the torso. Same parts and function irrespective of the color or material or cost. The essential features of basic-level objects are typically evident from their shapes, that is, their parts: the seat, back, and legs of a chair; the sleeves, neck, and body of a sweater; the legs, body, and head of a dog. Those parts of objects are the fundamental features that characterize basic-level objects. The parts are clues both to perception, to recognizing the object, and to function, to what they do or what we do with them, to our interactions with them. Parts form a bridge between perception and action. Chairs have seats and legs and backs. Seats and legs and backs look different from each other and serve us in different ways. The seat of a chair is the right size and height for sitting, the legs support the seat, and the back of the chair supports the back of the person. Chairs *afford* sitting. The sleeves, neck, and body of a sweater look different from each other and are meant to be used by different parts of our bodies. Same for the dog: its distinctive parts, legs, body, and head, serve it in distinct ways. As do our own.

There are so many more things than names for things. The basic level is about naming things in the world, though referring to things that way undoubtedly helps learning to discriminate them in the world. We can distinguish far more things than we can name or describe. Those names are usually sufficient for ordinary conversation, but it is clear that the eye takes in much more. The eye can tell how ripe the banana is and if the fabric of the sweater is soft or harsh and whether the seat of the chair is the right height and if the table is well constructed. The eye can tell if the screwdriver will fit the screw or the shirt fit the baby. The eye recognizes thousands of properties of countless numbers of objects, properties that have significance but that can't easily be named, and even if they can, the knowing comes before the names.

PEOPLE

Like objects, people have shapes, and the shapes have parts, including faces and bodies. It is hard to overestimate the importance of faces and bodies in our lives. Who is that? Friend or foe? Old or young? Sick or healthy? Native or foreign? Drunk or sober? Rich or poor? What are they feeling? What are they thinking? What are they doing? What are they going to do? So much of that vital information and more is right there on the surface, on the face or in the body. Insides make their way to outsides. We turn to some of that information now. We need to absorb it quickly because it guides our own behavior. And we do absorb it quickly. Quick appraisal doesn't guarantee accuracy. Remember the **First Law of Cognition: No benefits without costs.**

Here the benefit is speed, necessary in the savannah or on a dark street or even on a well-lit one—you must flee danger and greet a friend, but not a stranger, who might interpret your smile as an invitation. Identical twins create this problem; I was once miffed when a friend didn't greet me only to realize that it was his twin, who quite understandably had no idea who I was. Speed and accuracy trade off in just about everything we do; the trick, as with all trade-offs, is to find the sweet spot. That depends on the costs of both errors, falsely greeting a twin stranger warmly or failing to greet a friend. Mistaking a coyote for a dog can be costly, but mistaking a dog for a coyote less so.

Who: Faces

Try this. Describe a person you know to someone who was at a party with that person but who isn't sure whom he or she is. Not easy. Easy only in those rare cases when someone has a distinctive feature, neon hair or unusual glasses. In general, everyone has eyes, noses, mouths, and ears. We have good words for those, but they don't distinguish one person's face from another's. We don't have good words for the features that do distinguish one face from another, the subtle differences among eyes, noses, mouths, and ears, or the subtle differences in their configurations and expressions. Like their parents, each of my three children has "blue" eyes. Five pairs of eyes, five shades of blue, and I'd never confuse them. Despite the near impossibility of describing individual faces, most of us can recognize thousands of them. That disparity says loudly that face recognition can't be based in language. We don't normally bother describing faces to distinguish one from another. Rather, we give each face an arbitrary name, a name that has something to do with the person's family but nothing to do with the person's appearance. And that disconnect between the vivid appearance and the disconnected name is part of why so many complain that they never forget a face but can't remember names.

Recognizing faces is fundamentally different from recognizing objects. For one thing, whose face is important, but which chair or which hammer is usually not. Chairs and hammers are typically interchangeable, but individuals, for better or worse, are not. Silhouettes work for recognizing chairs and giraffes and shirts and bananas, but shape won't do for faces. All faces have more or less the same shape. Recognizing faces depends on what's inside the shape, but not just the features themselves, again because we all have those, and so do dogs and monkeys. Key for faces is the qualities of those internal features, eyes, nose, mouth, and how they are arrayed. That's a hard problem, one that the fusiform gyrus, tucked underneath the cortex, is good at solving. Other areas of the brain, the occipital face area (OA) and the superior temporal sulcus (fSTS), respond to face parts in any configuration, the kinds kids have fun making, but the fusiform face area is sensitive to properly configured faces.

Now a few interesting facts about memory for faces. Memory for faces is specific to faces, independent of other abilities. It is stable over time, and doesn't seem to be trainable. Perhaps not surprisingly, it turns out to have a strong genetic base. Recognizing faces improves with age, especially through adolescence (ten to twenty years), and peaks at thirty-two.

Despite the importance of individual faces in our lives, not everyone's brain can distinguish and recognize individuals. What do Brad Pitt, Oliver Sacks, and Chuck Close have in common? Sure, they're famous. And supremely talented. But the exotic feature they share is *prosopagnosia*. Practice a bit and the syllables will roll off your tongue. Yes, it's Greek; *prosopon* is Greek for "face"; *agnosia*, for "not knowing." Face blindness. A problem in the fusiform gyrus. People with prosopagnosia can sense they are looking at a face but do not know whose. Painfully, some can't even recognize their spouses. If you suspect prosopagnosia, don't take it personally. It's the brain's fault; apparently, the neural circuitry that responds to faces in prosopagnosics differs wildly from the neural circuitry in those who recognize faces effortlessly.

Not recognizing faces is not just embarrassing but a serious problem. Prosopagnosics develop compensatory mechanisms, analyzing and memorizing critical features, attending to other aspects of individuality like voice, body, and clothing. Fortunately, more wonders of the brain, the inability to identify individual faces doesn't interfere with the ability to detect emotional states. Fascinating, isn't it, that recognizing identity and recognizing emotion are computed independently, in different areas of the brain?

Faces and emotion

If cooperation is key to the success of our species, emotion is key to cooperation. To work with you, I need to trust you, to like you, to think positively of you. There are widely diverse views of emotion, but there is one thing on which they agree: emotions can be readily divided into positive or negative. Like/dislike. And quickly expressed in behavior. Positive means approach; negative, avoid. Emotions come on quickly, expressed by the face, the body, the voice. Emotions are rapidly recognized and hard to suppress. e e cummings famously opened a poem, "since feeling comes first," an insight later supported by research (and contributing the Third Law of Cognition). People viewing random meaningless forms have gut feelings about them before they know whether the forms are familiar. And they feel more positively toward the forms they've seen even when they fail to recognize them. Recognition and emotion are separate systems that are slow to talk to each other. The essence of emotion, positive or negative, is a rapid distillation of the essence of social glue, approach or avoid. This fundamental dimension has been anointed with a term from chemistry, *valence*. In chemistry, valence underlies the bonding of molecules; in psychology, the bonding of people. Emotional valence is the great reducer, the bottom line. **Third Law of Cognition: Feeling comes first.**

Emotions not only come on quickly in ourselves and are sensed quickly by others, they are also contagious. As are yawns, even for dogs. Remarkably, dogs are more likely to catch yawns from familiar people than unfamiliar, strong evidence for social empathy. Both people and dogs seem to catch stress from others, for example, we and they respond similarly to crying babies by increasing cortisol levels, a response to stress. It's not just emotions that are contagious but also emotional states, like stress. If experiencing others' emotions is the starting point for empathy and if emotions are contagious, then we seem to be wired for empathy. It can even be located in the brain, in the catchy TPJ (temporal parietal junction, just behind the ear). Note the qualifications: the *ifs* and the *seem*. Not all emotions, not all people, not all the time. And not with the same intensity.

Here's something else to try: walk down the streets looking at the faces coming toward you. Smile. Most likely, your smile will be returned. Like many people, I squint when there's sun in my eyes.

Squinting makes me smile, though I'm not aware of it and often wonder why so many people walking toward me are smiling at me.

Given the crucial role of emotion in social interactions, the diversity of views of emotion is not surprising. As we noted earlier, people like to categorize and even need to categorize; there are simply too many different things in the world. One venerable view, personified and immortalized in the animated film *Inside Out*, is that there is a small set of basic emotions: anger, fear, disgust, sadness, happiness, surprise. That these are universally recognized from facial expressions, that they have an evolutionary history evident in other species as social signals, and that the basic facial expressions are distinguished by the activity of specific and specifiable muscles. Experiments worldwide using photos of faces frozen in these poses have shown that judgments of these emotions are rapid and that deliberation does not improve judgments—strong evidence that judgments of basic emotions, like recognition of people and things, are direct and unmediated.

Others agree that emotions are rapidly expressed and recognized but claim that, like flavors of food, there are countless nuanced emotions. That they are hard to name. That appraisal of them is tempered by context and culture. That we can and do experience and can and do express more than one emotion at the same time, disgust and surprise, sadness and anger, fear and happiness. That emotions are expressed in the body as well as the face and that, not infrequently, the emotions displayed by the body override those on the face.

Taste, too, is said to have five basic categories: sweet, sour, salty, bitter, and a recent addition, umami (savory or brothy or meaty), with several vying to be sixth or seventh. Now, we must explode an urban myth: these basic tastes are *not* sensed by different parts of the tongue. Even more significant, these tastes appear in combinations, and those combinations don't begin to capture the myriad different flavors people can sense, as chocolate lovers and wine tasters and mole poblano makers and curry consumers will attest.

Categories are so much easier than continua. They are so much simpler, there's so much less to be kept in mind. Distinct and different groups rather than many subtle gradations. This tension between a few basic categories and the myriad variations that we can sense in the world holds even for a far simpler quality, color. There is evidence for a basic set of colors whose centers or best examples are agreed on across cultures and whose names enter languages more or less systematically, though there are disputes about the order: first dark and light; then red is added, then green and yellow followed by blue, then brown, then purple, pink, orange or gray. In the case of color, there is evidence for heightened sensitivity for the basic colors. Basic colors notwithstanding, people recognize many subtle shades of colors whose names carry neither transparency nor agreement. Crayola crayons, used by generations of children and nostalgic adults, has expanded its box of colors with these: *melon, mahogany,* and *manatee,* and also *wild blue yonder, bittersweet shimmer, purple mountains' majesty,* and *unmellow yellow,* the last barely distinguishable from *laser lemon.*

Returning to emotion, there are the Ekman-Friesen six (+/−): anger, fear, disgust, sadness, happiness, surprise. Yet, our faces and bodies and words and tones of voice express far more emotions and more articulated emotions than the six proverbial basic emotions (recently recognized by Ekman, who has expanded the list). Think sympathetic, apprehensive, annoyed, disappointed, remorseful, suspicious, anxious, proud, pleased, bored, hostile; the list is long and the list is only words. Describing emotions is not always easy or straightforward. Appraisal of emotions depends not just on the face but also on how they emerge and fade on the face and the body and the voice. And, as we said, appraisal of emotion also depends on the larger context and on the culture.

Film lore has it that Kuleshov, an early Soviet filmmaker, paired a frame of the expressionless face of a heartthrob film star in a sequence with a frame of either an attractive woman reclining seductively on a sofa or a bowl of soup or a child in a coffin. Viewers interpreted the same face as desire, hunger, or sorrow depending on the juxtaposition. The effect (alas, like so many) sometimes replicates, sometimes not, but there is plenty of other research showing that interpretation of emotions from faces, both frozen and animated, is tempered by culture, by voice, by words, by the body, by others, by setting. Long as this list is, it's undoubtedly incomplete.

Do the eyes have it?

Some old proverbs just might be true, in this case the one about the eyes being the window to your soul. If you are interested in how well you can read faces, there's a five-minute test you can take and that thousands of others have taken, the *Mind in the Eyes* test. It shows you photos of only the eyes and eyebrows of real people and asks you to select which of four emotional states the eyes express. On average, more-educated people outperform less-well-educated people, women outperform men but only slightly, and neurotypical people outperform people with conditions that compromise recognition of emotion such as Asperger's, schizophrenia, and anorexia. An analysis of more than eighty-nine thousand people who completed the test and volunteered their genetic information confirmed a genetic basis. A separate study showed that performance of identical twins is more similar than performance of unrelated people, more evidence for a genetic basis.

What is it about the eyes? There is still much to learn. And, in fact, the eyes learn, by scrutinizing the world. When eyes open wide, they take in a wide range of information. When eyes narrow, they achieve sharper acuity, but for only the small region in focus. Squinting is all too familiar to those of us who are near-sighted. Try both. New research connects the information-gathering functions of the eyes to emotional expression. Wider eyes appear for such opposing emotional states as fear and surprise. Both fear and surprise naturally stimulate a broad search for information. Other emotions associated with wide eyes include awe, puzzlement, cowardice, anticipation, and interest. By contrast, the unrelated emotions of disgust and anger are associated with narrowing of the eyes; the sources of disgust and anger are quite clear, in focus. Other emotions associated with narrow eyes include annoyance, disapproval, suspicion, and pride.

When people viewed photos of faces in which the expressions of the mouths were discordant with those of the eyes, people's judgments of emotional state followed the eyes, though the effects were reduced slightly due to the discordance.

Faces and traits

In a surprising and disturbing series of experiments, students were shown a series of pairs of photos of faces for a fraction of a second and asked to judge which of the two people was more competent. The photos were the candidates for eighty-nine previous gubernatorial races. Students were also asked whether they recognized any of the faces, and if they did, those data were dropped. Remarkably, the candidate whose face was judged more competent won better than chance, around 55 to 58 percent of the time. These judgments were rapid, as requested, and a replication asking participants to carefully deliberate their judgments actually reduced predictability. Competence judgments don't just account for election results after the fact, they also predicted more than 68 percent of the gubernatorial and 72 percent of the senatorial races in 2006. And this happens in other countries, not just the United States. Rapid social judgments of competence or dominance (the judgments of these traits turn out to be related) from faces appear to have broad consequences on our lives; they correlate with sentencing decisions, hiring decisions, salary, and military rank. Our brains seem to be wired to make these evaluations automatically, as we casually go about our business, without an explicit intention to judge.

That was the surprising part. Now the disturbing part. These judgments have no validity. That is, people judged to be more competent or dominant are not necessarily more competent or dominant. The judgments are not borne out in behavior. There is some good news, however. The biases can be countered by other information. Remember that these are studies on frozen faces. In real life we can hope to have more information about people than a single facial expression for important decisions and other information can counter the biased judgments. However, we must be wary and remember the facts. Rapid judgments of frozen faces by participants in academic laboratories do predict voting decisions made by other people, and seem to predict other life-changing decisions like employment and promotions.

Bodies and emotion

Bodies, too, express emotion. Bodies have large advantages over faces: they are larger. Bodies can make bigger expressions and they can be seen from a greater distance. Normally, bodies and faces work together, as integrated units. Conveniently, experiments can separate and realign face and body. When face and body are congruent, expressing the same emotion, appraisals are more accurate. If face and body are incongruent, expressing different emotions, the body carries more weight than the face in judging emotions.

When they conflict, emotion expressed by the body can override and even reverse emotion expressed by the face. A striking example comes from competitive tennis matches. Players typically react strongly to points they win or lose. When a winning body is paired with a losing face, people see the reaction as positive. And vice versa: when a losing body is paired with a winning face, people interpret the reaction as negative. Impressions go with the body when the face and the body conflict. In these cases, the face alone, without the body, even when viewed close up in a photograph, is not reliably judged for positive or negative affect. For this situation, what comes through from the face is intensity, but not necessarily valence.

Faces cannot be discounted as carriers of emotion. Tennis matches require forceful actions of the body and are played to a crowd, so the dominance of the body over the face is natural. Tennis matches are only one of a vast range of situations that elicit emotion. Many encounters, both intense and casual, involve people sitting or standing face-to-face, where emotion is carried primarily by the face and voice and less by the rest of the body. Human communication is typically redundant, presumably at least in part to reduce error; if you miss part of a message, say, in a noisy restaurant, you might get another part, enough to understand. Like many expressions and communications, emotion is expressed in the face, voice, and body and redundantly even within each mode. People who are blind can grasp emotion from voice, both prosody and words; people who are deaf can grasp emotion from face and body.

Bodies and action

Bodies do more than express emotion. As we saw in Chapter One, bodies gesture, creating countless communications. They also act in the world, doing the myriad things that need to get done, also discussed in Chapter One. Of course, the brain is involved: the EBA, the extrastriate body area, that is, the lateral occipitotemporal cortex, responds selectively to bodies and body parts, but not to faces and other things such as objects and animals. Significantly, still photos of bodies caught in motion, such as throwing a javelin, also activate an area known to respond to actual motion, MT/MST, or medial temporal/medial superior temporal cortex. Photos of static poses do not activate that area, a strong indication that moving bodies have a different and special status from stationary ones.

Bodies convey action, but they also convey intentions of action, and in exquisite detail. In one set of studies, people were shown videos of the hand of another person reaching to pick up a block for different reasons: to take it for themselves, to give it to someone else, or to grab it before a competitor grabbed it. The videos were stopped before the hand actually reached the block. Despite the subtle differences in the actions of the body, viewers could reliably distinguish those three possibilities. The differing intentions were apparently evident from the shape and action of the hand and the direction of the actor's gaze.

In continuous natural actions such as making a sandwich or washing dishes, the head and eyes of the actor shift to the next object to be acted on before the hand begins to reach. The hand is often busy completing the previous action while the actor is already preparing the next action. So, the head and eyes of an actor show the actor's intent and provide good clues to the next action.

Just as for the face, people, tiny ones and adults alike, quickly process the direction of eye gaze and the actions of hands of others and use that information to infer and understand what others are thinking, doing, or intending to do. Yet another example, an important one, of information conveyed by the body that others absorb and even act on without the need for language.

PLACES: SCENES FOR ACTION AND EVENTS

The first question that people seem to ask on the phone these days is: Where are you? Knowing where someone is tells us so much about their present state. And so many times when we arrive at a distant place, we call a friend who was last with us there. Places are different yet again, not like objects, not like faces, and not like bodies. As for objects, faces, and bodies, there are areas in the brain that are selective for scenes, the parahippocampal place area (PPA) and the retrosplenial complex (RSC) primary among them.

Scenes surround us, usually richly populated. We are always embedded in a scene. Scenes are the settings for activities, and most of our activities take place in specific scenes. Scenes both constrain and enable activities, in part through the objects that are present in scenes. Scenes include many of them, and typically include faces and bodies. Scenes are the settings, the background, for all the events of our lives, for the stories of our lives, the mundane and the monumental. They are the settings for historical events, mundane or monumental. So, scenes are especially informative. What we see and do in a restaurant is very different from what we see and do in a post office or what we see and do in a classroom or what we see and do in our living rooms. Like objects, scenes have a basic level, the level of school, store, home, park, beach, forest, where parts, objects, and activities converge. Some are indoors, some outdoors, and *indoors* and *outdoors* are the superordinate categories that encompass the basic-level categories.

Like our memory for faces, our memory for scenes is extraordinary, so extraordinary that for a number of years, there was a competition in the literature, how many pictures of scenes can people remember? The prize went to ten thousand pictures. In general, recognition of pictures was excellent, even better for vivid pictures, and in both cases, far better than recognition of words. Now a caveat. Memory was tested in two ways. In one design, participants saw pairs of pictures, one that had been viewed and one that was new. The task was to select the old familiar picture in each pair. In the other design, pictures were presented one by one. Half were old and half were new, mixed randomly. Participants judged each picture in turn as *old* or *new*. Typically, the new pictures of scenes were very different from the old ones, making the task of distinguishing the old and the new fairly easy. When pictures are more similar, recognition accuracy naturally goes down. Think of identical twins.

Change blindness

Now, what might seem to be a paradox. We're so biased to pick up the gist of scenes that we ignore the details. We don't notice when features of a scene change, even important ones, a phenomenon known as *change blindness*. There are many demonstrations online; try them. Several demonstrations show pairs of photographs of richly inhabited scenes, in a city, on a lake, at an airport, in rapid alternation. The paired photos are identical except for one important feature that has changed in one of them, for example, one of the engines of a large jet is missing or the battery of a motor boat has disappeared. Viewers often sense that something has changed but rarely know what it is even after seeing many repetitions of the pairs of pictures.

Change blindness happens in real life in real time. In one impressive demonstration, passersby on a college campus were stopped by a twenty-something male student asking for directions. As the passerby explains the way by gesturing on a map, a crew carrying a large door passes between them. Using a magician's trick, the inquiring student switches places with another student, another twenty-something male who had been part of the crew carrying the door. Fewer than half the passersby noticed the change. Yes, both were young men, of similar build and dress, and yes, the passerby was looking at the map, not at the student's face. But still. This trick, of changing a central feature of a live situation without the participant noticing, has been demonstrated numerous times. When we look around us, we see a richly detailed world. But that's just it, we're seeing it, not remembering it. As long as we can see that rich world, we can reference it, and we don't need to remember it. It's there. We just need to know where we are.

Change blindness is yet another example of the **First Law of Cognition: There are no benefits without costs.** Here the benefit is rapid ascent to meaning. If I know the meaning, I know what to expect and how to behave. The cost: the details. It's a field in a park and there's a game on the field, I'd better walk around it. Whether or not there are trash bins or lights for night play isn't relevant at the moment. I'm helping yet another confused stranger find the way on campus, I'm concentrating on explaining the route on a map, I'm never going to meet that person again. It's a shopping street I'm approaching. I'd better be prepared for crowds. Whether or not there's a shoe repair shop or a dry cleaner isn't important unless that's what I'm looking for. It's troops boarding a plane. Of course, engines are critical for the airplane, but not for me. Not now.

CATEGORIES ARE EASIER THAN DIMENSIONS

The world gives us more than categories; it gives us continua, dimensions on which things differ. Food isn't just sour or sweet; there are gradations of each. People aren't short or tall; they have heights. What we've seen in this chapter is how quickly the mind forms categories of the people, places, and things most central to our lives. Many of those categories are overdetermined; that is, category members have many features in common and differ from other categories by many features. Shirts share many features and differ from pants on many features. Ditto potatoes and tomatoes, chairs and carpets, football stadiums and grocery stores, beaches and post offices. The features come in bundles; they are highly correlated. Members of frequent categories such as furniture and clothing typically have many features in common, features that are not shared by other categories. Birds have feathers, lay eggs, and fly. Dogs do none of that. And I've picked close examples, examples from the same superordinate. Musical instruments and vegetables are far more extreme in common and distinctive features; they have far fewer overlapping features. Sharing many features and differing from others on many features allows categorization to proceed with both speed and accuracy. It also allows for many expectations and inferences that are likely to be correct. Be careful with knives. Drink from glasses. Sit on chairs. Have a bite of an apple. Kick a soccer ball. Categorical thinking makes carrying out the activities of life easy and fluent. Once we know that something belongs to one of that kind of category, we know so much about it and about what it can do and what we can do with it. Categories are incredibly useful. We use them to organize our belongings as well as our minds and our lives.

But there are important things in our lives that can't be so neatly put in bins and boxes. There aren't bundles and boundaries created by common and distinctive features. Rather, exemplars that belong to different categories might differ on an important feature, the one underlying the category, but might not differ on others. Yet categorical thinking persists. Take citizenship. Citizenship is a highly meaningful category, with large implications for our lives. It also allows certain inferences about ourselves and about others. The diet, housing, and clothing of people in countries in the far north are likely to differ from the diet, housing, and clothing of people in equatorial countries. There might even be evolutionary differences due to adaptation to the different climates. People in far north Sweden, whose diet heavily relied on milk from herding animals, developed genes that allowed them to digest milk in adulthood. People in China, whose diet was crop-based, remain lactose-intolerant. Nevertheless, people in Sweden and people in China have heads and arms and legs, eat, laugh, get dressed, grow up, form families, work, and enjoy friends.

Citizenship, then, may allow some inferences and good guesses about correlated features, but because human beings across the world are the same and different in innumerable ways, innumerable features are not correlated with citizenship. The same is true for other ways we categorize, especially the most important things in our lives, people. Children and adults. Urban and rural. Politicians and journalists. Democrats and Republicans. Cubs fans and White Sox fans. Christians and Muslims. Poor and rich. Female and male. Categories that are as charged as they are important. People who vote or worship one way or another might share some features, but there are far more ways they differ from each other and far more ways they are similar to those in other categories. The uncorrelated features are likely to be far greater in importance than the few that are correlated. Yet thinking about subtle gradations along dimensions is much harder than lumping things into gross categories; there's so much more that has to be considered and kept in mind. Categories are easier on the mind. But beware the **First Law of Cognition, benefits come with costs.**

The beloved physician and professor of global health at the Karolinska Institute in Sweden, Hans Rosling, was dismayed by the many misconceptions people, even distinguished political and economic leaders of the world, had about the state of the world. His TED talk, telling the dramatic story of world economic development in recent times as if it were an ongoing tight soccer match, went viral. Many of the misconceptions that people held about economic and social development came from categorical thinking, especially dividing the world into rich and poor. Poor countries had no electricity, education, clean water, or health care. Rich countries had all that and more. Nothing in between. Wrong! Highly educated people vastly overestimated the percentage of the world that is poor, failing to update what was true of the world in the sixties to the world of the twenty-first century. They also saw poverty as all-or-none, not in gradations. Rosling found two ways to help people think dimensionally rather than categorically. First, by dividing the world into four categories instead of two and labeling them *levels* to signify a fluid dimension, not two rigid bins. Next, he used vivid depictions. Population of the world depicted as icons of people, each representing a billion, seven in total. Levels of wealth depicted in photos showing how the people at each level get water, move about in the world, cook, and what they eat. Life at Level 1 does resemble our image of dire poverty: people earn one to two dollars a day, carry water by foot in buckets from rivers, grow the crops they eat, gather firewood for cooking. But in 2017, only one billion of the seven billion people in the world lived at that level, not the large numbers that most educated people estimated. The three billion at Level 2 earn four dollars a day, get around by bicycle, have cannisters of fuel for cooking, grow more than they can eat, and eat a varied diet. Importantly, the children attend school. Even the girls. The two billion at Level 3 earn sixteen dollars a day, have running water, electricity, and a motorcycle. They might work multiple jobs, but the kids go to high school. As for Level 4, we know it intimately; we are among the one billion at Level 4. Take note that the key to jumping from level to level is means of motion, of getting from place to place in the world: from foot to bicycle to motor scooter to automobile.

Rosling relied on two compelling devices, both rooted in spatial cognition, to correct categorical thinking and misconceptions. The first was using a small number of levels rather than two dichotomous categories. Four categories fit neatly into short-term memory, we can hold four in mind, but holding many nuanced gradations is difficult. The second was creating understanding of the levels and the numbers through striking depictions. Perhaps Rosling's methods can encourage dimensional thinking and dispel misconceptions in other domains of our lives.

There's another lesson to learn from Rosling's analysis: economic mobility is tied to mobility in space. Moving farther in space opens economic possibilities, and even more, it opens opportunities to learn more pathways in space, to encounter new perspectives, to meet new people, places, and things, to learn from interacting with them. Moving farther in space opens opportunities to increase well-being in all aspects of what makes life worthwhile.

THE MIND CAN OVERRIDE PERCEPTION:
UNCERTAINTY, HYPOTHESES, AND CONFIRMATION BIAS

Back to perception of the world around us. The various demonstrations of change blindness show two important phenomena: that we have the impression that we are taking in a vivid, clear, coherent, and complete image of the world and that in fact we aren't. In many cases, the immediate impression is based on inference rather than perception: if it's a kitchen, it has a sink and a refrigerator; if a classroom, desks and white boards. Plausible inference fills in for direct knowledge in every domain of thought. Hence: the **Fourth Law of Cognition: The mind can override perception.**

That is, what's in the mind can override what's perceived, or more generally, hypotheses override perception. First, a striking demonstration from perception of familiar objects. Years ago, students viewed blurry, out-of-focus photographs of fairly familiar objects. The students were asked to guess what they were seeing and to keep guessing as the photographs were gradually brought into focus. Another group saw the focused photographs. Of course, you'd think that the group that had previews would be faster to recognize the objects, perhaps even before they were fully focused. You'd be wrong. Those who saw the blurry photos tended to generate false hypotheses about what they were seeing, and those false hypotheses got in the way of recognizing the objects in clear view. Presumably, viewers continued to interpret what they were seeing in terms of their original hypotheses.

This phenomenon, that hypotheses can override facts, occurs in cognition as well as in perception, like so many perceptual phenomena. The hypotheses or presumptions or beliefs that we hold bias our interpretations of the facts, of what we see. Here's another example; there are dozens and dozens. In a classic experiment, both Princeton and Dartmouth students were asked about an especially rough football game between the rivals, a game in which there were many penalties and several serious injuries. When asked who started the rough play, 86 percent of the Princeton students but only 36 percent of the Dartmouth students said Dartmouth did. Similarly, 93 percent of the Princeton students but only 42 percent of the Dartmouth students thought the game was rough and dirty. Viewing a film of the game later, Princeton students detected more than twice as many violations by the Dartmouth team as Dartmouth students. The inevitable conclusion is that Princeton and Dartmouth students didn't see the same game.

Since that study, numerous other studies have shown that our own starting points, our perspectives or our hypotheses, bias our very perceptions. We are more likely to notice evidence that supports our hypotheses than evidence that refutes it. When we find counterevidence, we are likely to discount it, to explain it away as aberrations. We—*everyone*—are prone to *confirmation bias*: we actively seek confirmation of our hypotheses and ignore disconfirming evidence, and we do that even when we have no personal investment in the hypotheses. Gathering evidence that a claim is true seems to be at the very heart of understanding a claim. Off in the distance, is that the cousin we haven't seen in years? Right height. Right hair. Right build. The surprising story we hear about a friend or news we read about a politician or a scientific discovery, could it be true? We first look for information consistent with the cousin's appearance or the story. We can't begin to reject a claim until we have some confidence in it. Looking for confirming evidence can make sense as a starting point; if there isn't any confirming evidence at all, the hypothesis should be dropped. But looking for confirming evidence shouldn't make us blind to counterevidence, fail to search for evidence that might counter the hypothesis, or dismiss it out of hand when confronted with it. Doing that can have dire consequences.

One reviewer of dozens of experiments presenting evidence for, and some against, the confirmation bias put it this way:

> Finally, I have argued that the confirmation bias is pervasive and strong and have reviewed evidence that I believe supports this claim. The possibility will surely occur to the thoughtful reader that what I have done is itself an illustration of the confirmation

bias at work. I can hardly rule the possibility out; to do so would be to deny the validity of what I am claiming to be a general rule.

That we naturally seek support for our hypotheses and that our hypotheses make us blind to counterevidence is rampant in perception, and what is true of perception is true of all thought. **Fifth Law of Cognition: Cognition mirrors perception.**

We'll return to this theme over and over. Spatial thinking is mirrored in abstract thought, in social thought, in cognitive thought, in thought about what makes people tick, in thought about art and about science. Thinking is thinking, whatever the domain, and spatial thinking is core to our very existence. Getting food into our mouths, finding our ways in the world. Carrying out most of the quotidian tasks that living entails, arranging our belongings, moving about in the world. We are far from perfect spatial thinkers, we don't perceive everything—too much is there, too much happens too fast—so we rely on plausible inferences. There is no guarantee that our inferences and judgments are veridical because we don't have objective measurement instruments built into our bodies or our brains. So, we must rely on other mechanisms and they are imperfect and can be biased. We saw this in representations of the body and the space around the body, and there are more biases to come in representations of the larger world. Even so, we are far better and more experienced at spatial thinking than at abstract thinking. Abstract thought can be far more difficult in and of itself, but fortunately it can often be mapped onto spatial thought in one way or another. That way, spatial thinking can substitute for and scaffold abstract thought.

PEOPLE, PLACES, THINGS

We are surrounded by the things most central to our lives: people, places, things. They compose the settings for the events of our lives. We distinguish people we know from those we don't know; we divine what they are thinking, feeling, doing, and communicating from their faces and their bodies. We know how to interact with

the objects around us—the objects tell us. We know what objects
and actions are likely in the places around us. The brain has specialized areas for recognizing people, places, and things, allowing
us to identify what they are in the briefest glance with nary a movement of the eyes. Both the brain and the mind like to put things into
boxes. Boxes are so much easier than dimensions. What's surprising
is how much meaning they carry, right there on the surface. Faces
and bodies carry identity, emotion, intention, action, communication. Things carry affordances: what they can do for us and what we
can do with them. Places tell us what they are and what we can do
in them. Meaning arrives without words, too fast for words. We use
that meaning to understand what is happening and to orchestrate
our own behavior. And we use it to imagine worlds that have never
been. Just as meanings can be wordless, so can thinking, an insight
Richard Feynman came to as a child:

> When I was a kid growing up in Far Rockaway, I had a friend
> named Bernie Walker. We both had "labs" at home, and we would
> do various "experiments." One time, we were discussing some-
> thing—we must have been eleven or twelve at the time—and I said,
> "But thinking is nothing but talking to yourself inside."
>
> "Oh yeah?" Bernie said. "Do you know the crazy shape of the
> crankshaft in a car?"
>
> "Yeah, what of it?"
>
> "Good. Now, tell me: how did you describe it when you were
> talking to yourself?"
>
> So I learned from Bernie that thoughts can be visual as well as
> verbal.

CHAPTER THREE

Here and Now and There and Then: The Spaces Around Us

In which we examine the ways that the space around the body and the space of navigation are represented in the mind and the brain, providing support for the premise of the entire book, that spatial thinking is the foundation for abstract thought.

THE WORLD AROUND US

Understanding the space around us seems easy. We only have to look at it. It's right there in front of our eyes. But our heads keep moving, our eyes keep moving, and so do our bodies. That rich world around us keeps changing as our eyes move, as we move. Even when we can't see it, we keep track of the world that was once in view and no longer is. What's there and where it is. You probably know what's behind you now without looking. Whenever you sit on a chair without looking backward, whenever you go up or down stairs without staring at your feet, whenever you return to the house to fetch the umbrella you left in the closet, you're relying on a world in the mind, but not in view. If I'm walking in midtown Manhattan and somebody asks me how to get to Carnegie Hall—that really happens!—I resist saying, "Practice," and tell them how to get there, even though Carnegie Hall is nowhere in sight. The world that is in the mind but not in sight is a skeletal world, not as precise or richly detailed as the one in sight. That sense of where things are in the world around us is carried in the mind in a mental spatial framework, a framework that gets updated as we move and enlarged as our experience is enlarged.

The mind creates and carries several different kinds of spatial frameworks. Like real-life frameworks, bookshelves and cabinets and networks of trains and roads, the formats of mental spatial frameworks can be used and reused, and what's arranged on them can be changed and rearranged. Mental spatial frameworks can be used to store and organize ideas, any kind of idea, not just places and landmarks. **Corollary of Fifth Law of Cognition, Cognition mirrors perception: Spatial mental frameworks can organize ideas.** Any ideas.

Centered inside one basic type of spatial framework, a three-dimensional one, is you, or a stick figure of you. This is a body-centered framework, one that represents what is around the body relative to the body. Not to the encompassing world. The mind creates a mental spatial framework, an imaginary stick figure extending from the three axes of the body, front-back, head-feet, and left-right, and hangs what's around the body on extensions of those axes. As the body moves and turns, the mental spatial framework is updated. It goes with you.

Just because you're at the center of your spatial framework and keeping track of everything around you relative to your own body doesn't mean you can't get out of your spatial framework and into someone else's, doesn't mean you can't take someone else's perspective. On the contrary, it's exactly because we're so good at keeping track of the things around us that we are also good at jumping into someone else's framework, at taking a different spatial perspective, even when it flies in the face of our own. We just hang different things on the front-back head-feet left-right framework and enter a different world. This is why you can give directions from your office to your home when you're sitting in neither.

Spatial frameworks allow taking perspectives that are entirely in the imagination. This is how you create the movie that runs through your mind as you read a novel. Creating a movie in the mind from words is in fact how we found support for the strong statements I just made, and that rightfully have you wondering, What's the evidence? Evidence meant going into the laboratory.

We began with two questions whose answers converge. We wanted to understand the model of the world around the body in the mind and we wanted to understand the nature of mental imagery created only with words, that movie that runs through your mind when you read. Up till then, most work on mental imagery had begun with pictures, not words. Most work on mental imagery had focused on visual images of things, animals, objects, and the like, and less on spatial imagery. People blind from birth may have excellent spatial imagery without any visual imagery at all. Studying spatial mental models created by language confronts more challenges than studying mental images created by pictures. Our stories were not nearly as engrossing as those on the best-seller list, but they worked. We wrote narratives placing first "you" and later fictitious others in a variety of environments, in a museum, at the opera, at a construction site, and more. Each narrative put "you" in the center of a bubble, with objects located above, below, in front, in back, to your left, to your right.

Here's the beginning of one of our narratives. The critical objects are highlighted here, but they weren't highlighted in what participants read.

You are hobnobbing at the opera. You came tonight to meet and chat with interesting members of the upper class. At the moment, you are standing next to the railing of a wide, elegant balcony overlooking the first floor. Directly behind you, at your eye level, is an ornate **lamp** attached to the balcony wall. The base of the lamp, which is attached to the wall, is gilded in gold. Straight ahead of you, mounted on a nearby wall beyond the balcony, you see a large bronze **plaque** dedicated to the architect who designed the theatre. A simple likeness of the architect, as well as a few sentences about him, are raised slightly against the bronze background. Sitting on a shelf directly to your right is a beautiful bouquet of **flowers** . . .

After people learned the environments, various versions of the narratives rotated them in place, rolled them on the floor, turned them upside down. This was imaginary, no acrobatics required. Remarkably, people had no problem learning these environments and even more complicated ones, and no trouble imagining themselves moving in them and keeping track of everything around them as they did. After each move, people were asked what was now in each direction from the body. What's in front? What's above your head? What's on your right? The task was easy. People easily kept track of what was around them as they moved in their imaginations; they rarely erred. What interested us was how quickly they retrieved the objects in each direction. The narratives were agnostic with respect to locations, the locations of the objects had been chosen by coin toss, but we suspected that some directions from the body would be faster than others. We also asked people how they did it, but their reports were vague and in many cases contradicted their own data. In any case, as good scientists, we trusted their data to tell us what their minds were doing. And they did.

Before data, some theory. If spatial thinking were like mathematical thinking, all directions would be equipotential, equally fast. But spatial thinking is not like mathematical thinking, and some directions turn out to be systematically faster than others. Which directions are faster depends on asymmetries of the body, of the world, and of the alignment of the body to the world. The body has three axes, and they differ considerably in both perception and action. Two of the body's axes, front-back and head-feet, have salient asymmetries, both of perception and of action. Of those, the front-back axis seems more critical as it separates the world that can be readily perceived and easily manipulated from the world that cannot be seen or easily interacted with. Our eyes face forward, so do our ears and our noses. And our arms and legs. Unless we are highly adept magicians, our arms and hands are more facile at doing things in front of us than behind our backs. Walking backward is awkward. Our heads swivel, but not all the way, so turning backward requires the whole body. Thus, both input and output, both perception and action, are asymmetric and oriented forward. After the front-back axis, the head-feet axis. More asymmetries, though not quite as strong. Our heads with much of our perceptual apparatus, eyes, ears, and nose, are at the tops of our bodies. Moving in space is controlled by our feet; most of us don't spend too much time walking on our hands. Finally, left-right. For the most part, our bodies are symmetric left-right, two arms, two legs, a symmetric torso, a symmetric face. True, most of the world is right-handed and handedness is important no matter which hand is dominant. But heavy lifting requires both arms and hands, and walking, both legs and feet. All things equal, objects in the more salient and distinctive directions should be faster to access.

But all is not equal. If it were only our bodies, then front-back would be fastest followed by head-feet, with right-left the slowest. But the body is in the world. The world, too, has three axes, but only one is asymmetric, the up-down axis conferred by gravity. Gravity, of course, exerts enormous constraints on our bodies, both our appearance and the appearance of everything in the world, and our actions, pulling us to the earth, making uphill harder than downhill. When we're upright, rather than lying on the couch or tossing and turning in bed, head-feet, our second most salient axis, is aligned with gravity. And when it is, when we're upright (remember, this is in imagination), we're fastest at finding what's above and below us followed by what's front and back. Left-right is most confusing, and slowest. But when we're lying down and rolling around, no axis of the body is aligned with gravity, and we respond fastest to objects in front or back followed by those at head or feet and slowest for objects left or right.

TAKING OTHER PERSPECTIVES

Now that this paradigm was working, we worked it hard. We wrote stories that put the objects around inanimate things like refrigerators rather than people; our participants had no trouble taking the perspective of refrigerators. We wrote stories that filled two bubbles

with different objects around two separate characters and asked people to take each of their perspectives in semi-alternation. Participants
didn't confuse which objects were around which characters and could
keep track of where the objects were as the characters' orientations
changed. We asked people to take the perspective of stick figures in
diagrams and Homer Simpson dolls in front of their eyes. Those, too,
were easy. The patterns of times differed somewhat for some of the
versions but in predictable and predicted ways. The essential finding
was that, in imagination, people could take many different perspectives, even that of a refrigerator, even that of a Homer Simpson doll
in front of them, with ease.

Yet, all the searching and finding was in imagination. We next
asked what happens when people search real environments that
actually surround them. The answer was different, depending on
whether the environments were brand new or had been learned.
When people first entered a new environment (simulated in a lab
room), they needed to look to see what was where in order to answer
each question of what's in front, what's above, what's to the left.
When they looked, they were fastest to find the objects that were
closer to their viewpoint. When the environments were new, people
were fastest to report what was directly in front of them, next to report the objects 90 degrees displaced, above their heads, below their
feet, to right or left, and slowest to report what was behind them. But
people quickly learned the environments and stopped looking; they
knew where everything was. Then their answers were faster and fell
into the same pattern as that of people who had learned the environments from language: fastest to head-feet because of asymmetry and
gravity, next to front-back because of asymmetry, last to right-left.

This is another example of the **Fourth Law of Cognition: The
mind can override perception.** We don't always look, even when the
answer is right in front of our eyes. Memory overrides perception.
It's sometimes faster to find information in the mind than to find it
in the world.

That bubble surrounding the stick figure framework of objects is
transportable. Rather than keeping us locked in our own here-and-

Figure 3.1. "In relation to the bottle, where does he place the book?"

now perspective, it enables going then and there. It allows taking any number of other perspectives, imaginary and real, as long as we can hang objects and landmarks on the appropriate appendages. It allows taking the perspective of someone right in front of us, even when that perspective conflicts with our own. Here's the task that shows that. People were shown a photograph like the one in Figure 3.1 of a young man, let's call him Patrick, seated a table that has a water bottle on his right and a book on his left. He is looking at the book.

His left hand, palm pointing downward, hovers just over the book. Participants were asked, "In relation to the bottle, where does he place the book?" We were interested in whether people would say "left," that is, answer from the Patrick's point of view, or say "right," answering from their own point of view. Many theorists and laypeople alike proclaim or assume that our own egocentric perspective is primary and that taking other perspectives is unnatural and effortful. This view is intuitively compelling. After all, we see the world from our own eyes, we experience it from our own bodies, from our own egocentric point of view. Virtual reality is giving us opportunities to see the world from other points of view, somebody else's ego, but even then, the experience is from a single point of view. Theories, intuitions, and proclamations notwithstanding, more participants took Patrick's perspective than their own egocentric perspective. More answered "left" than "right," as if in Patrick's place instead of their own. Spontaneously reversing right and left is all the more impressive because distinguishing right and left is hard—they are frequently confused. The key seems to be action. When the question didn't imply action, that is, "In relation to the bottle, where is the book?" many, but fewer, people took Patrick's perspective. When Patrick disappeared from the scene, the vast majority of participants took their own perspective. A couple of people out of sixty-four participants seemed to take the perspective of the opposing wall, but it's more likely that they just mixed up left and right.

Simply watching someone act induces us to take their (spatial) perspective. The research on the mirror system, reviewed in the first chapter, showed that viewing action resonates in the viewer's body; that is, we are programmed to internalize the actions of other people. But perspective taking is more than that: it's putting yourself in the place of the actor. Watching action can elicit perspective taking for two key reasons. I might take your perspective in order to understand your actions so that I can perform them myself. We learn so many diverse actions from watching, even imitating, others, from tennis serves to working a ticket machine. I might take your perspective to understand your actions so I can prepare my own. Are you tossing something to me? Then I reach out to catch. Are you throwing something at me? Then I'd better duck.

FLATTENING THE FRAMEWORK: MAPS

The body-centered framework, even if transportable, has limits, serious ones that evolution caught onto ages ago. The body-centered framework locates objects and landmarks relative to you, the stick figure in the middle, but not to each other. The body-centered framework is egocentric. To think about space more generally, we need to take the ego out of the space and form an allocentric representation. An egocentric body-centered framework is helpful for keeping track

of what's where as you move about, it's helpful for taking the perspectives of others, and it's helpful for imagining other perspectives
and other places. But it's not an efficient way to represent where
objects and landmarks are relative to each other. And of course we
can do that, as can rats and other creatures, by flattening the framework onto a plane and removing the stick figure. Like a map, flattening the framework to a plane not only swallows the stick figure
in the middle but also swallows height, the vertical dimension. That
flattened framework in the mind is more like a schematic network
of places than the GPS map you have in your phone. But networks
qua networks don't capture distances and directions among places,
and the mind captures some of that, with, as shall be seen, some
simplifications and distortions.

One of the more remarkable feats of humankind is the creation
of maps in the world, making a miniature representation of a large
space, a space too large to be seen from one place, abstracting and
shrinking that space, and putting that miniature into the world on a
virtual page. Our primary experience of the world is from the bubble
that encompasses us, updated as we move, our surroundings relative
to us. Yet, millennia ago, people began making egoless maps, broad
views of landmarks and paths (the flattened framework) relative to
each other, views that brought in far more than could be seen from
a single place. Creating a map means integrating many different experiences and flattening them to a plane. Some of those experiences
come from the moving bubble, but others may be indirect, from
other people's reports or sketch maps.

The new new thing keeps changing, that's a given. But the oldest
old thing keeps changing too. As new archaeological sites are discovered, the oldest known map keeps moving backward. Of course,
we are unlikely to find the really and truly oldest maps because they
were probably arrangements of sticks and stones or drawn in the
sand or gestured in the air and are unlikely to have survived. Those
that have survived are in sturdy forms, inscribed in stone or painted
on the walls of caves. The current oldest, a carved stone found in
a cave in northern Spain, dates back 13,600 years, far predating

written language. You can see it in Chapter Eight. It shows both the terrain—mountains, rivers, paths—and animals, encouraging speculation that it was a hunting aid or perhaps a tale of hunting. What's remarkable about this one as well as many of the previous contestants for oldest map is that they show two perspectives at once, overviews of paths, rivers, and mountains and frontal views of significant features of the environments, mountains, buildings, and in this case, animals. Many maps throughout history and to the present day do the same. They by no means conform to the standards of official cartography. Rather they appear to tell stories of the territory they depict, stories that can be entered and exited in diverse places. They can be used to tell many stories.

MAPS IN THE BRAIN: SPACE AND BEYOND

So, too, the maps in the brain. We go now from mind, from the thoughts and judgments and behavior of organisms, to brain, to the neural substrates presumed to underlie them. It's almost impossible to separate mind and brain. They are connected through behavior; it's by looking at the brain as organisms behave that we are able to infer the neural substrates. Now a pivotal example, the neural underpinnings of navigation. It will pivot us from real spaces to conceptual spaces.

Years ago, neuroscientists learned how to place tiny electrodes into single neurons to record what excited each one. The procedure has frequently been used in rats and allows them to roam freely, oblivious to the apparatus appended to their heads. Rats live in nests and scavenge for food, so they need to keep track of where they are and how to get home from wherever they are. The key components are places, how to recognize stable points in an environment, and the spatial array of places, how you go from one place to another. Single-cell recordings from neurons in rat hippocampus and neighboring entorhinal cortex have revealed both, single cells that respond to places in the former and spatial arrays of cells that correspond to spatial arrays of places in the latter. Since the seventies, dozens of studies have shown cells in rat hippocampus that fire when rats are in particular places in a field they are exploring, some cells for one place, other cells for other places. However, the place cells are not spatially organized in the hippocampus, so how the hippocampus could serve as a cognitive map, as claimed, wasn't clear. In the nineties, cells in rat brains that organized the place cells spatially were discovered bordering the hippocampus and richly interconnected with it, in entorhinal cortex. These cells have been called grid cells because they are laid out on a two-dimensional surface like the grid of a map and the pattern of firing looks grid-like. It is movement, the scampering of tiny feet as rats explore environments, that establishes the spatial layout of places on the grid cells. The grid cells then serve as a map, allowing the rat to go from one place to another in any order. The boundaries of the grid correspond to natural boundaries in the environment currently being explored. When rats explore a new environment, the set of grid cells is reused to map the new boundaries and locations of places. Those boundaries serve as a frame of reference for the set of places within, and both that frame of reference and the array it supports keep changing. The currently active set of grid cells is oriented with respect to the local environment, not to the coordinates of the world, as some of the hype implied. The important bottom line is that grid cells can be reused, recalibrated, and reoriented.

Those discoveries, place cells and grid cells, earned a Nobel Prize in 2014 for John O'Keefe, May-Brit Moser, and Edvard Moser. O'Keefe and Nadel had done the seminal research on place cells as well as header cells that responded to the rat's head direction, both in the hippocampus. The Mosers, as post-docs in O'Keefe's lab, led the research on grid cells.

Grid cells representing local cognitive maps are active in people when they explore environments, typically a virtual world in a scanner. In fact, the grid-cell substrate for representing cognitive maps seems quite similar in many mammals. What's important is that the spatial representation in grid cells is place-to-place and egoless, that is, allocentric, and that allocentric representations of space are created from the get-go, even in infants.

Those two components, place cells and grid cells, underlie spatial disorientation as well as spatial orientation. Losing either can be disorienting: not recognizing your surroundings, a feat that depends on place cells, or not understanding how your surroundings fit into the larger world, a feat that depends on grid cells.

At the other extreme, there are the super-oriented. London taxi drivers are legendary. London is a sprawling city with paths going every which way connecting what once were dozens of villages. To become a taxi driver, candidates need to learn at least 320 basic routes through more than 25,000 streets including more than 20,000 landmarks. It typically takes two to four years of intense study to master. That intense education changes the brain! A headline-making piece of research reported that the posterior portion of the hippocampi of taxi drivers grows larger and larger the more years they drive taxis.

Evolution likes to give new functions to old structures. Think of the mouth, originally for eating. We still use our mouths for eating, but we probably spend more time using our mouths for talking. Many of us learn to whistle and some of us can sing or play the flute. So for the brain: old structures pick up new functions both in evolution and in development. In rats, hippocampus and entorhinal cortex are used primarily for navigation, for remembering places and the paths among them. In humans, the hippocampus, entorhinal cortex, and other nearby cortical structures get used for remembering places and organizations of places, but different subregions are used for remembering and organizing many other things, including the events of our lives and the relations among ideas. Concepts and relations that are concrete and concepts and relations that are abstract alike.

The tragic case of H.M. provided fascinating information about the roles of these structures in forming new memories. In 1953, before neuroscientists knew better, large parts of his hippocampus, entorhinal cortex, and other nearby regions of the brain were resected in an attempt to control his epilepsy. The damage was crippling; he could form no new memories, so every event of every hour of every day was a new one. People and places were unrecognized even after many encounters. He had to be cared for the rest of his life, and was.

The hippocampus and entorhinal cortex are critical for remembering the past. It turns out that remembering the past is critical for planning the future. The same regions that are used to remember the past are also used to plan the future, so that damage in those regions affects both retrospective and prospective memory. It's not that we need specific information from the past to plan the future; we can plan trips to places we have never been. The dual dependence on these brain structures for both remembering the past and planning the future is most likely due to the roles of these brain areas in organizing and representing the separate items of information and in integrating them in meaningful ways.

FROM SPATIAL MAPS TO CONCEPTUAL MAPS

Now some audacious neuro-speculation. A shameless and gross oversimplification that focuses only on a small part of the brain when far more of it is necessarily involved. In humans, the hippocampus and entorhinal cortex enlarge and differentiate to represent not just places and space but also episodes in time. Recent research has expanded those roles even further, to associative and conceptual spaces. There are two key facts, one about place cells, the second about grid cells, that allow them to represent different real spaces and, later in evolution, abstract spaces. Place cells in hippocampus represent integrated sets of features, whether places, episodes, plans, or ideas, as individuals, independent of how they are interrelated. Grid cells represent relations among those places or ideas, spatial, temporal, or conceptual. Like grid paper, grid cells are a template that can be reused, remapped. Voilà! the same neural foundation that serves spatial thought serves abstract thought. It's as though the hippocampus created checkers or tokens for places or memories or ideas and entorhinal cortex provided a checkerboard for arraying the relations among them in space. Significantly, the array of grid cells, the checkerboard, is two-dimensional, flat, perhaps one reason why thinking in three dimensions is challenging for most people. I repeat: the same brain mechanisms in humans that represent actual places in real spaces also represent ideas in conceptual spaces. Spatial thinking enables abstract thinking.

We are now ready to proclaim (trumpets, please!) the crucial, central, fundamental tenet of the book: **Sixth Law of Cognition: Spatial thinking is the foundation of abstract thought.** The foundation, not the entire edifice. We show some of the implications of the Sixth Law in the next section, which recounts many curious and systematic distortions in people's cognitive maps, distortions that are mirrored in people's social maps. But the main focus of the second half of the book, Chapter Six and onward, will be the spatial foundation of abstract thought.

MAPS IN MINDS: COGNITIVE COLLAGES

The exciting research on place cells and grid cells has shown forcefully that the brain does not have a file drawer of cognitive maps that it pulls out as needed. Instead, cognitive maps are constructed and reconstructed on the fly, from pieces that are distributed in the brain. Grid cells represent spatial relations, but approximately, not exactly, and relative to a frame of reference that keeps changing as the environment explored changes. Collecting disparate pieces to navigate or make judgments is true in spades for humans. But people have far more pieces to use to construct mental maps beyond personal exploration, beyond place and grid cells. People can use specific memories of places they have visited or routes they have taken, but they can also use descriptions of places and routes in language and depictions of them in maps. They now can use mobile phones and augmented reality and who knows what else in the future. People can use spatial schemas, general knowledge about layouts of cities and towns, not just of their own regions and countries but also of other regions and countries. Once I visited Prague and Budapest in succession and realized that they have the same map: a river running north and south, with an old town and a castle on the west bank and a "new" town and art nouveau museum on the east bank. I couldn't use the maps interchangeably for finding the castles and the museums, but I could use the general schemas to understand the layouts of the cities. Japan has its own distinctive way of organizing cities: into quadrants, labeled the equivalent of NW, NE, SW, SE, with each quadrant divided geometrically into smaller units that are systematically labeled. Once you understand that organization, you can understand the clever and transparent address system, so different from Western systems.

When making decisions about navigation or judgments of distance or direction or sketching maps, people can make explicit inferences as well as implicit ones. This makes spatial judgment and navigation the same as solving any problem: gather whatever information seems to be relevant and try to make sense out of it.

Spatial thought, abstract thought

What follows are some of the proxies people use to make judgments about distances and directions in space or to sketch maps of space. Like our representations of the body, like our representations of the space around the body, the judgments are not random perturbations of physical measurements but systematically biased by the proxies and processes used to create them. Same for biases in the judgments of the larger spaces that we cannot see from one location. That's significant on its own, but it attains greater significance because the biases in spatial judgments are directly mirrored in biases in social and cognitive judgments in accordance with the **Fifth Law of Cognition: Cognition mirrors perception.** Earlier, in the discussion of the space around the body, we noted that the mind creates spatial frameworks to keep track of where things are relative to each other. Those spatial frameworks are essentially networks and can be used to keep track of relationships among any set of ideas; ideas in conceptual spaces are like places in real spaces. Similarly, the same processes used in spatial judgments will be shown to be at work in abstract judgments, judgments that are social or cognitive. These parallels between spatial thought and abstract thought strongly support the premise that spatial thought is a foundation for abstract thought. Much more on that in Chapter Six.

Rotation

We know about people's understandings of space from the judgments and inferences and decisions and sketch maps that they make. Now let's look more closely at those tasks, their findings, and their implications. We begin with perceptual processes that bias judgments, processes rooted in the gestalt principles of perceptual organization, *common fate* and *grouping*. Common fate is the expectation that objects that are related should be oriented in the same way. If one slants, they all should. According to common fate, the slant or orientation of a geographic entity should be close to the orientation of its frame of reference. For geographic entities, the frame of reference would be the encompassing structure, in this case, the canonical cardinal directions. This implies that the mind should mentally rotate the geographic entity to be oriented more like that of its frame of reference, here, the cardinal directions. Naturally, the world did not evolve to conform either to grouping or to common fate; other forces determined its evolution. So it turns out that many (if not most) geographic entities, like South America, Italy, Long Island, the San Francisco Bay area, and Japan, are tilted with respect to their encompassing frame of reference, the cardinal directions. The encompassing frame of reference might be an approximate proxy for the true orientation, but it's still approximate. People think of Milan as in the north and Naples as in the south of Italy, and that's true, but Naples, on the Mediterranean side of Italy, is way east of Milan and even Venice, which is on the Adriatic side of Italy.

To find out if minds use common fate even though geography doesn't, we developed geography quizzes especially designed to make people get them wrong. One asked a group of Stanford students to draw a line to indicate the direction from Stanford, on the west Bay, to Berkeley, on the east Bay. Other Stanford students were asked to draw a line indicating the direction from Stanford, which is inland, to Santa Cruz, which is on the Pacific. The Bay Area actually slants relative to N-S. Even though the correct map was on the road maps that people used then and in the weather maps published in the daily papers, a significant majority of students who lived in the area got the answers wrong. The majority drew lines showing Stanford west of Berkeley and Santa Cruz west of Stanford. Incorrect in both cases. The wrong answers come from rotating the major axis of the Bay Area to be more north-south than it actually is. The Bay Area actually runs almost diagonally with respect to the cardinal directions, but people's minds rotate it to be more upright relative to a north-south axis. In an informal test of an Italian audience, most raised their hands when asked if they thought that Naples (on the west coast of Italy) was west of Venice (on the east coast of Italy). Those Italians were wrong and surprised to learn that they were wrong. Just as Bay Area residents are surprised to learn that Berkeley is west of Stanford and that Palo Alto is west of Santa Cruz.

Similarly, people upright South America in their minds; its true orientation seems tilted. When students were given cutouts of South America and asked to paste the cutouts in a rectangular frame oriented north up, a significant majority uprighted South America. You can check your own memory. We then taught students new maps, made-up ones in which the geographic entities were tilted with respect to the canonical axes. Sure enough, when participants were asked to remember the directions between pairs of cities or to orient the map from memory, they made errors in the direction of rotation, of using the canonical axes as proxies for the actual orientations. We found the same error when participants were presented with map-like blobs. Ditto for school-aged kids; for these errors, kids and adults look alike.

Alignment

A core gestalt organizing principle is grouping similar things together. Objects in close proximity are seen as grouped, and objects that are similar by some attribute such as shape or color or size are seen as grouped. Now another brief geography quiz, taken from an experiment. Which is farther south, Rome or Philadelphia? If you answered "Rome," you are in excellent company. A majority give that answer. Their reasoning is reasonable, but the answer is wrong. For this question and many similar ones, people seem to rely on a perceptual inference, grouping by proximity. The mind groups the first row of x's into two groups of three and the second row into three groups of two.

xxx xxx

xx xx xx

When groups aren't quite aligned, the mind treats them as virtually aligned. And so for large geographic bodies, like Europe and the United States. The mind groups them and aligns them along an east-west axis even though most of Europe is north of most of the United States. Philadelphia is located in the northern part of the United States, Rome is located in the southern part of Europe, so people make the not unreasonable inference that Philadelphia should be north of Rome. But it's not. Grouping works north-south as well as east-west. Mentally aligning the United States and South America leads the majority to say that Boston is east of Rio because Boston is far east in the United States, and Rio is below Brazil's bulge, so not on the easternmost part of South America. This bias, to group similar geographic entities, has been termed *alignment*.

Like rotation, spatial alignment appears in other tasks. When people are asked to select which of a pair of maps is correct, the correct one or a world map in which the United States and Europe are more aligned, the majority select the incorrect but more aligned version. The same error shows up for North and South America. When asked to select which of a pair of maps is correct, the correct one or one in which South America is pulled eastward (or North America westward) to be more or less under North America, the majority select the incorrect map that is more aligned.

People make the same rotation and alignment errors when remembering new fictional maps or even meaningless blobs that are not interpreted as maps. They incorrectly remember new fictional maps and blobs as more aligned, and they incorrectly remember "cities" located on the fictional maps as more aligned. When sketching maps of their own familiar surroundings, surroundings they have traversed many times, they align streets, sketching them as more parallel than they actually are. These errors are widespread and persistent in the face of experience.

Hierarchical organization

You may have noticed that grouping, perceiving similar things as a group, is essentially placing them into a category. Although geographic space is mostly flat, we humans group geographic entities into categories such as continents and subcategories such as countries, then states, then cities, then neighborhoods. Out of flat space, minds—or governments—construct hierarchies of spatial categories. Spatial hierarchies are partonomies, not taxonomies like the categories of objects, events, and scenes, discussed in Chapter Two. Partonomies are hierarchies of parts; taxonomies are hierarchies of kinds. Cities are parts of states and states are parts of countries just as fingers are parts of hands and hands are parts of bodies.

We saw earlier that categories and hierarchies of categories allow reducing the amount of information in the world. Instead of thinking about each and every apple or dog or outing to the grocery store individually, we can think about apples and dogs and grocery outings in general. We can go up a level and think about fruit and domestic animals and shopping as categories. Categories are efficient for another reason. They allow broad inferences. If I learn that a kinkajou is an animal and I know that animals breathe and reproduce and move about, then I know that kinkajous do all those things (in case you are wondering, kinkajous are mammals with enormously long tongues that live in Central and South America). This kind of reasoning is especially important for new information. If you encounter a mangosteen and a grocer tells you it's a fruit, you know it is likely to grow on trees; have seeds, peel, and edible pulp; and so on. Categories are an efficient way to organize and store familiar facts and to learn new ones.

Like taxonomies, partonomies allow inferences, but inferences of containment, not of properties. If a knee is part of a leg and a leg is part of a body, then a knee is part of a body. Direct measurements of distance and direction, the kind surveyors do, use flat space, so spatial partonomies are irrelevant. But people, who don't store zoomable maps or, for that matter, any maps in their heads, use them as proxies, in the absence of direct measurements. Here's an example, another quiz. Note that, as before, it's the systematic errors that demonstrate the phenomenon.

Is Reno east or west of San Diego? Hard. Again, there are no complete and accurate maps in the mind that can be consulted. But, wait, there's an easy way to figure it out. Use hierarchical reasoning, the same kind of reasoning that allows us to infer, on being told that a kinkajou is an animal, that kinkajous breathe, eat, and reproduce. Here the hierarchy is spatial. And here's how people seem to reason. Reno is in Nevada, San Diego is in California. Nevada is east of California. So, Reno must be east of San Diego. Good reasoning but wrong answer. To make things worse, or maybe better, a wrong answer that the majority agrees with. The inference from location of state to location of city, from larger category to smaller, would be correct in many cases, but not in the case of Reno and San Diego. The problem is that the southern part of California cuts east, so that Reno, northwest in Nevada, is actually east of San Diego, far south in California.

This brings us to the **Seventh Law of Cognition: The mind fills in missing information.**

Spatial categories are used as proxies for distance estimates as well as for direction estimates. Distances of pairs of locations that are within a spatial group like a state or a country are estimated to be smaller than distances of pairs of locations between spatial groups, even when pairs are deliberately chosen so that the between-group distance is smaller than the within-group distance.

You might think that because hierarchical organization can lead to systematic error only novices would rely on hierarchical organization and experts would not. In fact, experts, namely, experienced taxi drivers, have more refined and better hierarchical knowledge of the environments they traverse than novices. This is not to say that experts make more errors than novices. Experts have also developed ways to counter the errors. Hierarchical knowledge is not the only method to determine routes or estimate distances, and experts have many methods at their disposal.

Significantly, the bias that within-group estimates are smaller than between-group estimates occurs for groups that are defined functionally rather than spatially, groups that have no spatial integrity at all. In Ann Arbor, the home of the University of Michigan, buildings belonging to the university are interspersed among commercial buildings that have no association with the university. Students in Ann Arbor give smaller distance estimates to pairs of university buildings or to pairs of commercial buildings than to pairs formed from one university building and one commercial building. Similarly, Israelis, both Palestinian and Jewish, estimate the distances between two Jewish settlements or two Palestinian settlements to be smaller than the distances between one Jewish and one Palestinian settlement even when the latter are in truth smaller than the former. In both cases, then, within-group distances are perceived as smaller than between-group distances, yet here the groups are functional or political rather than spatial.

Even more support for the spatial foundations of abstract thought comes from studies on similarity within and across social groups. Similarity is distance in conceptual space. Just as politically similar settlements are judged to be closer in space than politically different settlements, so people who happen to be in the same social or political group are judged to be more similar to each other even on an irrelevant dimension than people who happen to be from different social or political groups. Inferences that are natural but that can lead to trouble.

So far, we have described three mechanisms that are used for judgments of space, rotation, alignment, and hierarchical organization. Each acts as a proxy or heuristic for judging distance or direction or selection of the correct map in lieu of direct measurement. Each biases judgments systematically in ways that would be difficult to show unless you knew how to find them. Rome and Philadelphia, Berkeley and Stanford, Reno and San Diego were deliberately chosen for the geography quizzes. There are other heuristics spatial reasoning takes. There is *straightening*. Even long-time residents of Paris straighten the curvaceous Seine in their sketched maps and in their mental maps. One can only imagine the numbers of hours of extra walking and liters of gasoline this distortion has cost. Next, we turn to systematic errors due to reference points and perspective.

Reference points

Yet another proxy for estimating distance is using landmarks. Every city seems to have them, and they often symbolize the city. Think of the Eiffel Tower in Paris or the Empire State Building in New York. Landmarks frequently serve as reference points. Because they are familiar, other places are located with respect to them. I might approximately locate a restaurant for you by saying it is near the Piazza del Duomo in Milan or the Pantheon in Rome.

Spatial reference points are larger than themselves. This isn't really a paradox: landmarks are themselves, but they also define neighborhoods around themselves. In a paradigm that has been repeated on many campuses, researchers first collect a list of campus landmarks from students. Then they ask another group of students to estimate the distances between pairs of locations, some to landmarks, some to ordinary buildings on campus. The remarkable finding is that distances from an ordinary location to a landmark are judged shorter than distances from a landmark to an ordinary location. So, people would judge the distance from Pierre's house to the Eiffel Tower to be shorter than the distance from the Eiffel Tower to Pierre's house. Like black holes, landmarks seem to pull ordinary locations toward themselves, but ordinary places do not. This asymmetry of distance estimates violates the most elementary principles of Euclidean distance, that the distance from A to B must be the same as the distance from B to A. Judgments of distance, then, are not necessarily coherent.

Cognitive reference points work the same. Cognitive reference points are convenient: a composer might be compared to Bach or Beethoven and an artist to Picasso or Pollack. Somebody's the new Babe Ruth or David Bowie or Spike Lee. Like spatial reference points, cognitive reference points are larger than themselves; they serve as genres or prototypes. Cognitive reference points create asymmetries of judgments of similarity just as spatial reference points create asymmetries of judgments of distance. Similarity, after all, is a measure of conceptual distance. People judge magenta to be more similar to red than red to magenta. Red is the prototype, it stands for a category of colors that are red-like in the way that the Eiffel Tower stands for a neighborhood. Magenta stands only for itself. Ditto Pierre's house. Moving from the perceptual to the cognitive, people judge a son to be more similar to his father than a father to his son. They see North Korea as more similar to the People's Republic of China than the PRC to North Korea. Fathers and the PRC are like red or the Eiffel Tower, they are prototypes, endowed with a broader set of qualities than sons or North Korea. Another set of examples of the **Fifth Law of Cognition: Cognition mirrors perception.**

Perspective

When you are high on a mountain or a tall building taking in the vast panorama in front of you, you might notice that things that are far from you seem closer together, more crowded, than things closer to you. The dispersion of close things and crowding of distant things occurs for imagined perspective as well. Students from a university somewhere between the coasts of the United States were asked to imagine themselves either in San Francisco, on the Pacific coast, or in New York, on the Atlantic coast. Then they were asked to estimate the distances between several cities scattered along an east-west axis between San Francisco and New York. Those who imagined themselves in San Francisco gave a longer estimate for the distance between San Francisco and Salt Lake City than those who imagined themselves in New York. Conversely, those who imagined themselves in New York gave a longer estimate for the distance between New York and Philadelphia than those who imagined themselves in San Francisco. It's as if distances were telescoped, larger when close, smaller when far. Remember that the students were actually in neither place. What's remarkable is that this distortion happens solely with imagined perspectives, irrespective of where people are actually located in space.

That same distortion, finer discrimination for things that are close to us than for things that are far, occurs for judgments of people on social dimensions. People judge members of their own social group, a close group, to be more different from each other than members of other social groups, faraway groups. Individuals in our university, our political party, our country are quite different from each other, but those in the rival university, another political party, and surely another country, they're all alike. It's natural; we've had far more experience with our own social groups than with others.

Expertise matters. Bird experts and car experts make far greater distinctions in their areas of expertise than the rest of us. It seems inevitable that we discern more differences for the close and the familiar, and see the distant and less known in generalities. But then, there are times we need to think in generalities, to see the broad strokes rather than the fine detail. Those cognitive trade-offs again.

COGNITIVE COLLAGE

Cognitive map is an old notion. It came from Tolman's pathbreaking work on rats: he showed that when rats solved mazes they made spatial inferences, they took shortcuts when given the opportunity, as if they had map-like representations in their brains. As does at least one young child, despite being blind from birth. Yet it seems that whatever people have in their minds that they use to estimate distances or directions or to sketch maps are constructions of the mind, from pieces, often from different experiences and different kinds of information. Because people's minds lack direct measurements and lack map-like mental representations of the world, they bring together whatever information seems to be relevant for the task at hand. That information is useful in general, but piecemeal and approximate. Many cities in Nevada are east of many cities in California, but not Reno and San Diego. The United States is generally aligned east-west with Europe, but Rome in southern Europe is actually north of Philadelphia in the northern United States. The Bay Area is closer to running north-south than east-west just like the state of California, but inland Stanford happens to be west of coastal Santa Cruz. Pierre's house can't be closer to the Eiffel Tower than the Eiffel Tower to Pierre's house. These proxies are independent for the most part, and so are the consequent errors. Because they are independent, the errors can cancel each other, so sketching a map of many spatial relations is one way to increase accuracy. The more constraints that are fulfilled, the greater the accuracy.

Yet, ultimately, these proxies—alignment, rotation, hierarchical thinking, perspective, landmarks, and more—can't be resolved in a flat Euclidean map. Rather than cognitive maps, the mind seems to have cognitive collages.

Why do these errors persist? Because the mind doesn't have ways to correct them, short of measuring the world, and when accuracy is crucial, the world gets measured. Measurements can overcome many biases in natural judgments, not just these. Because in many cases, the errors are not large and don't matter. Because when we're actually navigating on the ground, the environment itself can correct us.

Even if incomplete, ambiguous, inconsistent, and biased, our mental spatial frameworks play crucial roles in our lives and in our imaginations. They allow us to envisage other worlds, worlds we have not seen, that no one has seen, even impossible worlds. Metaphoric worlds where places are replaced by any kind of entity or idea and paths by the relations among them. The worlds of fiction, of the arts, of science.

CHAPTER FOUR

Transforming Thought

In which we distinguish *representations* of thought from *transformations* of thought, then analyze spatial transformations and what they are good for (plenty!) followed by spatial ability and how to get it.

NOW WE LEAVE THE BODY IN THE WORLD AND ENTER THE MIND. We've populated the mind (and the brain) with the things that are central to our lives: faces, bodies, objects, scenes, events. We've put them on the mind's stage for the mind to use, to ponder, to perform, to transform. Once the players, any sort of object or thing, are on stage, we can play with them. We can turn them into symbols in mathematics, words in poetry, particles in physics, molecules in chemistry, buildings in a neighborhood, dancers on a stage. We can change their shapes and sizes and properties. We can change where they are and what they do. That stage is the stage of imagination, and it can carry us far.

Thinking starts somewhere, with an idea or a problem, vague or precise. Then you do something to the idea, you transform it some way, and *voilà!* a new idea. After that, you can begin to work on the new idea. And so on, until you're done or reach a dead end or are simply worn out. Sometimes thinking comes with instructions: multiplication and piano music and waltz steps and chemistry problems. That doesn't mean that following the instructions is trivial—instructions aren't always clear. It can take concentration and thought to follow instructions, but there are instructions. There's a script that tells you what to do at each step. Like following a recipe or assembling Legos or furniture. Recipes and assembly instructions are a sequence of actions on real objects that transform them step-by-step into something else. The right sequence of actions on butter and sugar and eggs and flour and baking powder takes glop and transforms it into cupcakes. Pieces of wood can be turned into a desk or a bookcase. Lego blocks, into houses and robots.

Assembly is actions on real objects. Thinking is mental actions on mental objects—ideas. Actions on ideas that transform them into something else. That's how we talk about thinking, as if it were actions on ideas. We put ideas aside or turn them upside down or inside out. We split them into parts or pull them together. We arrange and rearrange, enlarge, stretch, reverse, join, copy, add, scramble, subtract, lift, glue, push, fold, mix, toss, embellish, separate, nail, scatter, bury, eliminate, turn, elevate, and poke holes in both real objects and mental ones. Intriguingly, we will see soon and in the chapter on gesture that performing the actual actions helps the mental ones, the thinking.

Of course, not all cooking or assembly follows scripts. Chefs, professional and hack alike, improvise new recipes on the fly or invent them studiously. Rauschenberg famously took junk he found on the streets and turned it into art. Le Witt made art by systematically and methodically arranging lines and boxes and cubes. If you or I tried to do what they did, alas, it probably wouldn't be art. No script for Rauschenberg or even the more methodical Le Witt. Instead, trial and error, practice, skill, expertise, and, yes, talent. Same for thinking. No script for creating a good novel or a catchy melody or a gripping film or an elegant teapot or an unreturnable tennis return. No script for figuring out what you want to do on your visit to Rome, no script for figuring out why an election turned out this way instead of that way, no script for rearranging the furniture in your living room or deciding your next move in chess. There are schemas, constraints, rules of thumb, educated hunches: what spices work together, what makes a balanced composition, what chess moves are likely to succeed. The truly interesting and challenging kind of thinking can't follow a script; there isn't any.

REPRESENTATIONS AND TRANSFORMATIONS

Now some jargon. What I've been calling *ideas* psychologists often call *representations*. Representations are in the mind rather than in the world, though they often come from the world. Representations are regarded as something static, something you can look at and contemplate, something you can alter in your mind. Of course, there aren't really representations in the brain; it's just a useful way of talking. A representation captures the information that is central for an idea or a problem. Representations are schematic, like maps. Aerial photographs don't make good maps; good maps select the information that's important for the task at hand, say, driving, hiking, or bicycling, and they simplify, amplify, and even distort that information. Roads, for example, wouldn't be visible at scale on many maps, so they are enlarged. Small bends in roads don't appear on maps. And maps often add information like names of streets and cities, borders between states or countries, coloring for altitude or depth.

Representations in the mind can come from outside the mind, from perception, the view you have of the city you're exploring or the face in the distance you think you recognize or the chess board on the table. What you put in your mind isn't all that you can see; rather, what's in your mind is abstracted from what you see, usually embellished with interpretations from the inside, like the name of the person or the roles of the buildings, bank, department store, church. Representations can also come entirely from the inside; you might be thinking about chess moves or rearranging the furniture in your living room or the route you want to take home to do your errands. Representations come in many formats: Some lean toward depictive, like the chess board or music score or scene in front of your eyes or the living room in your mind. Others lean toward descriptive, like the words of a song or your lines in a play or a list of errands. Still others might be musical, the song's melody, or motoric, the finger movements to play a piece on the piano or open a lock or the body movements to perform a dive or a tennis serve. Many representations are essentially mixed media.

Although the number of representations is boundless, the number of kinds of representations is not. And there are varieties and combinations of each kind. Representations can be regarded as internalized perceptions, so visual representations carry some visual properties like color, spatial representations carry some spatial properties like composition or size or distance, auditory representations carry some acoustic properties like pitch, and verbal representations carry semantic and syntactic properties.

What I've called actions on ideas psychologists often call *transformations*. Sometimes we use the term *operation*, lingo borrowed from computer science. Just as there are countless real-life actions on real objects, there are countless mental actions on ideas or transformations of representations. Recall the list, a partial one: pull together, raise, toss out, arrange, and so on. Some transformations are loosely tied to domains like arithmetic or cooking or music or language or gene splicing or chess, but many are generic. And so very many of them are based on actions by the body in space, whether actual or imagined. In fact, a useful way to think about mental transformations is as internalized actions. Just as representations can be regarded as internalized perceptions.

MENTAL ROTATION

Now decide whether the *F*s and *R*s and *5*s in Figure 4.1 are the same or mirror images of each other. Then think for a minute how you decided.

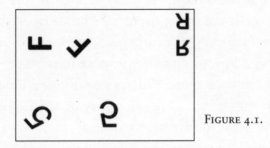

FIGURE 4.1.

Mental rotation entered the world in 1971 to great fanfare. You got a feel for it when you decided whether the *F*s or the *R*s or *5*s were the same or mirror images of each other. Doing so is a very different kind of thinking from the thinking needed to decide that because Socrates is a man and all men are mortal, Socrates is mortal. It is entirely different from deciding which movie to see or whether or not to buy a dog. It is not so different from adding 5 + 7 to get 12 because it turns out that mathematical thinking has a layer of spatial thinking. You might have done what I did, imagine a mental ruler with numbers going horizontally from 1 on the left, each marked with a vertical tick, longer ticks for 5s and 10s. My mind slid to the 5 tick, then to 10, then 2 more to get 12.

Mental rotation is a distinctly visual-spatial transformation. It has been likened to watching something actually rotate in space. Now some gritty detail on the first dramatic study. Rather than letters or numbers, that study used pairs of ten linked cubes with two bends, each a different direction. Neither easy to describe nor easy to mentally rotate. The figures appeared at different angles, either in the picture plane or in depth. When rotated to the same angle, half were the same and half were mirror images. Participants were shown many pairs of those figures, half same, half mirror image, over many days. The angular difference between the pairs varied from 0 to 180 degrees. With so much practice, some participants became highly skilled at the task. Their performance became quite regular and they made very few errors. The data of interest were the times to decide whether the two figures of each pair were the same or mirror images as a function of the difference in angle. One way to decide is to mentally rotate the pairs to the same angle and to "see" if they overlap or diverge. If people do mentally rotate the figures into correspondence, then the greater the difference in the orientation of the two figures, the longer it should take to respond. Exactly that happened. Twelve disparities in orientation, varying from 0 to 180 degrees, yielded twelve data points lying on a straight line, showing increasing response time with increasing disparity in orientation. It was as if the brain had a turntable that continuously rotated and you simply put a shape on it and turned it on. That striking claim about the mind, however, turned out to be an oversimplification.

The discovery of mental rotation was especially striking on the background of the field at the time. The cognitive revolution that began in the late fifties and sixties had released the shackles of behaviorism and allowed entry into the mind. The challenge was (and still is) to show what was happening in the mind by putting the mind into the world. Yet the field of thinking was (and in many ways still is) dominated by language. It's easy to get people to read or listen and to talk or write and then to make inferences about their thinking from their words. Also, when people think about thinking, they think they are thinking in words. So how to study imagery, spatial or visual? Or auditory or olfactory or tactile? How to get it out of the head and into the world where it can be objectively observed? Words can't do justice to images. Drawing won't work, it's too hard for many to draw their imagery. Then there are so many people who say they have no imagery, so spatial and visual thinking can't be tied to subjective experience. Reaction times to perform spatial or visual or acoustic tasks provided a way to put the mind into the world. In the case of mental rotation, a continuous spatial process perfectly predicted the times.

These remarkable findings seemed to imply that people smoothly mentally rotate the figures into congruence as if they were watching the figures rotate into congruence. However, there are perfectly intelligent people who can't perform the task easily; several of them dropped out of the experiment. Others say that they don't smoothly mentally rotate; rather they look back and forth part-by-part. Eye movements confirm those reports, going back and forth between segments of the figures as if checking part-by-part. Of course, this is still visual-spatial reasoning even if it's piecemeal rather than holistic. Those whose eye movements and subjective experience indicated holistic mental rotation performed better on a battery of tests for spatial ability than those whose eye movements and subjective experience suggested part-by-part comparison. Since then, a variant of the mental rotation task has become one of the major measures of spatial ability. More on spatial ability soon.

Mental rotation, imagining something in front of the eyes in a different orientation, is more than an arcane skill studied in the laboratory. We use it when we are lying down, when we recognize objects that aren't upright, and when we read at an odd angle. We use it when we solve puzzles or organize shelves and drawers or pack a suitcase or put together a bicycle or assemble a piece of furniture or put a key in a lock. Surgeons, plumbers, electricians, football coaches, mathematicians, fashion designers, urban planners, gardeners, physicists, fire fighters, architects, basketball players, interior designers, dentists, and so many more use mental rotation and other forms of spatial reasoning regularly in their work. Or their play. But not to worry if you're at the low end. Remember that mental rotation can be done in many ways, piecemeal or by trial and error. What's more, although some fortunate folk seem to be born with the skill, it can be acquired, in the usual way: practice. Moreover, lawyers and journalists and historians and accountants and executives and philosophers and poets and translators don't seem to need mental rotation in their work.

The intimate connection between mental actions and physical ones is evident watching people attempt mental rotation tasks. When they try to solve mental rotation problems, many people spontaneously rotate their hands as if rotating an object. When they do, their performance is faster and more accurate. As they practice and get better at the mental rotation task, hand rotations tend to drop out. Presumably, physical rotation helps to internalize mental rotation. In other studies, participants rotated a wheel clockwise or counterclockwise while solving mental rotation problems. Mental rotation was faster and more accurate when the direction of manual rotation was the same as the optimal direction for mental rotation. But when the direction of manual rotation was in the opposite direction, mental rotation times and errors increased. More evidence that mental actions resemble physical ones comes from neuroimaging studies showing that mental rotation activates motor areas of the brain. Mental actions do not merely resemble physical ones; it turns out that making the parallel physical actions helps perform the mental ones.

TWO PERSPECTIVES: OUTSIDER AND INSIDER

When we solve mental rotation problems, we are outside looking at an object. We can mentally rotate all sorts of objects, familiar and unfamiliar, meaningful ones like letters and chairs, meaningless ones like shapes, 2D or 3D. They vary in difficulty and in patterns of reaction times. For example, deciding whether pairs of asymmetric letters like R and G at different orientations are the same or mirror images doesn't give linear reaction times. Rotating a letter to 90 degrees from upright hardly increases reaction time, but turning it upside down slows time considerably. Apparently, we get pretty good at reading sideways.

But when we imagine our own bodies in different orientations, we take an insider perspective. Look at the body in Figure 4.2 to decide which arm is extended, right or left.

If you are like most people, you imagined your own body in that position and then figured out whether your left (correct) or right arm would be extended. Many everyday situations require that kind of thinking, such as when you tell someone how to get from your office to your home or figure out a route from a map. At each choice point,

FIGURE 4.2. Which hand is outstretched?

you have to decide whether to turn left or right. Doing this is more like spatial-motor imagination than visual-spatial imagination. You can feel it in your body as you think. If you're like me, you might even turn your body a bit. Think back to being a child and figuring out how to put on a jacket or sweater. Or which way to turn a lid. Or which hand is your right one, still a problem for many grown-ups. Then there are soccer moves and tennis serves and dance and yoga and gymnastics. Playing the piano or violin, using your hands to raise clay on a potter's wheel or do calligraphy. How to twist your body and your shoulder and your hand to reach an object that found its way under the bed. Or how to throw your opponent off in a combat sport.

Thinking about how your body moves and turns in space can be brought into the laboratory as a visual-spatial task, no gymnastics required. Like the one you just tried. On each of many trials, people view bodies like the one above in various orientations with one arm outstretched; their job is to say whether the right or left arm is outstretched. Or they view hands in various orientations and say whether it's the right or left hand. Even though the stimuli are visual, deciding whether an arm or a hand is right or left seems to rely primarily on spatial-motor imagination. That is, people imagine themselves or their hands in those orientations in order to make the right-left judgment. Just as for mental rotation of objects, the times to perform these tasks yield regular patterns of reaction times but quite different patterns from those of imagining rotation of objects. The patterns of response times reflect imagining motor actions rather than watching spatial transformation. For hands, it takes people longer to make left-right judgments when the hand positions are awkward than when they are comfortable. Both tasks, mental rotation of objects and mental rotation of bodies, have been brought into the scanner. The two tasks activate partly overlapping but partly different brain areas. Somewhat the same, somewhat different.

Intriguingly, people who have lost an arm can perform these tasks, that is, they can decide which arm is outstretched and whether the depicted hand is right or left, but they are slower than people who have all their limbs. Presumably, the loss of physical motion diminishes imaginal motion, further support for the close relation between imagination and action. More to come.

Just as actually rotating a hand can facilitate mental rotation, actually turning the body can facilitate imagined turns of the body. In one set of experiments, people made or imagined a short route with two turns. Then they were asked to point back to where they started. When they only imagined the turns, they made large errors, but if they actually turned, even blindfolded, they were far more accurate. In both cases of mental rotation, rotation of objects or rotation of bodies, actual actions facilitate imagined ones. The actual actions need not be identical to the imagined ones, but they are congruent with the imagined ones, rotating the hand for imagining rotating an object and rotating the body for imagining rotating the body.

Although actual rotations help imagined ones, actually moving straight forward or backward doesn't seem to help imagining moving forward or backward. Rotation in space leads to dramatic changes in the spatial relations of the things around us to us: what was in front might now be to the right, what was on the left might now be in back. Mimicking the motion apparently helps us update those spatial relations. Moving forward or backward, translation in space, can change what's in front and back but doesn't change what's right and left. Updating spatial relations when imagining translation in space is apparently easy enough that it doesn't benefit from the support of actual movement.

All of this points to the difficulty of mental rotation, whether of our own bodies or of objects in front of our eyes, and to the roles congruent actions of the body can play in supporting that thinking.

CREATING IMAGES: DRAWING IN THE MIND

Mental rotation generated tremendous excitement and sparked more exciting research in spatial thinking. If the mind can imagine mental rotation, what other wonders can the mind perform? Perhaps we can imagine things changing in size, location, shape. Or adding parts, taking them away, reorganizing them. Perhaps we can scan them to make judgments, like size and distance. Yes, people can do those mental manipulations and more, with greater or lesser ease. Try this one. Imagine half a grapefruit, dome side up, flat side down. Now imagine hanging a capital *J* from the middle of the flat side. What do you have?

You just built something in your head from a description in language, without any visual input. Mental construction, like physical construction, appears to be a step-by-step process. Consequently, the greater the number of parts, the longer it takes. For example, the figure in Figure 4.3 can be described as having two parts, the intersection of two rectangles, or as having five parts, five squares in a specific array. Same figure, but when described and conceived of as two parts, it takes less time for people to create an image in the mind than when described and conceived of as five parts.

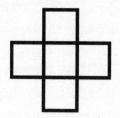

FIGURE 4.3. Image to be formed from a description with two or five parts.

Mental construction mimics physical construction in that it's step-by-step from parts. But the analogy goes deeper. First, another task, one familiar from grade school, geometric analogies. Try the analogy in Figure 4.4.

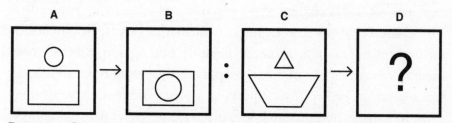

FIGURE 4.4. Geometric analogy requiring two spatial transformations for solution. From Novick and Tversky, 1987.

The answer requires moving the small upper figure (the circle or triangle) inside the lower larger one (the rectangle or trapezoid) and enlarging the smaller one. Or changing the size of the smaller one and then moving it into the larger one. The order of moving or changing size doesn't matter. Just like adding a set of numbers.

We asked people to solve geometric analogies like this one. Each required two or three transformations drawn from a larger set of possible transformations. After solving each, people told us the order in which they did the transformations. Although they were free to choose any order, the order they chose agreed, the same order for nearly everyone. We then asked another group of people to do the transformations in that preferred order or in some other order. When the new group of students used the preferred order, they were faster and more accurate. Because there are no mathematical constraints on the order of applying transformations, the constraints must be cognitive, and we puzzled over what they could be. Maybe people did the harder ones first, while they had something to look at, and then did the easier ones that had to be done entirely in the mind. So, we asked people which transformations were harder. We also determined which ones took more time, another measure of difficulty. It was a good idea, but the data didn't support it. People preferred first to *move,* then to *rotate* or *reflect,* then to *remove* a small part, then to *add a half* or change *size,* then to add *shading,* and finally to *add a small part*. The fastest and easiest transformation was the first, *move,* but the slowest and hardest was the second, *rotate or reflect.* So, neither time nor difficulty explained the order. We continued to puzzle.

Then we had a change of perspective and an insight. You probably realized that putting a capital *J* under the grapefruit half forms an umbrella. This feat required mental construction, albeit simple mental construction, not as complicated as imagining structures from Lego or Tinker Toys. Applying a series of mental transformations to solve geometric analogies is also a mental construction task, a 2D one, akin to mental drawing. If mental drawing is internalized physical drawing, then drawing order should account for transformation order. And it did. We asked another group to imagine drawing a simple object, for example, a cane. Then we asked them to tell us their drawing order; it compared nicely with the transformation order. Drawing has built-in constraints. If you're drawing, you first need to decide where to put your pencil on the page, that is, where to place the object; that's *move*. Then you need to decide what direction to begin drawing, that is, how the object you are drawing is oriented; that's *rotate* or *reflect*. Next, you need to decide how far to draw, that is, how large the object is. That's *remove* or *add half* or *size*. After you've drawn the object, you can *shade* it or *add a small part*. With that, mental construction, in this case, drawing, accounted for the perplexing order of performing the mental gymnastics needed to solve geometric analogies. And simultaneously revealed the origins of some of the marvelous creativity of the mind. Imagining elaborate scenes is like internalized drawing.

ANIMATING IMAGES: STEP-BY-STEP

Step-by-step mental construction is an amazing feat our minds can perform to create an endless array of objects in the mind and to alter them and their configurations and actions. The very gifted among us, choreographers, topologists, engineers, Ping-Pong players, seem to be able to mentally animate those changes, that is, to imagine transformations in parts, shape, and location as they happen. Bodies dancing or diving; mechanical systems like pumps or brakes. It might seem that way, but closer examination suggests otherwise.

We ordinary folk need to imagine motion whenever we cross the street as a car is approaching; do we have enough time to cross—or will the driver slow down? A complicated judgment, part spatial, part social, and the cost of error is high. Sadly, both pedestrians and drivers are reliably unreliable in these judgments despite extensive practice. According to the National Safety Council, approximately forty thousand people died in traffic in the United States in 2016. Almost six thousand were pedestrians. Of course, not all deaths were due to unreliable judgments, either by pedestrians or by drivers, but misjudgments are likely to have contributed to many.

Baseball outfielders ought to be expert in mental animation, in imagining the path of a fly ball as they dash to catch it. They are indeed pretty good at it, or they wouldn't have lasted on the team, but they don't seem to mentally animate the trajectory. That is, the brain doesn't seem to have an algorithm that accurately computes the ball's trajectory. Rather, outfielders seem to have developed heuristics, or approximations, for estimating what direction and how far they need to run to catch the ball. The estimations are modified "on the fly" as outfielders are running. Frisbee-catching dogs, and presumably Frisbee-catching people, seem to do the same.

The paths of fly balls or oncoming vehicles are single objects in motion. Perhaps we are better at imagining mechanical systems in action. Alas, those are difficult for most people as well. People animate them step-by-step, sometimes with great effort. Take pulley systems; they run smoothly and continuously. You pull on the rope, the rope turns the pulleys, and the weight attached to the rope rises. Now suppose you see a static diagram of a set of pulleys and have to answer which way each pulley rotates. If you are watching the pulley system in action, you can immediately see whether each pulley is going clockwise or counterclockwise. But most people can't mentally animate a pulley system from a diagram of the system. To decide which way each pulley is rotating from a diagram, they animate each pulley step-by-step, discretely. What's perhaps even more interesting, there's a bias to begin at the conceptual beginning, with the person pulling on the rope, even when beginning at the "end" with the weight would be faster and more efficient for the last pulley.

Mental animation, like mental drawing, seems to be conceptually driven and step-by-step rather than a smooth and continuous analog transition.

SPATIAL ABILITIES

I was once asked to write a book on spatial ability: what it's good for, do you have it, and how to get it. I replied that it would be either a very brief book or a long, tedious one. Here's a summary of the brief book. Spatial ability is good for football, basketball, sharp-shooting, Go, hockey, science, math, engineering, design, art, fashion, stage sets, choreography, carpentry, and surgery, just for starters. You probably have it if you did the mental rotation tasks easily. Otherwise, practice; it works.

Now a slightly longer version, hopefully not yet tedious. First to dispel a pop psych myth: people don't split into verbal or visual thinkers. Verbal and visual thinking skills are pretty much (note: I said *pretty much*) independent. You can be good at both or bad at both or good at one and bad at the other. Next, like verbal ability, spatial ability isn't unitary, it has many flavors.

Finally, like musical ability and athletic ability, and just about every other ability, some fortunate people seem to come into the world with it, but the rest of us can work hard and get better. Studies of twins show—no surprise here—both genetic and environmental influences on spatial ability. Even those who come into the world blessed with abilities have to work hard to excel. No amount of musical ability can make someone an instant violin virtuoso, no amount of athletic ability can make someone instantly into a soaring high jumper, no amount of spatial ability can turn someone instantly into a Frank Lloyd Wright or an Einstein. Expertise as well as abilities can be quite specialized, as anyone who has built a baseball team or a symphony orchestra or a design team knows. Sports provide an elegant lesson: both what you come into the world with and what you do with those qualities matter. To be an elite high jumper or shortstop or quarterback, you need special physical characteristics and the talent and the training. All of the above.

Measuring spatial abilities

Spatial ability is intimately tied to spatial transformations and other forms of spatial reasoning. Although there are no standardized measures of spatial ability, versions of mental rotation are widely used. So are other measures of mental spatial manipulations, like geometric

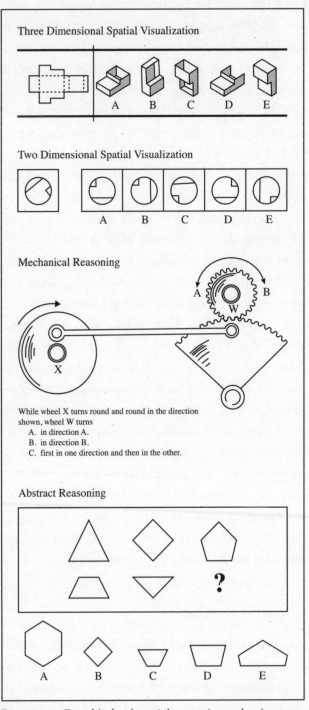

FIGURE 4.5. Four kinds of spatial reasoning tasks. Answers:
1. A, 2. A, 3. C, 4. D.

analogies or imagining how to fold a flat diagram into a box or which way a part of a mechanical system moves. Some of these tasks are shown in Figure 4.5.

Other measures use jigsaw puzzles or finding a simple geometric figure like a triangle hidden in a larger intricate one. Some rely on understanding the spatial world. Here's one. People are shown a picture of a tilted but empty water glass and asked to draw a line showing the top of the water in the glass. Some people mistakenly draw the line parallel to the tilted bottom of the glass instead of parallel to the ground. The trick for this one is using the right reference frame, using the world, which is not in the picture, as a reference frame rather than the glass, which is in the picture.

The different measures of spatial ability go together to some extent, that is, people who do well on one tend to do well on another—but not always—and the lack of standard measures can make it difficult to compare across studies or draw generalizations. Rather than a single spatial ability, there seem to be many spatial abilities. Naturally, there have been many attempts to make sense of the various spatial abilities, to develop a taxonomy, but none has proved satisfactory— yet. On reflection, this is not surprising. It wouldn't be easy to come up with a taxonomy of sports or music or literary abilities.

We can't escape the gender question. Yes, males perform somewhat better on mental rotation tasks. And slightly better on the tilted-glass problem. Playing fast action video games, the kind boys are more likely to play, improves performance. As does other kinds of training, which reduces the differences in mental rotation. So does removing time pressure, but neither seems to eliminate the male advantage entirely. However, plenty of women surpass plenty of men in these tasks, and as we saw, they can be solved in different ways.

Women, however, aren't about to be undone. Women excel at recognizing objects and object locations. Perhaps even more important, women, from infancy, recognize faces and facial expressions better than men. Again, the differences aren't large, and there's considerable overlap in the distributions, that is, there are plenty of men who surpass women.

What is spatial ability good for?

One very impressive endeavor, Project Talent, followed a sample of four hundred thousand (!) US high school students for eleven years. Students' spatial skills were assessed using variations of the test you just saw. Their verbal and math skills were also assessed using standardized measures. Naturally, math skills were important for success in science, technology, engineering, and math (fondly referred to as STEM), but spatial skills gave an extra boost. That is, when students were equally high in math skills, those with superior spatial skills were more likely to reach higher educational goals and careers in STEM fields. The spatial-STEM connection receives further support from the twin research, which shows moderate correlations between specific spatial skills and mastery of certain mathematical concepts. Other research shows common brain underpinnings for some spatial skills and some mathematical skills.

Laboratory experiments support the STEM–spatial thinking connections. Many studies have shown that people excelling in spatial skills also excel in understanding explanations of assembly procedures and mechanical systems. People with good spatial skills are also better at creating visual and even verbal explanations of assembly procedures and the actions of STEM systems.

But spatial skills should be important for many other talents and occupations beyond STEM. Choreography, all sorts of sports and coaching all sorts of sports, all sorts of design, art, carpentry, board games like Go and chess, surgery, filmmaking; the list is long. Which skills for which activities? There are bits and pieces of tantalizing data. There seem to be some people who excel at visualizing spatial transformations, and others, at visualizing intricacies of objects. And of course, some are pretty good at both. Mathematicians and physicists seem to be especially adept at spatial transformation of objects and artists especially adept at visualizing details of objects. Designers seem to be pretty good at both.

To add to the puzzles, none of the popular tests of spatial ability predicts navigational abilities. What does predict way-finding abilities is self-report, that is, our own ratings of our navigational abilities. For navigation, too, there are small but persistent gender differences, more in style than ability. Women tend to prefer routes for navigation and for giving directions; men tend to rely more on cardinal directions.

Acquiring spatial skills

For years, I taught an honors program in psychology, an elite group of students who went on to stunning careers in many fields, not just psychology. One year we carpooled to the Exploratorium, a wonderful science museum with excellent hands-on psychology demonstrations. This was in ancient times before mobile phones and navigation systems—we relied on paper maps. I sketched one for the carpool drivers. One of the student drivers said, "I don't do maps." I wrote out verbal directions; they worked. One of my colleagues, a distinguished member of the National Academy of Sciences, lived not far from me. I told that person about a shortcut that had opened up to drive to campus. The reply: "Please don't confuse me." Very smart people can have trouble thinking spatially. We notice when people are brilliantly articulate or the opposite, but only in unusual circumstances do we discover that someone has trouble thinking spatially.

Not only can spatial skills be developed, but according to no less than a committee of the National Academy of Sciences, they *must* be developed. Spatial skills are fundamental to so many professions, tasks, and activities. Reading, writing, and arithmetic are proverbially taught in schools, but what about understanding and creating maps, graphs, assembly and operation instructions, and visual explanations of not just science and math but also literature, history, social sciences, and more?

Enhancing spatial skills is a no-brainer: acquiring spatial skills is fun! For kids—and their caretakers—all sorts of spatial play: puzzles, construction toys like Lego and Tinker Toys, board games like Chutes and Ladders, computer games like Tetris. Even often dismissed computer games, action ones like *Grand Theft Auto,* can have benefits; they improve allocation of attention and perceptual speed.

Wrestling places high demands on spatial thinking to get out of complex holds. Learning and practicing wrestling turns out to improve spatial skills. It wouldn't be surprising if other sports that demand spatial thinking also improve spatial skills. It is known that expertise in various sports correlates with various spatial tasks. But those data don't tell us whether the sports improved spatial abilities or those with better spatial skills do better in sports. The causality is not clear, but it is likely that it goes both ways: some spatial skills are needed to excel in athletics and attaining expertise boosts spatial skills.

Parents, teachers, and caretakers can do much more than provide opportunities, sports, toys, games, and more. Crucially, they can enrich the experiences with spatial talk. Calling attention to spatial details and spatial relations and comparisons, to similarities, differences, symmetries, analogies. Querying the child about those relations, similarities, differences, symmetries, and analogies. Using gestures: pointing to details, using back-and-forth gestures for comparisons: similarities, differences, and analogies. Playing the opposites game: in/out; up/down; forward/backward; over/under; inside/outside. Using gestures, even whole-body movements, for those concepts. Naming shapes, describing their characteristics using the *P* words, *parallel, perpendicular, perimeter,* the D words, *diagonal* and *diameter,* and others, *area, circumference, radius.* Guessing games: which is taller, wider, closer? Measuring almost anything. Lining up shoes or blocks or toy cars by size. Drawing. Asking or, better yet, working with children—and adults—to create visual-spatial representations, perhaps starting with heights of people and things, then maps, then how something works or how to do something, continuing to a multitude of concepts, on paper or with any objects that are at hand. Bar graphs of books read or glasses of milk consumed, networks of family relations. Wonderful art projects. There are so many opportunities in everyday life: the shapes and sizes of everything; the ways bodies twist and move; the patterns of spots on butterflies and giraffes, of windows on buildings; the speeds of ants and dogs and cars; shadows; all sorts of fastenings: buckles, hinges, keys and locks, snaps, zippers, knots, screws, and lids.

Of course, these activities aren't just for kids. A painstaking analysis of over two hundred studies showed that spatial thinking skills can be improved in anyone by many different training techniques. That the effects of training were long-lasting and, in many cases, transferred to other spatial skills, skills that were not directly trained. Hopeful and encouraging findings.

SCOPE OF SPATIAL ABILITIES

We have a bit of a quandary here. We now know that there are many spatial abilities and that some of them seem to hang together. We also know that training improves various spatial skills and that training one skill can improve performance on another. But we still don't have a taxonomy of spatial skills.

Let's zoom out now and consider the range of spatial abilities. They seem to fall on a continuum from seeing to doing, from perceiving to acting. There is the talent many artists and designers have for seeing—and often producing—fine details of the visual world, catching slight asymmetries in faces, the proportions and layerings of bodies and landscapes, the tilt of a head and the curve of a road, in depth. There are judgments and comparisons: Which is taller? Wider? Farther? There is that talent athletes in team sports need, keeping track of moving things—the players on each team and the ball or Frisbee. Which is faster? Higher? Then there are the various imaginings in the mind. Imagining what an object will look like under various transformations like rotating or folding or stretching, imaging what the playing field will be like, imaging the trajectory of a moving object, skills tied to seeing but adding motion in imagination. Now we slide into skills that involve actions of the body in space as well as perception: imagining navigating, wrestling holds, broad jumps, violin sonatas, gymnastics tricks, knitting, or knotting, The continuum: seeing, imagining, doing.

That continuum from perception to action is really a spiral, an upward one. The perceiving helps the imagining, the imagining helps the doing, the doing helps the perceiving. To use another metaphor, they bootstrap each other. You draw the curve of a smile or a body or a hill as you see it; you look again at the world and at your drawing, and you adjust. And adjust until you are so practiced at seeing and drawing that you do it right the first time. As a result, you probably see the world more clearly. You practice tossing the Frisbee to where you imagine your teammate (or your dog) will be until you get that right. That tight connection between perceiving and doing is a hallmark of spatial thinking. It's not just doing and perceiving, it's doing and knowing. Remember that making circular gestures with the hand helps mental rotation. And that drawing lines and dots with the hands to make a schematic map helps people understand and remember environments. The spiral is enriched: perceiving and acting and knowing.

MEANING

I've shown you some of the amazing mental gymnastics our minds can perform. Those mental gymnastics transform what we see in the world and what we imagine in our minds into countless ideas, from the elementary and mundane needed to catch a ball, cross the street, or pack a suitcase to the spectacular and arcane used to create magnificent buildings or fantastic football plays or theories of particle physics. Marvelous as they are—and they are marvelous—buildings and football plays and zooming particles have a physical presence of one sort or another. But spatial thinking has even more wonders to reveal. Spatial thinking underlies how we talk and how we think, about space to be sure but also about time, emotions, social relations, and much more. Turn the page.

PART II

THE MIND IN THE WORLD

CHAPTER FIVE

The Body Speaks
a Different Language

In which we consider how actions of the body, especially the hands, turn into gestures that act on thought, our own and others, and provide the social glue underlying cooperation.

> The Winter's Tale *act 5, scene 2, First gentleman:*
> *"There was speech in their dumbness, language*
> *in their very gesture."*

WATCHING PEOPLE, EVEN FROM AFAR, YOU KNOW WHAT IS HAPPENing. You know what they are doing and you know what they are feeling, happy, angry, energetic, anxious—no need to hear. You know their intentions. You know their relations. One couple huddled arm-in-arm, another erect and apart. You see people in conversation. One head tilts, quizzically. Someone leans forward, in confidence. Another leans back, yielding the floor. One shakes a fist at another, the other steps back. One minute the exchanges are slow and relaxed; another they are rapid and intense. What others are doing tells you what to do. You go to the back of the line at the theater, skirt around teams fixing potholes, and cross the street to avoid a fight. These coordinated actions of bodies are often as subtle, as highly articulated, as exquisitely timed as a virtuoso string quartet. They are actions, but not actions on things, like making dinner or getting dressed. They are unlike the other myriad actions that we perform throughout the day that change things in the world.

Our bodies perform an astonishing assortment of actions. We prepare food and consume it; we dress and undress; we arrange books, clothing, food in cabinets and closets; we assemble furniture and sew clothing; play pianos, flutes, and drums; operate vacuum cleaners, cars, and bicycles; we walk, run, dance, climb trees, chase dogs, shoot hoops and rapids, do yoga, and ski. Some are actions by hands that can even change the world, like assassinations; others are actions by feet that simply change where we are in the world. But there's another set of actions that neither change the world nor our locations in it. These actions change thoughts, our own or those of others. These are gestures. Intriguingly, many gestures are abbreviations of the very actions that change the world or our locations in it: putting, taking, raising, pushing, turning, splitting, mixing, and countless more. As gestures, they express actions on ideas rather than on objects. We talk that way, too, as if ideas were objects and thinking were action on objects. We pull ideas together, put them aside, tear them apart, turn them over or inside out.

Despite the extraordinary expressiveness of the body, the face, and the hands, when we think about thinking, we typically think of words. We teach them to our children, we write them to our friends, we post them on refrigerators, we speak them with strangers. We learn the rules of grammar and composition for organizing words into sentences and sentences into discourse of all kinds. We consult dictionaries for meanings of words and style manuals for techniques of composition. Not so for gesture. There isn't an authoritative dictionary for the meanings of gestures as there is for the meanings of words. There aren't rules of grammar for organizing gestures into sentences; there aren't sentences.

Gestures come first, before words, both in evolution and in development. An insightful, if speculative, theory of the evolution of language from monkeys to people begins with actions that are significant in the lives of monkeys, such as throwing and tearing. A remarkable experimental program has found single neurons in monkey motor cortex that fire when the monkey performs one of those actions and when the monkey sees someone, even a human, perform the same action. Mirror neurons they are called. They unite the doing of action and the seeing of action in single neurons, different neurons for different actions. The brain basis for understanding action. Some speculate that actions are also the foundation for language, for expressing action. A truncated version of an action like throwing or tearing could signal an intention to perform that action. The truncated action becomes a gesture. The area in monkey cortex representing the hand overlaps an area in humans that represents spoken language. The theory then speculates that the voice came to take over for the hand, both because it has greater articulatory power and because it can project across distance.

If gesture precedes language in evolution, then perhaps it can be seen in primates. The trick is to find it in the wild, not the laboratory where "natural" behavior has been contaminated by interactions with humans. In fact, painstaking observation has shown many cases of communicative gestures by chimpanzees and bonobos in the wild. The intentions of ape gestures seem to be requests for attention, sex, grooming, or companionship. Requests to stop some behavior have also been observed. So far, no one has found apes counting or giving directions. Given that there is cultural transmission of tool use and food foraging in apes, it would be exciting if continued observation found cases of using gesture to teach or explain.

Communicating with the body is ubiquitous but usually implicit. You don't have to think about it; it happens by itself. Somebody asks you a question you can't answer. You shrug your shoulders. "How's school?" I ask D., a five-year-old granddaughter. Her answer: one thumb up, the other down. Body-to-body communication is more direct than word-to-word, performed by one body and understood viscerally by another, often without awareness. I glance at the door, your head and eyes follow my glance. I cross my legs; soon you do the same. As we converse, we increasingly use each other's words and gestures, a phenomenon called *entrainment*. Entrainment undoubtedly serves to make sure we understand each other, to create mutual understanding or common ground. It is also a form of social mimicry.

When we imitate each other, we like each other more. It goes both ways: we're more likely to imitate someone we like. Mutual imitation encourages cooperation. Social mimicry is social glue.

But there's even more to imitation, explicit or implicit. You smile or wince and I feel your pleasure or your pain. I might even smile or wince, automatically, mirroring your emotion. Even babies do this. Emotional mirroring is fundamental to empathy.

Body-to-body communication goes far beyond mirroring. It is often complementary. At a cocktail party, you spot a group of friends chatting. You approach. The circle widens to include you and you enter. During a seated discussion, one person stands, ending the meeting. At a disturbing presidential debate in 2016, the larger of the candidates added drama to a wordy event by circling in place like a lion about to pounce on a prey, a show of power to the audience and a threat to the smaller candidate. What's gesture, what's body language—there's no way to separate the hands from the head from the body, they're all connected. Bodies can be seen from afar; whether the person approaching is young or old, drunk or sober, friendly or aggressive is evident from a distance. Faces and hands require closer viewing. We talked about faces in Chapter Two, when we considered the world the body enters. Hands are especially agile, their many joints and muscles performing remarkable feats on pianos and surgery tables and cutting boards and weaving looms. Those supremely articulated movements of hands and fingers also participate in subtle gestures that express subtle meanings. We turn to those now.

THE HANDS SPEAK

No less impressive than the large performances of the body, small gestures of the hands turn out to be chockfull of meaning. Even in babies, or maybe especially in babies. Babies gesture to communicate before they speak. Many parents complain of becoming slaves to their babies' points, requests to take me there or bring me that. Some gestures by babies are less demanding. C., at eighteen months, is exploring her grandmother's (that's me) overnight kit. She pulls out a toothbrush and then a small tube she thinks is toothpaste. She tries to open the tube but fails. She hands it to me, that action a request to open it. I say, "C., that's not toothpaste, it's lotion." C. looks at me and rubs her arm up and down as if putting on lotion to show she understands. Another example. A., at the same age, spots a small decal of an airplane on a motorcycle. She makes sure I am watching, points to the picture of the airplane, and then points emphatically to the sky as if to say, airplanes go in the sky. Two-"word" sentences, where one is uttered and the other gestured or where both are gestured, are common in babies just learning to talk. They are also an invitation to an adult to provide the words: "Right, A., airplanes go in the sky." In fact, such multimedia productions are a harbinger of spoken language. Babies who gesture to communicate early usually speak early.

Now consider B., an adult who has been blind since birth. She's been asked for directions, how to get from one place to another. As she speaks, her hands show each part of the route in sequence. She can't see her gestures and can't know if you are looking, or know if they help you understand.

Another example—you see this every day: people walking down the street jabbering, one hand holding a small, flat rectangle, the other one gesturing emphatically in the air. Although we are not party to the conversation, we can see the gestures, but the conversation partner cannot. And we no longer regard such behavior as loony.

Why do people gesture? The answer is simple. Gestures express so many meanings directly; words take time to find and to assemble. Words are arbitrary. Except for a few onomatopoeic words, words like *buzz, hiccup,* and *gurgle,* words bear no relationship to their meanings. It's all the more remarkable that we learn so many of them so early and so quickly when they are only arbitrarily connected to the meanings they express. Gestures, by contrast, more often than not bear immediate relations to their meanings. C. expressed lotion by pretending to put lotion on her arm. A. expressed "airplane" by pointing to a picture of an airplane. She then expressed "in the sky" by pointing to the sky. What could be more direct than conveying an object by pointing to it or showing how it's used? These gestures seem to do what words or short phrases do in spoken language. The gestures essentially substitute for words; they're easier to produce than words certainly at that age, before the fluency that allows words to pop out before the thought has finished—often with regret. In fact, for babies, many gestures of this kind will eventually drop out and be replaced by words.

The gestures made by B., the blind adult, are different. They accompanied her speech; they expanded her speech, presenting more or less the same information but in a more natural format. Her gestures worked with her speech or more likely her thinking. Her gestures didn't substitute for words. As she spoke, her gestures sketched the route segment by segment, drawing straight lines for the streets and bending her hand for turns. Strung together, her gestures formed a map of the route. Did her gestures serve her own thinking, or were they meant for her unseen and unseeable listener?

On the one hand, gestures can represent thoughts that can be conveyed by single words, as when C. rubbed her arm to represent *lotion*. On the other hand, gestures can serve to create an overall structure in space, as in B.'s gestural sketch of a route. That spatial structure, unlike *airplane,* can't be expressed in a single word; unlike *in the sky,* it is even difficult to express in several words. Her gestures followed a logic quite different from the logic of language. They created a continuous diagram that organized and expressed an integrated set of thoughts. Their structure was not the structure of language. Gestures don't follow the rules of grammar. It probably hasn't escaped you that the expression I used to create a dimension of the breadth of meanings for gestures was a set of words describing a pair of gestures: on the one hand, on the other. That pair of gestures creates a virtual diagram in space, a horizontal line representing a continuum of expansiveness of meaning.

THE HANDS DRAW

Gestures do so many things. One of them is to draw in the air, and there are fundamental similarities between gestures and graphics such as sketches, drawings, diagrams, charts, paintings, and models. Both gestures and graphics are created by actions in space. Both are used to represent something other than themselves, though on occasion—think painting and dance—they have dual roles: they both represent and are objects of contemplation in and of themselves. Both follow a different representational logic, a more direct one, from that of language. Crucially, both resemble what they represent. Of course, there are differences between gestures and graphics as well. Gestures draw, but in broad strokes, strokes of the fingers or the hands or the body, not of a pencil or fine brush. They necessarily lack the refinement of paintings or sketches. And they quickly disappear. Graphics stay there but stay still—except for animated graphics, and those have problems of their own. Yet another significant difference: gestures are performed in the here and now. Depictions and graphics of all sorts are free of the momentary context of here and now; crucially, they can represent things and events not in the present, things and events that are in the past or future, an advantage they share with language.

That gestures can show so little and show it so imprecisely forces abstraction. At a minimum, abstraction entails slimming the information, not uniformly but by selecting the essential features of the ideas and eliminating the irrelevant (I hear you saying, *But so do words*). For gesture, that also means selecting features that can be enacted or spatialized. Graphics, too, force selecting what to show and what to ignore, but they can show far more, sometimes too much, overwhelming viewers and forcing them to search and further select. In contrast to graphics, gestures are fleeting, they don't hang around to be explored. But graphics require implements, pencil and paper; gestures require no more in the way of implements than the body we carry with us. And quite frequently, the surrounding world. Finally, gestures are actions, often abbreviated actions in the world, and as such better suited to show action than static graphics. These features of gestures—that they use actions in space to create meaning, that they represent something other than themselves, that they can resemble what they represent, that they are abstract and schematic, that they are fleeting, and that they are in and of themselves actions—all these features help us to understand what they communicate and how. And how they affect thought both in those who create them and in those who see them.

KINDS OF GESTURES

Everyone likes to put things into bins, to make piles of like things and separate them from unlike things. That is, taxonomies, dictionaries, catalogs, categories. They're so useful. Putting information into bins and the bins into bigger bins makes everything simpler. But there's no way to produce a neat catalog of gestures much less of all the ways that our actions in space create meanings. Except for a small set of frozen gestures like "okay," "thumbs up," and "high five," gestures are constantly—indeed, typically—invented on the fly and adapted to the situation. Of course, words, too, can be invented on the fly— when did *email* and *spam* become nouns and then verbs? But words tend to be invented from other words, and invented words conform to parts of speech; they're nouns or verbs or adjectives. There is no syntax for gestures, no grammar, nothing that corresponds to parts of speech. Sentences are almost always invented on the fly in conversation or carefully crafted in poetry, and there is no comprehensive catalog of sentences. There are, however, typologies of utterances and of discourse, and even of gestures. These typologies aren't rigidly defined; many gestures fall into more than one category. Nevertheless, they are useful. For gestures, the commonly accepted types are emblem, beat, deictic, iconic, and metaphoric. The features that distinguish the types are partly form, partly function, partly semantic, partly a combination.

Emblems are frozen gestures that are word-like: the signs for "okay" or "thumbs up" or "peace." Nodding the head sideways back and forth for "no" and up and down for "yes." Waving to say hello or goodbye. Emblems typically serve as crisp replies or greetings. As such, they usually stand alone; they rarely combine with other gestures or words to form longer utterances.

Beats are rhythmic gestures that accompany speech, typically at phrase or clause breaks. They can serve to structure the discourse and advance it; they can serve to emphasize. Although they are regarded as not having semantic content, they often do. The repeated pounding on a lectern timed with each of the faults of the opponent in a political debate are beats. The emphatic hand slices that accompany a list, first, second, third . . . are also beats, but because those beats usually proceed along a horizontal line in space, they carry semantic meaning by establishing a dimension along which a set of things is ordered, events in time, teams by order in a league, movies by ticket sales. The human mind does like to order and to rank.

Deictic gestures point. The word *deictic* and the noun form *deixis* derive from a Greek word that means to show or demonstrate or prove or point to. Oddly, despite its origin, *deixis* was first used with respect to words, not gestures. *Deixis* refers to words like *here, there, me, this, that, next,* and *now,* words that rely on the current context, the here and the now, to be understood. The *now* in the previous sentence is no longer now.

One fundamental role for points is to bring the world, the here and the now, into the conversation. Points simultaneously direct attention to something in the world and refer to that something in the world. Airplane <point sky>. Eat <point cookie>. Go <point outside>. Daddy <point shoe>. So much conversation, especially with children, is about the here and now. But pointing to bring something in the world into the conversation isn't just for children. Adults point: to show someone which way to go, to indicate which dessert they want, to designate whose turn is next.

Points are often regarded as the simplest gestures. What could be simpler than extending a finger in the direction of the focus of one's thought? That's their meaning, right there in front of our eyes. Babies point early and proficiently. But simple points are not. Suppose while talking I point to a book. I could be referring to any old book, to an object that could be used as a door stop, to a recent purchase, to something a friend forgot, or to that specific book. If to that book, I could be referring to its title, to its contents, to its author, to the pleasure it brought me, to its influence, to its size or its cover or to countless other features associated with the book. Context can clarify.

To complicate things further, pointing is not a single gesture. It needn't even use the pointer finger. We can point with a finger or a hand or our heads or our shoulders or even with our eyes. How we point varies. Perhaps we've been told that pointing isn't polite or perhaps pointing with the head or the eyes is more private and can't easily be seen by others. A sweep of the eyes toward the door can signal a companion to see what's going on there or that it's time to leave. How we point depends on so much, on who the point is for, on what is pointed to, on the surrounding context, physical, social, and conversational.

Even odder, points can be directed at something that isn't there at all. A nod in the direction of the place of someone who has left the room or a dish that has been removed from the table can refer to that absent someone or that absent dish. But more than that, I can set up an imaginary world with points, a remembered world or a completely hypothetical world, a concrete world or an abstract one. And I can continue to point to the imaginary things I've arranged in my imaginary world, even rearranging them using moving points. Setting up an imaginary world and animating it is in fact a feature of American Sign Language.

Iconic gestures depict. They show properties of objects, spaces, or actions. The prototypic iconic gesture is the "big fish" gesture, the drawing out of the hands to indicate the impressive length of the fish that was caught or that got away. Iconic gestures do not and cannot exhibit all the features of an object or action. The big fish gesture shows the length and horizontality of the fish, but it doesn't show the shape of the fish or its swimming motion. Iconic gestures can also represent actions as in "he walked into the room looking as if he owned the place" while swaggering and strutting.

Metaphoric gestures express depictable but nonliteral properties or abstract concepts. There are *big* fish and there are *big* ideas. Of course, ideas can't literally be big. Ideas might be big because they are inflated or because they encompass many other ideas or because they have many implications. A gesture accompanying *big idea* would be different from one accompanying *big fish*. Fish have shapes and orientations; ideas don't. How do you indicate that something, an idea, can be regarded as an entity but that it has no particular shape or orientation? A sphere. So, a *big idea* is more likely to be conceived of as something rounded rather than something elongated like a fish. For *big idea,* the fingers might be curved as if holding a ball. Actions can also serve as metaphoric gestures. A head bobbing this way and that can depict a person who bounces from idea to idea. A flattened hand wobbling up and down signals uncertainty, like a teeter-totter.

Metaphors of all kinds permeate our thought and our talk, and our gestures as well. One reason metaphors work is that they use something that is familiar to represent something that is unfamiliar, something that is concrete to represent something that is abstract, something understood to represent something that is not. Many metaphors are so common—often called, metaphorically of course, "dead"—that we don't notice them as such: the heart pumps, the brain computes, life is a journey, political candidates are at war. During a recent presidential campaign, a political commentator remarked that one of the major candidates had a driver's license, the other not even a learner's permit, and a third-party candidate was without a car. Shakespeare was the master metaphor maker: life's a stage, Juliet's the sun, life's a web. Of course, metaphors do not transfer all senses to their targets. What transfers from *web* to *life* is a complex network, a network of events and relationships, not of strands of filament extruded from the nether parts of a spider. Similarly, Juliet lights up Romeo, but she isn't a glowing ball in the heavens. So, too, for metaphoric gestures: only some features transfer. Gesture can make explicit which ones.

GESTURES REVEAL THOUGHT

My husband was a paratrooper in the Israeli army. One of the training exercises was to be dropped alone in the desert in darkness without a map. You found your way back or . . . He had an uncanny sense of direction. Many years later in more benign environments that were paved and well lit on the rare occasions when I was the driver and he was the navigator, he would tell me to "turn right" and point left. Or vice versa. It didn't matter what language he was speaking. Since the body is faster than the mind, I knew to go with his hand, not the words. The relationship between words and action is arbitrary, but the relationship of pointing to action is direct, it's in the body and the world. You point the way you want to go. Sometimes people's gestures contradict their speech. In those cases, pay close attention to their gestures.

This is true in spades for children because they are often less adept at explaining in words. Here's an example from young children in a standard Piagetian conservation task. Two equal rows of checkers are lined up in front of the child. The experimenter spreads out one row and asks, "Are there more checkers now [pointing to the widened row] or are they just the same?" The experimenter also asks why. Very young children say more; older ones correctly say same. But some children say one thing and gesture another; the researchers called these discordances *mismatches*. For example, a kid might say *more* but make a gesture pointing to corresponding pairs of checkers in the two rows. That one-to-one gesture suggests the kid is on the cusp of grasping conservation. In this case, the mismatched gestures don't contradict the words, as in the case of my husband and *left* and *right*. In many mismatches, the gestures and the words simply carry different information.

The same happens in school-aged children learning to solve arithmetic equations. Some kids calculate incorrectly but point to both sides of the equation with a V gesture, suggesting nascent understanding that the two sides of an equation must be equal. Significantly, children's mismatches predicted leaps in understanding in both cases. That is, a child pointing to two sides of an equation will soon understand that the two sides of an equation must be equal or that stretching the row of checkers doesn't change the quantity of checkers. What's more, teachers seem to pick up the discrepancies between words and gestures and use them in teaching, by helping the child articulate their understanding. Teachers sense that these are teachable moments and give more instruction to children who produce mismatches.

Students' gestures provide other information that is helpful to teachers, notably their problem-solving strategies. When children are asked to gesture as they explain how they solve equations, their gestures reveal strategies not explained in speech, for example, which numbers in the equations they are summing. It's a bit like asking students to show their work. They are then more likely to benefit from instruction.

Conversely, children learn better when their teachers provide two different problem-solving strategies, one in their words and another in their gestures, than when their gestures and speech match or when both strategies are conveyed by speech.

GESTURES PUT THOUGHT ON A STAGE

Gestures reveal thought, often far better than words do. This turns out to be especially important for really big thoughts, like the (Kantian) Big Three: space, time, and causality. Each of these is a multifaceted concept that can be spatialized, and spatialized in different ways. Setting up a schematic space of ideas is one of the great powers of gesture. Much research on gesture has analyzed single gestures focusing on hand form or simply counted gestures. Insightful as that work has been, that narrow focus overlooks the force of an integrated sequence of meaningful gestures that put ideas on a stage, poised to interact.

What's missing from the Kantian Big Three is emotion. Emotion was not one of Kant's fundamental *a prioris*, space, time, and causality. If space, time, and causality are successively more abstract, then emotion is even more so, though not on the same conceptual continuum. Emotion is on its own conceptual continuum. Or continua. If expressing space, time, and causality uses sequences of integrated gestures, usually of the hands, emotion often takes only a single gesture, typically of the face. Still, emotion is part of every perception and every thought, and this cannot be forgotten.

Countless nuanced and nameless emotions can be expressed by the body and the face, even just the eyes and eyebrows. *Raised eyebrow,* either as action or an expression, has become a synonym for skepticism. We discussed emotion in Chapter Two, when we populated the world around the body. Here, we only give lip service to emotion. And the lips play roles, they smile and frown and yawn and pucker. Words emit from them. Suffice it to say that we often experience the emotions of others the way we experience actions of others directly, through mirroring by the body and the brain.

Space. Using space to represent space is a no-brainer. Nevertheless, if you're in psychology nobody trusts you unless you do an experiment. So, we did. We brought people into the lab, gave them schematic maps to study, and asked them to describe the environments represented in the maps to a video camera so that someone watching the video would know where everything was. As expected, most (but not all) gestured. Many produced a long string of integrated gestures that laid out the places and paths in the environment in a spatial array, some on a virtual vertical blackboard, some on a virtual horizontal table. Predominating the gestures were lines for paths and points for places.

Now *time.* Time is usually abstracted to a single dimension, a line. But which one? Depending on the language and the situation, the line might be gestured from left to right or right to left, it might go sagittally from the front of the body to behind the body or vice versa. The direction depends on how time is conceived. In some languages, the future is in front because conceptually we are moving toward it or it is coming at us. In other languages, the past is in front because it is known and the future is behind because it cannot yet be seen. In Mandarin, time might be gestured vertically, earlier up and later down, like a calendar. Arraying time from left to right or right to left is convenient on a page or in some social situations where the sagittal front/back is complicated to represent. Whether time goes from left to right or vice versa appears to depend largely on reading/writing order.

Causality. Causality is much, much harder; there are so many different kinds of causes and so many of them are invisible. But many causes and consequences of causes are actions, inviting iconic gestures. Back to the lab to see how people gesture when they explain causal systems. In one experiment, students studied the rock cycle or the workings of the heart and then made a video explaining the system. Typically, they first used gestures to create a large virtual diagram that located the parts of the systems, much like the way people create a map of locations in space or a timeline of events using gestures. For causality, gestures can do more than map in space or time. Gestures were used to show the actions of the parts of the system and the causal chain of actions in the system. Thus, gestures do double duty in representing causality, making them all the more important in explanations of causality.

We'll stop here, with examples from the Big Three, but it should be clear that this is only the beginning of ways that gestures can put thought onto a stage. But gestures representing space, time, and causality do far more than put thought on a stage—they have the power to change thought in those who make them as well as those who see them.

Second General Fact Worth Remembering: Representations created by hands and by words are wildly different.

Presumably by now I have convinced you that people spontaneously gesture and that gestures can express a multitude of different kinds of ideas more directly than words can. Yes, all over the world. And, yes, there are also cultural differences. As for just about everything. Now I need to convince you that gestures make a difference, that they are effective and effective beyond words in communicating both to others and to one's self. Fortunately, there's plenty of evidence for both. And that research gives more insight into how gestures work.

GESTURES HELP US TALK

Try this. Sit on your hands. Then explain out loud how to get from your house to the supermarket, train station, your office or school. This isn't just a thought experiment; it works in highly controlled laboratory experiments. When people are asked to explain or describe spatial relations while sitting on their hands, they have trouble speaking. They can't find words.

People blind from birth, both children and adults, gesture, even when speaking to each other. They have never seen gestures nor have their conversation partners. They seem to gesture for themselves. Gesturing by people who are blind, as for the people with sight in the previous experiments, seems to help them speak. But it turns out it isn't just word finding people have trouble with when they can't use their hands. Preventing gesturing doesn't just disrupt speaking, it disrupts thinking.

GESTURES HELP US THINK

There is a perhaps apocryphal story about the venerable poet Wallace Stevens, who walked to his work in an insurance company. As he walked, he wrote poetry, in rhythm with his thoughts. The story is that when he revised a line, he walked backward to where that line had begun in his mind, and then forward again as he rewrote.

Now from poetry to a far more mundane activity of the mind, counting. Try counting a bunch of pennies sprawled on a table without pointing to or moving each one as it is counted. Children are taught to point to each object in turn as they count, and doing so makes counting more accurate and faster. When adults' hands are tied as they count, they count with their heads. And, undoubtedly, if the head were immobilized, people would count with their eyes. Pointing while counting allows keeping track of the count. Is pointing to count an action or a gesture? It seems to be both.

Making the case that gestures help thinking requires gestures that represent thought. And more: that people gesture when they are thinking, but not talking, that when they do so, they think better, and that preventing gesturing disrupts thinking. There's an added bonus. Seeing the kinds of gestures people make when they are thinking also reveals the thinking and does so directly, without the use of machines that peer into the brain.

To do all that means going into the laboratory. We began a research program in which people were alone in a closed room and given problems to solve or complex descriptions to remember. We know that people gesture when they talk about such things, but in our studies, there was no one to talk to.

First, we gave people problems to solve. Here's one of them: *There's a row of six glasses. The three on the left are empty, the three on the right are full. By moving only one glass, change the configuration to empty-full empty-full empty-full.*

Did you figure it out? While thinking about that problem, the majority of students gestured. Their gestures represented the problem, three empty glasses, three full glasses in a row, but in different ways. Some put out three fingers on each hand, side-by-side. Others used an index finger to lay out two separate groups of three along a row on the table. Either way, their gestures represented the problem. These gestures aren't single gestures like deictic or iconic or metaphoric gestures. They are much more; they are a coordinated sequence of gestures that form a spatial representation of the problem, a virtual diagram of the problem. That was an interesting finding in and of itself. But there was another finding, much more surprising. The people who gestured were more likely to solve the six glasses problem than those who didn't gesture. Why should gesturing help problem solving?

Before trying to understand why gesturing helps problem solving, we need to know how general the phenomenon is: Will people gesture to understand and learn other kinds of information? Because it's known that people gesture when they describe environments, we turned to those, roads and landmarks in a small town or the configuration of various exercise rooms in a gym. Environments are inherently spatial, but they are abstracted both in the mind and on the page—into the paths and places of sketch maps. Dots and lines. Would people, alone in a room, gesture to represent and remember descriptions of environments, and would their gestures form sketch maps? The answer to both questions is yes.

Just as they did while reading problems to solve, most (but not all) people gestured while reading spatial descriptions to remember. Whether or not they gestured didn't depend on whether the environment was indoors or outdoors, large or small. It didn't matter if the description took a perspective from above or from within the environment. Just as for the six glasses problem, people's gestures made virtual sketches of the environments, but their styles of gesturing differed. Some gestured on the table, some in the air, some under the table. Some traced lines or pointed with the index finger, some used an entire hand. But the gestures were similar at a semantic level. Everyone used line-like gestures to represent paths and point-like gestures to represent landmarks. Other features of the environments, like parks or schools or weight rooms or pools, were rarely represented. Only the skeleton, much like sketch maps.

Again, gesturing helped people think. Those who had gestured answered more questions about the environments correctly than those who hadn't. And they answered faster. Those who gestured made more accurate inferences; they were better at answering questions from perspectives they hadn't read. Several people gestured for some but not all descriptions; they performed better on the descriptions they had gestured. To cinch the case for gesture, we asked another group of students to read and remember the descriptions while sitting on their hands. Sure enough, those who sat on their hands performed worse than the group allowed to gesture.

The environments were rich and complex, as were the gestures. Most people produced a long string of gestures, sometimes revising as they worked out their understanding. They rarely looked at their hands, and when they did, it was a brief glance. That means that the gestural representations were spatial-motor, not visual. Given that, it makes much more sense that people blind from birth gesture. What matters are the movements in space, not what they look like.

Surprisingly, gesturing while reading didn't slow reading, even though people were doing two things at the same time. Doing two things simultaneously is supposed to increase cognitive load and lower performance. Not so for gesturing and thinking. Paradoxically, adding to the cognitive load reduced the cognitive load.

Understanding the explanations was hard; it took effort to figure out where everything was. Words march one after another in horizontal rows; they bear only symbolic relationship to the environments. But the gestures resemble the environments, they put the places and paths in a virtual map step-by-step. In essence, the gestures translated the language into thought.

Will gesturing facilitate any kind of thinking? Our guess is that gesturing can help thinking that is complicated and that can be spatialized. Research on understanding elementary actions in physics and mechanics supports those ideas. A string of gears works because adjacent pairs of gears go in opposite directions: a gear that rotates clockwise is surrounded on both sides by gears that rotate counterclockwise. This is called the parity rule. Gesturing helps people grasp the parity rule, that in a chain of gears, each successive gear reverses the direction of rotation.

Gesturing helps people understand the water level problem, that when a glass is tilted, the water level stays parallel to the ground, it doesn't tilt with the glass. Imagining tilting the glass didn't help understanding, but tilting the hand as if grasping a glass did. This is a crucial, if puzzling, distinction. Imagination, that is, visual-spatial reasoning, was not as effective in understanding that the level of water in a glass stays parallel to the ground even when the glass is tilted as was making a tilting action.

Rotating the hand in the right direction also helps some people solve mental rotation problems.

Our own work is venturing farther, beyond the inherently spatial. We have given students descriptions of all sorts of things to remember and reason from: party planners' schedules, people's preferences for film genres, orderings of countries by economic growth, explanations of how a car brake or a bicycle pump work, multiplication of two 3-digit numbers, and more. In each case, about two-thirds to three-quarters of participants gestured as they read, and their gestures formed virtual diagrams of the problems. The formats of their virtual diagrams varied widely, but the essence of the information represented did not. In all cases, gesturing while studying speeded answering questions at test, indicating that the gesturing consolidated the information. For the mechanical systems, the car brake and bicycle pump, gesturing at study improved performance on the tests as well. We've also found that people gesture when given diagrams rather than descriptions of the mechanical systems and maps of the environments. That is, even when provided with visualizations, many people use gestures to make spatial-motor models of the systems and environments they are trying to learn.

Watching people's hands as they read and understand feels like watching their thinking. Better than peering into the brain, it's all out there before the eyes. Some of our students used the joints of their fingers as the rows and columns of a table for representing preferences or schedules. Others made virtual tables on the table. The gestures that represented the mechanical systems, the car brake and bicycle pump, were remarkably creative and diverse (just as were people's diagrams, as shall be seen). Despite the diversity, the gestures (and the diagrams) abstracted the underlying structure and dynamics of the systems. As before, we required half the participants to sit on their hands. Remarkably, almost a third of those asked to sit on their hands couldn't comply; they could not stop gesturing! It was as if they couldn't think if they couldn't move their hands. Some told us exactly that.

How curious and surprising that we think with our hands. But gesturing is no panacea. It does not guarantee success. Telling people to gesture doesn't necessarily improve performance. The gesturing has to be part and parcel of the thinking, to represent the thought. And the thought has to be correct. If the thinking goes astray, so do the gestures and so does the correct solution. Another problem we gave students illustrates this nicely. Try it yourself: A ship is moored in a harbor. A rope ladder with 10 rungs hangs over its side. The distance between each rung is 12 inches. The lowest rung touches the water. Because of the incoming tide, the surface of the water rises 4 inches per hour. How soon will the water cover the third rung from the top of the ladder?

This problem *seems* like one of those rate X time problems we struggled with in junior high. But it's not. It's a trick, but most of our very bright undergraduates fell for it. A majority of students gestured while trying to solve this problem. Typically, they used one hand to keep track of the rungs of the ladder and the other to calculate. Those who gestured succeeded in computing the wrong answer more accurately, that is, the time at which the water would rise to the third rung from the top—if the boat were attached to the floor of the sea. But the boat floats! So the level of the water relative to the ladder doesn't change as the tide comes in. The answer to *When will the water cover the third rung from the top?* is: Never. Realizing that the boat floats doesn't require gesturing. That's a fact that has to be drawn from memory. So, in this case, those who gestured were more likely to solve the problem incorrectly because their gestures were driven by incorrect thinking.

To be effective, gestures need to represent the thought in the right way. If gestures that are congruent with thought augment thought, then it should be possible to design gestures that can help people comprehend, learn, think, and solve problems. One such gesture is routinely used in teaching physics. Students are taught to form three axes by holding their thumb and two adjacent fingers at right angles and to rotate them to solve vector problems. In school settings, children were taught a gesture designed to help them understand that the two sides of an equation are equal. Children made a V gesture with their index and middle fingers, each pointing to a side of the equation. Children taught that gesture showed greater understanding of the underlying principle of equality.

Touch pads provide an excellent opportunity to induce students to make gestures that are congruent with the desired thinking. For example, addition is a discrete task, each number gets a count. By contrast, number line estimation is a continuous task. In a number line estimation task, people are presented with a horizontal line representing the numbers from 1 to 100. They are given a number, say 27 or 66, and asked to mark where that number would be on the number line. Children performed better when the addition task was paired with discrete one-to-one gestures and when the number line estimation task was paired with a continuous gesture.

HOW REPRESENTATIONAL GESTURES WORK

We've shown that the gestures people spontaneously make for themselves can help them think. That gestures embody thought. That they map thought directly. They represent thought, not in words or symbols but as actions in space. This is the mysterious part. It's not just motor memory, the kinds of gestures that dancers or pianists or surgeons or tennis players or typists might make to jog their memories. Those gestures are miniatures of the actual actions they would make. Making a map of an environment with hands and fingers isn't at all like walking through an environment. The hands and fingers are used to *represent* the environment. The mappings are abstractions. When we walk through environments, we walk on paths. We can think of the paths as lines and then we can represent lines by moving a finger, moving a hand, or making a discrete chop with a finger or a hand or an arm. We can abstract places to dots and make dots in a variety of ways. Similarly, we can think of each movie genre as a dot, and we can represent our preferences for genres by ordering the dots on a line. We can use that same mapping to represent events in time; each event is a dot ordered on a line. Maps of environments, preferences for movie genres, events ordered in time—and much more—all use the same representational primitives. They use dots to represent places or ideas and use lines to represent relations between them. There's more, circles and boxes, and even more. We'll return to this when we get to graphics in Chapter Eight. The same sorts of mappings are used on the page.

The gestures people make as they think have another boon: they allow seeing thought in action. Others can watch our thinking and we theirs. In real time, as it happens. Can the kinds of gestures that serve our own thought also serve the thought of others? We turn to that now.

GESTURES CHANGE THE THOUGHTS OF OTHERS

We start with babies again. Babies whose caretakers use gesture and speech simultaneously (rather than unaccompanied speech) acquire vocabulary faster. It could be that gestures like pointing clarify the referents of the speech. It could be that gestures enact or depict the referents of the speech. It is probably both and more. When babies see more gestures, they gesture more themselves, providing, as we saw earlier, yet another route for increasing vocabulary.

Parents are so proud when their toddlers can count. But then they are baffled. Despite getting all the number words in the right order, their young prodigies can't answer: How many? What counting means to the toddlers is matching a sequence of words to a series of points to objects. It's rote learning like the alphabet song, with the addition of a marching pointing finger. It isn't yet about number as we understand number. Don't get me wrong, this is a remarkable achievement. That they can do one-to-one correspondence, one number for each object irrespective of the object and increasing numbers, at that, is impressive. Other primates don't do that. But one-to-one correspondence is only part of the picture. When they can't answer how many, they don't yet understand *cardinality,* that the last number word, the highest number, is the total count for the set. If you show them a picture of two sets, say Jonah's candy and Sarah's candy, and ask them to tell how many pieces of candy each child has, they often count Jonah's and without stopping, continue on to count Sarah's. Gesturing a circle around each set of candy helps them to count each set separately, an important step toward understanding cardinality. The circular gesture creates a boundary around each set, including the candy in Sarah's set and separating hers from Jonah's. Children are more likely to stop counting at the boundary.

Now we jump to bigger people. When we explain something to someone else, we typically gesture. Those gestures are usually larger than the gestures we make for ourselves, there are more of them, and they work together to form a narrative that parallels the spoken narrative. If speakers make larger gestures for others and link them in a narrative, then it's likely they think the gestures help their listeners. We certainly depend on gestures when someone tells us which way to go or how to do something. But that kind of gesture depicts actions we are supposed to take in the world. What about gestures that are meant to change thought, to form representations in the mind?

For this, we turned to concepts that people of all ages and occupations need to learn and that are difficult. Complex systems. The branches of government, what each does, how laws are passed, how they are challenged in courts. How elections proceed, how babies are made, how the heart works. Shakespeare's plays, the main figures, their social and political relations, what each did and how others reacted. Diverse as they are, underneath each is a complex system with a structural layer and a dynamic layer. Structure is an arrangement of parts. Dynamics is a causal sequence of actions. Structure is space; dynamics, time.

Dozens of studies have shown that it's easier to grasp structure than dynamics. Structure is static. Dynamics is change, often causality. Novices and the half of us low in spatial ability understand structure, but it takes expertise or ability or effort to understand dynamics. Structure can readily be put on a page. A map of a city. A diagram of the branches of government, the parts of a flower, a family tree. Networks of all kinds. Action doesn't stay still, it's harder to capture and harder to show. The actions are diverse and the causality is varied and might not be visible, forces and wind.

Gestures are actions; could gestures that represent actions help people understand dynamics? For a dynamic system, we chose the workings of a car engine. We wrote a script that explained its structure and action, everything that would be needed to answer the questions we asked later. Then we made two videos of the same person using the same script to explain the car engine. One video had eleven gestures showing structure, such as the shape of the pistons. Another had eleven gestures showing action, say, of the piston. The same rudimentary diagram appeared in both videos. A large group of students watched one or the other of the videos. Because structure is easy, we didn't expect effects of structure gestures, but it was important that both groups of viewers see gestures.

After viewing the explanation of the car engine, participants answered a set of questions, half on structure, half on action. Then they created visual explanations of the car engine. Finally, they explained the workings of the car engine to a video camera so that someone else could understand. Viewing action gestures had far-reaching consequences. People who had viewed action gestures answered more action questions correctly, even though all the information was in the script. The differences in the visual and videoed explanations were more dramatic. Those who had seen action gestures showed far more action in their visualizations: they used more arrows, they depicted actions like explosions, intake, and compression. They separated the steps of the process more cleanly. In their videoed explanations, they used far more action gestures and most of those were inventions, not imitations. They used more action words, even though they hadn't heard more action words. Viewing straightforward and natural gestures conveying action gave students a far deeper understanding of action, an understanding revealed in their knowledge, in their diagrams, in their gestures, and in their words.

Put simply, gestures change thought. Gestures that we make as well as gestures that we see. Next, we turned to concepts of time, using the same technique: identical script, different gestures for different participants. Perhaps because words come one after another, people can have trouble grasping that two steps or events aren't strictly ordered in time. They may be simultaneous in actual time or their order might not matter. When the stages of a procedure are described as, first you do M, then you can do P or Q in either order, and finally you do W, people often remember that P precedes Q (or vice versa). When the description of the steps in time was accompanied by a beat gesture for each step, people made the error of strictly ordering the steps. However, when the description came with a gesture indicating simultaneity, unordered steps were remembered correctly, as unordered.

Another temporal concept that doesn't come easily for people is cyclicity. Think of cycles like the seasons, washing clothes, the rock cycle, and this one: *the seed germinates, the flower grows, the flower is pollinated, a new seed is formed.* When given the steps of cycles like these and asked to diagram them, people tend to draw linear, but not circular, diagrams. People do understand circular diagrams of cycles perfectly well, but they produce linear ones. Gestures change that. When we presented one of the processes with gestures that proceeded along a line, the linear tendency strengthened. But when we presented one of the processes with gestures that went in a circle, a majority drew circular diagrams. Importantly, they weren't simply copying the gestures. We repeated the experiment with another group and instead of asking them to create a diagram after the last stage, we asked them: *What comes next?* Those who had seen circular diagrams usually went back to the beginning of the cycle and said: the seed germinates. But those who had seen linear gestures tended to continue to a new process, like gathering flowers for a bouquet. So, seeing the circular gestures did change the way people thought.

These studies are only a drop in the bucket of the research showing that the gestures we view change the ways we think. The trick is to create gestures that establish a space of ideas that represents the thought felicitously. That gestures have the power to change thought has powerful implications for communication, in the classroom and outside.

GESTURES DO MATH AND MUSIC

Fingers and toes and other parts of the body have been used for counting all over the world for eons. At first, one finger for one thing, much like a tally. The one-to-one use of fingers and toes is an elegant example of a congruent mapping, one thing to one finger. But the

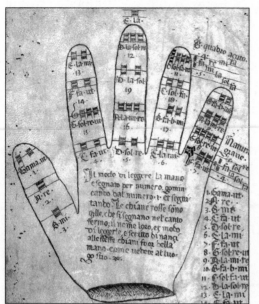

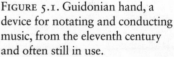

FIGURE 5.1. Guidonian hand, a device for notating and conducting music, from the eleventh century and often still in use.

number of things can go far beyond the number of fingers and toes, and even shoulders, knees, and every other joint in the body. People eventually came up with the bright idea of using some joints as multiples of others, so some joints became tens, hundreds, thousands, and so on. That transformation left a one-to-one congruent correspondence far behind. Going even further, the hand itself became the first slide rule or calculator. It took practice, just like using a slide rule does, to become adept at bending and straightening fingers in order to add, multiply, subtract, and divide. Like playing the piano. Pianos also have a congruent mapping, the left-to-right order of the keys to the increasing frequencies of the notes the keys play. Using the hand as a calculator began as spatial congruence and evolved into performance congruence, one that mapped hand actions to arithmetic operations.

Continuing with music, not the piano, but singing. Another fascinating use of the hand was to represent musical notes and to lead a chorus, the Guidonian hand, so-called because it has been attributed to an eleventh-century monk, Guido of Arezzo. You can see a version in Figure 5.1.

Guido is also responsible for the way music is annotated to this day: do re mi fa so la ti do. Leading a chorus meant inscribing the notes on the fingers and palm, and pointing to the appropriate notes for the singers. Although the Guidonian hand fell out of use with the availability of printed music, it is making a comeback today.

The gestures used to calculate sums or to lead a chorus are not spontaneous; they are highly codified, even more than language. Nevertheless, like spontaneous gestures, they are intricately involved with thinking.

GESTURES AS SOCIAL GLUE
Conversation

That gestures are social glue is apparent from watching conversation. Gestures of the head, face, hands, and body keep conversation going. You say something and pause, looking at me. I nod my head to indicate I'm with you, or if I'm not, I raise my eyebrows or tilt my head and squint in puzzlement. When I'm ready to give you the floor, I lean back. Instead of answering a question I can't answer, I might shrug my shoulders. If we don't give this silent feedback to each other, conversation is awkward.

Collaboration

Conversation is one form of collaboration, but there are other explicit collaborations where gesture is key, notably where collaboration is facilitated by something in the world that can be pointed to or manipulated. Here's one example: pairs of students were asked to find the best route to rescue wounded people after a hypothetical earthquake. They were given a map of the campus with locations of wounded people and blocked roads. They were asked to sketch a map of the best route. Some pairs worked side-by-side huddled over the same map. Their conversation tools were hands, map, and voice. Although they were deep in conversation, they rarely looked at each other's faces. Instead they looked at their hands. Their hands took turns suggesting and editing routes on the map, annotated by the voice. The voice said things like: go here, turn there, now this way, not there—expressions that made sense only by looking at what the hands were doing on the map. Their gestures got abbreviated. Initially, participants would trace a whole route; as collaboration proceeded, they just pointed to the successive intersections. They picked up on each other's gestures, a common phenomenon termed *entrainment* that is evident in words as well. Other pairs also worked side-by-side with identical maps but with a thin curtain between them. For those pairs, the only conversational tool was the voice. The first group of pairs, those who could gesture on a shared map, were more interactive, enjoyed the experience more, and produced better maps. The pairs separated by a curtain worked hard to agree on a route—students took this task seriously and enjoyed it. Yet, fully a third of the pairs came up with routes that differed substantially between partners.

Words can be and all too often are ambiguous, even words describing something as basic as space, the surroundings we carry with us at all times. Gestures, by contrast, are explicit. They show the exact places and trace the turns and paths. You already know what gestures predominated: point-like gestures for places, line-like gestures for paths. Zero-dimensional and one-dimensional. A third kind of gesture was also used, a two-dimensional sweep of the hand, to denote an area. The gestures didn't work alone, they worked with an external representation of the task, in this case a map. But remember that we saw earlier that gestures can create a virtual external representation that serves as a platform for gestures. Whether actual or virtual, an external representation creates common ground and serves as a stage for the hands to reason and deliberate.

Design

Here's another case, design. Small, experienced teams of designers were asked to redesign a device that detected properties of materials. Each team was seated around a table and given an engineering drawing and eventually a tangible model to work with. Needless to say, there was considerable use of gesture, on the drawings and the object. A few of the groups had "radical breaks," sudden changes in design ideas. Insights. Flashbulb moments. These were accompanied by a cascade of new metaphors and new ideas, and notably an explosion of gestures, a switch from small ones on the table to large ones walking around the room enacting interacting with the object. Sometimes the narrated enactments were sketched rather than gestured, again showing the close relations between the two forms of expression, gesture and graphics.

Dance

The entire body participates in dance—dance is inherently and fully embodied. As such, it can readily represent itself. Yet choreographers and dancers have developed other embodied ways to represent dance when they are referring to dancing, techniques they call *marking*. Marking is often done with the fingers of one hand on the palm of another. The fingers dance as the legs would, showing a step to someone else. The whole body can also mark, performing what is essentially an embodied sketch of a dance or a segment of dance, for example, to sketch out position on the stage for lighting or to show in exaggerated fashion a dip of the torso or the stretch of a leg to a dancer. Surprisingly, sketching by marking an entire sequence of dance moves turns out to be a better way to remember the sequence than fully dancing the sequence. Sketching the sequence allows dancers to concentrate on the sequence, per se, rather than on both the sequence and the full expression of the movements.

Conducting

Now consider conducting, a vivid case for which gestures are the social glue. If the job of gestures on maps was straightforward, to express places and paths and areas, the job of gestures in conducting is straightforward but also nuanced and subtle. Among so many other things, conductors synchronize the tempo, oversee the dynamics of the music in space and in time, control the volume and intensity, and cue the entrances and exits of musicians. It is said that the left hand typically sets the tempo, and the right hand does the rest. But actual practice is far more complicated, and in no way systematized. Hand gestures vary wildly across conductors, many use a baton, some don't. Many use their faces, backs, legs, and even their lungs, the rhythm of their breathing. Leonard Bernstein famously conducted Haydn, entirely with his head and plastic face, especially his eyebrows, with hardly a movement of his arms or body. Van Karajan conducted with his eyes closed. Esa-Pekka Salonen dances. The diversity of styles is astounding, all the more so because, according to some research, hundreds of years of social interactions of this sort should have converged on a common language.

Conductors conduct the audience as well as the orchestra. Audience perception of features of music such as expressiveness, articulation, and dynamics are enhanced when emphasized by conductors. Even though the contribution of a conductor is entirely visual, when audio is kept constant and conducting varied, the experience of audiences changes accordingly. For example, conductors could lead listeners to attend to overall melody or to a repeating theme (*ostinato*). When conductors emphasized overall melody, listeners were more likely to describe the piece as connected and regular, but when conductors emphasized repeating themes, listeners were more likely to describe the same piece as disconnected and irregular.

Although conductors only create visual performances, musicians create both sound performances and visual performances. Remarkably, sometimes the visual is more powerful than the sound. Here's a dramatic case: determining the actual rankings of the top three finalists of a piano competition from audio alone, video alone, or both. Make your own prediction about which is best, but be prepared to be surprised. Both experts and novices were most correlated with the actual rankings when they had viewed only the video! This is, of course, despite their beliefs that the sound is more important than the visual.

Moving from music to art. Let me end the discussion of gestures as social glue with da Vinci's iconic *Last Supper*. You can find many copies in Google images. Better yet, go to Milan, to the church of Santa Maria delle Grazie and spend half an hour enjoying the real thing. A double session because the fifteen-minute standard session isn't enough time. Follow the complex interactions of the bodies, the eyes, and the hands. You can see who's talking to whom, how they are related, what they are referring to, how they are reacting. You feel the intensity of the interactions of the groups of guests and the calm detachment of Jesus. This is where we began, observing social interactions from afar, now exquisitely captured by da Vinci.

AFTERTHOUGHT

We can think with our bodies, but can we think great thoughts with our bodies? Yes! There's da Vinci thinking through designs for flying machines and bridges and parachutes. There's Einstein, imagining himself flying on a beam of light, the imagined flight that enabled his insights into spacetime. There are magicians who imagine making knots that undo themselves and surgeons who imagine one-handed knots that don't come undone. Houdinis imagining escapes from locked boxes and thieves imagining cracking safes. Then there are choreographers, football coaches, fashion designers, military strategists, wrestlers, artists, engineers, actors, and mathematicians. All (or most) thinking great thoughts with their bodies.

CHAPTER SIX

Points, Lines, and Perspective: Space in Talk and Thought

In which we consider how linear language describes space, using a perspective, either an inside, body-centered perspective or an outside, world-centered perspective. For insider perspectives, we show that surprisingly taking another's perspective is sometimes easier and more natural than taking your own.

> *The goal is not only the destination but also the path that takes you to it.*
>
> —PAUL ANDREU, from Lao Tzu

TALK AND THOUGHT

Talking isn't thinking. Talking can reveal thinking and talking can change thinking, but it shouldn't be confused with thinking. Talk is only one way to express thought; there are others. Laughing, gasping, and screaming emerge from the mouth bursting with meaning but are not talk. The face, the hands, the body—all express thought. As do sketches and diagrams and models and arrangements of things in space. Then there are times that our thoughts get stuck in our heads—they can't seem to find their way out. We are speechless, at a loss for words.

But talk can take us far; it's where we'll begin. Talk is words, one after another. Words are symbols, arbitrary and indirect expressions of meaning, expressions of meaning that are highly condensed. There simply aren't enough words. Words do not show their meanings in the ways that facial expressions, gestures, and depictions do.

Unfettered by meaningful perceptual features, words reach effortlessly to abstraction. Because of the abstractness of words, there are
so many more meanings than words. Talk still provides a window
to thought. That window is a narrow one but, under scrutiny, a
revealing one.

We begin with talk about space. Talking about space is quite like
exploring space. Talking about space takes us on a journey from one
place to another. Space should be one of the easiest things to talk
about—we spend our lives in it. Navigating in space is essential to
survival. We have nouns for places and kinds of places, adjectives
for describing them, verbs to express exploring them, prepositions
to convey spatial relations within and between them. Despite the
solidity and tangibility and ubiquity of space, talk about space is
subtle and prone to ambiguity. Watch my words and yours. Talk
and thought about space serve as foundations for talk and thought
about so much else. That foundation is embedded in the brain. If you
missed that, go back to Chapter Three, the **Sixth Law of Cognition:
Spatial thinking is the foundation of abstract thought.** We saw the
foundation in the brain; now we show it in talk.

TALK AND THOUGHT ABOUT SPACE
Perspective

We start with an ordinary, everyday request: someone asks you where
something is. Your bike. Their keys. Cell phone. Glasses. Your house
or office. Think how you would answer. "On the kitchen table" or
"leaning against the right side of my house." But you can't give those
answers without being sure that you and that someone have a shared
understanding of which kitchen table and house, and where they are
located. That is, you need a shared perspective. You need a common
way of looking at the world as a starting point. In fact, it's likely
you can't talk about anything without taking a perspective, implicit
or explicit, and making sure that perspective is shared (n.b.: *shared*
does not mean *agreed*). A number of different disciplines arrived at
the same two basic perspectives if by different routes: *egocentric,*

that is, with respect to a specific body, typically yours, and *allocentric,* that is, with respect to the surrounding world. The most familiar allocentric perspective is north-south-east-west.

Egocentric perspective. Let's say a friend wants to borrow your bike and you're not home, so you need to tell your friend where your bike is. You might say, "If you're facing my house, you'll see the bike leaning against the right side of the house." Here the perspective is explicit, it's facing the house. If you had said, "The bike's to the right of the house" it wouldn't be clear whether *right* was from the point of view of someone facing the house or someone leaving the house. You also need a frame of reference. Here, it's your friend's egocentric perspective, your friend's right-left front-back above-below, those imaginary axes extending from the body that we talked about in Chapter Three.

But that presupposes that your friend knows where your house is. Explaining how to find your house may require a longer description. Like all spatial descriptions, that one has to begin with a shared perspective, one that is known to your friend, one your friend can take. You might say something like, "From your hotel, turn right onto Cowper. Go down Cowper about half a mile until you get to Embarcadero. Turn right on Embarcadero, then left at about the third light onto El Camino. Go down about half a mile. Turn right onto Stanford Avenue . . . " Here, the perspective is still the egocentric perspective of your friend, the traveler. Although "your" viewpoint keeps changing, the changes are explicit and the frame of reference is always "your" body, your left-right front-back head-feet.

For good reason, perspective and reference frames are core concepts in linguistics, psychology, geography, and more—history, literature, art, everywhere you look. The perspective illustrated above, that of an observer embedded in a space, and the frame of reference described above, extensions of the axes of the body, are typically called *egocentric*. The center, the starting point, of the perspective is the ego. Ego keeps moving along the route, and the reference point moves along with ego. Now for a technical term, from linguistics. That center, ego's position in space and time, is called the *deictic* center. *Deictic,* right, Greek again, "to point or show." Knowing the deictic center is essential for understanding words like *here, now, there, next, this,* and *that.* Put differently, grasping those terms depends on knowing ego's location in space and time. No wonder that the first question we usually ask the caller on the cell phone, "Where are you?"

The extended use of an egocentric perspective to give directions, to tell someone how to get from A to B, is often called a *route perspective.* Route descriptions are procedures, explanations, directions for getting from A to B. They take you from where you are to where you need to be in space. But also in time. Writers address their readers as *you* when they want to put you smack in the middle of a scene, when they want you to experience the action as if you were there, as if the action were unfolding step-by-step before your eyes.

Route perspectives can be used not just to give directions but also to give an overall impression of an environment, to describe the layout of your apartment or locate the major landmarks of a city. Here's one of midtown Manhattan. "Start with Lincoln Center at your back and make a right onto Broadway. Go down about seven blocks until you get to Columbus Circle at 59th Street. You'll see the statue of Columbus in the center, surrounded by fountains. To your right, you'll see Time-Warner Center and on your left the edge of Central Park. Turn left onto 59th Street and walk along the park until its end, at Fifth Avenue. Go right on Fifth Avenue and continue to 53rd Street. Go right again on 53rd and you'll see the Museum of Modern Art half-way up the street on your right." I've taken you from landmark to landmark, place to place, point to point, along a path. Travel guides do this more vividly. Take my word for it, it's a nice walk.

You probably noticed that route descriptions are built from pieces, like Lego blocks. And like Legos, each piece has two parts, a link to the previous part and a link to the subsequent one. The parts of each route segment are a path and a place. The path is a link from the previous part and the place becomes a link to the subsequent one. Just as Lego parts can be connected to create smaller or larger edifices, so route parts can be connected to create smaller or larger descriptions. Paths are the way you get from place to place, the actions you take to get from place to place. At places, actions can change; for routes, the change is typically change of direction. Places, choice points, are often street intersections but could be other landmarks, churches or piazzas, subway stops or restaurants. Another way to think about paths and places: actions and consequences of actions, the places actions bring you to. "Make a right onto Broadway." "Turn left onto 59th Street." Segments of places and paths can be added, as many as needed, like links in a chain. Points and links, places and paths, form the skeleton of routes.

Sketch maps have that same structure, pieces that connect places. We asked hungry students to sketch maps or write down directions from where they were to a nearby fast-food restaurant. Although sketch maps could represent distances and directions and turns and wiggles in paths in an analog fashion, they don't. They are discrete in the same ways that directions in words are discrete. Sketch maps elongate distances where there are many turns, just as verbal directions are longer for many turns. Sketch maps straighten wiggles in roads and draw turns as 90 degrees regardless of their real angle, just as verbal directions say "go down" without specifying wiggles or say "turn right" or take a left" without specifying the angle of the turn. In short, the same schematic mental representation of a route seems to drive both the verbal route directions and the sketch maps.

Your perspective or mine? The *you* that I've dragged to find my bike or to explore midtown Manhattan is a hypothetical *you*, any *you*, even me. But what about face-to-face situations when I choose between your perspective or mine? Say there are two wine glasses on the table and you ask, "Which is mine?" I'm more likely to answer from your perspective than from mine, even if it means switching right and left, which is, as you know, a difficult switch. Taking your perspective rather than mine might be in part a matter of politeness, though Japanese people, members of the most stereotypically polite culture, take your perspective no more than Americans, about 70 percent of the time, depending on the circumstances. And that's just it—whose perspective seems to depend on the circumstances, in particular, on the relative cognitive loads, yours and mine. In the case of the wine glass, I know whose is whose, but you don't, so your cognitive load is greater than mine. You have to both understand the utterance and map it to the glasses; I know the mapping and only have to create the utterance. On the other hand, if my cognitive load is greater than yours, say, you know the answer but I don't and I'm asking you, I'll favor my perspective, "Is mine on my right?" If we are offered a neutral way to specify the location, neither your perspective nor mine, we'll both prefer that one. If the designated glass is closer to the salt shaker, we'll use the salt shaker as a landmark and say, "Your glass is the one closer to the salt shaker."

Fans of route descriptions claim that they are common and compelling because they are natural: routes are the way we experience the world, by moving through it.

Then, in order to describe where things are in an environment, we reexperience it, we imagine ourselves moving through that environment and describe where everything is from our changing point of view. Persuasive as that claim might be, and it did persuade many, people have made maps for eons, and mapmaking requires an allocentric perspective, one from above. Sure enough, when people describe environments and even routes, they often adopt an allocentric perspective in part or in whole.

Allocentric perspective. Mapmaking has to be one of the truly remarkable achievements of the human mind. No one has found a chimpanzee who makes maps—yet. In contrast to exploration, maps don't use an egocentric perspective, they use an *allocentric* perspective, an egoless "other-centric" perspective, one outside the body and typically one from above. The most general frame of reference that ordinary mortals use is the one of the world, north-south east-west. Geologists and meteorologists and some other -ologists add a third dimension, altitude. Sailors use the coordinates of the vessel, port-starboard (left-right) and bow-stern (front-back). Actors and directors use those of the stage from the point of view of an actor, facing an audience. Hence, *upstage*. Neuroscientists and physicians, those of the body, naturally obscure terms derived from Latin, *dorsal/ventral, caudal/rostral, medial/lateral*. In case you're curious, *dorsum* means "back" and *venter* means "stomach." No wonder they use Latin.

Before we can draw maps, we need to conceive of them. We need to imagine the world from a perspective above the world, a bird's-eye or survey or overview perspective. We experience the world from within it in bits and pieces but can imagine the pieces patched together from outside, a feat accomplished by the hippocampus working with nearby entorhinal cortex. For the details, go back to Chapter Three. Don't worry about the names, they are simply parts of the brain and the brain has far too many parts for most mortals to remember. Our brains can extract our egos from their place embedded in the world and arrange things relative to each other rather than relative to ourselves. That is, we, in common with rats, can enter a room or a neighborhood from different directions and know where things are. Unlike rats, we can shrink that world in our minds and then put it out in the world, onto a page.

Add language to a map-like mental representation and you can talk about the world from an allocentric perspective. Tourist guides also use allocentric perspectives to give readers an overview of the interesting landmarks in a city. Here's a way to describe the heart of DC: "The National Mall is bounded by the Washington Monument on the west and the Capitol on the east. From west to east on the north side of the Mall are the National Museum of American Art, the National Museum of Natural History, and the National Gallery of Art. From west to east on the south side of the Mall are . . . " You get the picture. This perspective has been called a survey perspective or an overview perspective or a bird's-eye perspective or even an absolute perspective. Instead of locating landmarks relative to "you" using body coordinates, the reference frame of a survey perspective locates landmarks relative to each other using an external perspective, typically the cardinal directions, north-south and east-west. I made things easier by using a simple environment, one that doesn't have landmarks on many different streets that are parallel and perpendicular. By the way, did you pick up that the description started in the west, on the left, and proceeded eastward, rightward, in (Western) reading order?

Back to the bike. Using an allocentric perspective, I could've said, "The bike's against the south side of the house" (after giving you an allocentric description of the house's location). So many complexities in what seems like a simple task: Where's my bike? And I've only told you the easy parts. I've skipped many other fascinating and revealing opportunities for ambiguity, error, and confusion. Just in descriptions of space. This is one of many subtleties that keeps linguists in business. An aside: this is why we use gesture to locate things when face-to-face. Gesture has dual benefits: it's more direct and it's less ambiguous.

You might be discouraged by the complexity of crafting descriptions for what should be straightforward, describing locations in space. You might think, *Just give me a map.* And you'd be right: how simple and straightforward it is to sketch the relative locations of the landmarks. The simplicity of the depiction in contrast to the clumsiness of the description. Both to create and to grasp. For one thing, maps use space to represent space, a direct mapping. They can show many spatial relations all at once, not just a single route. They enable taking many different perspectives and exploring many different routes. Indeed, maps typically give us overhead or survey perspectives, but we often use them to create routes, routes that can start and end in many different places. We can also use maps, in the mind or on the page, to estimate distances and directions, so maps are not only far more compact and direct than descriptions but also far more informative.

Real-life in-the-world on-the-ground spatial descriptions. Back to talk. How do people actually talk on the ground in real life? The descriptions I provided are clearly concocted. Real-life spontaneous descriptions and directions, like any real-life talk, are messier. Even written ones: here's how a package sent from Sweden to Kabul, the capital of Afghanistan and a city of millions, in 2017 was addressed: "To Atta Mohammed, next to Sajadee Mosque." "Next to"—no clear perspective, vague frame of reference. And where is Sajadee Mosque? To make things worse, Atta Mohammed is a common name. It took hours of detective work and many false turns by a postal worker on a bike, but, amazingly, the package was delivered. It turns out that uncertain addresses are not at all unusual. On a recent Scandinavian Airlines flight, I was informed by the September 2018 *Scandinavian Traveler* that "half the people on our planet, or four billion individuals, lack a precise address." SAS is funding a group to rectify that (http://mapproject.se/).

When people actually talk, they casually mix frames of reference and switch perspectives, and they do that without signaling. Even more surprising, the rest of us understand the mixed perspectives and mixed reference frames and make sense out of them. This flies in the face of claims and presuppositions not only in psychology but also in linguistics: that we need a uniform, coherent perspective not only to talk and understand but also to think. Apparently not so. Actually, people quite frequently—though not always—make sense even out of nonsense. It's the sense we're after, the meaning.

A simple laboratory task, describing an assortment of environments learned from maps, showed decisively that people don't consistently adopt a unified perspective. We gave people many maps to study, a convention center, a small town, a museum, an amusement park, and more, and asked them to study each map and then describe each environment in turn from memory. The spontaneous descriptions were quite good, complete and accurate enough for other people to sketch more or less the same map. Most of the descriptions mixed perspective and frame of reference, that is, they used both egocentric and allocentric perspectives, without signaling when they switched. Skip the examples below if you trust us—they're fragments, the environments aren't real, you don't have the maps, and spatial descriptions, even when they're simple, are hard.

Convention center fragment:

After you pass the bulletin board (on your left) and Camera Stores (on your right) there is an office in the back of the building in the left-hand corner. Right next to it on its right side are restrooms and a Cafeteria, respectively.

The Cafeteria is in the far right corner of the building and the restrooms are between the office and cafeteria. Next to the Cafeteria along the North side of the building is a CD store and a Stereo components store. The Stereo component store is in the NE corner of the building. There are TV and VCR stores across from the CD Store and Stereo component store.

Small town fragment:

The River Hwy. runs E-W from the river to the Mountain Rd. and further; it is to the S of the mountains. Going E on the River Hwy., at the intersection with the Mtn. Rd., there is a gas station and a restaurant on the left. On the right, before the intersection are the stables. Going N on Mtn. Rd. from the intersection towards the mountains, to the right is the town hall and to the left is the park with a gazebo.

Mixing perspectives seems to be the rule rather than the exception. It can take us a bit more time to understand descriptions that use mixed perspectives rather than consistent ones, but once we have, our own perspectives are more flexible. We get good at switching perspective. Our mental representations become perspective-free. Then we are equally fast and accurate answering questions from each perspective, irrespective of the perspective we studied. While we're listening, it might take us longer to understand mixed perspectives, but if they are reasonably consistent and unambiguous, we can get them. Making sense of mixed perspectives might be difficult but ultimately has benefits: it makes our own thinking more flexible. Reverse the **First Law of Cognition: Every cost has a benefit**.

Different languages, different perspectives. Now an important qualification on frames of reference. Many of you will be wondering about other cultures, other languages. The answer is fascinating. We take the primacy of an egocentric perspective for granted. After all, we begin with our own bodies, we experience the world from our own viewpoint. There are so many voices in the research literature—I won't name names, they're friends!—claiming that it takes extra effort to get out of our own egocentric perspective. Yet, there are languages scattered all over the world that don't use an egocentric perspective at all. If there are two glasses of wine on the table and the person across from you asks you whose is whose, you're likely to say something like, *Yours is on your right.* If you happen to be from the outback of Australia and speak Guugu Yimithirr or if you happen to be from the highlands of Mexico and speak Tzeltal or if you happen to be from rural India and speak Tamil, you would be more likely to say, *Yours is the north glass.* These languages don't use an egocentric reference frame. Instead, they use an allocentric reference frame based in the cardinal directions and sometimes called an *absolute* reference frame because it is a fixed reference frame, one that doesn't depend on any individual's perspective.

What's especially notable about people who speak languages that rely solely on an absolute reference frame is that they know where they are with respect to the rest of the world. We're so often clueless. They seem to keep track of their orientations in space much better than those of us who frequently rely on an egocentric frame of reference. To say or understand where one thing is relative to another, they need to know where things are relative to north-south east-west. If you blindfold them, lead them hither and thither, and then ask them to point home, they can! Do the same to residents of Amsterdam, and they're hopeless, they point almost at random.

This fascinating discovery is the best evidence so far for the Whorf-Sapir hypothesis, the idea that the language you speak affects the way you think. There is more, but that's for a different book. And all of it is controversial. Naturally.

Addresses and devices. Many of you are rolling your eyes again, all of this talk about talk about navigating in space is archaic. It's like doing arithmetic; who does arithmetic anymore? Just give me an address. But an address can't be used without an enormous amount of shared information, map-like information, maybe even a map. An address locates a building in a network of streets, it doesn't have a start point or a way of navigating. Okay, then pull out your smartphone: that has both. But smartphones and other navigation systems depend on that same map-like information. It happens to be in the brains of the smartphone instead of in yours. Just as the operations of multiplication and division are in the brains of a calculator rather than burdening yours. You've outsourced parts of your brain. Soon even smartphones will be archaic; all the knowledge we will need will be embedded and updated in our minds or our bodies. We will never lose our glasses or smartphones because we won't need them; we'll never lose our kids in a mall or our friends in a museum because the knowledge embedded in us of where they are will be updated continuously with AI programs that understand us and our lives. Maybe we won't even have to clarify whose wine glass is whose. We'll see.

Places and paths. Talk is linear, one word after another. Thinking seems that way, too, one thought after another, however chaotic the order. We talk about and think about routes as sequences of nodes and links, where the nodes are places and the links are the paths that connect them. Years ago, some anthropologists asked river traders in New Guinea to sketch their routes. The traders had never been to school and had never seen a map. They drew a line for the river (straightening it!) with small circles, dots, along it for the settlements where they stopped to trade. Beads on a string.

Survey descriptions have that same character, nodes and links, places and paths. Routes arrange points, landmarks, along a single line, often turning in space to take you from A to B. Survey representations are like maps: they have many lines and many points, they arrange landmarks along multiple lines, parallel or intersecting or not connecting at all. A network.

There isn't a single path; there's the possibility of many. But as we said, talk is one word after another, so describing forces us to linearize a space, irrespective of perspective. Otherwise, route-like thought and survey-like thought differ deeply: a single path for a specific set of actions versus a web of paths for many possible sets of actions.

These different views, insider or outsider, a single path or the possibility of many, have enormous consequences.

We began with talk, talk about the endlessly rich and complex and variable spaces in the world, the spaces that we experience constantly, that we cannot escape. Despite their variability and complexity and richness (or maybe because of it), the mind abstracts them to a simple form, a network composed of places linked by paths. For networks of places, as well as for networks of events or networks of people or networks of just about any concept, we can assume a perspective from within or from without, from inside or from outside, egocentric or allocentric. Perspective, real or imagined, crucially determines what we can see. Things near our perspective loom larger: we see them more clearly and see the differences among them more clearly. Things in the distance get jammed together. Seeing things from within is vital for orchestrating our lives. Where we've been, where we're going, what we just did, what we are going to do. Seeing things from above is fundamental to planning our lives and to maintaining orientation with things out of view. Switching perspective from inside to outside isn't straightforward; we can do it if only we have the larger picture, but even then, switching perspective from inside to outside, from the here and now to the general, or from outside to inside, from general possibilities to specific plans, takes effort.

That simple structure, nodes and links, scaffolds thinking but in and of itself is devoid of meaning; the meanings of the nodes and links need to be filled in. A multitude of concepts beyond strictly spatial ones, paths, and places, can be mapped to that simple structure, and we turn to some of them in Chapter Seven, beginning with time. But even before that, a broader view, a detour to ways we organize the stuff in the world and the stuff in the mind. The same ways! Networks are only part of the story.

CHAPTER SEVEN

Boxes, Lines, and Trees: Talk and Thought About Almost Everything Else

In which we reflect on the ways simple geometric forms, dots, boxes, lines, and networks, capture thought about space, time, number, perspective, causality, and just about everything else.

> George is a deep thinker, but his thoughts rarely come to the surface.
>
> —TOM TORO, cartoon in *The New Yorker*, April 2, 2018

TALK ABOUT SPACE

Talk about space is as ancient as it is common. There is literal spatial talk: telling someone what a place looks like or where something is or how to get there. It's an old neighborhood, the streets lined with four-story pastel stucco apartment buildings with bay windows, some with small shops and cafes at the corners. Your keys are in the right-hand pocket of your jacket. The symphony is one block west and one block south of City Hall. Go right on Broadway, down seven blocks, turn left, and cross the street to get to Central Park. There is figurative spatial talk: she's on a path to success, he's on top of the world, the government took a sharp turn to the right, those ideas are worlds apart. Underlying both kinds of talk, literal and figurative, is a simple structure: nodes for ideas and links that connect them. Nodes are boxes, they can be packed with people, places, things—any idea for that matter, singles or collections. Links connect them in myriad ways, sometimes specified, sometimes not. The architecture of the brain is like that, in the small, neurons linked to neurons. In the large, the hippocampus for ideas and the entorhinal cortex for arrays of ideas.

Boxes and links turn out to underlie an enormous swath of talk and thought, maybe all of it. Links can fall into patterns: lines, trees, networks, circles, zigzags, spirals. Networks organize into clusters, hubs, and neighborhoods. Curiously, the boxes and links we create in the mind are mirrored by those in the world. Inside the body, the network of arteries and nerves. On earth, the network of paths of rivers, of traders, of automobiles, of airlines. Of phone lines and the internet. Then there are those that we put in the world, like maps and diagrams, to enlarge and enhance or instill those in the mind. Thoughts that we put in the world are the focus of the next chapter, Chapter Eight, but before the world, the mind.

THE GEOMETRY OF THE MIND: FORMS

We've had Cognitive Laws and Facts Worth Remembering. Now we add *forms*, abstract geometric structures that pervade talk and gesture and all the other ways thought is expressed. First, and central to this chapter, points and lines. Practical words that are spatial at their core and expand and enrich and enlighten every which way. We added boxes and networks and we'll add arrows, circles, trees, spirals, and maybe a few more. Then we'll need qualities of forms: center, periphery, symmetry, synchrony, repetition, pattern. Each has aliases that carry nuances. Points are otherwise known as dots or nodes or places or ideas; lines can be called links or paths or connections or relations; boxes can be termed regions or areas or containers. Center is also known as middle, focus, core, crux, hub, foreground. Yeats's poignant line: *Things fall apart; the centre cannot hold* (from *The Second Coming*). Susan Sontag asks us to reflect on the difference between being in the center and being in the middle. Same geometry, radically different meanings. *Center* contrasts with *periphery,* another fundamental idea that comes in many forms.

Some lines are *edges:* they can be boundaries, barriers, separating one set of things from another, or they can be seams where one set of things rubs up against another.

These abstract geometric ideas—points, lines, arrows, boxes, circles, center, periphery, symmetry—are building blocks. They can be arranged to create forms or frameworks in the mind or in the world. Those frameworks represent structures of thought. These forms organize thought and especially organize carefully crafted thought, thought in the mind or put into the world with forethought in the form of language, gesture, diagrams, design, and art. It's not just linguists and mathematicians who have been captivated by these forms. They have captivated poets, writers, artists, designers, architects, and others who closely observe their practices. They have inspired generations of mystics. Points and lines are the basic elements of drawings, of language, of thought, and of the brain. In language, subjects can be represented by points with lines linking them to predicates. Ideas can be represented by points and connections to other ideas by lines. Neurons linked to neurons. What could be more fundamental?

Points and lines, and also arrows, boxes, circles, and the like, are simple geometric figures. Familiar patterns. Good gestalts. At the same time, they are abstractions, generalities representing the essences of a panoply of ideas. We'll return to abstractions, but first, we consider some specifics. Thought does that, meander around from general to specific to general again.

BOXES: CONTAINERS FOR STUFF AND IDEAS

Before boxes and lines, there's the stuff we put into boxes and connect with lines. People, things, places, events, ideas. Boxes are so much easier than continua, than dimensions, but they can obscure nuances that are meaningful and important. That **First Law of Cognition** again, **no benefits without costs.** Dots can be placeholders for just about anything you can imagine. Depending on the context of course. We don't see the world as a helter-skelter array of dots, of people, things, places, events, and ideas. We make order out of them, we put them in boxes, string them along lines, hang them on trees. We connect the dots.

Boxes in the world and in the mind: Kinds

Here's one way to organize the stuff in the world and the stuff in our minds. Put similar things together. Those are the categories of Chapter Two. The brain and the mind do love boxes; they simplify the world by putting a multitude of different things together. We begin at home, in our bedrooms and kitchens. Socks in one drawer and sweaters in another. Plates on one shelf and glasses on another. All too often we procrastinate putting the stuff into the boxes and leave them in stacks, sometimes organized by type. It even happens in department stores, though usually they are organized, clothing in one department organized by type, bedding in another. Same for online stores. In a zoo, monkeys in one cage, giraffes in another. In counting money, bills and coins, each sorted by amount, on a table or in our wallets. We organize the activities of our lives as well as the things in our lives, sleep at night, work and dine in the day, go out or zone out in the evenings. There are boxes in time, night and day, week and month, the seasons.

The mind declutters and organizes in the same way. Socks and shirts, glasses and plates, monkeys and giraffes, eating and working are categories, useful ones because the items in them share appearance or function or both so they are easy to identify and to group. These categories are known to a community, so we can call them names. I just did that. We label the boxes: clothing, food, tools. The labels are informative: they tell you what the things inside look like and act like, and how they relate to you. In the world, we literally put one kind of thing in one box—or drawer or shelf or, sadly, cage— and another kind in another box. Those boxes are inside larger ones, a drawer for socks and another for sweaters inside a chest of clothing, a shelf for plates and another for pots and pans inside a kitchen cabinet. That's in the world. Boxes inside boxes not only store our stuff but also represent a *taxonomy*, a hierarchical arrangement of kinds. Kinds and kinds of kinds.

Boxes in the world and in the mind: Places and parts

Here's another way to organize the stuff in our minds and our stuff in the world. We mix up the categories. Not randomly, but for a purpose. Bedrooms have beds and bureaus and closets and night tables. Kitchens have stoves and refrigerators and cupboards. Bathrooms have sinks and tubs and toilets. We sleep and dress in bedrooms, prepare food in kitchens, bathe and brush teeth in bathrooms. These are places, places that contain different kinds of objects that are appropriate for certain activities. We can call the whole complex, places with objects selected for certain activities, *themes*. Rooms are also boxes inside a larger box, a home. Furniture stores might arrange furniture by categories, but our homes arrange furniture by themes. Of course, within the themes we have categories; we just noticed that we organize closets and bureaus by kinds of clothing and kitchen cabinets by kinds of utensils. More themes: supermarkets have aisles and packages of food and checkout counters (who knows how long that will last?), theaters have box offices and seats lined up in rows; parks have grass and benches and swings and slides. Disparate kinds put together to serve a common purpose. These boxes inside boxes also form hierarchical networks, not of kinds but of parts, *partonomies*. You may remember them from previous chapters (Two and Three). The partonomy most familiar to us is our own body. And partonomies, like taxonomies, form trees, trees composed of a hierarchy of nodes and links. The analogy to the living tree is direct.

TREES: BIG IDEAS DIVIDE INTO PARTS OR KINDS
Trees

The tree idea, the tree visualization, the tree name, come from the world: the trunk of a tree, embodying a whole, the large branches splitting into smaller branches, literally embodying parts and parts of parts. The parts and parts of parts emerge from the whole through a biological process. That process isn't evident to the eyes, but the thick, stable trunk and the thinner and thinner branches are visible in trees large and small, wide and narrow. That abstraction, trunk and branches, has been borrowed to represent origins and branches of thought since ancient times and proliferates today.

Real trees are everywhere. They teem with life, providing fruit and seeds and remedies and shade and fuel and boards and homes for birds and beauty. Insects, too. Independently, faiths across the world have conferred trees with mystical and mythical powers. They have been called the Tree of Life for abundant reasons, for reasons of abundance. Although trees have long had rich symbolic meanings, using the branching of trees to represent the branching of knowledge seems to have originated with Aristotle and was explicit in the writings of the third-century Greek philosopher Porphyry. No diagrams remain from Porphyry's writings, but his description of Aristotle's categories and subcategories was sufficient for later philosophers to construct a tree diagram of the scales of being, which came to be known as the Porphyrian tree. Tree diagrams, often with new content, became a standard for study and memory in the high Middle Ages and thereafter.

The process that generated the branching is not always clear. Some seem to be partonomies, some taxonomies, many a mix, some neither. Family trees seem to have originated in medieval representations of the genealogy of Jesus and, later, monarchies and dynasties of rabbis. Bacon, Descartes, Linnaeus, da Vinci, and Darwin are among the many philosophers and scientists who relied on trees to organize, understand, and explain their investigations. Rivers form trees, as does the circulatory system. The brain is a tree, both macroscopically and microscopically. Macroscopically, the branching of the major structures and their functions. Microscopically, the branching of neurons and their interconnections. Freud was a neuroanatomist before he was an analyst, developing staining techniques for microscopic scrutiny and drawing what he saw, essentially neurons and their branching. Freud's drawings of neurons and his insights from the drawings were crucial not only to his later theories but also to the work of the great neuroanatomist and drawer Ramón y Cajal.

The enormity of the influence of tree diagrams on the accumulation and dissemination of knowledge has not been fully recognized. Trees, knowledge, brain. By now their uses are uncountable and their visualizations myriad. The Big Bang, phylogenetic trees, corporate trees, occupational trees, decision trees, diagnostic trees, linguistic trees, knowledge trees, probability trees, family trees, the list goes on. And on.

Networks

Trees are a special kind of network that emanate from a single source. Conversely, networks can be thought of as decentralized trees. Networks have no origin. Nevertheless, networks are often referred to as trees. Typically, networks don't link every node directly to every other node; if the nodes were all interconnected, there would be no reason to create a representation. Network representations are useful when some connections are direct and others indirect. Your link to your parents and siblings and offspring might be direct, but your links to your MD and dentist are not; you need to go through their administrators to make an appointment and through their assistants when you arrive. To fly from where you are to somewhere else, you have to go through certain airports, hubs, and you have to get to and from the airports. Even driving from one place to another is constrained by the networks of roads; normally, you can't just drive directly, the way a bird can fly directly. But even birds don't fly directly; their actual paths depend on the network of winds, a network fundamental to sailors as well. To get to the entertainer you adore or the boss of the company you are applying to or the president of your country might require many links, one of the raisons d'être for social networks such as Facebook and LinkedIn.

Social networks: Six degrees of separation

How many links separate one random person from another? In research that became a meme, the influential social psychologist Stanley Milgram conceived of an experiment that would reveal how closely Americans are interconnected. He sent packages to people in the Midwest and asked them to get a letter to an individual in Boston through people they knew on a first-name basis. A postcard was sent back to Milgram at each link in the chain. Of course, many chose not to play the game and many letters never arrived, so the results remain controversial. Nevertheless, the average number of links in successful chains was around six, a number that has replicated. The meme, however, seems to have come from John Guare's 1990 play with that name, *Six Degrees of Separation,* in which one character ruminates on the phenomenon, the ultimate closeness of each of us to each other. Psychological research on Broadway! The field, the analysis of social networks, has proliferated, not without controversy, using more direct ways of tracing social (and other) networks.

When asked to diagram their social networks, people do interesting things. They quite naturally put themselves in the center. Center. They quite often put their parents above, and their siblings and friends sideways or below. Their diagrams aren't copies of traditional family trees; for one thing, all the links emanate from the person in the center. Everyone in the network is directly connected to the person doing the diagram. The lengths of the lines reflect closeness, shorter lines to those the participant feels closer to. The ease and naturalness of the task show clearly that social relations are readily thought of as spatial relations. Behavior, too, not just thinking. We stand and sit closer to those we feel closer to, and we use the proximity of others to infer their social relations.

The applications of networks are as diverse as they are vast. Their proliferation and complexity pose challenges to visualization, providing work for many clever scientists, journalists, and designers, among others. How can you visualize a family tree of thirteen million people? Researchers have done that.

LINES: PUTTING IDEAS IN ORDER
Lines in the mind and in the world

Simpler than trees to both eye and mind are lines. The books on our shelves alphabetically or by topic or size; events in history and events in our lives by time. We form lines at bus stops and in supermarkets; in supermarkets, we leave our carts as placeholders when we go to grab an item we'd forgotten. Those lines are spatial as well as temporal. We line people up by height or age or status. Wines and washing machines by quality. Countries by population or GNP. Movies and video games by sales. The landmarks along a route. The steps of a process. Again, nodes and links, places and paths, dots and lines, but now arrayed on a line. Lines for time, for quantity, for size, for cost, for preference, for any dimension on which things can be ordered.

Ordering things on a line requires abstraction. The line selects a single dimension along which disparate things can be ordered, no matter how different they are from each other in other ways. *Nota bene:* These are only orders. They don't have values or amounts. The dots along the lines represent the order of things, they don't represent the distances between the things, only what comes before or after what. They aren't metric, they don't come with numbers that indicate exact values. Impressively, ordering things and even judging the relative magnitude of pairs of things are things other animals can do. You don't need language. More on that soon.

Time on a line

One of the earliest concepts to be placed on a line is time. Depictions of sequences of events in time, like making cheese or planting, growing, and harvesting wheat, lined the walls of tombs more than three thousand years ago in ancient Egypt. Aztec and Maya codices depict their histories, step-by-step, along a line.

Jumping from space to time is easy. Space has two, or really three, dimensions; time has only one. A line. Not a plane or a volume. Because of Einstein, we know, even if we don't understand, that space and time trade off; time is the fourth dimension of space. We talk about events in time using the language of moving in space. We treat a landscape of events in time like a landscape of places in space. *After* the Washington Monument we come to the Reflecting Pool; *after* Xmas we come to New Year's. We are looking forward to seeing the Washington Monument; we are looking forward to the new year. We *put* events on calendars as though they were books on a shelf. We arrive *in* time and *in* place. Life is just one damn thing *after* another (source disputed). We passed quickly through the mall. Time *passes* quickly when you're having fun. We've *moved past* the worst; the best is yet to *come*. We raced *through* the summer; the summer raced *past* us. This from the *New York Times:* "With Thanksgiving behind us, the country is rapidly slipping towards the year's end." Note the change in perspective.

We think about time as movement on a line in space. "We're marching through time." But there's also "Time marches on." Which is it? What's moving, time or us? Are we moving through time, the way we move through space? Or is time moving past us? Are we sitting in place, like a king on a throne, with events coming to us, like subjects in the kingdom? Or are we moving through a crowd, like a politician before an election, hugging babies one after another? We face the future—it is in front of us (in English, but not in at least one other language). Do we boldly walk forward or do the events approach us? Actually, both, and there's the confusion. Consider the Famous Ambiguous Question asked in many experiments: someone tells you that next Wednesday's meeting has been moved forward two days. When is it? Half answer Friday—I am moving toward the meeting time; half answer Monday—the meeting time is moving toward me.

These two metaphors for thinking about time have been called *moving ego* and *moving time*. For *We've moved past the worst; the best is yet to come,* the first clause uses *moving ego* and the second, *moving time*. Did you notice that switch the first time you read the sentence? In both, you are embedded firmly in the middle of the time line, you are facing forward in the deictic center separating the past from the future. The future is in front of you; the past is behind. Both moving ego and moving time take egocentric perspectives on time.

Answers to the Famous Ambiguous Question depend on what's moving, you or things in the world. If you are moving or have just moved, you are likely to be biased toward the moving ego metaphor and answer Friday. If you are stationary and watching something else move toward you or away, you are likely to be biased toward the moving time metaphor and answer Monday. Movement in space biases thought about time, but not the other way. More generally and central to the **Sixth Law of Cognition: Spatial thinking is the foundation of abstract thought,** thought about space biases thought about time, but not vice versa. Space, moving in it or watching motion, is the foundation. The rest follows. A highly significant consequence of the mapping of time to space is order. With our eyes, we can see that places are ordered in space; it is our movement from place to place that orders events in time. We cannot see events in time; ordering events in time is conceptual, the mind does it. Same for ordering by quantity or preference or power.

Both ways, either way, one common way we talk about events in time is as though they were landmarks on a line in space, a space we move through or one that moves past us. Both metaphors, moving ego and moving time, place us inside, on the time line, just as route perspectives place us inside space. The path through time is lined with events just as the path through space is lined with landmarks. But in our minds and in our talk, we can get out of time and above it, just as we can get out of space and above it.

Allocentric perspective on time

Not every statement about time is ambiguous, just as not every statement about space is ambiguous. Outsider perspectives can reduce ambiguity. Let's meet at the NW corner of Broadway and 42nd at 7:45 p.m. (yes, there's still ambiguity; we didn't specify where on the NW corner, nor did we specify the second). Just as there's an outside perspective on space, there's an outside perspective on time, an egoless, allocentric perspective. Another analogy from space to time. We can call it a calendar perspective. Or an absolute perspective. It can come with dates, hours, minutes just as space can come with names of locations or GPS coordinates. A calendar gives an overview of a swath of time just as a survey perspective gives us an overview of a swath of space. There's no ambiguity about which day in the calendar view: we simply move Wednesday's meeting to Friday. Or to Monday.

Instead of a single line—a route—through space or a single line through time, an egoless overview gives many possible routes through space or lines through time. We can schedule lunches every Tuesday at noon and classes Monday, Wednesday, and Friday at three. That egoless calendar perspective on time surfaces in many places. In novels, newspaper reports, history books, in time lines on museum walls and in textbooks. One event after another, viewed from outside, not from a specific temporal perspective inside. Think of graphs of some variable like population or GNP changing over time; think of musical scores. Now think of the gestures we make or observe as someone relates events in time, a story or a procedure for doing something. Slices of the hand moving along a line, each slice a new event, viewed from the outside, the ego looking on.

Distortions

Because thought about time is based in thought about space, it should not be surprising that many of the distortions and biases we saw for space hold for time. There are landmarks in time just as there are landmarks in space, and ordinary events are judged as closer to temporal landmarks than they actually are, just as ordinary buildings in space are judged as closer to landmarks in space than they actually are. Remember Pierre's house and the Eiffel Tower? College students tend to remember events like going to the movies or exams as closer to the beginnings or ends of semesters than they actually were. Events in time get telescoped, just like places in space. Events in the distant past are judged relatively closer together in time, and more recent events are judged relatively farther apart.

But, alas, like most analogies, the analogy from space to time runs into trouble. Unlike space, time as we know it is unidirectional. Many's the time that we wish we could go backward in time, to revisit the good times or revise the bad ones, the same way we can go back in space to revisit the good places and maybe even revise the bad ones.

Cycles: Circular time?

Many of you are undoubtedly balking at this point. What about seasons, cycles? What about other cultures? Think of clocks. We thought similarly. So, we asked dozens of people to think about a familiar repeating process, cyclical events like the seasons, washing clothes, the events of a day, or seed to flower. We then asked them to represent each on a page. We got many adorable diagrams with whimsical depictions (so much for least effort), but the vast majority were lines, not circles. We next pushed hard, giving events that began and ended with the same event, say seed-to-flower-to-seed, and listing the events in columns rather than rows. Even so, linear diagrams always outnumbered circular ones. For those of you who believe that Asian cultures think about time circularly, we collected data in China. Chinese participants responded the same as Americans, overwhelmingly creating linear representations of cyclical events.

Okay, ordinary people (and extraordinary people as well) aren't inclined to spontaneously use circles to represent cyclical events—but do they understand them? After all, cyclical events are so often depicted as circles in newspapers and textbooks. We asked large numbers of people to interpret a variety of circular diagrams of cyclical events, scientific, like the rock cycle and cell division, and everyday cycles, like the seasons and washing clothes. Fortunately, they had no trouble interpreting circular diagrams; they simply didn't spontaneously produce them. They could even fill in templates of circles with cyclical events like seed to flower or cell division or the seasons.

But those circles weren't never-ending, with no beginning and no end. On the contrary, they had beginnings and ends; they began at twelve o'clock and proceeded clockwise.

After many attempts, we finally succeeded in getting a majority of participants to create circular representations of time. Perhaps you remember that from Chapter Five. The trick was gesture. We sat with them and explained the events using a circular gesture, putting the first stage at twelve o'clock, the second at three, the third at six, and the last at nine. Then we gave them a piece of paper and asked them to put something on the page to represent the events. In that case, a majority of people made circular diagrams. Interestingly, that set of gestures not only changed their diagrams but also changed their understanding. In a follow-up study, we explained the sequence of events, the seed to flower, with circular gestures for half our participants and with linear gestures for the other half. Then we asked, "What comes next?" Those who had viewed circular gestures went back to the beginning. They said things like, "A new seed is formed." Those who had viewed linear gestures continued to a different event. They said things like, "I gather the flowers for a bouquet for my girlfriend." Gestures changed their thought!

It was a struggle to get people to produce circular representations of familiar cyclical events, like the seasons and doing laundry. When you think about it, circular diagrams of cyclical processes defy time. Time doesn't go back on itself. Nor does the process. The seed that generated the flower isn't the same seed that the new flower forms. Each winter is a new winter. Perhaps even deeper, we think about processes in time as having beginnings, middles, and ends—outcomes. You start somewhere and end somewhere else, with something different. A journey. An explanation. A story. A process that creates a product. Circles are never-ending—they have no beginning and no end.

That linear bias, the strong tendency to see and explain events as unfolding in time, as linear processes with beginnings, middles, and ends that are outcomes, has dominated the conduct of life, including the conduct of science. But that linear bias has also impeded progress in science. Remember the **First Law of Cognition: There are no benefits without costs.** One enormously important phenomenon that is not linear and that appears across the sciences is self-regulation, processes that oscillate to support a steady state, typically represented by circles. For self-regulation, the circles are true to geometric circles; they have no beginning and no end. Self-regulatory systems are crucial in biology under the rubric homeostasis. Homeostasis wasn't recognized until the late nineteenth century by Claude Bernard and only popularized by Cannon half a century later.

A familiar example of homeostasis is the maintenance of body temperature: when it gets too high, processes set in to lower it, and when it gets too low, other processes set in to raise it. A thermostat is similar but simpler: sensors that detect room temperature send messages to turn up the heat when the temperature gets below the set point or to turn on the AC when the temperature gets above the set point.

Representations of brains as well as computers are still dominated by linear conceptualizations. For the nervous system, sensory input → central processing → motor output. For computers, input → throughput → output. Yet feedback, also self-regulatory, is as fundamental to the workings of the brain as it is to computer systems. So strong was the input-throughput-output model of the brain that only after years of studying the feedforward pathways from sensory areas to central areas of the brain and from central areas to motor ones did neuroscientists notice that there are as many feedback pathways as feedforward pathways. This discovery has opened exciting new research: How does feedback modulate feedforward? And feedforward feedback? It feels a bit like defying time. After all, this is circular. Or perhaps a spiral. Either way, the change of perspective, from linear to circular, enabled new discoveries. Biases can impede perception and certainly discovery. Change of perspective like this underlies many leaps of creativity. More on that in Chapter Nine.

Directionality

Back to barebones time. We've seen that for the most part, people think of events in time as linked one after another on a line. But which way does the line go? Vertical or horizontal? If horizontal, does it go sagittally, sideways, across the body, or coronally, through the body, in front or back of the body? The answer seems to be all three, depending. Depending on whether we're talking or drawing or gesturing. Depending on the language we speak. Whatever the direction, the time line never goes diagonally and, as we have seen, only rarely circularly. Lines like stability, either supported horizontally or balanced vertically. Now a closer look.

Talk about time: Is the future in front or behind?

In English and many other languages, the future is in front of us whether we are moving forward or events are moving toward us. The past is behind us. Motion in space is key to putting the future in front. We are facing forward whether we are moving past events or we are greeting events moving toward us. *Now* is in the middle of the time line, like *here* in space. For at least one other language, notably Aymara, an Amerindian language spoken in the Andes in South America, perception of space rather than action in it is key to talk and thought about time. The horizontal plane representing events in time goes the opposite direction. The past lies in front because it can be seen; the future is behind because it cannot be seen. Whether this is a curiosity of a single language or more general remains to be seen.

Talk about time: The future is down. Calendars and some spontaneous sketches of time use the vertical dimension, with earlier events higher and later events lower. There is no "now," no deictic center in a calendar. In speech, Mandarin uses the vertical plane in addition to the horizontal plane. Earlier events are sometimes spoken of as *up* and later events spoken of as *down.*

On the page and in the air. Hundreds of kids and adults were asked to put stickers or marks on a page to represent the times for breakfast, lunch, and dinner. Most, even the preschoolers, ordered the meals of the day on a line, a horizontal one, but the starting point depended on reading and writing habits. Those who spoke a language written left to right, namely, English, lined up the events left to right, starting with breakfast. Those who spoke a language written right to left, namely, Arabic, lined up the events right to left, starting with breakfast. A sizable minority of the Arabic speakers used the vertical, as in a calendar, with earlier events higher and later ones lower. Intriguingly, speakers of Hebrew went fifty-fifty. Like Arabic, Hebrew is written right-to-left, but unlike Arabic, numbers increase left to right, as in Western languages.

Now to gesture, in the air. When describing events in time, speakers of languages written left to right do the same, their gestures line up the events horizontally across the body starting from the left. Interestingly, speakers' gestures go left to right from their point of view, so listeners see them as right to left. This is a general phenomenon for gesture: speakers gesture from their own points of view. We saw in the last chapter that in spoken languages, speakers frequently assume the perspective of listeners. However, in signed languages, speakers take their own perspective; speaker perspective is embedded in the syntax, so listeners often need to flip the direction.

Again, something that seemed simple has gotten complicated. Space has two (or three) dimensions, time has only one—why is time so complicated? There is a bottom line, and it is indeed a line: people order events in time on a line in talk, gesture, and graphics. Which way the line goes is where it gets complicated. For most cases, the line is horizontal and sideways. The preference for sideways in gesture and graphics is likely to be pragmatic; sideways is easier to see, both on the page and face-to-face. The order, from left to right or right to left, seems driven by a cultural artifact, reading and writing order. The front-back plane is used in talk but rarely in graphics; most languages seem to put the future in front, the direction of movement, but at least one puts the past in front, the direction of perception. The vertical dimension shows up frequently in graphics, notably calendars, and some in talk, in Mandarin and perhaps other languages. Time is a neutral dimension, in contrast to quantity, value, and preference. As we will soon see, neutral dimensions tend to land on the horizontal and dimensions with value tend to favor the vertical. The latter seems to have something to do with countering gravity. Countering gravity takes strength, power, health, wealth—all things that have value.

Ordering events on a time line entails abstraction; it means ignoring everything else about the events except their order in time. At the same time, ordering events by time makes order, in one's life, in the lives of others, in science, in politics, and in history. Ordering by time or any attribute allows comparisons and inferences. Importantly, what event precedes another. Roughly how far apart in time pairs of events are from each other; the more intervening events, the farther. This is a qualitative judgment, not a quantitative calculation. Which event preceded or followed another. Ordering allows *transitive inference*: if A came before B and B before C, then A came before C. Knowing which event came before another underlies inferences about causality. Except for some arcane theories of physics, causes precede effects. Ordering events in time is a fundamental first step to understanding causality. Without an appreciation of causality, we would not reach for a glass or lift our legs one after another to climb stairs. We would not try to catch a falling object or turn a door handle. Understanding causality is crucial to understanding ourselves and others and everything else that happens or happened or might happen.

ORDERS: WHO'S ON TOP?
Quantity, preference, value—anything that
can be ordered on a dimension

The worst time to rob a house and the best time to go out to eat is during the Oscars, the Super Bowl, the World Cup finals. People are obsessed with ordering: who's the best singer, actor, football player? Who's the wealthiest? The strongest? What's the best film, TV show, restaurant, wine, guacamole recipe, cell phone, car? Among chimps (and other species), who's the alpha male? Orders have enormous implications and enormous power. The alpha male gets the best pickings, ensuring his continued dominance. Prizewinning books, computer games, and movies can make fortunes. The runners-up, second-bests, also-rans—alas, soon forgotten. Reducing a set of people, places, or things to a single order leads to fascinating discussions or endless arguments. Ordering seems embedded in our biology, certainly in the biology of our ancestors: pecking orders, dominance orders. And it is certainly built in to our lives: elections, the World Series, the Olympics, contests that grip nations for weeks.

Ordering things by time is easy in contrast to ordering things by quality or preference or value. Time keeps happening whether we like it or not, and which came first can usually be determined—or measured objectively. Not so for qualities and preferences and values; we make those dimensions up. There's no objective way to measure them. As a consequence, not only do people disagree with one another, they often disagree with themselves: Is Michelangelo better than da Vinci? Picasso better than Matisse? Beethoven than Bach? Although ordering is hard, comparing things that are far apart on an order is fast and easy. Is Picasso better than Renoir? A fast and easy yes. On most orderings, Picasso and Matisse are likely to be close and Renoir more distant. Comparing Picasso and Matisse causes more wavering and takes longer than comparing Picasso and Renoir. It's parallel to it being faster to say San Francisco is farther from New York than from Salt Lake City. Placing things on a line of quality is quite like putting places on a line in space. Another example of anchoring abstract thought in spatial thought. Distance in space is real, but distance in quality or value is symbolic.

Once symbolic distance had been demonstrated, people looked for it everywhere. It was easy to find. Geographical locations, letters of the alphabet, social status, size of animals, and, importantly, numbers. All with spatial underpinnings.

Ordering isn't just for humans

Ordering things and making inferences from the orders are by no means limited to humans. Monkeys show a symbolic distance effect.

Monkeys, along with other primates, birds, rats, and foxes, make transitive inferences. They know that if *A* dominates *B* and *B* dominates *C,* then *A* dominates *C.* Intriguingly, animals with more complex social relations are better at transitive inferences, but here it seems that social behavior is driving cognition. The implications of lining things up in an order are huge. Once order has been represented for one aspect of life, the abstraction, an ordered line, can be co-opted for so many other aspects of life.

NUMBERS LINE UP

The ultimate abstract ordering is number. Number, the great equalizer, is devoid of content. Number is both easy and hard. There are two number systems, the approximate number system (affectionately known as the ANS) that doesn't actually have numbers, and the exact number system that does have numbers. The two systems are separable in development, in the brain, in evolution, and in cultural history. The approximate number system can answer: Which is more? Only the exact number system can answer: How many? The approximate number system depends on direct perception. The exact number system can act in memory as well as perception. Numbers summarize quantities and are an excellent mnemonic.

The approximate number system

Estimates turn out to be easy. Babies, primates, and pigeons can make approximate comparisons of quantities, by no means perfectly, but with decent accuracy. That means that some form of quantitative competence is deeply embedded in evolution, and that this competence doesn't depend on counting or exact numbers. It depends on ordering, by amount. What's hard are exact calculations. School math is hard; young and even older and former students struggle with multiplication and division, so-called simple arithmetic. The contrast between the two systems is revealing. Numerical accomplishments by organisms that do not speak or have other representational systems must be nonsymbolic; they can't be verbal or symbolic; they must be unmediated and direct.

The approximate number system bears strong similarities to the system that makes judgments about time, brightness, pleasantness, ferocity, and more. It is present in animals and present in humans. It is prone to error, especially as quantities get larger. Discriminating between large quantities or intensities is more difficult than discriminating between small quantities. Yet, it can do rudimentary estimation, addition, subtraction, and even multiplication and division. It can estimate over space, approximate number of items, and it can estimate over time, approximate number of events.

Not surprisingly, the various brain areas underlying these estimates both overlap and are partly independent. In particular, all comparisons activate a broad network, including the intraparietal sulcus, an area generally involved in spatial thinking. Relative to the other comparisons, activation for numerical comparisons is especially strong in the left intraparietal sulcus and right temporal regions. The partial overlap and partial independence evident in behavior is—necessarily—reflected in partial overlap and partial independence in the brain.

Implications of ordering

Forming linear orders is a crucial skill, both social and cognitive. Creating an ordering requires abstracting a single attribute from a set of different things and ranking them on that attribute, ignoring myriad other attributes. Once done, ordering allows inferences fundamental to behavior and thought.

Orders are only that—they do not carry exact numbers. They do come with several key features, each of which differs from exact numbers in significant ways. One is symbolic distance: comparing far instances is easier and faster than comparing near instances. For example, answering that 81 is more than 25 is faster than answering that 81 is more than 79. Next, semantic congruity: it's easier and faster to compare small quantities for "less" or "smaller" and large quantities for "more" or "larger." What's more, the low end of the number continuum is associated with left and the higher end with right in languages where numbers and reading are ordered left to right, a phenomenon known as the spatial-numerical association of response, or SNARC, effect. For languages where numbers are ordered from right to left, the correspondence seems to reverse. We've noted another signature characteristic of ordering, transitive inference: if A is more/greater/less than B and B than C, then A is more/greater/less than C.

Perhaps the most important feature of orderings in the mind is that sensitivity is greater at the low end of the continuum than at the high end of the continuum. For numbers, we are more sensitive to the difference between one and two than the difference between eighty-one and eighty-two. We and other creatures are more sensitive to differences in weight for light objects than for heavy ones, to differences between dim lights than bright ones. The perceptual differences, weight and brightness, are embedded even in the peripheral nervous system. Relatively more neurons fire for increases in intensity at low levels of intensity than at high levels of intensity. The greater sensitivity to differences on the low end of a scale than differences on the high end of a scale is known as the Weber-Fechner function. We are more sensitive to the differences in sweetness of crackers than in sweetness of baklava, to the differences between small sums of money than between large sums of money. We talk that way: *one or two, several, a few,* and then jump to *many, lots.*

Even highly educated people who make decisions about large sums of money show this bias. Formal numbers do not: the difference between one and two and eighty-one and eighty-two is always the same, one. The differences in distance between one mile and two miles and one thousand and one miles and one thousand and two miles are the same, and the same amount of gasoline will be consumed. People and other creatures have a fast and handy, broad and useful system for keeping track of and comparing amounts that is not based on formal numbers. Compared to numbers, which are indifferent to their place on the number line, the approximate number system distorts, conferring relatively greater weight to smaller quantities than to large ones.

The Big Question hanging in the air is: Is this irrational? If so, why didn't evolution correct it? Undoubtedly because it's a fast, useful, easy kluge. What can correct this bias—but not always—and many others is cultural evolution, the slow development of systems for measurement, counting, and calculation.

The exact number system

Even if evolution didn't correct the biases of the approximate number system, the exact number system (ENS) can. Numbers are indifferent to where they are on the number line. In budgets, every dollar counts equally. In building a bridge, every foot counts equally. The exact number system is necessary for counting and arithmetic and math and engineering and science and the humanities and the arts and the uncountable number of artifacts, norms, laws, rules, conventions, inventions, and discoveries that depend on an exact number system. Without a system of counting, and importantly, a system for recording, nearly everything we depend on for our daily lives would not exist. Yet humanity survived many millennia without an exact number system, and many pockets of humanity lack one to this day. They can estimate, but not calculate.

The exact number system is a cultural invention. In contrast to the approximate system, it has to be learned, in school or at home. Even the simplest mathematical task, counting, depends on representations for numbers, typically words. Surprisingly, there are communities today that speak languages that don't have them. One such community, the Pirahã, live an isolated existence in the Amazon. They even lack a word for *one*. Nevertheless, they can accurately compare the magnitudes of two sets of things differing only by one object if those things are lined up so that one-to-one matching is easy to do. In other words, they understand one-to-one correspondence even if they cannot count. But if the comparison depends on memory or if the objects are not lined up, performance drops dramatically. That task can't be done by one-to-one matching; it has to be done by counting. Another group indigenous to the Amazon, the Munduruku, has

number words up to five. Although they are excellent at approximations, they cannot do exact arithmetic.

Equally striking are the differences in neural substrates for the
approximate and exact number systems. Patients with brain damage
can lose one system and not the other. However, in intact brains, the
two systems interact and cooperate. Although the approximate and
exact systems are separate in evolution and in the brain, the systems
get integrated. Children who are better at estimates turn out to be
better at math. What's more, training the approximation system to
be more accurate enhances exact number performance.

The development of an exact number system depends critically
on developing a visible notation system, one external to the mind
that the mind can use. Many cultures scattered across the world invented elaborate notation systems for counting and even calculating
using objects such as tallies in stone or bone, knots, and pebbles. In
fact, *calculus* is the Latin word for pebble. Many cultures used the
body, especially the joints of the fingers, as instruments not only for
counting but even for calculating. Hands were the first slide rules,
if insufficient for square roots. In many languages, the body parts
became the names of the numbers they represented. *Digitus* means
"finger" in Latin. Many of us keep track and count with our fingers,
even with ubiquitous paper and calculators. The body might work as
an efficient calculator, but it doesn't leave a record. Knots and tallies
do leave records, but they are a clumsy way to represent numbers
and even clumsier for calculations. Symbols for numbers, like those
familiar to even preschoolers in literate societies, are more efficient,
but a richer notation system is needed for calculations.

It is accounting that drove the development of a notation system
for numbers and thereby drove the development of writing by Sume-
rians living in Mesopotamia in the fourth millennium BCE. Keeping
track of the number of sheep, cows, and the like of citizens was central to taxation, and taxation was needed for an organized society.

Every schoolchild today knows + and – as well as numbers, and
even 0, but these were hardly known only two thousand years ago.
Our current notation system has taken thousands of years to de-

velop and had many dead ends. Zero is an enlightening example. The Egyptians, Greeks, Romans, and Chinese built magnificent edifices without it. Mayans had a symbol for zero, but it didn't leave Central America. Similarly, there seems to be a zero in Angkor Wat, dating from the seventh century; it, too, did not spread further. Zero seemed to catch on—if slowly—after it was borrowed from India and used in records of Arab traders in the ninth century. It was brought to Europe early in the thirteenth century by Fibonacci, a—you guessed it—number theorist.

Mathematics and measurement begin with the body and in the world. The origins of hands to measure horses and feet to measure the ground are evident in their names. The simple act of counting is a sequence of actions, pointing to each item in turn or moving each item aside as it is counted. These actions create a one-to-one correspondence between items and number names. Notation systems allow calculations in the absence of the objects. Like language and graphics, notation systems, in this case for numbers, free us from the here and now. The notation system that eventually took over the world is inherently diagrammatic and spatial. Where a number appears in a sequence determines its value: 56 and 65 are not the same. The number on the left is multiplied by 10, so 56 is five tens and six ones. Arithmetic operations depend on getting the vertical columns lined up properly and on beginning the calculations with the rightmost column for addition, subtraction, and multiplication, the leftmost for division. The actions and the notation systems are at their foundation spatial, and the brain already knew that.

BOUNDARY: ANOTHER KIND OF LINE

Like so many useful words and marks, *line* has many senses. A sense that has had and continues to have enormous significance in history and politics is boundary, border. The contested borders of countries, the line in the sand, the metaphoric red line—crossing it will not be tolerated (or maybe it will). But borders can also be places where different things meet and interact. Crossing disciplinary borders makes interdisciplinary research. Crossing culinary borders creates fusion delights. Crossing subspecies borders can yield hybrid vigor.

Boundaries can be subtle, even imaginary. The artist Fred Sandback stretched one or two strings from the ceiling to the floor. Museum goers often look *at* the space created by the strings and the nearest wall, but don't enter it. That lone skinny string has become a barrier. When someone does enter the space, it gives permission to others to do the same, and many do. In a schoolyard or at a cocktail party, a group of people interacting creates a barrier. A line of people at a bus stop or a theater creates a beginning and an end, often one that keeps growing and sometimes endlessly. The line can even be tokens that represent the people, their backpacks or shopping carts. Those ordered lines are called queues.

ARROWS: ASYMMETRIC LINES

The first arrows are our eyes. They point in the direction of thought even when the thing we are thinking about is no longer in our field of view. The famous actor at a nearby table in the café, even when she's left the café. In that case, as our parents told us, it wouldn't be polite to point, but we can and ought to point when telling a stranger the direction of the nearest subway. And we can even use our entire hand. Much more on arrows (and boxes, lines, and trees) in the next chapter.

PERSPECTIVE

Perspective is another of those extraordinarily useful words that is consequently used with many senses. There's near and far. There's above and within, outside and inside. There's global and local. There's peripheral and focal. There's yours and mine (go back to Chapter Three). Each is spatial, and each goes abstract. Many are encapsulated into epigrams, not necessarily consistently, as for all epigrams. The big picture. The devil is in the details. To see the world in a grain of sand (William Blake).

Near and far

We begin with an old, but nevertheless true, aphorism: *Can't see the forest for the trees.* When we are close, we see the trees; only from a distance can we see the forest. From close, you see the details; from afar, you see the broad outlines. Now, which is better? The usual answer: it depends. But first, let's examine the phenomenon that imagined distance affects thinking in a range of tasks. In particular, a distant focus is accompanied by generalities, abstraction, and greater certainty, whereas a close focus is accompanied by specifics, details, and greater uncertainty. Here are a few of the studies that are consistent with that analysis. People are faster to read words denoting certainty, like *sure,* when they are located close in a drawn scene and faster to read words expressing uncertainty, like *maybe,* when the words are placed at a distance in a scene.

When they imagine the distant future, people judge that others and they themselves will be more consistent than when they imagine the near future. This implies that we are more likely to get out of ourselves when we take a distant perspective on ourselves. According to the fundamental attribution error, we see our own behavior as more dependent on external influences, so more variable and uncertain, but we see others' behavior is more dependent on traits, so more consistent and predictable. Distancing ourselves from ourselves makes us see our own selves like selves of others. People use more abstract words to describe their distant past than their close past.

Together, the studies show that taking a distant spatial perspective induces people to think more abstractly. This suggests that taking a distant spatial perspective should abet creative problem solving, and in fact, children and adults are more likely to solve insight problems after they have been primed with a distant perspective.

But distance is only one-dimensional, and space has three dimensions, though it's often flattened to two in the mind and on the page. Instead of thinking along a single line, let's now pop up overhead.

Above and within; outside and inside

Networks and lines are simple structures that contain and connect ideas. Networks are surveys, they provide outside perspectives from above, like maps. Lines are routes, we're on them, they give us inside perspectives. Surveys are spaces, routes are sequences of actions. Inside perspectives along routes vary in imagined distance, with consequences. People who imagine themselves on the East Coast judge the distance between San Francisco and Salt Lake City to be smaller than people who imagine themselves on the West Coast. Differences in distance between near things are exaggerated relative to distances between far things, which get minimized, a phenomenon you now know is characteristic of the approximate estimation system.

We saw that time, too, can be viewed from an inside point of view, with the future in front and the past behind, but time can also be viewed from an outside point of view, as in a calendar. Outsider and insider perspectives, maps and routes, networks and paths pervade many kinds of information.

Route/survey; path/overview; procedure/organization; solution/problem space

Routes are essentially sets of directions, sequences of turns at landmarks, strings of actions at choice points, paths or procedures that will take you from A to B. Directions to bake a cake or filet a fish or solve an algebra problem or put something together, be it Lego or furniture, are similar; strings of actions, here on objects rather than at landmarks. So are explanations of cell division or how an engine works. Or how to complete a tax form or buy a ticket online. Step-by-step actions that lead to an outcome. Guaranteed success recipes.

Maps aren't like that, they aren't instructions or recipes. They do not provide routes, procedures, or sets of actions. Maps are surveys of a space of possibilities. Maps provide an overview, a skeleton, of the organization of a set of places—or objects or times or organisms or ideas. Overviews enable the evaluation of many paths, perhaps to select one, but they don't favor any one. They tell you what's there and how it is arranged, they show you how things are related to each other, but they don't tell you what to do. You have to figure that out, but the overview gives you (or should give you) the information you need to do that. And much more, sometimes too much more, too many places or objects or ideas and too many relationships among them. Too many possibilities. Then it takes creativity to discover felicitous paths, to find a good solution. Where to start and how to proceed. Routes show a single set of actions; surveys show a large set of possible actions. Routes are active; surveys, static.

Routes are egocentric and maps are allocentric. Now extend those perspectives to spaces of organizations, say, that of the boss and that of an ordinary employee. We see the boss as on *top*, and employees as lower *down*, in varying degrees. Bosses are often seen as insensitive. Power is up, and power is, well, powerful. It's also complicated, and complex. But there's more than sheer power; there's a right-angle shift of perspective. First, a spatial example, spatial in two senses. If you're a mail carrier or a bus driver, all you need to know is your route, where you start, how you go, where you end. If you're the supervisor in charge of all the routes, you need an overview of possible routes and carriers or drivers to design the most efficient routes and to keep track of the carriers or drivers. If you're a salesperson, all you need to know is how to get to your customers. Not if you're the boss. If you're the boss, you need an overview of all the salespeople and all the customers. If you're the president, you need to oversee multiple government offices; if you are the secretary of one of them, you need your path to the president. At the same time, you need an overview of those you supervise, and each of those has their path to you. Supervisors, bosses, CEOs, presidents, and the president need to keep track of a large number of individuals as well as the goals and procedures of the organization they are in charge of. They become leaders—hopefully!—exactly because they are perceived to take everything into consideration, that is, to advance group goals and interests. Supervisors, bosses, and presidents have more power than the people they are responsible for.

Many complain that people high in power lack empathy. Perhaps this is inevitable. Remember route perspectives are egocentric; survey perspectives are allocentric, other-centric. People in power overview and oversee a large number of individuals, and they need to weigh the needs of each of them with the needs of the entire enterprise. Individuals oversee and only see themselves, their routes to the boss; they can't have the boss's survey perspective.

WORDS: OPENING THE BOXES

Pay attention to words. As the insightful art theorist Rudolf Arnheim said: words point to percepts. Hmm? All words? Those three certainly do: word, point, percept.

Here are two words that enter children's vocabularies early on: *see* and *look*. What's surprising is that these words appear in the vocabularies of children blind from birth at about the same age as for children who have sight. The implication: even children who cannot see understand that "see" means "understand." And "look" means "attend to." It's the mind's eye that sees and looks.

See and *look* are in excellent company. See (or look at) how many other words of seeing are used so often with nothing in sight but a thought in the mind: behold, distinguish, discern, detect, discriminate, eye, focus, gaze, glance, glimpse, inspect, notice, observe, peep, peek, recognize, regard, scan, scrutinize, search, spy, stare, survey, witness, view, watch. And here are more words of seeing that seem to be used mostly for seeing with the mind: envision, visualize, speculate, introspect.

You will remember that we observed that the mind regards ideas as objects. Now I propose a game. Below some words I plucked from the air. The list is suggestive, far from complete. They are all concrete words. Some are used to describe actions that the body performs on objects or in the world, some, actions of objects themselves. Others describe spatial relations among or between objects. Still others describe shapes of objects and their parts. For each, find a literal use, like *exploring* a city or *in* a store and then find an abstract use, like *exploring* an idea or *in* a quandary.

Ways whole bodies move in the world: explore, navigate, guide, lose/find one's way, confront, emerge, escape, surround, descend/ascend, fall, rise, float, move, approach/avoid, wander

Ways that bodies act on things: touch, blend, mix, combine, separate, join, gather, dump, ground, add, subtract, rotate, reverse, distribute, attach, take apart, fill/empty, overlay, lift, raise/lower, put, push, throw, stretch, grasp, kick, shove, toss, shred, cut, slice

Ways things in the world change: expand, contract, increase, decrease, disappear, spiral, circle, dissipate, dissolve, fall apart, come together, melt, freeze, boil, start/end, close/open, crumble, crack, sublimate, burst, blow up

Ways things relate to each other: meet, separate, adjoin, abut, surround, lower/higher, before/after, on top of/below, closer/farther, overlap, connected/disconnected, near, far, part of, inside/outside, in front of/behind, horizontal/vertical, parallel, diagonal, inward/outward, tangential, contain, collide, straddle, span, touch, penetrate, intersect, support, foreground/background

Where things are: far out, close, near, far, up, down, on top, above, below, in between, at the bottom, in the middle, here, there, everywhere, ubiquitous, in the clouds, under water

Things and shapes: forms of objects (e.g., tree, carrot-shaped, heart-shaped, snake-like), circle, spiral, square, other geometric forms, places, field, area, region, barrier

Size: big/little, tiny, infinitesimal, huge, enormous, gigantic, wide/narrow

Parts: body parts as prototype, head, hands, feet, arms, legs, fingers, belly, belly button, shoulders, fragments, pieces, periphery, center, focus, middle, edge, boundary, juncture, seam, membrane

Pattern: striped, dotted, speckled, rough, smooth, angular, craggy, cluttered, bumpy, piles, regular, uneven, symmetric/asymmetric, balanced, repetitive

Now that you are aware of how ubiquitous the language describing space and action in space is, you will hear it constantly. There's hardly any other way to talk.

LANGUAGE AND SPACE

Long ago, when I began to study cognitive psychology and for many years thereafter, the dominant view of thought was that it was language-like. Even images. Introspection agrees: when we think about thinking, we think we are thinking in words. The formal view claimed that units of thoughts were like propositions, minimal assertions that could in principle be verified as true or false, an idea taken from symbolic logic. Any actual sentence could have multiple propositions. "The quick brown fox jumps over the lazy dog" would decompose into: the fox is quick; the fox is brown; the fox jumps; the jumping is over the dog; the dog is lazy. All that packed into a sentence that uses every letter of the alphabet!

That view ran into trouble when it collided with images and other mental representations that couldn't be neatly decomposed into propositions. How on earth could you reduce the Mona Lisa's, or anyone's face, to propositions? Like many fiery disputes, it consumed itself. At the same time, views of the nature of language changed. Many now regard the spatial world as primary and language as rooted in the spatial world. A minimal unit of thought is a link between two ideas. But that's a path linking two places. In evolution, understanding the spatial world and action in it certainly preceded the development of language. Language is used to describe situations that exist in the world or existed in the world or might exist in the world. Language is meant to create mental models of those situations to evoke the past or describe the present or to plan the future. Naturally, the ways we think about the space of the world and the entities and events in it affects the ways we talk about the world. But it goes far deeper: it's not just that language is used to talk about the world, it's that the space of the world and the entities and events we perceive in the world structure language. It's not just that language structures space, as Talmy noted; it's that space structures language. Space came first.

THINKING AND THOUGHT

The two Fundamental Facts about space, *proximity* and *gravity*, and the myriad actions of the body in space quickly take on abstract meanings. Things that are close to us are more likely to be seen, reached, and interacted with. Things that are close to each other are more likely to be related to each other. On any dimension. Because of gravity, it's more effortful to go up than down. Going up takes resources: strength, health, and wealth. Spatial metaphors pervade our cognitive lives, our emotional lives, our social lives, and our scientific lives. We grow close to some people and apart from others. Someone's at the top of the heap; someone else has fallen into a depression. Ions attract or repel. New fields open up, uncharted territory. Others implode. Actions on thoughts are like actions on objects. We scan, focus, and scrutinize ideas; we turn them upside-down, we pull them together, we tear them up, we toss them aside. We move meetings forward or back, up or down. Some meander through life and others twist and turn; we put the past behind us, events rush toward us. Sales, popularity, and the economy go up or down, electrons spin around orbits, viruses invade and the immune system attacks. We spend our lives perceiving and acting in space. It is perceiving and acting in space that keeps us and kept our predecessors alive. The language and reasoning of space, perception, and action become the language and reasoning of all thought, spatial, social, emotional, scientific, philosophical, and spiritual.

CHAPTER EIGHT

Spaces We Create: Maps, Diagrams, Sketches, Explanations, Comics

In which we show how thought has been put in the world by arranging marks in space to create meanings that transcend the here and now. We zig and zag between the historical and the contemporary to draw lessons for designing and using thinking tools for thought about space, time, number, events, causality, and stories, highlighting comics, an explosively creative zany mix of storytelling

Art proves that life is not enough.

—Paraphrasing Fernando Pessoa

FIGURE 8.1. Petroglyph in Nine-Mile Canyon near Price, Utah, showing a hunting scene. Probably made by the Fremont tribe between 950 and 1250 CE.

PUTTING THOUGHT IN THE WORLD

It is hard to overestimate the significance of putting thought in the world. In the here and now, in the form of language, gesture, or graphics, it

189

allows us to share thoughts with others, critical for learning, teaching, coordinating, and collaborating. But putting thought in the world can do something far more consequential: it allows us to transcend the here and now. Putting thought in the world gives us ways to refer to the past and to plan the future. My guess for the first instance of putting thought in the world: telling someone else what to do or explaining how to do something. Putting thought in the world enables not just doing and wayfinding but also, and more far-reaching, the creation of society and culture. Thought put in the world allows disseminating knowledge and accumulating knowledge, all the more so if on the page.

We are unlikely to ever know what creature first developed language to represent what is not in the here and now or when in evolution that happened. But we do have an abundance of ancient evidence for the emergence of the ability to represent what is not present, paintings on the walls of caves, images inscribed in stone, tallies carved in bone, each found all over the world. They are a testament to the remarkable ability of humanity to represent ideas not in the here and now. Thrilling evidence for symbolic thought. And for the deep human need for art. Surprise: we, *Homo sapiens sapiens,* were apparently not the first.

Now to the quotidian. When the shopping list gets long, we write it down. When computing a discount, we pull out a calculator. When we're trying to work out how to arrange furniture or how to phrase an explanation or who to invite for a large party and where to seat them, we reach for pencil and paper. When we want to make sure we remember an appointment, we put it on a calendar. We don't rely on the mind for all that thinking; we use the world.

The mind is too small; the world has far more space. The **Eighth Law of Cognition: When thought overflows the mind, the mind puts it into the world.** We put thought in the world in many ways: in talk, in gesture, in actions. But these are ephemeral, they hold thought only for a moment. There are more lasting ways to put thought into the world. We make to-do lists, we place the things we need to take to work by the door, we sketch out ideas we need to work with, we add numbers with a pencil or a calculator. We put Post-it notes in strategic places (an aside on Post-its: they are a legendary example of design serendipity—how to make use of glue that doesn't stick). Putting thought in the world enlarges the mind, though not without limit because attention has limits: we still need to work with what we've put out there to make sense of it. Thoughts put in the world become thinking tools. A spiral: we put thought in the world, use it, revise it, use it again.

We put thought in the world for so many reasons. To remember, remind, and record. To inform, to influence, to boast. To contemplate, compute, organize, rearrange, design, and create. To plan the future. To reminisce about the past, or to use it to think about the present or to plan the future. To show others and collaborate, then we're literally on the same page and we can point to, gesture on, and move around ideas, more efficient and precise than using words. We create a joint idea, not yours or mine, so we are both committed. Thought can be expressed in arrangements of pebbles or lines in sand or scribbles on napkins or actions of the body or objects like sundials and abacuses and models. Canonically, thought is arranged on a flat surface like the wall of a cave or the face of a stone or a sheet of paper or the screen of a computer. Of course, thought has been put into the world in three dimensions as well: abacuses and water clocks and sundials and quipu and pebbles and slide rules and models of molecules and buildings. For simplicity, I will refer to all those ways of putting thought in the world as a "page." Putting it on a page or a stone or strings allows us to carry it with us or send it to others. Now much of it is in the cloud, accessible everywhere. Modulo connectivity.

Thought can be expressed in words, but spoken words hang in the air, and even those on the page express thought only indirectly, through arbitrary symbols. Marks in space and place in space on a page (and in the air) can express meanings more directly. Worldly expressions of thought allow molding and carving and construction of ideas much like the tools that mold, carve, and construct artifacts. Worldly expressions of thought are meant to be used, to be worked with.

Putting thought into the world changes our thinking and our lives in profound ways. Writing enabled masses to be educated and informed. Writing changed our understanding of language and, in turn, changed language. Math notation, which took hundreds of years to develop, enabled efficient calculating, which in turn enabled the formation of governments and the development of science and engineering. Maps changed our understanding of the world. It is hard to exaggerate the impact on our lives and on history of putting thought into the world. Maps, books, calculators, clocks, paper, artifacts, and the world itself: stop lights, bike lanes, store signs. And that's not all.

Putting thought into the world isn't new, and we have much to learn from ancient thinking tools. They were invented and reinvented in different places at different times. They were refined over generations through cycles of trial and error. No one has yet spotted a chimpanzee or bonobo sketching another chimp or bonobo or making a map or a tally. Maybe making thinking tools is the elusive difference between us and the other living primates. So much follows from the making of tools for thought.

Most of those early creations must have gotten lost. Maps in the sand and counting with pebbles don't last. Because they withstood wind and water, caves and stones and bones are the repositories of many remaining ancient expressions of thought. Impressions of hands, ladder-like forms, and faint animals were found in a cave in Spain and dated back 64,800 years. Because *Homo sapiens* arrived only twenty to twenty-four thousand years later, these intriguing forms must have been created by the extant denizens, the mistakenly maligned Neanderthals. Why hands? Handprints remain in caves all over the world. Perhaps, in the absence of writing, they were signatures, testimonials: That hand represents me. I was here.

Nevertheless, ancient remnants of externalized thought continue to be found scattered all over the world. Frequent among them are images of people, objects, animals, events, tools, maps, and tallies. The images may be decipherable even if their meanings elude us. Take note of the content: people, objects, space, time, events, and number, the mainstays of our lives and undoubtedly the most common content to this day. Glance at any newspaper or website and you will see representations of creatures and things, space, time, events, and number, concepts core to human existence. So core that the brain, too, makes special note of each of them.

Definition of sorts

Importantly, these worldly expressions of thought are representations. Like symbols, they stand for something other than themselves, though unlike many symbols, they bear resemblance to what they represent. Remember Magritte's pipe. They use place in space and marks in space to convey meaning. The marks can be depictions, icons, words, symbols, and simple geometric forms like dots and lines and boxes. The words often appear singly or in small groups; they aren't organized into sentences and paragraphs like the prose you are reading now. That is, maps, charts, graphs, diagrams, and sketches—graphics of all kinds—can be multimodal. Like conversation.

COGNITIVE DESIGN PRINCIPLES

New representations of thought are being created by the second: recipes, explanations of political conflict, stock market ups and downs, scientific phenomena, instructions for assembling or operating or dancing. Designers should consider how users will understand the representations and how they will use them, but clearly, designers of visualizations, like designers of anything, cannot anticipate all the ways people will understand and use their designs. In fact, the new understandings and new uses can be creative and significant in themselves. These goals can be incorporated into two **General Cognitive Design Principles.**

Principle of Correspondence: The content and form of the representation should match the content and form of the targeted concepts.

Principle of Use: The representation should promote efficient accomplishment of the targeted tasks.

Take note: the principles can and will conflict, that is, they can suggest radically different designs. Hence the generations of refinement as well as the evolution of different solutions. Consider written language. It began all over the world by mapping words to pictograms, sketches of things that resembled the things. Resemblance aligns nicely with the correspondence principle, but ultimately not with the use principle. There are thousands of words, so thousands of characters to learn. And how to find resemblance for concepts like beauty, justice, and revolution? Negations, qualifications, and hypotheticals? The typical solution was to add characters that represented sound rather than appearance. Only once in history, a different kind of representation was invented: map sound to sight rather than meaning. Voilà, the alphabet! Sung by toddlers all over the country. But difficult for people who are deaf.

Despite these shortcomings, logographic writing has survived; over a billion people read it daily. Poetry in logographic languages has a feature lacking in poetry in alphabetic languages. Alphabetic languages allow alliteration, word play based on sound. Logographic languages have that too, but they also have another layer that allows visual word play. How delightful!

There is an important lesson to be drawn from the development of writing. Rarely is there a single best solution. Nearly everyone struggles with English spelling. Recall the **First Law of Cognition: There are no benefits without costs;** each solution has advantages and disadvantages. The same is true for design by nature, evolution: fish swim, birds fly, snakes slither. Different ways to move in the world, and they all work. But not all the time.

SPACE: MAPS

Ancient maps reveal so much about thinking. Many early maps are more user-friendly than many designed-by-experts contemporary ones. Figure 8.2 shows what is currently thought to be the world's oldest map, a pocketable one incised on a stone block weighing about two pounds and left in a cave in northern Spain over 15,000 years ago.

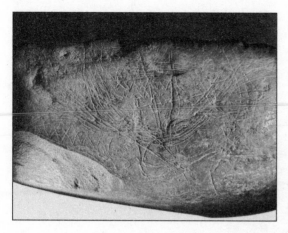

FIGURE 8.2. Paleolithic map, world's oldest, from Abauntz Cave, Spain, ca. 13,600 BCE.

Perhaps you can see what thrilled the archaeologists who found it, that the map depicts paths as well as features of the landscape around the cave, including mountains and rivers. Rather large landmarks. Harder to see are groups of animals on both sides of the river gorge. The archaeologists speculated that it might have been used to record a hunt or perhaps to plan one. Mountains, rivers, and animals are visible aspects of the scene, placed in a spatial array, so the representation is part a depiction of a scene and part a map of one. The map shows two perspectives at once, an overview of the terrain and head-on views of features of the terrain. This double-perspective and partly depictive representation is certainly neither as realistic as a scene nor as abstract as a map, but, just as certainly, it is a helpful one, both for orientation and for planning.

Our ancestors mapped not only the ground but also the sky. One can only wonder why. The cycles of the moon were the source for many early calendars. Mapping the stars is more puzzling; perhaps their awesome beauty. Perhaps a belief that celestial bodies, so high in the sky, observe us, guard over us, control us, beliefs shared by contemporary astrology. Ancient maps of constellations have been discovered in many sites. The famous Lascaux cave in southern France has a map of the Pleiades going back at least twenty thousand years, as does the nearby Tête du Lion cave.

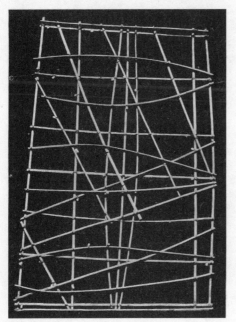

FIGURE 8.3. Stick and shell
map used by Marshall Islands
navigators.

Maps come in many forms. North Coast Native Americans made
maps by annotating their slightly cuffed left hand, placing cities and
towns along their index finger and thumb, Quebec at the tip of the index finger, Montreal at the joint, New York at the juncture of the finger
and thumb to the hand. Michiganders hold up their left hand, fingers
straight, mimicking the shape of the state, with Lake Huron occupying
the gap between the index finger and the thumb. They then point to the
location of their home town on their hand. Inuits who navigated the
coasts of Greenland carved pocket-sized maps from wood, with curves
matching the undulations of the coast. The maps fit inside a mitten and
could be followed tactilely—no need to remove the glove and freeze
the fingers. They floated in case they fell into the water. So clever!

Equally clever were the floating bamboo and shell "stick" maps
designed by Marshall Islanders in the South Pacific and used for navigating long distances on the open ocean, like the one in Figure 8.3.
The bamboo sticks represented the ocean swells and currents and
wind, essentially the highways of the ocean, and the cowrie shells
stood for the islands, too far from each other to be seen.

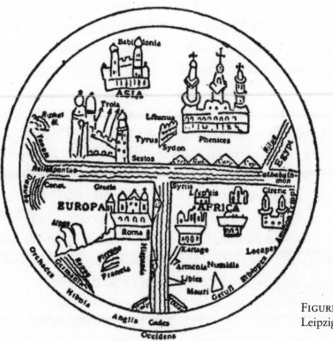

Figure 8.4. T-O map, Leipzig, eleventh century.

In the Middle Ages in Europe, cartography was schematic and the vast majority of the population traveled only in imagination, so maps seemed to serve spiritual, religious, and political ends. Maps like the one in Figure 8.4 were frequent, called T-O because of their form. The Holy Land, the birthplace of Jesus, is in the center. Note that *Oriens,* east, is at the top. *Oriens* means "rising," as in the rising sun, and as in Orient and orient. The horizontal bar of the *T* is the Indian Ocean separating Asia from Europe and Africa, and the vertical bar is the Mediterranean Sea separating Europe and Africa. A single ocean surrounds the world as was then known in Europe. The spatial locations and sizes are vague and boundaries are missing. Don't worry if you can't read the small print. What is important to see is that spatial layout is highly schematic: the Holy Land is in the center of the world, and the three continents then known are separated by bodies of water.

It is not clear why European maps were later turned 90 degrees so that north was and remains up, but that change in perspective happened around the time magnetic north was discovered. The even older maps attributed to Ptolemy were also north-up; some speculate that that was pragmatic because most of the land known at the time extended east-west. Maps don't just map space, they map so much more.

Diverse and imaginative as they are, these maps share core features. They aren't always to scale. They mix perspectives. They depict as well as map. They omit masses of information. This isn't just from ignorance or lack of technical sophistication, it's by design. What sparse information they show differs for the different examples. The precise ins and outs of the coastline for the Inuit canoeists. The ocean swells and islands for the Marshall Islands navigators. The terrain and animals for the Iberians. The spiritual for Europeans in the Middle Ages. What's included is exactly the information that the users of the maps needed, uncluttered by information they didn't need.

With those features in mind, let's skip a few millennia to a map used today by millions of people. The London Tube map. I can't reprint it here, but Harry Beck's map of the London Underground entered the world in 1931 and has since been imitated by transport systems all around the globe. In an odd way, it resembles the stick maps used by the Marshall Islanders only, instead of ocean currents and islands, we have underground lines and stops. It shows—but distorts—a simplified skeleton of the train lines, depicted as lines running vertically, horizontally, or diagonally, by no means an accurate reflection of their pathways. The insight that inspired the map came from electronic circuit diagrams, a fascinating instance of anachronistic analogical reasoning. Geography doesn't matter for electricity. What matters are paths and connections, gateways to other paths. The same for commuters, Beck reasoned. What commuters needed were the paths from station to station and the connections to other Tube lines, not geographic accuracy. His design met resistance (unintended pun) from the powers that be but was an instant hit with commuters. It's so legible. The Tube lines are color-coded. The horizontal, vertical, or diagonal lines are easy for the eye to follow. The stops are indicated by name and perpendicular blips, and the connections to other Tube lines are clearly marked by circles. There's even some geographic information, enough so I once used the Tube map to successfully get to a place that was off the street map I was using for navigation in the ancient times before ubiquitous smartphone maps.

Like the historic maps, the Tube map includes only a small fraction of the possible information. And again, like the earlier maps, what it includes is exactly what users typically need: paths and points where actions can be taken, specifically, switching Tube lines, entering, or exiting. The Tube map goes further: it distorts distances and directions. The alert reader will remember that memory for environments does the same. And that schematic maps, even distorted ones, can be helpful, even more helpful than veridical ones because they are easy to read, to understand, and to use. As such, well-designed schematic maps follow both **General Cognitive Design Principles.**

You might wonder whether the missing information and distortions confuse people. Like all diagrams and, for that matter, all communications, maps are designed to be used in a context. The context can be what's perceptible in the surroundings and it can also be shared knowledge in the mind. The context typically (but not always) provides the missing information and resolves ambiguity and distortion. That's in the implicit contract between communication partners. Users understand that maps and other diagrams work that way, that they're meant for a particular set of users in a specific context, known to both. The Tube map is meant to be used with the Tube, assembly instructions with the object to be assembled. We have the same understanding for language. If someone says, "Isn't it cold in here," it's understood as an indirect request to close a window or turn down the AC. If your passenger-navigator says, "Turn right," you know to turn at the next intersection, not right now.

The London Tube map also adds words and symbols. Most good maps and diagrams are multimodal, like natural conversation, which uses far more than words, such as intonation, gesture, and stuff in the world.

Maps can be designed for multiple purposes or different maps for different purposes. Maps can allow way finding and exploring

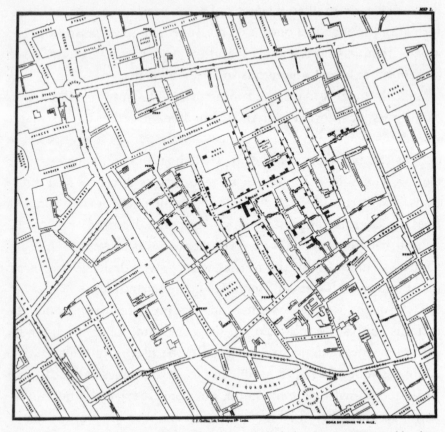

FIGURE 8.5. Snow's 1854 map of central London, with cholera cases represented by dots.

an environment and planning excursions and rerouting traffic and locating bike lanes and so much more. Maps can form a foundation for explaining history, as the Aztecs did in their codices, colorfully showing the migrations of their ancestors over space and time.

Maps can explain wars, as the newspapers did during World War II, showing the size and movements and alliances of troops in Europe day by day. They can track spread of disease, the first step in finding causality, as the dogged physician John Snow famously did in the cholera epidemic in London in 1854. No one knew then what caused cholera. Snow asked that each case be recorded on a map of central London, as shown in Figure 8.5. He observed that many cholera cases clustered around the Broad Street pump and ordered the pump handle removed.

That virtually ended the epidemic and, at the same time, initiated the science of epidemiology, still strongly based on maps. Maps can foster sleuthing and inferencing and discovery and prediction, whether it's spread of disease or tracking terrorists or paths of hurricanes. They can allow making sense of voting patterns, famine and flood, and demographic data like population shifts and economic disparities. They can allow explanations of social, religious, political, linguistic, genetic, and technological change and their consequences.

Try thinking of activities central to our lives that do not involve movement in space. Not easy. Maps are a natural for showing space, and because the eye quickly sees locations and clusters and direction—remember gestalt grouping and common fate—maps foster inferences about phenomena in space and movement in space. Space and movement in space are the ground on which individual, social, political, biological, chemical, and physical processes take place. We can also create conceptual maps, and maps for theories, that show relations among ideas and changes in ideas and relations.

RULES OF THUMB FOR DESIGN OF MAPS AND OTHER THINGS

Here are four **Rules of Thumb** for map design that we've gleaned from maps, ancient and modern. Most have been tested in one way or another. Together, they conform to the two cognitive design principles: they help to ensure that the representation corresponds to the targeted concepts and that the representation is straightforward to use for the targeted tasks.

> **Map elements and relations in real space to elements and relations in representational space.** That's the page, virtual or actual.
>
> **Include only the information that's useful for the task,** uncluttered by irrelevant information that can distract or confuse.
>
> **Exaggerate, even distort, the useful information** to make it easy to find and follow.

Add words and symbols where useful to clarify the critical information.

These rules of thumb apply to maps and to many other diagrams as well. These are best practices, gathered from observation, analysis, and experience. But there are more direct methods to determine cognitive design guidelines for specific cases, methods grounded in empirical research.

Cognitive design guidelines for route maps: Show paths and turns

Route maps are a special case of maps, but a common one. Route maps take you from A to B, from one location to another. Now a smaller jump in time, to the late nineties, for a bit of geographic scientific serendipity. Long before smartphones, a pair of grad students in computer graphics just down the street from my office came up with a prescient idea: develop an algorithm to generate route maps that would allow people to easily get from A to B. At the time, the custom routes that could be downloaded from websites were superimposed on highway maps and were almost useless. They were on a single scale, so the tricky parts, getting to and from the freeways, were too small to be seen and the route itself was buried in irrelevant clutter. The students had found our work on effective sketch maps. Together with the work of others, we had shown that people produced, preferred, and performed better with schematic route maps, ones that showed the relevant paths and places to turn, even if directions and distances weren't accurately depicted.

What characterized those maps came to be used as cognitive design guidelines specifically for maps. Cognitive design guidelines can be developed empirically for any thinking tool. For maps: clearly show the paths and the points where actions are taken, typically landmarks. Exact distance and direction are less important. Agrawala and Stolte applied those principles to create a terrific algorithm, one that produced an enormous number of A's to B's quickly and that was loved by users in beta testing. Applying those principles did double duty: it earned one of the students a PhD and it was sold and used by millions. Perhaps even more, it was the beginning of rapid-paced developments in map technology. And it served as a paradigm case for using empirical methods to reveal cognitive design guidelines and applying them to other design cases.

The Three Ps for finding cognitive design guidelines: Production, preference, performance

We developed an empirical program that co-opted experienced users as designers to uncover specific design principles. Here's the program, applied to route maps. Production: one group of experts creates maps, in this case, route maps. Nowadays just about every literate adult is an expert in using maps. Preference: another group rates them for quality. Performance: a third group uses the highly rated maps for navigation. If the features gleaned from the productions are also preferred and go on to help performance, then, bingo! we have the cognitive design principles for route maps and the program for designing other graphics and more. The Three Ps Program to reveal cognitive design principles has since been applied more generally, with a string of successes. Another paradigm case was developing cognitive design principles for instructions for putting something together, and we'll get to that soon.

NUMBER AND NOTATION

We turn now from maps, one of the most concrete of external representations, to math, possibly the most abstract. One of the earliest external forms of representing numbers (after fingers) was a tally. Like schematic maps, tallies seem to be a human universal; they were invented over and over by cultures dispersed in time and space.

Tallies are abstractions, one mark for one thing, whatever the thing. No depiction, so you can't tell what's being tallied. Like maps, tallies appeared in many forms: incisions in bones, stones, or sticks,

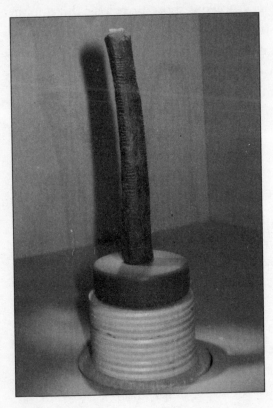

FIGURE 8.6. Ishango bone with tallies found in Congo, dating back at least twenty thousand years.

knots in strings, piles of pebbles. The one in Figure 8.6, two sides of the Ishango bone, is a tally and perhaps more.

The bone is the fibula of a baboon, found in a cave in what is now the Democratic Republic of Congo and dating back to at least 20,000 BCE. It can be seen in the Royal Belgian Institute of Natural Sciences in Brussels. The markings are grouped in curious ways, and that has led to speculation about what they represent. Prime numbers? Unlikely, as that would be astonishingly advanced mathematics. Lunar months? Also unlikely, as another bone found later in the same cave seemed to be arithmetic. Indeed, the consensus that emerged from the academic back-and-forth is that the groupings are arithmetic, perhaps used for calculation. One can't help but wonder if the creators of the tally would understand what was represented many years later. Not infrequently, I am perplexed by some of the notes I wrote myself.

Tallies, knots, and pebbles provide a visible, long-lasting record of counting, an enormous advantage over counting out loud or with the body. This one has lasted a remarkable twenty-two thousand years, far outliving its makers, and some are even older. But take note: tallies do not give a sum. You have to re-count the marks or line them up with whatever is being tallied. Tallies are one-to-one correspondences. Number names or symbols are needed for totals. At some point, preschoolers can count up a storm, but if you ask them how many, they are flummoxed. Until they make that leap from attending to each item to attending to an entire set of items, from one-to-one correspondences to cardinality, they can't answer how many. The cognitive system that underlies counting a set of things is separate from the cognitive system that underlies giving a total for a set of things. This separation strikes us as odd because the systems are so well integrated in us adults.

Yet the uses of tallies and totals are different. Tallies keep track of individuals: did each of my sheep return from pasture? Are there enough people to hold a meeting? Are there empty seats in the theater? Comparing individuals one-by-one to a tally answers those questions. Next time you ask the host if there's a table for two, look at the chart the host uses; it's usually a tally. It shows the tables and chairs in the restaurant, with marks where they are occupied. The host doesn't count and the host doesn't need to count—the total number of people in the restaurant isn't relevant for the problem at hand. The host looks for a free table and then adds marks for your party. You've been tallied.

Intriguingly, in many cultures, there are taboos against counting, especially valuables like people and cattle. For one thing, counting reduces individuals to numbers; for another, it can be seen as indication of riches and might then bring the evil eye. Using tallies of one form or another obviates the necessity of counting.

Final counts, totals, though, are necessary for calculations. Notable among them: How much tax do you owe? Or, if each sheep is worth five shekels, how many shekels for twelve sheep? Accounting depends on calculations, as do engineering and architecture and science and mathematics. For complex calculations, two ingredients serve the notation system in wide use today: symbols for numbers, and position in space. Independently, cultures all over the world transformed tallies into numerals of varying utility for computation. Initially, most systems invented symbols for ones, tens (or twelves, depending on the base), hundreds, thousands, and so forth. You can already see problems with the "and so forth." The representation of 7,846 would have 7 of the thousands symbol, 8 of the hundreds symbol, 4 of the tens symbol, and 6 of the ones symbol. This is called an additive system. It's cumbersome. Neither easy to read nor easy to work with. Look how we do it now, using only nine symbols for numbers, zero, and spatial position for ones, tens, hundreds, thousands, and so forth from right to left. A multiplicative system. All you need to represent 7,846 is that. Easy to read, easy to work with.

The Babylonians around 2000 BCE, then the Chinese around the beginning of the Common Era, and then the Maya around the third to fifth centuries independently invented efficient systems for representing numbers and using spatial position for calculation. Abacuses and counting boards use spatial position; they are at their core tables. The rudiments of the current system using ten symbols and spatial position for ones, tens, hundreds, and so on were developed in India around the fifth century and brought to Europe by the thirteenth century. Symbols for the arithmetic operations, addition, subtraction, multiplication, and division, came centuries later.

Taking counting out of the mind and putting it into the world first helped counting and keeping records of counting. But once it was in the world, it became a tool of thought, and like so many cognitive tools, one that could be worked with, designed, and redesigned. Those brilliant inventions, symbols and spatial position, that seem so natural to us now depended on generations of transactions between the mind and the page, trial and error, give-and-take, with many false turns and dead ends. It is hard to overestimate the importance of transactions between the mind and the arrays in the world. Those transactions depended on putting math on a virtual permanent page—abacuses and counting boards count—so that there was something to look at, contemplate, and rearrange. Mental math and the hand and body weren't sufficient. Taking counting and calculations out of the mind and into the world, placing symbols in spatial positions on a page, in turn allowed complex developments in society, agriculture, engineering, science, and math.

Mathematics is regarded as the most abstract way both to reason and to represent reasoning. It works because of symbols and place in space. Landy and Goldstone said it in the title of one of their papers: "Formal notations are diagrams." They found that people use spacing, even when irrelevant, as a clue to grouping when solving algebra problems. As they put it, "Algebra is a story about objects moving in space. Proofs tell a story about these objects." Mathematical proofs are stories. Hmm.

Math diagrams and culture

A slight digression to cultural differences in math diagrams. The Asian street scene is rated as more complex than the Western street scene by both Western and Asian observers. Perhaps coincidentally, perhaps not, Asian societies are more interrelated, more socially complex than individualist Western societies. We wondered if the tendency for greater complexity in Asia would carry over to diagrams, specifically, math diagrams. We collected the first ten diagrams for each of the four arithmetic operations, addition, subtraction, multiplication, division, by entering those terms in Google Images and in Baidu Images (dominant Chinese browser). We took out any words and gave the images to European American and Chinese raters. We ran the study twice, a few years apart. The Chinese arithmetic diagrams were rated as more complex than the American ones by both groups of raters. One can't help but wonder if the complexity of the street scene or the complexity of social and familial relations enable people to better comprehend complexity in other domains.

As mentioned, math notation stands in stark contrast to another early cognitive tool, maps. Maps transform large spaces into small ones, shrinking distance and direction in the real world to distance and direction on the page. A direct mapping of space to space. Not so for math notation. For math, using place in space to code value in ones, tens, hundreds, and so forth is far more indirect and symbolic. Neither the marks, the symbols for the numbers, nor the spatial relations bear similarity to anything relevant in the world. Tallies do, if abstractly. Specifically, the more items, the more marks, one-to-one. But there is nothing in the form of 9 that would indicate it represents 3 more than 6. Space in a map reflects space in the world, even if sometimes distorted. Space in math, the columns that we need to line up properly when we do arithmetic, are ordered, increasing right to left, and represent relations in a purely conceptual world, and a complicated mapping at that. Tallies are highly congruent with quantity, one-to-one, but they are highly inconvenient to use in calculation. For math notation, the two principles conflict and the Principle of Use overrides the Principle of Correspondence.

Math notation has been and is hugely important in every aspect of our current lives. Remember from Chapter Seven that people, in common with many other animals, have an approximate number system that allows seat-of-the-pants estimations and comparisons when both sets are visible. However, that system is not only approximate but logarithmic, that is, the same difference for small numbers is more influential than for large numbers. This holds not only for judgments of numerosity but also for judgments of brightness, loudness, and more. The way to correct those errors is with an exact number system, a way to measure and compute. There are cultures without numbers to this day, and it took modern culture centuries to develop the sophisticated systems in use today, even by children in school. Perhaps it's surprising that evolution did not wipe out these widespread systematic errors of the human mind's estimation system. Undoubtedly, the approximate number system has served us in other ways. For better or worse—and truth is almost always like that—these are not the only systematic errors of the human mind. Some, but by no means all, can be corrected or reduced by measurement and calculations.

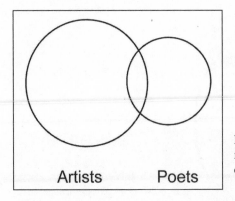

FIGURE 8.7. A Euler diagram for reasoning about sets of entities.

NOTATION: LOGIC AND PHYSICS

So much I've had to leave out. Fascinating developments in notation for math, for logic, for physics, chemistry, statistics, and many other domains. Geometry, a mixed system, part literally spatial, part abstractly spatial, part symbolic. Interestingly, for Euclid, the proofs were in the diagrams; the text simply annotated them. Unfortunately, the original diagrams were lost.

For logic, one tool is Euler diagrams, circles that represent sets of things, with overlapping circles representing partially overlapping sets, separate circles indicating separate, independent sets, and inclusive circles representing inclusion. Even the language is the same. Think of how many inferences can be made from the simple Euler diagram in Figure 8.7. Each circle represents a set of things, for example, Artists and Poets. The overlap, called the intersection of two sets, indicates those who are both Artists and Poets. What's outside the circles are those who are neither.

Here are a few inferences readily apparent from the diagram: some Artists are Poets, some Poets are Artists, some Artists are not Poets, not all Poets are Artists, and so on. Those relations are transparent in the diagram. The diagram enlivens those lifeless propositions directly, so much easier than imagining them from the statements. It has been well documented that people can construct spatial mental models from clear (well-designed!) prose but doing so takes time and effort. Euler diagrams save that effort.

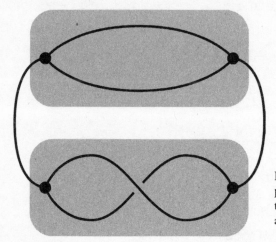

FIGURE 8.8. Feynman diagram that physicist Mark Wexler imagined twisting with his fingers to "prove" a theorem.

A priori arguments aside, empirical support for the superiority of Euler diagrams over statements in reasoning has been mixed. It is likely that the representation interferes with the reasoning process, which is sequential and in parts. The visualization shows all the relations simultaneously; for large sets of relations, it is difficult to separate into parts the separate propositions that would be used in an argument. A list of statements does that—it separates the entire set of relations into discrete parts. This seems to be another case where the Principle of Use overrides the Principle of Correspondence.

The ease of reasoning from well-designed diagrams has encouraged new fields to blossom, endeavors to make mathematics, logic, physics, and computer science diagrammatic, yet rigorous, in order to capitalize on our extraordinary abilities to see spatial relations and to reason about them. The rationale is the same, that diagrams use the power of spatial-motor reasoning for abstract reasoning. Mark Wexler, now a cognitive scientist working on perception and mental imagery, used to be a physicist. When he was a physicist, he was working with the Feynman diagram in Figure 8.8. Each gray blob represents a separate universe. For the universes to be coordinated, the twist in the lower blob had to be undone. He imagined grabbing each of the lower ellipses with his thumb and index finger and twisting them in opposite directions, a bit like Cat's Cradle. Doing that made him realize that untwisting the lower one twists the upper. The only way to remove the twist is to cut one of the attachments. This conclusion has implications for spacetime and quantum gravity, but that's beyond me and thankfully beyond the scope of the book. His intuition turned out to be right, as he later showed in a rigorous line-by-line proof.

Feynman diagrams are admittedly abstruse, as is the physics they represent, but once they are learned, like all effective visual spatial representations, they become a powerful thinking tool.

NOTATION: MUSIC AND DANCE

Like the alphabet, music notation maps sound to sight. Like written language and math notation, there have been many systems developed across the world in ancient and modern times. Music has deep cultural as well as personal significance. Singing unites people; its rhythms keep us moving together for joyous occasions like weddings as well as agonizing ones like forced marches. Good notation helps the creation, the learning, the remembering, and the performance of music. The system that so many children learn all over the world maps music primarily in two dimensions, convenient on a page. Increasing pitch is mapped to the vertical, a natural mapping both because lower notes are produced lower in the vocal tract and because higher notes have higher sound frequencies, though the latter fact would not have been known when music notation was invented. Time is mapped horizontally, consonant with the way most cultures think about time. Pitch is categorized into discrete notes, resonating both with the way music is perceived by the brain and with the way it is performed on most instruments. Standard music notation, then, conforms to both principles: correspondence and use. The mapping of pitch vertically and time horizontally is only the rudiments; music notation has been and continues to be enriched to capture subtler aspects of music.

Dance notation has been far harder. Ballroom dancing is intended to be performed by amateurs, so it does not demand the skills and knowledge of ballet and other dance performance forms. Ballroom dancing is primarily small, simple movements of the feet on the floor and those are relatively easy to portray, exactly in that way. But many of the kinds of dance that elate us involve elaborate movements of arms, legs, head, and torso as well as complex tempos. Add to that duos and trios and ensembles. Creating a system to annotate dance has attracted many people across the world. The dancer, choreographer, and dance theorist Rudolf Laban invented what came to be called Labanotation in the early part of the twentieth century. Bodies are divided into parts with horizontal lines, much like a musical staff, with stick figures depicting the positions of each part. The system has been adapted to show other kinds of movement. However, it is difficult to learn and difficult to use and cannot capture many aspects of dance, so it is not a standard part of practice. The same for similar systems such as those developed by the Beneshes in England and Eshkol and Wachmann in Israel as well as groups in other countries. Dance remains primarily in the Homeric age, passed down from choreographers and dancers to choreographers and dancers, but with the increasing help of video.

TIME

Clocks follow us everywhere, on the streets, on walls, on our appliances, on our wrists, on our ever-present devices. We check the time constantly. Everything we do and everything we understand seems to depend on the time. All our actions are predicated on their predictability and their consequences, and those causal predictions are keyed to time. Merging with traffic on foot or in a car, catching a ball, entering or ending a conversation. Comedy, timing and all that.

We can't directly estimate time the way we can directly (if erroneously) estimate space, by eye. Time isn't visible. We can only measure the effects of time, processes that occur in time and that go hand-in-glove with the passing of time. We can count seconds silently: one one thousand, two one thousand, but we wouldn't use that heuristic for hours much less for days. Sundials, water clocks, hourglasses, the burning of oil (remember the eight days of Hanukkah) or a candle ("out, out brief candle") have all been used to measure time by observing the visible consequences of processes that occur in time. T. S. Eliot's J. Alfred Prufrock: "I have measured out my life with coffee spoons." More recently, the decay of radioactive substances. What's especially elegant for these is that they are self-measuring. Time is correlated with visible changes we can read. In Egypt, obelisks were not only monuments to the sun god but also sundials, providing the approximate time of day and year to those at a distance. Undoubtedly, because of the significance of agriculture in our lives, Stonehenge and Mayan temples are aligned with the solstices and equinoxes. Capturing the movement of water, sand, or shadows captures time. These are self-illustrating instruments; they visualize time directly. On a larger scale, the phases of the moon, the rotation of stars, and the angle of the sun all can be used to indicate time.

In contrast to sundials and water clocks and hourglasses and grandfather clocks, calendars are not self-illustrating. They needed human creators. The history of calendars is a surprising mix of cognition, astronomy, agriculture, religion, and politics, unfortunately too much to relate here. Recall from Chapter Seven that cultures all over the world think about time, talk about time, and gesture about time linearly, typically horizontally in the order of reading and writing. Although seasons are cyclical, spring and winter return each year, our own lives do not repeat, they are linear, each spring is a new one. So are calendars, with some exceptions. The stunning Aztec calendar wheel is the highlight of the impressive archaeology museum in Mexico City. Maya, Aztec, and other Mesoamerican calendars were sun-based and round, representing the cyclicity of the year. Who they served and how is unknown. By contrast, oracle bones depicting Chinese calendars dating from 1400 BCE were linear tables.

The typical (Western) calendar of today arrays time linearly and hierarchically: months left to right, and within each month, weeks in a vertical stack top to bottom, with the days of each week arrayed

left to right. Time lines within time lines organized by Western reading order, left to right, top to bottom. As we saw in Chapter Seven,
we think about time as a line dotted with events, the way we think
about space as a plane dotted with places.

Causality

Understanding causality crucially depends on time. Except for baf-
fling arcane cases, causes precede effects. Understanding causality is
fundamental to understanding ourselves and the world. If I let go of
a cup, it will fall. Babies in high chairs love to practice that maneuver,
to their delight and to the annoyance of their caretakers. Watching a
sequence of events is the first step in understanding the causality, and
controlling it the second. An excellent research method. Causality is
crucial for understanding our own behavior, for understanding the
behavior of others, for understanding phenomena in the world, for
controlling the world.

EVENTS, PEOPLE, PLACES, AND THINGS

Depictions of events are widespread in archaeological and historic
places all over the world, stelae in ancient Egypt, caves in Europe and
South Africa, frescoes in Crete, temple friezes in Angor Wat, petro-
glyphs in Hawaii, arches and columns in ancient Rome, scrolls in
China, tapestries in Europe, vases in Greece. They show people, tools,
animals, and the like engaged in everyday activities, mythical events,
or historic ones. A petroglyph found recently in Kashmir records a
single striking event that occurred around five thousand years ago, a
supernova, that is, an explosion of a star. To those on the ground, this
apparently looked like two suns in the sky. The petroglyph depicts
an entire scene: the two round heavenly bodies emitting rays above
a hunting scene; to the left, a stick figure of a man aiming a bow and
arrow at a large animal with antlers, to the right, another stick figure
pointing skyward and a smaller animal, perhaps a dog.

FIGURE 8.9. Wall painting from the tomb of Menna in the Valley of the Kings in Egypt from 1420 to 1411 BCE, showing scenes of daily life in Egypt.

In contrast to the petroglyph depicting a single dramatic event, wall paintings in Egyptian tombs often portray repeated events, such as the one in Figure 8.9, from the tomb of Menna in the Valley of the Kings, dated back to 1420–1411 BCE. It is essentially a step-by-step diagram showing how to make bread, from sowing the wheat to the finished product. This single painting also portrays many of the different kinds of activities that constituted the complex society of Egypt in that early era, from agriculture to measurement and taxation. The depictions of the events are stylized, and the different events are distinguished by their backgrounds, the spatial groupings of the participants, and their tools, activities, and dress.

Recall from Chapter Two that these features of perception and action characterize different scenes and events. What will appear in later depictions are explicit frames or boxes that include all the features of one scene or event that separate one from another as well as move in a consistent direction in space.

Events take time to happen, some glacial, some instantaneous. Either way, depictions suspend events—they capture a critical moment or string of moments that epitomize the event. We distinguish *event* from *action*: events have a beginning, middle, and end. Actions don't. Running is an action; running a race is an event.

The mind, too, freezes events into critical moments. The mind transforms the continuity of events to sequences of steps. When people are asked to segment videos of everyday events such as making a bed or putting a piece of furniture together, they easily segment the continuous set of actions into units and subunits, and agree with one another on where the segment boundaries are. The segment boundaries correspond to large visual changes in the action that beautifully correspond to accomplishments of goals and subgoals. Thus, the segments link perception with meaning so that one can be used to infer the other. Notably, time has only a background role in segmentation. When asked to describe what is happening, people report a sequence of actions on objects, for example, spreading the bottom sheet, tucking in the corners, spreading the top sheet, tucking in the bottom corners, putting on the blanket, stuffing the pillowcases. Those units and subunits may take different and variable amounts of time; what counts are the accomplishments. The event units are connected in a causal chain that accomplishes the overriding goal, making the bed. When people are asked to list the steps for making a bed or assembling a piece of furniture, they list the same steps.

EXPLANATIONS

It's a short hop from describing events step-by-step to creating instructions to do them. The wall painting from the Valley of the Kings has both. Instructions, visual ones especially, should be simple and straightforward, but all too often, they are not. Many of us have spent frustrating days and nights trying to put together a kid's bike or a new barbeque, swearing at the confusing instructions that came in the box. Many of the instructions that come in the box are just exploded diagrams of the objects. So many parts and nary a hint as to the order of assembling them, the sequence of actions.

The separate groups that had worked on map design joined forces. We thought we could do better, and even dared to think that we could discover design guidelines for creating effective instructions. Assembly instructions seemed a perfect paradigmatic task that would be familiar to most people and that most could accomplish, and one that represented myriad similar tasks that required following instructions. We chose an easy one, a piece of knock-down furniture, a TV cart. Not from IKEA, but similar. Hundreds of undergrads assembled the TV cart across the many variants of the experiments we ran, and we have a closet-full of broken ones to prove it. We think putting together a piece of furniture was an important part of their education.

The initial set of experiments had a similar format. Undergraduates first put together the TV cart using only the photograph on the box. Everyone succeeded, some more efficiently than others. Once they were experts, they were asked to act as designers, to create instructions so that others could easily put together the TV cart. Some were asked to use only diagrams, some only words, some a combination. We also assessed their spatial ability. One fascinating finding was that those high in spatial ability not only assembled more efficiently, they also produced better diagrams and even better verbal instructions. That is, people high in spatial ability seem to better understand the spatial transformations involved in assembly, and they are better able to articulate that understanding both in words and in diagrams.

The assembly diagrams of one high-spatial participant appear in Figure 8.10. As you can see, this set of diagrams leads you through step-by-step, they show the perspective of action, and they show how to perform each action using arrows and guidelines. Each new step is adding a new part. Not this one, but many others began with a "menu" of parts, like a recipe, and ended with sparkly lines, so the better diagrams had a narrative, told a story, there was a beginning, middle, and end. The diagrams of those low in spatial ability were

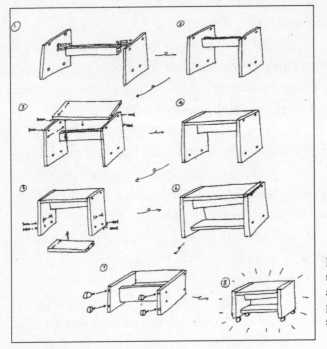

FIGURE 8.10. Instructions for assembling a TV cart made by a participant high in spatial ability.

flat, no perspective, no action. Sometimes nothing more than a menu of parts.

Although the diagrams of the high spatials made the rules of thumb quite clear, we followed the Three Ps and went on to test preference and performance. Indeed, the qualities of the high-spatial diagrams—show each step, show action, show perspective—were preferred by a new group of participants asked to rate a large and variable set of instructions, high and low spatials alike. Finally, we held our breath and tested performance. We began with a new group of participants, only low spatials, as the high spatials were whizzes. Half saw the instructions that came in the box, which weren't bad, but not nearly as good as ours. Those who used ours performed better and faster—whew!

Note the beauty of "our" (that is, the computer scientists') instructions in Figure 8.11. They were created by a clever algorithm developed by the computer scientists. The algorithm began with a

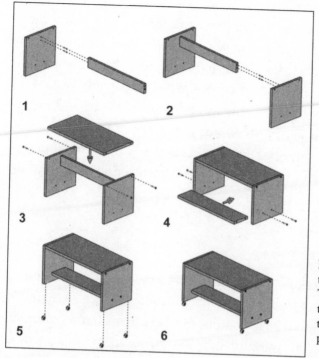

FIGURE 8.11. Instructions for assembling the TV cart produced by the algorithm following the cognitive design principles.

model of an object and decomposed it into parts. Then it created assembly instructions using the rules of thumb. Transparency in the diagrams affected the prescribed order of actions; the diagrams and the actions had to be designed together because they work together. The algorithm tackled other objects, including Legos, the gold standard for visual instructions, and produced the Lego instructions. I'd like to say whatever works for kids all over the world should work for grown-ups, especially grown-ups who used to be kids, but that would be reckless. Many of us put our kids to work assembling knock-down furniture—they're better.

These, then, are three **Rules of Thumb** for assembly instructions:

Show each step: Each new part is a new step.
Show the actions: Use arrows and guidelines.
Show the perspective of action.

These rules of thumb have far more generality. With minor variations, they can be applied to visual explanations of how things happen as well as instructions for how to do something, explanations
of how the heart works, how rain happens, how laws are passed,
how revolutions take place. And you've probably already picked up
that the same rules of thumb apply to verbal instructions and explanations as well as visual. Implicitly or explicitly, IKEA instructions
follow these rules of thumb. You can search the Web to find a tantalizing video of a pair of robots using IKEA instructions to assemble
an IKEA chair.

SEMANTICS OF DIAGRAMS

We are now ready to sketch a theory of diagrams. Diagrams use place
in space and marks in space to convey meaning. Place in space is
primarily left-right, up-down, center-periphery. Rows and columns.
Marks in space are meaningful graphic forms, depictions, icons,
words, symbols, dots, lines, boxes, arrows, circles, networks, and the
like. Often, the marks are referred to as *glyphs*. Icons acquire meaning through resemblance or through figurative correspondences such
as metaphor (scales of justice) and synecdoche (part representing
whole, as in crown for king). Dots, boxes, lines, and similar simple
abstract forms acquire meaning through their geometric and gestalt
properties. They can get combined to create familiar forms like networks, flow charts, and decision trees.

We have already seen many of the common meanings combinations of these visual spatial elements express—space, number, time,
creatures, objects, events, causality—to describe, explain, or retell.

Diderot

Depictions came early, but diagrams came late, perhaps surprising
because representations of space, time, events, and number came
early. The turning point for diagrams was a principled set of diagrams in the ambitious and remarkable oeuvre edited by Diderot and

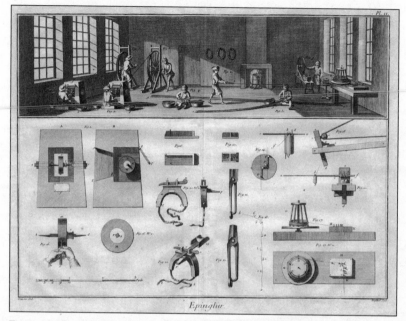

FIGURE 8.12. A pin maker's factory from *L'Encyclopédie* of Diderot and d'Alembert, late eighteenth century. Remarkably, the diagram does double duty: it shows the activities of the factory and it provides a visual explanation of what a diagram is.

d'Alembert, the *Encyclopedia, or a Systematic Dictionary of the Sciences, Arts, and Craft,* affectionately known as *L'Encyclopédie.* It was printed and published in secret over some twenty years in the late eighteenth century under the shadow of the political and social upheavals that preceded the French Revolution. It is regarded as epitomizing eighteenth-century Enlightenment values. The subtitle of a recent book on the topic put them perfectly: reason, science, humanism, and progress.

More than three thousand diagrams were created for *L'Encyclopédie* and they were created systematically, many with a uniform design. They were elegant visual explanations of various industries, like the one in Figure 8.12, a pin-making factory.

The editors apparently thought the concept, diagram, needed explaining and invented a system for explaining the concept of diagram within the diagram. Each diagram, then, is both a diagram and a lesson in diagrammatology. You can see that this diagram has two parts, each enclosed in a box. The top part depicts a scene, a large room with light entering the windows, a door, a fireplace, and decorations on the wall. Inside, factory workers are carrying out their tasks with the appropriate instruments. The scale and locations of the figures and tools are proportional, the lighting is natural, the scene is in depth. Like a painting of a landscape or a scene in a home, art that would be familiar to readers. The bottom part is quite different, not at all a scene. It is flat like a wall; it shows only the tools, and they are lined up neatly in columns and rows. They are sized so viewers can see their parts, not proportional to their natural sizes. They are grouped by their function, not their locations in the factory. The light and shadows are inconsistent, meant to show the features of the tools, not to reflect natural light. There are labels and there is a key to information outside the diagram. Some measurements are added.

None of this is difficult for our eyes, but it might have puzzled eighteenth-century eyes. It's a catalog or a web page. For eighteenth-century eyes, the diagram taught how to see and interpret diagrams by contrasting a diagram to a natural scene, which would have been familiar to eighteenth-century eyes.

Appropriately, *L'Encyclopédie* began with a set of tree diagrams, dividing knowledge into three branches: memory, reason, and imagination, and each of those further. Remember that trees are a special case of networks, networks with a single origin: large ideas and subdividing into smaller ones. That a monumental treatise of the Enlightenment regarded memory, reason, and imagination as the fundamental branches of knowledge is at once thrilling and at the same time daunting to the current enterprise, indeed to cognitive science as a whole.

As you have seen, Diderot's diagrams used many of the ingredients of diagrams: place in space, array in space, marks in space, depictions in space, words and symbols all deliberately remodeled for communicative ends. What's more, they explained what they had done and how to interpret it diagrammatically.

Place in space

Many of the spatial structures that reflect language and capture thought get put out into the world to represent thought. Like lines and boxes and networks. Anyone who's looked at graphs, and there's no escaping them, has noticed that time ordinarily goes left to right and that increases in any quantity go from down to up. This seemed to me more than a convention; it seemed to reflect how we think about time and how we think about more, of anything. As we saw earlier, people think about time as a line running horizontally. The direction of that line varies but often corresponds to reading and writing direction, a cultural artifact. Upward reflects the resources needed to counter gravity; more of just about anything does that—height, strength, health, wealth. Trees and elephants and people get stronger as they grow higher, healthy people stand erect, more money makes a higher pile. Good reasons why most good things go up. On good days, we're on top of the world, on bad days, down in a slump. For the most part, neutral dimensions like time generally run horizontal and value-laden dimensions like health and wealth run vertical.

Spontaneous graphing: Vertical carries value, horizontal is neutral, reading order matters

If these correspondences are natural, time running horizontal in reading order and increases running upward, perhaps they would show up in young children and cross-culturally. Years ago, when I first became fascinated with the ways people put thought into the world, I found myself on sabbatical in Israel. Israel provided a unique opportunity as most of the population are schooled in languages that are read and written right to left, Hebrew and Arabic. On my return to the United States, we added English readers, for a sample size of more than twelve hundred, from four years old—prereaders—to college age. We asked them to array temporal, quantitative, and preference concepts, concepts that are increasingly remote from spatial thinking but that can be and are spatialized, even by preschoolers. We sat side-by-side with the children, asking them to place stickers on a square sheet of paper to represent the concepts. For example, for time, we would say, "Think about the times you eat breakfast, lunch, and dinner. I'll put a sticker down for lunch and then you'll put down stickers for breakfast and dinner." The experimenter would place the lunch sticker in the middle of the page, and then ask the child to place a sticker for the other meals, one-by-one, in counterbalanced order. For quantity, we asked about the amount of candy in handful, bagful, shelfful. For preference, about a food they were indifferent to or loved or hated. We asked children to map two examples for each concept.

First, we wanted to know whether children would map these abstract concepts to space. The answer was a robust yes. The kids arrayed stickers on the page with little hesitation and, for the most part, systematically. Then we wanted to know if they would see time, quantity, or preference as a dimension. If so, they would array the stickers on a line. If not, they might put the stickers on top of each other or all over the page. Placing stickers randomly rather than on a line suggests categorical thinking, an easier form of thinking, rather than dimensional thinking. Some of the four- and five-year-olds did exactly that, but most arrayed the stickers on a line, meaning they understood that the instances were ordered on an underlying dimension. They lined up time at a younger age than quantity, and quantity at a younger age than preference; that is, more abstract concepts were mapped on lines in space at later ages.

Horizontal is neutral and can follow reading order. Our next question was the direction of the line. When you do research, you never know what will happen, and we were surprised by what we found. Only time corresponded to reading/writing direction. English speakers tended to map time left-to-right and Arabic speakers mapped time right-to-left, a finding that has been replicated by others. Hebrew speakers split. Could be because numbers are taught left-to-right in Hebrew-speaking schools but right-to-left in Arabic-speaking schools; could be because of greater exposure to Western languages.

Now the surprise. Reading and writing direction did not influence direction of ordering quantity or preference. Nor did graphing conventions; people's arrangements were their own inventions. In all cultures and at all ages, increases were mapped upward or leftward or rightward, but never downward, so the association of up with more was at play, but neither reading order nor graphing conventions were.

These results aren't as neat and tidy as we'd like, but adding them to the considerable evidence from language provides evidence that some graphing "conventions" are not arbitrary but are rooted in the ways that people think: *time*, a neutral dimension running horizontal, *more*, a value-laden dimension running vertical and upward, against gravity. These practices can conflict and can be overridden. Economists graph unemployment and inflation, both undesirable, upward, hopefully not because economists are perverse but presumably because the numbers go up, and numbers take precedence.

That cultural artifact, reading/writing direction, turns out to have far-reaching consequences on cognition. Years ago, I saw a lovely exhibit of court paintings from northwestern India in the British Museum. Many of the paintings depicted a bevy of attractive women following—actually, chasing—an elegant self-satisfied Maharajah. In the early set of paintings, the chase went leftward, but at some point, the chase switched to going rightward. The switch in the direction of the chase seem to have happened about the time that the local written language switched direction. Movement in the direction of reading order is seen as smoother and more natural; movement in the opposite direction is seen as forced and effortful. In the first version of the cover of this book, that energetic human raced leftward. Reversing the direction to rightward instantly made the action more graceful and fluent. Like Hebrew and Arabic, Japanese is read and written right to left, so that when Japanese comics, manga, are translated to Western languages, reproducing the images always presents problems. Western soccer referees are more likely to call fouls when viewing leftward action.

Motion is not the only characteristic that is influenced by reading and writing order. Preference and agency are as well. Images that are preferred or more powerful seem to appear more often on the left in Western languages, for example, men slightly more often than women on the left. Both preference and power go hand-in-hand with language, where preferences are often listed in order, most-preferred first, and declarations about action typically begin with the actor.

Center/periphery

Practices like *center* as focal and *periphery* as, well, peripheral come straight from vision: we simply see things in the center of our visual field, in the fovea, more clearly and in greater detail than things in the periphery. Presumably, whatever we focus on is, at that moment, most important to our thinking. Some maybe whimsical support for the idea: when people draw their social networks, they put themselves square in the middle. There is a perhaps apocryphal story of an African ruler at the beginning of the twentieth century who wanted to be modern and who had his country surveyed. When he learned that the capital wasn't at the center of the country, he had it moved to the center—on the map! Far easier than moving the capital itself.

Marks in space: Glyphs

From Diderot, we have boxes, lines, trees/networks, and tables—rows and columns. Diderot of course was not the first to use these devices but was in good company. To enrich a semantics of diagrams, we need to add icons, symbols, dots, blobs, arrows, and a few more. These have meanings, shared by a community and related to their geometric or gestalt properties. Consider the basic three: dots, lines, enclosures; they correspond to zero, one, and two dimensions. Their senses are captured by the English prepositions, *at, on,* and *in.* Those prepositions have spatial meanings that are extended to time and more: at the corner, at two o'clock, at attention, at risk. On the tennis court, on your mark (get set, go!), on time, on drugs. In the train station, in an hour, in a muddle. The meanings of many of these devices have been established in research that can only be called empirical semantics. Some of it appears below.

There isn't a good term for these meaningful marks, so we will adopt a term in use, *glyph*. Some glyphs are synonyms. Parentheses, for example, enclose and separate, like boxes. There are many forms on our keyboards; (), [], {}. Parentheses are naturally interpreted as enclosures as they are arcs of circles facing each other and surrounding the set of things they enclose. Text turns out to be full of meaningful visual and spatial devices, like parentheses and indentation. Some glyphs (like some words) are polysemous. A circle can represent an enclosure, a general one, with an unspecified and irrelevant form. But by considering only the perimeter and not the inside, a circle can represent a cycle, a process that goes round and round with no end. Lines can connect one place to another, as in a route map, or relate one idea to another, as in a network. But lines can also be boundaries, borders, lines in the sand or red lines, lines that disappear in the tide or that are crossed despite the threat, but also boundaries that cannot be crossed.

Elements of route maps: Points, lines, blobs

Before we go too abstract, let's go back to the real world, continuing to establish empirical evidence for the meanings of these devices. Years ago, we caught hungry students outside their dormitory around five o'clock and asked them if they knew where a popular fast-food place was. If they did, we asked half to sketch a map and the other half to write down directions to get there. We got highly diverse sketches and directions, some lengthy and detailed, some brief and crisp. Two appear in Figure 8.13.

Despite that delightful diversity, we wondered whether both depictions and descriptions had the same underlying structure, and they did. Both were segmented by actions, in this case, turns. The turns were typically to new paths. Exact direction and exact distance didn't matter, even for the sketch maps. Because they were sketches, they could have been analog, they could've reflected distance and

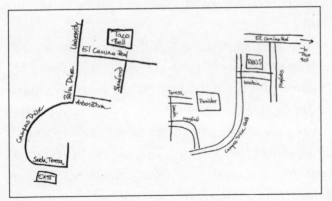

FIGURE 8.13.
Sketch maps of two
participants.

direction quite accurately, but they were far from it. The route directions, in sketch or in words, consisted of a start point followed by a
list of actions at choice points, usually turns to a new street or path
at landmarks or intersections, ending at the desired location. Taco
Bell, in this case. The sketch maps were a string of lines with some
context that represented the paths or streets and points or blobs that
indicated the landmarks or choice points. A part of a network. And
in fact, when people in another experiment were asked to sketch a
map of an entire region, they sketched what looks like a network, a
configuration of points and lines, places and paths.

Points

Points don't move, they just stand there. At attention. An intersection, a train station, a city on a map. You or trucks or trains move
from one to another, on a line, but points stay where they are. A
server in a network; the server stays in place, but information goes,
in a line, from server to server. Points represent anything that can be
regarded as stationary, an idea in a concept map, a person in a social
network. Momentary stability in a world of constant change. Lines
can connect points by moving, moving from one place to another,
one person to another, one thought to another.

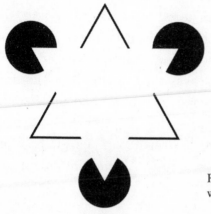

FIGURE 8.14. Kanizsa triangles
with illusory lines.

Lines

Lines are everywhere, inside and out, and I am obsessed by them.
There are the lines the hand draws on a page. The lines the eye sees
where there are none, called Kanizsa figures after the man who
demonstrated them. You can see one of his figures in Figure 8.14.
The lines we create with our bodies as we move in the world. The
lines in the world, streets and buildings and bridges, the flat earth
and everything parallel and perpendicular to it. Lines in the design
of the world: shelves for books and toys, strings of seats in a theater,
chains of buildings lining streets, rows of windows on their facades.
Lines in maps and graphs.

I am not the only one obsessed by lines. Mondrian's *Broadway
Boogie Woogie,* immortalizing his fascination and delight in the parallel and perpendicular, vertical and horizontal lines of Manhattan.
Klee and Kandinsky, Bauhaus legends, were obsessed by these simple
geometric figures, point, line, and plane. They are not simple geometric figures, they are rich concepts. Especially lines. Lines are replete
with meaning and create meaning. They can be stretched and bent
and curved and combined to create everything we might draw and
an endless number of things we might imagine. Both Klee and Kandinsky were visual artists whose art itself did not move. Yet for both,
their art was dynamic, moving. The lines did it. Klee: "A line is a dot

that went for a walk." And Kandinsky: "The line is, therefore, the very antithesis to the prototypic pictorial element—the point." To create a line, you move your hand. Movement is inherent in lines, and lines can convey all kinds of movement. For both Klee and Kandinsky, movement, motion, moving was the elemental and natural state of the world. Both used drawing to explore and understand movement and to create it.

Lines alone, upward, downward, straight or jagged, lines in groups, harmonious or dissonant, like music. All ways of moving.

Containers: Blobs, circles, squares, bars

Bar graphs and line graphs appear all over the place, from austere journals to the popular press, even as jokes. Sometimes their uses are puzzling. We wondered how viewers made sense of them. We reasoned that bars and lines are communicating different ideas even if displaying the same data. Lines show relationships; they say the points on a line have different values on the same underlying dimension. If so, lines should be interpreted as trends. By contrast, bars are containers; they say there are separate sets of things. If so, bars should be interpreted as discrete comparisons. We presented one of the graphs in Figure 8.15 to large groups of people and asked them to tell us what the graph was saying.

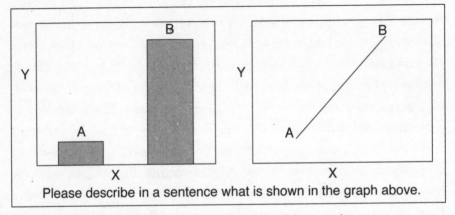

FIGURE 8.15. Participants were asked to interpret one of these graphs.

In some cases, the graphs were labeled: height of eight-year-olds and ten-year-olds or height of women and men. When the "data" were presented as lines, people gave us trends: there's an increasing function from *A* to *B*, height increases with age, and the like. When the "data" were presented as bars, people gave us discrete comparisons: the *B*s are greater than the *A*s, ten-year-olds are taller than eight-year-olds. If these are the meanings, they should go the other way too. We asked another group to draw graphs for trends or for discrete comparisons. Sure enough, people drew lines for trends and bars for discrete comparisons. The graphic forms, lines or bars, were a larger factor in producing and understanding than the underlying data, continuous, like height, or discrete.

Lines and boxes

Next, we extended the investigation of the semantics of visual forms to exploration, inference, and discovery, important uses of displays of information. One task that parents, managers, and detectives share is keeping track of different people in different places at different times. One possibility is to arrange people in a time-by-place table. But if you are interested in tracking individuals over time and place, you might prefer a line graph for each person over the places. Our Three Ps (production, preference, performance) gave some support for this. We added another task that our participants enjoyed enormously. We gave them either line graphs or tables and asked them to generate as many inferences as they could. Counting inferences turned out to be more complicated than we'd thought (as I've said, research always brings surprises), but it seems that the tables generated more diverse inferences as well as more inferences than the line graphs. Tables gave us fascinating social and personality inferences that went far beyond the actual information, far more than line graphs. If two people were together in the same place at the same time, they must be pals. Those who went to the gym at night must be night owls. Those who didn't go to the gym must be flabby.

Tables constrain thinking less, but because they don't suggest many inferences, they require more thinking from viewers. Lines biased interpretations toward temporal inferences. Now designers have a choice: Do they want to constrain what viewers infer or do they want to support many kinds of inferences but require viewers to explore more? A trade-off.

Arrows

From research on route maps, we have points, lines, and blobs—enclosures. One line has a special property, an arrow. It is asymmetric. It has a pointer, typically only at one end, and it is used to express an asymmetric relationship. Just as lines show paths as well as relations on the page, arrows show asymmetric paths and relations.

Arrows have some foundation in experience. Arrows shot from bows fly in the direction they point. There are arrows in the sand, made by the erosion of water. Yet, unlike dots, lines, and boxes, arrows do not appear in antiquity or even the Enlightenment. Nevertheless, there were feet that walked and hands that pointed the way. The footsteps carved in the stone paving of Ephesus show the way to the brothel. Hands point in medieval texts. The arrows familiar to us now seem to proliferate only in the twentieth century. And how they proliferated! Artists like Klee and Bacon put arrows in their paintings. Math and chemistry have formalized uses of arrows. Arrows appear in road signs, sometimes confusingly so. In Venice, one of the hardest cities to navigate, signs at choice points meant to guide you to the major sights, like San Marco or Rialto, often have arrows pointing in both directions. One of many examples appears in Figure 8.16

By now, arrows have accumulated numerous meanings. Even before they can read, American preschoolers correctly interpret arrows that indicate the direction of movement, up or down a ladder, even when the depictions are ambiguous with respect to direction. Similarly, they understand arrows used to indicate a temporal sequence of events, even when the depictions alone are ambiguous.

FIGURE 8.16. Which way to go? Arrows indicating directions in Venice.

To uncover the semantics of arrows, we ran pairs of studies, interpretation and production, as before. We began with tried-and-true diagrams we and others had used in previous research: a bike pump, a car brake, and a pulley system. We redesigned the diagrams so we had two sets, one with arrows showing the action, one without. We gave large groups of undergrads one of the six diagrams and asked them to describe in words what the diagram showed.

The presence of arrows completely changed the meanings of the diagrams. Those who saw diagrams with arrows gave us step-by-step causal descriptions of the actions of the system. Part of one description of a diagram of a bike pump with arrows read: "When you push down on the handle of the bike pump, it forces air into the cylinder. That opens the valve so air can flow into the tube connected to the tire." Notice the verbs, *push, force, open, flow*: all verbs of motion. One description of the pulley system with arrows included: "When the rope is pulled, the upper pulley moves, causing the middle pulley to move, which causes the lower pulley to move." Those who saw diagrams without arrows described the structure of the systems using verbs like *is* and *has*. For the pulley system, one participant who viewed a diagram without arrows

FIGURE 8.17. Diagrams produced from descriptions. The diagram on the left uses labels (don't worry if you can't read them) and was drawn by someone who had read a structural description of a car brake; the diagram on the right uses arrows and was drawn by someone who had read a functional description.

began: "There are three pulleys. One is attached to the ceiling." For the bike pump, a participant who described a diagram without arrows said: "A bicycle pump is made of a cylinder and a handle with a piston attached at the bottom." We coded the descriptions as structural or functional (action/behavior/cause) simply on the basis of the verbs.

We then ran the reverse experiment with new participants. We gave each one either a structural description of one of the systems or a functional description of one of the systems. Their job was to sketch a diagram of the system from the descriptions. Two examples appear in Figure 8.17.

Sure enough, those who diagrammed functional descriptions used arrows, the sketch on the right. They did not label the parts. In contrast, those who diagrammed structural descriptions did not use arrows and labeled the parts, the sketch on the left. In short, arrows are understood to indicate a sequence of causal actions and are produced to diagram the same. Production and understanding (performance) mirror each other. The semantics of arrows, just like that of lines and bars, goes both ways.

While we were working on arrows and animations, Rachel Mac-Kenzie, an industrious undergrad, collected hundreds of diagrams appearing in STEM textbooks—biology, chemistry, physics, engineering. Although there have been claims of more than a hundred meanings to arrows, our large survey turned up around seven: to connect, for example, labels to parts; to show the next step in time; to show the next step in causation; to show motion; to show kind or direction of motion (e.g., wavy arrows); to show increases or decreases; to show invisible forces, like wind or gravity. In many cases the different uses weren't clarified and often diagrams used arrows with three or four different senses in the same figure. You simply couldn't know if an arrow in a diagram of the rock cycle or the nitrogen cycle showed movement or the next temporal step or an invisible force. Imagine how difficult these ambiguities are for students!

Animation

You might be thinking, as many have, why bother with arrows, just use animation to convey processes that unfold over time. After all, using change in time to show change in time follows directly from the Principle of Correspondence. You wouldn't be alone in that thought, and that thought led to the creation of educational animations for just about anything you can imagine, so many processes take place in time. The trouble was, when they were carefully and appropriately compared to static graphics, animations were no better for understanding and learning. This puzzled us, and we tried various simplified animations, but still found no advantages to animated graphics. We did find, as have many others, that good diagrams were better for learning than good descriptions. After looking at many animations, we realized that they violate the Principle of Use. Things happen too quickly to make sense of them. Sometimes we didn't even know where to look. In addition, animations just show, they don't explain. Good explanations segment processes by actions on objects, causes, and outcomes. Animations typically unfold in real time, but causes and outcomes don't necessarily occur in equal time segments. This is not to say animations can't be effective. They have proved themselves in helping people keep track of simple changes in time or space. However, creating effective explanatory animations takes thoughtful design—and checking to make sure they do what they are supposed to do.

Interacting with interfaces: Gestures

Gesture interfaces have caught on so quickly, undoubtedly because they take advantage of the natural urge of humans to use their hands to express meaning. And that's the trick, to make the gestures correspond to the meaning. One example. We found that young kids performed discrete math problems, namely, addition, better with discrete than continuous gestures on an iPad. Conversely, they performed estimation tasks better with a continuous gesture.

Memorability

So many of the graphs and charts in textbooks and the media look alike. It's no wonder: they all spew forth from the same graphics software. To make something memorable, make it distinctive. Unadorned points and lines and boxes are lifeless. One way to give them life is by turning them into pictograms or icons. Sometimes graphics of networks of politicians or actors use their faces as points. Hand-drawn graphs and charts can be distinctive, beautiful, and memorable. In the optimistic international spirit that tragically preceded World War II, philosophers and linguists of the Vienna Circle worked to create universal linguistic and depictive communications, Esperanto and Isotype (International System of Typographic Picture Education) among them. Otto Neurath, who later escaped to England, invented Isotypes, simple pictograms, for example, of tractors or factories. Neurath's diagrams filled the bars of bar graphs with them, making it easy for viewers to see what variables were being compared in the bar graphs.

Diagramming is blossoming everywhere. One interesting use is in conflict resolution or conflict prevention. A facilitator gathers different groups, listens to their issues, and sketches them on a huge white board, altering them as the discussion progresses. In articulating

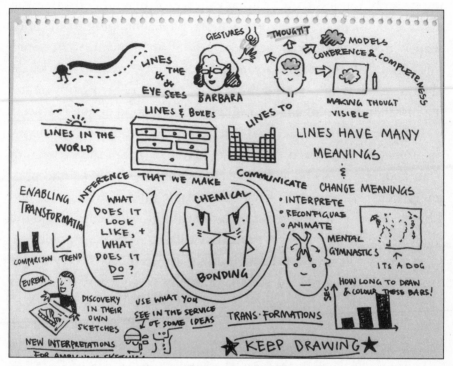

FIGURE 8.18. Visual notes of a talk of the author's by Yoon Bahk.

their issues to the facilitator, people work through them and clarify them for themselves and for the others. Seeing the points of convergence and divergence on the white board often helps the interested parties see solutions. It can be quite magical!

Here's another, a new job for artists and cartoonists: visual scribe. Figure 8.18 is a lovely example of visual notes sketched by Yoon Bahk from a talk I gave a few years back at an awesome drawing-art-cognition gathering at the Metropolitan Museum in New York City. Some of the content previews the next chapter.

GOOD DIAGRAMS WORK

An enormous amount of research over many years has showed that diagrams are effective for learning, teaching, memory, and even persuasion, typically far more effective than unadorned prose. This holds for teaching, learning, and explaining a wide range of topics, STEM importantly among them. The advantage of diagrams over text is easily explained: diagrams are a more direct mapping of meaning than words. That makes diagrams a boon in showing what something looks like, how to do something, or how anything works. As always, good design is important; we hope we are giving tips on doing just that. Same, of course, holds for prose; good design is crucial.

If you prefer stories to data, I have a good one: a very simple diagram that has saved millions of lives. In 1997, the *New York Times* columnist Nicholas Kristof wrote that a column he had written changed the mission of the Bill and Melinda Gates Foundation from distributing computers to world health. Kristof later found out that it wasn't his heartfelt prose but rather a simple graphic, designed by Jim Perry. We tracked it down. It was indeed a very simple graphic, mostly words, no bars or lines, just a table with the header Death by Water. A column below and to the left listed four kinds of waterborne diseases and the number of deaths per year each caused. To the right, another column lined up with each cause described the painful course of each disease. The total count of deaths for 1997 was 3,530,000. I doubt that there has been a more influential graphic (or paragraph of prose) than that one.

CREATING EFFECTIVE DIAGRAMS, GRAPHS, CHARTS, TABLES, INFOGRAPHICS

The fundamentals: the message and the audience. What do you want to say and to whom? We've revealed the tools, many design principles, guidelines, and rules of thumb. The forms: dots, lines, boxes, bars, networks, trees, tables (arrays of boxes) each of which has meaning, in context. A line on a map doesn't have the same meaning as a line on a graph. Just like *line* in a clothes*line, line* of work, or a ticket *line*. Use the forms separately or combine them. Consider their meanings and the inferences they are likely to promote. Think about place in space. Add appropriate icons, words, sentences, and symbols. You can use other elements of meaning: color, texture, font style and size, and more. If you want your graphic to be remembered, make it distinctive. Whatever you do, make it beautiful—or try to. Check your design intuitions with real people, ideally using the Three Ps. Bear in mind that there is no single best way. Just as there are many ways to be beautiful, many ways to sing, many ways to be a good athlete or business person or actor, there are many designs that work. That's why they keep coming! Now to the messages.

FORMS OF DISCOURSE: DESCRIPTION, EXPLANATION, AND STORY

Recall that large survey we did of diagrams in college textbooks. We found a small number of discourse forms, essentially descriptions, explanations, and stories. Descriptions included labeling the parts of a leaf or a cell and examples of different kinds of leaves or cells. Explanations included photosynthesis and cell division. Stories included Mendel's discovery of genetics or Watson and Crick's double helix of DNA. Yes, they can be diagrammed.

The big three, descriptions, explanations, and stories, are also the big three that characterize discourse purely in language. Each of these builds on and expands the previous kind, and any particular piece of discourse, descriptive or depictive, may include a mix of the three kinds. *Descriptions* present a state of affairs in space or time. A map or a time line. *Explanations* add causality. How a pulley system works or how to register to vote. *Stories* have all that and then some: crucially, a narrative voice, but also suspense, drama, emotion, protagonists and antagonists, and more. In case you hadn't noticed, *story* is a current buzzword; everyone's looking for stories. Everyone's writing about stories (those are usually descriptions and explanations—like this one). For good reason. Stories have enormous impact on us. Stories typically have characters, good ones we root for and villains we hate. Like us, the characters have desires and goals and emotions that sometimes conflict, they get in and out of trouble, they try and fail or try and succeed. Stories have suspense and emotion to engage us; they have vivid detail for memorability; they have morals or lessons or takeaway messages to keep. That's a lot of bang for the buck. Remember that **First Law of Cognition,** benefits come with costs, advantages come with disadvantages.

The big, big trouble with stories is that they override facts in people's minds. Stories are colorful, engaging, and memorable. Stories stand in sharp contrast to facts, to data. Data reduce individuals to dots or numbers. Stories have life and are about life. We can learn life lessons from stories. Data are dry, numbers are easily confused. One story of one terrorist attack puts millions in fear. One story of one lucky lottery winner gets millions to buy tickets.

There are two more forms of discourse I should mention, *conversation* and *argument*. *Conversation* is interactive; it entails alternating contributions from each party. It's not appropriate for one person to dominate. At the same time, there's less control over the content and the direction; conversations can and do meander. One hallmark of "modern" media is claims of interactivity for diagrams, infographics, animations, literature, music, theater, art. The reader-viewer-listener is expected to participate in meaning making. And does. But this kind of interaction is often only one-way, so calling media interactive can seem puzzling. The idea seems to be that you look (or listen), get a thought, and look again, but you look differently the second time because of that thought. Another spiral, and one that underlies many of the creative enterprises described in Chapter Nine.

Next, *argument*, familiar from politics and courtroom dramas. Academia, too, is not without polemics, arguing for or against a theory or position or prediction. In making a case, building an argument, people bring to bear the evidence or analyses that support the position they are promoting. They may anticipate counterclaims, but usually only in the service of their position, to counter the counterclaims.

STORIES: COMICS!

For more on storytelling, we turn to comics, the most inventive form of storytelling around. Because comics use all sorts of depictions and all sorts of verbals, what we say applies far more broadly, to stories in prose, to visualizations. Comics typically show bodies acting in space, the foundational theme of this book. Comics are also diagrams: they use boxes to contain and separate, they line up the boxes in rows and columns and group them on pages. They use language and symbols in many ways.

Graphic storytelling is everywhere. The superheroes are still around; they've become myths that transfix their fans with new episodes. Serious works of fiction in comic format are inspiring excellent authors and reaching mainstream audiences. There are superb cartoon guides to history, psychology, philosophy, physics, chemistry, statistics—just about any topic you can think of. Comic journalism is proliferating. Comics for kids, toddlers and up, are increasingly purchased by parents, teachers, and librarians, and loved by kids.

Comics are good for us and good for our children

Like all stories, they offer pleasure, they can be poignant, exciting, or funny. They can successfully educate and inform. They can match the media to the message, using all kinds of depictions when depictions are likely to be effective, all kinds of language when language is likely to be effective, and both for a double-whammy. Unlike stories in prose, they teach us how to look and what to look for, so important for a world that is increasingly using visual forms of communication. Comics can draw in readers, especially young reluctant ones. By now, dozens of studies have shown that comics are effective teachers. I have to go out of my way to say this because for years they had a bad rap; even the US Congress joined the fray. Even if comics didn't turn youth to violence or communism, they were too easy, they weren't really and truly *reading*. Low culture, to be disdained. No way! They're an art form.

Many have explained what comics do and how they work, legends like Eisner and Spiegelman. McCloud, another master of the medium, penned a comic on comics that has become a classic. What follows draws on their insights as well as research on cognitive science. I will highlight reasons for their success, some of the many astute devices and practices they use, but keep in mind that the meta-rule of comics is: break the rules!

Pictures are remembered better than words

Depictions are an important part of the advantage of comics. Pictures are not only remembered better than words, they are more distinctive than words, and they communicate faster and more directly—recall Chapter Two. They show nuances of action and emotion and setting that defy words. Witness the explosion of emojis, which have far overtaken internet slang like LOL and OMG; see the popularity of GIFs: one billion per day in 2016; watch the enthusiasm for Instagram, ninety-five million posts a day in 2018. Set images loose and there's an explosion.

Depictions can show and words can speak

Spiegelman calls it Co-Mix, emphasizing the confluence of media, of depiction and description, allowing each to do what it does best, but even more, allowing them to work together, to interact, complement, supplement, contrast, contradict, meld, and blend. In that sense, comics bear resemblance to film or theater or computer games, but unleashed. Comics get away with more than the other multimedia. The medium allows, indeed, encourages and celebrates, unconventional, wildly creative ways of using each and both.

Comics encourage and reward scrutiny

The richness of the medium demands close study of each and both together. Those habits of looking and seeing can transfer to understanding real life—people, scenes, situations—and life on the page— maps, charts, visualizations, diagrams. Like comics, face-to-face communication is rich and multimodal, a mix of sound stuff—sighs, laughter, grunts, words, phrases, and sentences varying in intonation—and visual stuff—smiles, frowns, shrugs, nods, pointing of fingers, and enactments of hands and body.

STORIES HAVE BEGINNINGS, MIDDLES, AND ENDS

Stories, as far back as Aristotle's *Poetics,* are said to have a narrative arc, visualized as a triangle by Freytag, action rising to a climax where tension is resolved, and then falling to a denouement where the strands are sewn together. The narrative arc gives stories distinct beginnings, middles, and ends. Yet, as Jean-Luc Godard famously said, "A story needs to have a beginning, middle, and end, but not necessarily in that order."

Beginning

First, engage. Comics often begin with *splash* pages, fragments of the story splashed onto the page, usually a two-page spread. Splash pages are like an overture to an opera or ballet, hints of what's to come artfully arranged. Like the cast of characters and settings for a play or the ingredients of a recipe. These overviews of the whole tell you what to look for, what to expect; they entice you, whet your appetite for what is to come.

Middle: Segmenting

The mind segments, connects, and sometimes reconnects everything it perceives in the world. Bodies segmented by their parts connected by their joints. Same for objects, connected by glue and nails. Events by goals and subgoals. Sentences into clauses and phrases, marked by pauses in speech and punctuation on the page. Often the segmentation is hierarchical, parts and parts of parts. Years by months, months by weeks, weeks by days, days by hours. Understanding just about anything begins with taking apart and putting together. The separate parts have separate meanings, as do the wholes.

Comics segment stories explicitly and hierarchically, with boxes and pages and chapters. Comics put pieces of time into boxes that march in rows across the space of the page. Prose does it with paragraphs (note that indentation is a visual device) and chapters. Comic artists often think in two-page spreads of boxes; that's what readers encounter when they turn a page. The contents have to work as two-page spreads and also box by box. Boxes are used systematically, forming a spatial structure for the story.

Then there are those gaps between the boxes, colorfully referred to as the *gutter*. The boxes lack joints or glue; the gutters between them are empty, waiting to be filled in by the reader. Or hold the reader in suspense.

It's not just gutters in comics that need to be filled in. What we get from the world is always incomplete; we are constantly completing, jumping to conclusions from partial information. We see part of the face of a friend or only hear their approaching footfalls. A child hears "homework" and knows what to do. A siren from an unseen source; you know there's an emergency. A shadow from behind. We don't just fill in objects, we fill in context. If we see a close-up of an object like a garbage can, we remember it as if from farther away, we fill in the scene. Remember the **Seventh Law of Cognition: The mind fills in missing information.**

Boxes in comics can do more than segment and contain. Their very forms can carry meaning. They can vary in size and shape; they can disappear entirely; they can tilt; they can be circular or elliptical, smooth or jagged, narrow or wide—any shape for that matter; they can overlap or go inside another box. They can turn into arrows and point, or circles and roll. These variants can be used to great effect in telling a story.

McCloud classified box-to-box transitions in comics: moment-to-moment, action-to-action, subject-to-subject, scene-to-scene, aspect-to-aspect. And non sequitur, but one wonders if there is such a thing—people can find connections between anything, and odd combinations invite that. Someone could try that classification to see if it works on paragraphs of prose. His classification jibes with the work on event cognition: people segment live events when there's a new action, a new object, a new person, a new scene. Moment-to-moment entails breaking up a larger action into small pieces, prolonging the moment and creating suspense. A spider crawling ominously up a body. Aspect-to-aspect has a similar effect, by pausing the action to scan the space from different perspectives, pondering the entire scene rather than the action, per se. Different objects, different characters, and what the characters are seeing. Authors can use these transitions to set the pace, from slow and contemplative and mysterious to fast and chaotic . . . and mysterious. Creating mystery is mysterious.

Middle: Connecting

Language needs to be coherent to make communication fast and easy. It has explicit ways to bridge sentences or parts of sentences. You might not know the term *anaphor,* but you probably use it and understand it. It means "carry back." All the "its" in the previous sentences are anaphors. If you understood them (anaphor again), you understand anaphor. The prototypic anaphor is a pronoun. *It. Them. They. She. He.*

Comics can and do use visual anaphors to establish continuity and coherence. Something that appeared in one frame is carried over to the next one. Effective visual instructions do that. Adrian Tomine's *New Yorker* cover *Shelf Life* (February 25, 2008) is a comic format story about the life of a book, from writing to publishing to printing to buying to tossing in the trash to burning to warm some street people. Rather discouraging for authors. Throughout the frames of the story, the red book, carried from panel to panel, provides continuity as well as focus: the story is about the book.

Middle: Disconnecting

Comics don't have to connect. Because they are discrete parts, and not continuous like film or theater or prose, they can jump with ease and with effect. Film can do it with cuts, theater with acts, prose with paragraphs and chapters, but within each of those large parts, the pragmatics of the medium induce expectations of continuity. The pragmatics of comics allow large jumps even without signaling.

Middle: Inside the frames

The real art of comics is inside the frames. You need to advance the story, the action, to establish context, to create visual interest, an engaging pace, a changing rhythm. One important choice is whether to emphasize action or context. There are surprising effects of culture and language on that choice. Eastern cultures are regarded as more interconnected than Western, which are regarded as emphasizing individualism. Actions, like hugging or hitting or chasing, show relations between people, so Eastern comics should depict action more frequently than Western. There are languages, like English and Chinese, that are rich in ways to express manner of motion: *swagger, slink, scamper, sashay;* and there are languages, like Italian and Japanese, that have words for enter, exit, ascend, and run, but very few verbs for expressing manner of motion. Comics in languages with rich vocabularies for expressing motion should portray action more frequently. We had fun going to comic stores all over the world collecting comics in those languages and cultures. We took out the words and asked European Americans and Asians to rate each panel: Is it mostly showing action or mostly setting a scene? The raters agreed despite differences in cultural backgrounds, and both predictions were supported. More action in comics of Eastern cultures and more action in comics of languages that have many words for expressing manner of action. Chinese comics, produced by an Eastern culture with many verbs of manner of action, came out on top.

Ends

Because we had ratings of action from throughout each of the comics, we could look at the narrative arc, and indeed, overall, we found that action rose to a climax and then fell to a resolution.

CREATING MEANING

Comics have a multitude of unique ways of establishing meaning. I highlight some below, with visuals when they are in the public domain.

Multiple views

Sometimes comics can do both, show action and set a scene. *Gasoline Alley,* a long-running strip originated by Frank King, frequently superimposed time on space. One of his many elegant examples appears in Figure 8.19.

The entire page shows the background for the story, an overview of a scene, say, at the beach or in the neighborhood. The story is superimposed on the scene in the boxes arrayed on the scene, the usual way. You get the setting in the background and the story frame-by-frame at the same time, in the same space. Film of course does this, but comics give background and close-ups of characters in action at the same time, and they stay put so you can look and look.

Frames can depict two stories at once, by splitting a frame or by interleaving pieces, where one story is the background for the other, and figure and ground flip. This technique can be used to tell events that are simultaneous but separate or to give the background events for the ongoing events. Here's a poignant one. Foregrounded in a cluttered living room is an unshaven young man intensely scanning a dating site on his computer, oblivious to everything else. In the background, his attractive mate carrying overflowing suitcases is exiting their home and their life, with determination. Splitting a scene was common in Renaissance art in the Netherlands. Pieter de Hooch often depicted the interior of a home and what was outside in the same painting, giving viewers much to compare and contrast, much to think about, both visual and social.

Frames can show two perspectives simultaneously. A panel of Gene Yang's *American Born Chinese* shows, on the left, what the students in a class are seeing, the teacher introducing a small bespectacled Chinese boy to the classroom; on the right, what the boy sees,

FIGURE 8.19. Comic cover by Frank O. King showing space and time simultaneously. Not to worry if you can't read the text.

the unfriendly white faces of the kids in the class. Mirrors and cameras can do the same. In one, a young woman is proudly showing the large fish she caught to a camera, but the camera is focused on her halter top, not on the fish.

One master of these techniques is Chris Ware, building stories on and in buildings (puns galore) showing wholes and parts and insets of parts of buildings and people and objects, from close and far, changing focus, changing perspective constantly, the way the eye and the mind do.

Words, etc.

Comics can use bits and pieces of written language in a multitude of ways, many downright whacky. There are the familiar speech balloons, with curved arrows pointing downward to the speakers, and thought balloons, bubbles rising to them from the thinkers. Their arrangement in space shows the action in space, so comic artists have great fun creating comics just from speech and thought balloons and nothing else. You have to fill in the rest. There is often narration, rows of standard text usually at the top or the bottom of the frame, itself surrounded by a smaller frame. There can be noises and smells and unprintable expletives—#%$&. The lettering itself can be expressive, bold or timid, violent or gentle. Sharp, jagged forms, like the nonsense word *tekata,* suggest strong punctuated events. Think Malevich, Kandinsky. Soft, smooth, blurred forms, like the nonsense word *meluma,* suggest gentle slow ones. Think Rothko.

Contrasting word and picture

As McCloud and others have noted, the words and pictures can complement, supplement, contrast, or even contradict each other. The last can create dramatic irony. In Marjan Satrapi's *Persepolis,* nine-year-old Marjan overhears her parents describing the torture of an uncle in prison. He was "cut to pieces," she hears, but what she understands is depicted: her uncle laid out on a butcher's table, cut like a chicken at the joints. In *Violent Cases* by two Brits, writer Neil Gaiman and artist Dave McKean, a child about the same age, nine, is transfixed by tales of Al Capone, told by a visiting uncle. The uncle says someone crossed Capone and was therefore "rubbed out." In Brit English, *rub out* means both *erase* and *murder*, but the child only knows the former sense and imagines a gangster face being erased. You read the chilling words and see the picture of the thoughts.

Figures of depiction

Comics and cartoons use more figures of depiction, pun, metaphor, simile, synecdoche, alliteration, than the Greeks had names for. Winsor McCay made stunning use of them, a Manhattan street rolling into a treadmill that a proper businessman walked into. Here, in Figure 8.20, Little Nemo is asleep and caught in a dream, as if transported by the bed. When the dream ends abruptly, before the ending, the bed dumps Little Nemo back in bed. Look also at the resonating multiples, bringing to mind the music of Stephen Reich and Philip Glass. Any similarity of this work to another wonderful visual artist, Maurice Sendak, is real; Sendak adored McCay, and borrowed freely, a visual show of respect.

Then there are what might be called self-describing comics or visual alliteration. See Winsor McCay's *Little Sammy Sneeze* in Figure 8.21. When Sammy finally sneezes, the box around him cracks—to his bewilderment.

To show a reckless breathless chase, the frames in Krazy Kat run diagonally downhill in the example in Figure 8.22.

Comics can embody, impersonate, animate. Larry Gonick does this zanily in his Cartoon Guides to various academic topics like genetics, history, algebra, and chemistry. Mendel explains elementary genetics to you. Peapods get arrayed into diagrams that get progressively more abstract. Hills turn into slopes in graphs. Then they turn into sticks that can be rearranged as slope is explained. A

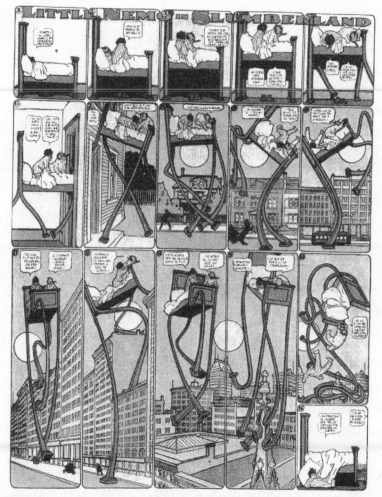

FIGURE 8.20. *Little Nemo* by Winsor McCay. Nemo's dream transports him to another world, and then dumps him back in bed. As before, not to worry if you can't read the text.

fish proudly crawls out of the water bragging, "I will be the first on land," but the fish just behind him says, "Hmm, it appears that the bugs are already there." Elements grow heads and arms and legs; they talk to each other and explain and enact how they bond to form molecules. Weak ones are skinny and strong ones are muscular. A function is an input-output device personified as a chick who eats and excretes. Memorable depictions and colorful words seamlessly woven together, in sharp contrast to the typical textbook.

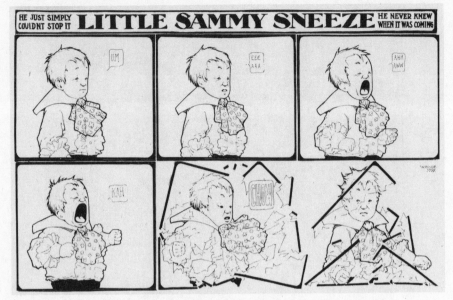

FIGURE 8.21. Sammy's sneeze cracks his panel borders.

Multiple meanings

Visuals have another trick, to express many meanings at the same time, without the wince that accompanies a pun. In a page from a superwoman hero, she is shown at the left talking on an old-fashioned phone, one with a curly cord. The cord wraps around three smaller adjacent panels to the right, each someone she speaks with. The cord serves as a literal phone cord, it serves as the frame for the boxes enclosing each of her coconspirators, and, as a whole, it serves to show that she has brought them into conspiracy. In Jim Ottaviani's *Two-Fisted Science: Stories About Scientists,* Galileo is shown in his study, behind him a circle divided into quarters. Three of the sections are parts of the heavenly bodies discovered by Galileo's telescope. The lower right quarter is part of the circular window from which he saw them, telescope nearby. Circles and other forms suggest so many meanings, as we have seen. In Spiegelman's *Breakdowns,* every chapter begins with a circle, his eye, a baseball. A circle serves stunning triple duty in Bob Staake's cover of *The New Yorker,* November 18, 2008, after Obama's thrilling first election. The cover is black except

FIGURE 8.22. To amplify the sensation of Krazy Kat's speed, George Herriman drew sloping panels.

for a bright circular moon, the O in *Yorker*, and the O of *Obama*, showering light on the Lincoln Memorial. In the reflecting pool before the memorial, blurry shadows of bars.

Everywhere, comics break the rules. The practice: putting story in the boxes, marching across the page in time. But you can break the frames and you can play with time. In Ottaviani's story of Feynman, a frame on the left shows his girlfriend at Columbia, dancing with a man, and a frame on the right shows Feynman at MIT, entertaining a circle of women (got that?). In between the two is a frame with a map of the East Coast. Feynman's arm is reaching back out of his frame across the map to hand a letter to his dancing girlfriend. Matt Feazall uses a similar visual device, breaking one frame and entering another, to go to a future time while staying in the past. Finding himself hungry but out of cash, he drops a fishing line out of his current frame and into a future frame to hook some cash to pay for dinner. To the annoyance of his future self.

So, if you want to exit the story, all you have to do is exit the boxes. In Wiesner's delightful *The Three Pigs*, the first pig did exactly that after the wolf ate him. From a safe place in the gutter, he poked his head back into a frame to tell the second pig to get out and join him. The third pig got out, too, and together they threw the frames of the story on the ground and stomped on them in protest. Children get this, that the story resides in the boxes, so getting out of the boxes is getting out of the story. And then you're in another story, a story about a story.

Crockett's beloved tiny book *Harold and the Purple Crayon* may be the sweetest. Harold, a cherub any child and most grown-ups can identify with, sets out on an adventure with a purple crayon, drawing the world he traverses. Hungry, he draws a tree with apples, but wants to go on, so he draws a dragon to guard the apples. The dragon frightens him. His hand, holding the pencil, trembles, inadvertently drawing waves. Harold finds himself in the water and rescues himself by drawing a boat. So it continues, until he is safe in bed, guided home by a moon of his own creation. Perhaps it was all a dream.

The brilliant South African artist William Kentridge has an actor's refined understanding of it all, bodies and thoughts moving in space creating stories. He invented a new art form. Find his videos on YouTube as well as in museums and opera houses all over the world. He draws a scene with charcoal, photographs the drawing, changes the drawing, and takes another photo, eventually stringing the photos into an animation. There are characters, a fat, cigar-smoking industrialist, his beautiful wife, an attractive artist—yes, an affair. Tere are migrations of animals and migrations of people—hordes of displaced colored people, marching. There are places, rooms and offices and city streets and beaches and savannah. Things morph into things, just like thoughts: migrations of animals turn into flowing water, bodies become landscapes, stars get connected by lines that become heads, a bare lonely room becomes an outdoor scene of mourning. The artist's thoughts fly on newspapers in the wind to his lover. Birds rise from the dead. The stories speak loudly, viscerally, without a single word.

CHAPTER NINE

Conversations with a Page: Design, Science, and Art

In which we join art and science through drawing. We watch people put thought on a page to hold a wordless conversation involving eye and hand and marks to see, to think, to clarify, and to create. We leave the page and return to the mind to reveal the key to creativity.

> To know what you are going to draw, you have to begin drawing.
>
> —Picasso

> Whatever is valuable in painting is precisely what one is incapable of talking about.
>
> —Braque

DRAWING TO SEE AND DISCOVER

Leonardo da Vinci drew constantly. He drew to see, he drew to think, he drew to create. Even his prodigious mind wasn't large enough to imagine his phenomenal ideas; his hand had to put them before his eyes. Drawing could reveal the structure of things, and even more central to Leonardo's thinking, drawing could reveal the action of things, how they work, what they could do. Static drawings could be active. He drew muscles and ligaments attached to bones and joints in humans and other animals to determine how bodies move. He drew the branching of trees to learn how they grow and split and in so doing, discovered the proportional rule of branching. He drew the branching of arteries to learn how blood flows. He drew plans for a multitude of devices, pumps and musical instruments and flying machines, to work through their mechanics. He drew water, over and over, to see it and to understand how it swirled and churned. Vortices drew him in and he drew them. He realized that the drawing motions of his hand mimicked the motions he was trying to understand and used his hand to understand them. Lacking mathematics, his thinking was visual and spatial, he reasoned from patterns and forms and analogies of forms, the curls of hair and the swirls of water, a fetus enclosed in a womb and a seed enclosed in a shell. He drew and looked and thought and drew again. And again. Leonardo used drawing to explore and refine ideas as well as to create new ones. He was one of the first to intentionally use drawing as an empirical method. Others have followed and continue to do so.

Drawing forces abstraction, far more than painting. No color. Just lines that the mind conceives and that the hand makes. The world might have too many lines or too few, the drawing might be from the mind, not from looking. Either way, the mind decides which lines to draw, how to draw them, and what they represent. Picasso can evoke a body with a few curving lines; Giacometti a face with a multitude of frenetic short ones. For both, more is missing than what is there. Abstraction leaves open many possibilities. Viewers fill in what's missing, and they might fill in differently from each other and each time they look. Perhaps it's that that makes good art interesting.

Leonardo was a prescient neuroscientist and psychologist. He knew the prevailing theories of cognition and emotion and searched for their places in the brain and in the body. Those theories affected what he saw and what he drew. Like everyone, he first looked to confirm them. But ultimately, his drawings of the brain and body refuted those theories and he stood with his drawings. Drawing was a form of empirical research. It wasn't enough to look at skulls and bones and muscles and hearts and ventricles. You didn't really see them and certainly didn't know them until you drew them and revealed their forms and how they were connected. Other scientists pored over his drawings to learn from them.

Some of his designs were dismissed at the time but proven hundreds of years later, a parachute sketched in the margins of a manuscript, a graceful wooden bridge he proposed to the Ottoman sultan to span the Golden Horn. The sultan thought it impossible and rejected the proposal. The plans went missing for four hundred years, and when they resurfaced, the Norwegian artist Vebjørn Sand was determined to use those plans to replace a pedestrian bridge in Norway. The elegant arching structure has been in use since 2001.

In using drawing as an empirical method of inquiry, Leonardo has not been alone. Although Goethe was a wordsmith, renowned for his novels, plays, and poetry, he was also a drawer. He believed that his drawings, not his words, best expressed his thoughts. He loved nature and everything in it, in and of itself and as allegory. Like Leonardo, he believed that nature revealed its function through its form, and that drawing was the way to discover both. He, too, was taken with similarities of form, suggesting similarity of function.

We know the artist Paul Klee through his endlessly inventive and playful paintings, but Klee was fascinated by motion, and many of his drawings were studies of movement, ways to capture its essence and understand it. The contemporary artist Gemma Anderson has adapted the drawing techniques of Goethe and Klee, cycles of looking, thinking, telling, and drawing, as tools of discovery. She works with teams of biologists and topologists and other scientists to understand forms and their formation. These projects both advance science and create art, in the form of drawings and sculptures, a double boon.

DRAWING TO UNDERSTAND AND LEARN

Leonardo's techniques aren't just for rare geniuses or sophisticated scientists. Drawing ideas on a page works well for understanding science for ordinary people, including kids. Studies of our own showed that when science students create visual explanations of scientific phenomena, they understand and learn more than when they create the verbal explanations typical in classroom situations. Here's how

FIGURE 9.1. Student's visual explanation of chemical bonding.

we know. Junior high students were first taught a STEM concept, a rather difficult one, chemical bonding. They were taught in the usual way, through a textbook and through classroom lectures and discussions, both with ample visuals. Immediately after learning, their knowledge and understanding of both the structure of the molecules and the process of chemical bonding was tested. The students were then divided in half; half made visual explanations and half verbal explanations. This was followed by a second test of knowledge and understanding. The first surprising finding was that both groups improved in the second test, without any intervening teaching or learning. Students increased their knowledge and understanding simply by creating explanations. The second impressive finding was that those who created visual explanations showed far greater improvement than those who explained in words. Here are two of the visual

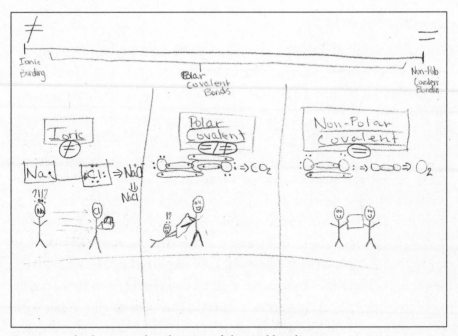

FIGURE 9.2. Student's visual explanation of chemical bonding.

explanations, one in Figure 9.1 and another in Figure 9.2. You will quickly see that these are creations of the students' minds, they are not copies of the diagrams and other visuals they saw in their textbooks or the class lesson. You also see delightful metaphors, sharks grabbing electrons or stick figures gladly giving them. They are woven into a narrative, a story of a process. Here, as before (and after), it's the depiction that's important even if the words aren't always legible.

Now we are free to speculate why creating visual explanations led to better comprehension and learning than creating verbal ones. The first part should be familiar to you: mapping processes in the world to the space of a page is more direct than mapping to words. A diagram has other benefits. It provides a check for completeness, are all the parts there? It also provides a check for coherence, does the diagram make sense? Most likely, Leonardo's practice also rested on these three features of creating sketches: directness of mapping, check for completeness, check for coherence. And a fourth, a platform for inference.

DRAWING TO CREATE

The truth is, sketching for thinking, alone or together, now, in the era of cheap paper, seems to be everywhere. There's the proverbial cocktail napkin, the one grabbed spontaneously in the conversations of scientists, football coaches, engineers, inventors, mathematicians, stage designers, architects, business innovators, and patent attorneys, to list just a few. Here's one headline: "Everything you ever needed to know about investing, scribbled on cocktail napkins." You can find websites and books that collect cocktail napkin drawings and other websites and books that tell you how to draw them and use them. You can enter yours into a contest. The *Architectural Record* has sponsored a contest for the best cocktail napkin sketches since 2010. There are science labs that use drawings and diagrams systematically to keep track of their progress, theoretical as well as empirical, with ? that denote the unknowns in the processes, the questions for future research.

Architecture and design rely on drawings. Drawings are the plans, the road maps, the instructions for constructing the buildings and objects. In practice, architects, engineers, product designers, and others depend on a range of different kinds of drawings and photos and simulations, annotated in different ways, depending on their intended use. Drawing serves as a thinking tool for designers and engineers, a way to work vague ideas into concrete ones as well as a way to check the coherence and feasibility of the ideas. Designers are said to have conversations with their sketches, cycles of thinking, drawing, looking, rethinking, redrawing, and so on, gradually refining a design. The conversations can be observed and studied by asking designers to talk aloud as they design or retrospectively and linking the thoughts, the drawing, and the looking throughout design sessions. Because the designing itself is for the most part interactions of the eye and the hand and the marks on the page, retrospective reports work better, as they do not interfere with the design thinking. The reports of the designers reveal fascinating aspects of the design process.

We wanted to capture that process as it unfolded to shed light on its underpinnings. To that end, two experienced and seven novice architects were asked to design a museum on a hillside to hold a hundred paintings plus a sculpture garden, ticket office, café, gift shop, parking lot, and more. They were filmed as they sketched. One of the design sketches appears in Figure 9.3. You can see that it is schematic and blobby; the structures and the layout are vague, in short, ambiguous. Ambiguity turns out to be one key to creative thinking because it allows, even encourages, reinterpretations. Abstraction plays a similar role for a similar reason. After the design session, the researcher went through the videos with each designer, asking what they were thinking each time they put pencil to paper to make a mark. The reports were painstakingly coded segment by segment for the content they were meant to represent: shapes, spatial relations, functional relations, background, and more. Segments with the same content were linked even when separated. Designers reported the general ideas they were playing with and the insights and changes in ideas they had as they worked.

The expert designers differed from the novices in two striking ways: whereas most of the observations and insights of novices were about perceptual relations, far more of the experts' reflections were about functional relations. In addition, far more of the experts' reflections were linked to other reflections. Perceptual relations are those directly apparent from the sketch itself, a shape or pattern or motif. Functional observations require inferences from the sketches, often animating the sketches. They cannot be read directly from the sketch, for example, the flow of traffic or the light changing throughout the day or year. This difference, that novices can see and work with what is present in sketches and diagrams and other visualizations but that it takes talent or expertise to use diagrams to imagine things that are not actually in them, is key to expertise. It characterizes expertise in other domains, like chess, engineering, and music.

Designers often report that they draw for one reason, and that when they look again at what they've drawn, they see new things.

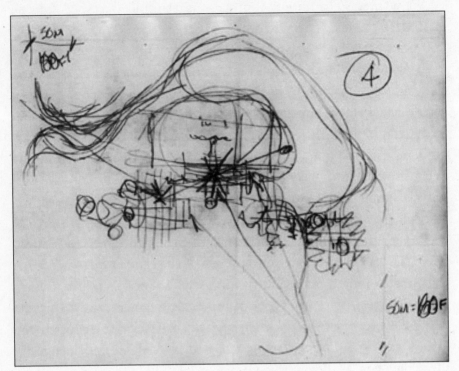

FIGURE 9.3. Architect's early sketch of a plan for a museum.

They make unintended discoveries in their own sketches. That is, they reinterpret their own sketches, a phenomenon encouraged by the sketchiness of the sketches. In fact, we were able to catch many unintended discoveries. A detailed analysis of the protocol of one expert revealed that unintended discoveries tended to occur when the architect regrouped elements of the sketch, when he saw new patterns, when new organizations emerged. Perceptual regrouping stimulated a virtuous cycle: regrouping led to new insights and new insights led to regrouping. Look at the sketch of one experienced architect in Figure 9.3. It is full of ambiguities, and it is those ambiguities that allow reorganization and new insights and discoveries. The highly rectified outputs of computer programs do not lend themselves to new interpretations.

To test that idea directly, we developed a task that ordinary people could do. We designed ambiguous sketches, those in Figure 9.4.

FIGURE 9.4. Sketches shown one at a time over and over to participants to generate new interpretations.

We showed each sketch over and over to undergraduates, asking them to come up with a new interpretation each time they saw the sketch. Half the participants were told that regrouping the parts was a good strategy for finding new interpretations. The other half was simply told to look carefully. We counted the number of new interpretations they reported until they gave up. Afterward, we asked them what strategies they used. Participants, like children and even adults, don't always do what they're told. Some of those instructed to regroup the parts didn't, whereas some told to look reported regrouping the parts. So, we regrouped, separating the participants into those who reported regrouping the parts and those who didn't. In fact, the participants who reported attending to and regrouping parts found nearly twice as many new interpretations as those who did not attend to parts. They also persisted longer as well, presumably because attending differentially to parts provided a useful strategy for generating new interpretations.

A follow-up study showed that experienced designers were more adept at finding new interpretations than ordinary people were. That led us to study effects of ability in addition to expertise. In yet another experiment, we found that two abilities predicted number of reinterpretations. The abilities themselves were unrelated. One was the ability to detect an isolated figure of a specific shape in a larger more complex configuration, a test called embedded figures. That skill is perceptual, requiring scrutiny of parts. The other was the ability to find remote associations among words, for example, what word is associated with *widow, bite, and monkey*? Spider. Or *sleeping, trash, and bean*? Bag. Or *duck, fold, dollar*? Bill. That ability is verbal or associative, requiring divergent thinking. On the one side, a perceptual skill, on the other, a cognitive skill. The first, bottom-up, the second, top-down. The two skills are integrated in what we have called *constructive perception,* that is, reconfiguring an external representation in the search for meaning. Possessing either skill increased the number of new ideas, and possessing both skills doubled the benefits. Constructive perception seems to be the key to a successful conversation involving the eyes and the mind and the marks on a page.

In later work we tried other strategies to encourage new interpretations. Interleaving the sketches with each other rather than repeatedly showing the same sketch increased production of new ideas. Interleaving or spacing presentations of the same sketch presumably allowed new associations to emerge, a phenomenon related both to incubation and to release from fixation, effects well known in creativity and problem solving. Interestingly, spaced practice is also better for learning than massed practice more or less for the same reason.

Reconfiguring parts is a bottom-up perceptual strategy. Because constructive perception involves both a perceptual and a cognitive skill, we reasoned that a top-down cognitive strategy should be effective at increasing the number of interpretations as well. As before, participants were presented with each sketch many times and asked to come up with a new interpretation each time. One group got the bottom-up instructions. They were told to reorganize or reconfigure or regroup the sketches to see them differently in order to think of new interpretations. Another group got the top-down instructions.

They were told to think of new domains, new settings, new kinds of objects or organisms in order to think of new interpretations. In this case, only the top-down strategy elicited significantly more interpretations than the no-strategy control participants. We think this is because ordinary adults have extensive top-down knowledge, so it is relatively easy for them (us) to generate new categories, new events, and new settings and to use them to reinterpret the objects in various contexts. However, ordinary adults are unlikely to have had extensive practice and experience deconstructing and reorganizing ambiguous sketches. Hence ordinary people could easily adopt the top-down strategy but wouldn't be as adept at using the bottom-up strategy. The bottom-up strategy is using the world in front of the eyes, on the page. The top-down strategy goes from the page back into the mind, with its vast store of people, places, and things and categories and transformations and networks and strategies, all of which can be activated to generate new ideas. We stay in the mind as we find the key to creativity.

CREATIVITY

Leonardo, architects, designers. How about the rest of us? There are many occasions where we need to improvise. A shoestring rips, an ingredient for a recipe is missing, the handle of a suitcase falls off. Improvising means finding a way to solve the problem, quite often with a substitute object, a safety pin or paper clip for the shoe, vinegar instead of lemon for the recipe, rope for the handle. A new, unfamiliar use for a familiar object. Finding new uses for familiar objects is a warm-up activity in design classes, like scales for piano or slalom courses for soccer. Like others, we turned to that task to see whether we could find strategies that would enable people to find more uses and more creative uses. We've left sketches in the world for sketches in the mind.

It seems that we can't escape our zeitgeists. Two key elements of early twenty-first-century zeitgeist poke their heads into research. Innovation and mind. Everyone and every country want to be

innovative. Some even use dropping out of Harvard as a strategy—
look what it did for Bill Gates! And everyone wants to boost the
mind. Some legally, some not. Any article or show mentioning mind
attracts immediate attention. It could be mindfulness or it could be
mind wandering; either way, people latch on and try, without seeing
the contradiction. Preview: the key to both innovation and mind is
perspective taking. You've noticed that perspective is another of my
obsessions.

There is a bundle of research claiming that mind wandering is
great for creativity. It has been shown to increase the number of new
uses for familiar objects. If only it were true, this would be good
news, just what we always wanted (dreamed about)—daydreaming
is good for us. Tell that to the baseball coach. Or the fifth-grade
teacher. Okay, maybe it makes sense that mind wandering could increase the number of ideas people have. After all, mind wandering
can release thinkers from fixation, from going around and around
in the same rut, a problem we've all had and one that experts have
too. Letting your mind go as it pleases, taking a break, going for a
walk, all help by bringing in new associations, some of which might
provoke new ways of thinking. But there's no guarantee that the
random associations of mind wandering or world wandering will
be relevant or productive. Mind wandering might get you out of a
rut, but it doesn't get you back on track. It doesn't give you a good
strategy for finding new solutions.

I once asked Paul Andreu, the visionary architect of Charles de
Gaulle Airport in Paris and more than forty stunning airports and
public buildings all over the world, "Where do you begin?"

"Inside," he said.

What he was saying is that he begins with you. You need to be
uplifted by the space you are in and you need to be guided effortlessly to where you need to go. As a designer, you must begin with
what you cannot design. You begin with the human (or other creature) who will use what you design. Design firms (like IDEO) that
work on real-life projects like water purification in remote areas or
cheap fuel for emerging countries or redesigning a shopping cart or

an electronic device use what they call a human-centric approach to design. Let's call it *empathetic* design. They study a community of users intensively to see what people actually do and what kind of new product or service might improve their lives, fit into their lives, and be sustainable. An empathetic perspective does provide a productive search strategy: think about people's lives, take the perspective of users.

We compared those two strategies, mind wandering and empathetic, for the standard divergent thinking task, finding new uses for familiar objects. We pretested our objects to make sure that people could find new uses for them. Our experiments used an umbrella, a shoe, a broom, a chair, a flashlight, and a smartphone. Participants were asked to find as many new uses for each object as they could. The mind-wandering group was told to let their minds wander. The empathetic group was told to think about ways that people in different occupations—gardener, artist, fire fighter, and so on—might use the object in new ways. In other words, take their perspectives, each a different one. Because those roles are well known, it wasn't hard for participants to put themselves in the others' shoes. Both groups were told, truthfully, that the recommended strategy had proven to be effective. We added a control group that was not given a strategy.

The hands-down winner was the empathetic perspective. The mind-wandering group was no better than the control group. In fact, many in the control group told us they just let their minds wander. Both perspectives appeared to provide strategies to release thinkers from fixation, but only the empathetic approach gave a productive way to search for new uses. Taking other perspectives led people to suggest more new uses and more creative new uses. Creative uses were those that only one or a few people came up with. Some examples: using an umbrella for shish kabob skewers or jewelry; using a shoe as a bird carrier or sound-proofing; using a flashlight as a meat tenderizer or martini shaker. As befits a chapter that begins and ends with art: the most productive perspective was artist! Artists can make art out of anything.

Perspective taking

The empathetic approach won't work for all design problems, certainly not for some of the natural-world challenges Leonardo faced, like harnessing the power of water and wind. But the core of the empathetic approach is perspective taking, in this case, taking the perspectives of different users. Perspective taking and perspective switching are strategies that are general enough to work for just about everything. The perspectives don't have to be human ones, even if it's humans who are doing the thinking and the creating. Mathematicians report one problem-solving strategy they use is to look at an algebraic problem geometrically or a geometric problem algebraically (Leonardo was all geometry, fitting).

Biomimicry encourages new perspectives. Architects and designers use biomimicry with outcomes that are as delightful as they are efficient. Snails have inspired stairways. The tiny "teeth" of shark-skin inspired a line of racing bathing suits. The beak of a bird the nose of the Japanese bullet train, the shinkansen. The burrs that stick to hikers' pants in the Swiss Alps famously inspired Velcro.

Changing medium changes perspective. Bronze, iron, aluminum, Teflon, reinforced concrete, titanium, silicon—all led to innovations. Architects have become amazing pastry chefs, structures so stunning you are reluctant to use your fork. Throughout history, technological advances have changed perspectives, changed ways of thinking, changed ways of living. Fire. Agriculture. The wheel and the arch and the cantilever. Writing. Math notation. The printing press, the compass. Cheap paper. Steam engines. Electricity. The internet. Telescopes, microscopes, X-rays, CAT scans, tunneling microscopes. The last few literally enable new ways of seeing, new perspectives. At first, these new materials and technologies and ways of seeing simply replace traditional uses. But soon they open up new uses. Think of the iPhone, hardly used for talking any more, but for thousands of other uses, some unintended and certainly not recommended, like walking into moving cars and other people.

The paradigm shifts in science noted by Kuhn are changes in perspective, quite literally. Ptolemy to Copernicus, Aristotle to Newton to Einstein. The idea of process, an initial state followed by a string of events culminating in an outcome, has been fundamental in many sciences, including biology. Processes make good stories, they have beginnings, middles, and ends. That perspective, seeing biology as processes, blocked seeing and understanding homeostasis, also core to biology and other sciences and engineering. Homeostasis is a continuous cyclical set of events that has no beginning and no end. The "outcome" is maintaining a steady state by countering changes with opposing changes. The prototypic case is a thermostat. If the temperature drops below the set point, the heat goes on. When it reaches the set point, the heat goes off. When the temperature goes too high, the AC kicks in. There's no beginning, no end (unless you turn it off).

Here's another example, vividly described by Siddhartha Mukherjee in *The New Yorker*. The dominant metaphor in treating cancer has been one of war. Foreign cells invade the body, they colonize and proliferate and attack other organs. Cancer, the ruthless murdering enemy, must be exterminated. The weapons of extermination are surgery, radiation, and chemotherapy. Sure, there's collateral damage, but this is war. Only recently have researchers taken a different perspective. There are cancers that implant (note the word) in the body, but do not spread. Many of those colonies are discovered postmortem in people who died for other reasons. Hmm. Why is that cancers colonize, but do not proliferate? Now the new perspective, a new metaphor. Cancer is a seed. It needs the proper soil to survive. If that's the case, look at the soil. Taking that perspective, the perspective of the soil, has led to new ways of doing research and new treatments: spoil the soil.

PREDICTION AND PERSPECTIVE TAKING

We turn now to predicting the future, to superforecasters. Patience; we'll tell you what they are soon. You have probably guessed it has something to do with perspective taking. Years ago, Phil Tetlock began to study professional forecasters, people who earn a living by predicting what will happen in the next year or ten, primarily economic and political predictions. The future is of great importance to economists, businesspeople, politicians, and, actually, to all of us. Economic and political events are notoriously hard to predict. As are which songs, films, tweets, books will go viral. Even the weather. Tetlock studied many self-proclaimed and well-paid expert forecasters over a ten-year period. They were no better than monkeys throwing darts. (Why are they consulted, much less believed? And paid?) In spite of their own findings, or maybe because of them, he and his collaborators changed perspective. They began to wonder whether there might be people who, in fact, *are* good at predicting. They ran and are still running prediction contests. In the contests, players, all volunteers, are given specific predictions like: What will the GNP of country X be in 20XX? Or, Will there be a revolution in country Z in 20ZZ? Predictions that can be checked. They found a small group of people, those are the superforecasters, who did succeed better than chance and better than others, not just once, but years in a row.

Naturally, the researchers—and the rest of us—wanted to find out what made these superforecasters so good. Sure, they were educated and smart, but far from off-scale. Sure, they were news junkies. Sure, they had a refined feel for probabilities, more articulated than the trinary: *for sure, maybe, no way*. Sure, they loved the challenge, they were curious and open-minded. And they stuck to it. Interestingly, they were humble. They understood how deeply uncertain the world is.

But to my (biased) eyes, the most important trait they possessed was perspective taking. They would carefully construct an analysis supporting their hunches. First, confirmation bias. Actually, not a bad first step: if there isn't strong support, then give up right away. Then they would challenge their own analysis: How could it go wrong? What's missing? An adversarial stance, no more confirmation bias. They would ask: What would X, Y, or Z, other known experts in politics or economics, predict? How would A, B, C, other theories, assess the situation? Superforecasters were open-minded enough to let the very different analyses of others alter their own predictions.

Others make similar recommendations. Writing in the *Harvard Business Review,* Schwartz advised: "Forever challenge your convictions." He called this *deepening* and added *widening,* take multiple perspectives, and *lengthening,* consider long-term consequences and implications.

Perspective taking is central to more than creativity and problem solving, or maybe it's that so much of life is problem solving and requires creativity. Diplomacy, international and domestic, right inside the home and the office and on the streets. Role-playing is perspective taking. So is cognitive behavior therapy. And empathy. I'm not saying it's easy. All too often it's really hard. Confirmation bias can get in the way. Self-protection can get in the way. Emotions can get in the way. Perspective taking doesn't guarantee success, but it's a good bet. Maybe it's hard, but in the end, perspective taking can actually overcome bias, diffuse emotions, and protect the self.

We've already seen many ways to find new perspectives. Reconfigure the parts. Take the point of view of different roles, places, events, categories, creatures, physical processes, materials, research methods, disciplinary viewpoints, nationalities, philosophies, religions, ideologies. Be your own adversary: challenge your own view. The list goes on. Some of this is stuff we know, from living and learning, so thinking from other perspectives often just needs a reminder.

PERSPECTIVES: INSIDE AND ABOVE

We can now jump above for a broad overview of perspective and perspectives. That lengthy list of ways to find different perspectives entails exploring the surrounding world, a conceptual world. The exploration follows a path through a space of ideas, with each place providing a different perspective. It's an inside perspective. Recall that one of the remarkable feats of the mind is to use exploration of the world from within to create a map as if from above. An overview encompasses many viewpoints, far more than can be seen from any viewpoint. Now remember the **First Law of Cognition:** gains inevitably come with losses. The broad overview necessarily loses some of the details of the embedded perspectives. What it gains is abstraction. An overview retains the core features of each place, each perspective, but loses detail. Individual features disappear and general ones remain. An overview shows the relations among the places, here, the ideas.

Here's how to find new perspectives:

Move around. Take different perspectives, those of someone else or something else.

Move above. Go abstract—find commonalities across perspectives; find connections among the perspectives. Change the commonalities, the features, the parameters. Change the relations. Regroup and repeat.

ART AND LIFE

Now we return from the mind to the page, we return to sketching and to art. Andrea Kantrowitz not only is a fine artist but also has studied the practice of other fine artists. Adapting the methods used in our research on architects, she videotaped nine experienced artists as they drew and talked through their videos with them afterward. She tried getting them to talk as they drew, but talking interfered with a process that wasn't verbal. The artists were engaged in that wordless conversation between the mind and the hand and the marks on the page. Instead, she looked on from the outside, recording the artists' hands as they filled the page. The patterns of hands filling space with marks revealed intriguing differences in style. Some artists went back and forth revisiting places that had been drawn; some charged through, rarely returning. All were exploring.

Going through their videos after the sessions, the artists had a lot to say about their process. They see drawing as a journey. The language artists used to describe what they were doing is one of exploration. Not wandering. At the beginning, artists are feeling their way, their marks are tentative, easy to change or to work into something else. No firm commitment yet. The artists have the confidence earned from experience that something will come of the mark making and exploration even if it isn't driven by a plan, or, more likely, exactly because it isn't driven by a plan. They say they can let themselves get lost or make mistakes. Some deliberately get lost, purposely get themselves in trouble, so they can't take the easy way, so they'll have to find a new one. Some say they enter an alternative world, one that is safe to explore. And just as for a journey, they sometimes realize they've made a wrong turn, go back to where the mistake was, and begin again. Most find mistakes and revise, some by erasing, others preferring to leave the archaeological layers as part of the drawing. Eventually, the drawing begins to take shape. At that point, artists say the drawing talks back to them. They are surprised by what they see, they get excited. They discover ways to join parts into wholes. Forms gradually emerge (note the passive), and spaces that need to be filled are spotted and filled. The drawing pulls itself together.

A journey of exploration, neither random nor predetermined, but improvised, perhaps a few wrong turns, perhaps a few missed places, a journey of discovery. The same journey of exploration and discovery for designers, to create a new building or product or business. The same journey of exploration and discovery for scientists or detectives or mathematicians or analysts or, for that matter, all of us, to solve a problem. For the artists, drawing is more than a journey, it is a story, with a beginning, middle, and end, full of twists and turns and emotional upswings and downswings and drama, surprises and disappointments and frustrations and uncertainty and discovery and elation and suspense. Like any creative endeavor. Like life.

CHAPTER TEN

The World Is a Diagram

In which we see that our actions in space design the world, that the designs create abstract patterns that attract the eye and inform the mind, that the actions get abstracted to gestures that act on thought, and the patterns to diagrams that convey thought. Actions in space create abstractions. A spiral we call **spraction**.

> *A city is a machine with innumerable parts made by the accumulation of human gestures.*
>
> —R. SOLNIT and J. JELLY-SCHAPIRO, *Nonstop Metropolis: A New York City Atlas*

FIGURE 10.1. The mind designs the world.

DESIGNING THE WORLD

My path to elementary school took me past an enormous oak tree with two prominent right-angle bends low in its broad trunk. According to legend, it was a trail marker made by the Potawatomi tribe in the late eighteenth century. The tree was in a large park. The rest of the park retained tiny pockets of wildness, but there

FIGURE 10.2. The world
designed by nature.

was another tree bent years earlier as a trail marker and there were
paved paths and a baseball diamond and the ice-skating rink where
I broke my arm twice in one week. The park was clipped and the
sides straightened, bordered by rows of tidy homes, my elementary
school, and a few shops.

In Figure 10.2 is the world as nature made it (minus the asphalt).
Look around at the world as it is now, in Figure 10.3.

How hard it is to find places in the world that haven't been designed by human actions. How different is our world from that of our
nomadic ancestors. Inside our homes we line books up on shelves.
We stack dishes in cabinets, arrange tools in boxes, and organize
clothing in drawers and closets. We don't just toss them on shelves
and in drawers, we sort them into kinds and kinds of kinds. Categories and subcategories. The plates go on shelves, with different sizes
in separate stacks. Same for the bowls. Categories inside larger categories: embeddings and hierarchies. Sweaters in one drawer, socks
and underwear in others. Inside separate drawers inside a chest of

FIGURE 10.3. The world designed by us.

drawers. Conceptual containers and boundaries as well as physical ones. Books ordered by topic or date or size. The books in one room, a bigger box, the dishes in another, clothing in a third, each room a different theme, different kinds of things brought together for a common purpose, reading, preparing meals, dressing and undressing. When we get dressed, we take one of each, underwear, something on the top, something on the bottom, something on the feet. When we set the table, we give each person a plate, a napkin, silverware, and a glass. One-to-one correspondences.

That's inside. Now look outside again. (See Figure 10.4.) Cities are patterns of streets, lined with buildings, grouped into residential, commercial, educational, recreational. More categories. Rows of windows or balconies on the facades of buildings: you can instantly spot the symmetries and repetitions and one-to-one correspondences. The patterns are created by actions of our hands. Those arrangements carry information, information that doesn't need words, that babies

FIGURE 10.4. Market, Piazza delle Erbe, Padua, Italy.

and children and foreigners can understand. A spatial language. **Ninth Law of Cognition: We organize the stuff in the world the way we organize the stuff in the mind.** The world mirrors the mind. And, as we saw early on, the mind mirrors the world. A cycle that is really a spiral.

DESIGNING US

We haven't just designed and redesigned the world, we have designed and redesigned us. First the body. For as long as anyone can tell, clothing. To protect us from injury and to keep us warm. Adornments of the body, paint, masks, jewelry, go far, far back in archaeological sites. The reasons are anybody's guess, and many have guessed. As a child I was mesmerized by a row of bronze statues in the Field Museum of Natural History in Chicago, portraying people from all over the globe, some with reshaped heads, chiseled teeth, body markings, necks so elongated by stacks of rings that the rings could not be removed. Foot binding ended in China more than a century ago but is still practiced by ballet dancers and aspiring ballet dancers. Young girls can't wait to pierce their ears, a rite of adulthood. What's yucky to one generation is cool to the next. Tattoos are old and new, now, like clothing and hairstyles, a burgeoning art form.

Moving farther and easier

Far more significant than designs for beauty—or cultural images of beauty—are the designs that enhance moving in the world, perceiving the world, and acting in the world. Enhancements of feet, senses, and hands. Shoes early on. Since ancient times, shepherds use walking sticks, mothers carry babes in arms or slings, people put baskets on their heads or on their backs or in their arms or carefully balance them on sticks slung across the shoulders. Palanquins transported nobility; commoners were transported on the shoulders or arms of family or in wheelbarrows or sleds. Horses, camels, donkeys, dogs, and reindeer took our premotorized ancestors farther distances than their feet could. Now strollers and wheelchairs and scooters and skates and planes and rockets do those jobs.

Recall Hans Rosling's work: the key to jumping up an economic level is moving farther in the world. At level one, you only have your feet. To get to level two, you need a bicycle; to get from level two to three, a motor scooter; to reach level four, an automobile. Moving farther in the world brings far more than economic opportunity. Moving farther in the world opens new vistas, new perspectives, new knowledge. Moving farther means collecting more places and people and things. More routes, a larger map. Moving farther expands all opportunities. For so many years, technologies were invented to allow more of us to move farther and farther. Some even to the moon, with the rest of the world watching.

And that's it, we no longer need to leave our armchairs. At the same time that technologies are allowing us to move farther and farther, other technologies are bringing the world nearer and closer, to wherever we happen to be. Letters, eons ago only for the wealthy, now instantaneous and always at our fingertips (a mixed blessing), enhanced by video and sound, replacing telephones, once an astounding resource. Now our bodies don't have to move at all; we can travel the world with smartphones, augmented reality, virtual reality. If we need to move, and physicians advise us to do so, we can move our feet on the treadmill in the gym, without going farther than getting to the gym. From the treadmill, we can enter a virtual world of our choosing, Machu Picchu without climbing, Bangkok without traffic, Beijing without pollution. Or we may prefer a social experience, chatting virtually with friends at a distant party or conferencing virtually with dispersed work colleagues. If, that is, we have the devices and high-speed internet that can take us anywhere virtually—it's just another way of moving. High-speed internet or high-speed jets? Yet experiences in augmented and virtual reality are enhanced by actual action. And actual sensation, so when we virtually visit Machu Picchu, we can feel the stones underfoot and smell the rarified air. All that without altitude sickness.

We've enhanced moving our bodies in space. We've also enhanced perception and action by hands. Many of us wouldn't have lasted long in this world without glasses. Glasses, telescopes, microscopes enhance seeing, allowing us to see farther, almost to the end of the universe and the beginning of time. They allow us to see smaller, almost to the most fundamental minute particles that compose everything in the universe. Of course, those particles are constantly in motion; astrophysicists go into caves deep in the earth to catch them. Microphones and hearing aids enhance hearing. Prosthetic arms and hands, robots, and apparatuses of other sorts augment actions by hand. Too many to list, and more and more accumulating.

Enhancing the mind

Even more important than enhancements of the world and enhancements of action and perception are enhancements of the mind. Teaching. Cooperating. Educating. These depend crucially on social interactions, and begin very early in life. They need nothing more than other human beings, though they are even more effective with books and toys and more. Sticks and stones work too. There's imitation, a phenomenon often laughable in small children. Chimps and bonobos imitate, too; that's how they learn from each other. One chimp figures out a clever way to crack nuts and the others imitate. Different tribes of chimps develop different methods. Interestingly, chimps will imitate another successful chimp, but they will not imitate a machine that accomplishes the same goal in the same way.

But chimps don't teach each other. People do. The foundations are put in place early in life, in games. Games like patty-cake involve more than imitation, they involve timing, synchrony, and alternation—turn-taking, like conversation. Those games are cooperative, they entail attending to each other, working together, and joint attention to the task. In humans, but notably not in apes, teaching and cooperating are enhanced by caretakers who show and guide. Gesture has a large role in guiding and teaching. Language comes to bootstrap those interactions, especially in Western cultures, but the naming game itself depends on joint attention and gesture, pointing, if not by the hand, by the eyes. There's so much more to say, but that would be another book.

THINKING

We spend our lives in space, acting in space, moving in space. For the most part, it's our feet that move our bodies in space. The paths of our feet as we move from place to place in the world leave traces on the ground and traces in our minds. Well-trodden paths get thicker. They make routes that can be turned into maps. The paths and places form networks, like the networks of neurons in the brain, blood vessels in the body, rivers on earth, information in computer systems, and power in governments. Frequented places become neighborhoods or hubs and they get thicker. Their boxes accumulate more actions. Sometimes one box takes charge, the brain, the heart, the president, and the network becomes a tree, with a single root. The patterns are patterns in time as well as in space, rhythmic points and lines, repetitions, orders, cycles. There's no separating time and space. Assembly lines, knitting, music, tennis games, cleaning the house. Sequences of punctuated actions, paths and places in time and space. They create the forms that are used to represent ideas and relations between ideas.

Now let's move to hands. For the most part, it's the hands that do the acting on objects, with remarkable agility. They touch, twist, raise, push, pull, put together, take apart, reach, organize, throw, scatter, mix, flip, rearrange, sort, construct, deconstruct, and act on objects in a thousand more ways. At the same time, our eyes glance, scrutinize, inspect, go back and forth. Pay attention to those verbs. They're the same ones we use to talk about thinking. Thinking is mental actions on mental objects—ideas—rather than physical actions on physical objects. All inside the mind. Now we move to gesture. Gestures are physical actions, but not on physical objects. Gestures are actions on invisible objects, on ideas, ideas that exist only in the minds of the person gesturing or the conversation partner, if there is one. I trust you remember the bottom line on gesture: gesturing helps thinking. If thinking is internalized action, then externalizing actions on thought as gestures that perform miniatures of the actions should help the thinking. It does. Our own thinking, and that of others.

The same is true for graphics of all forms, sketches, charts, graphs, diagrams, models, pebbles, cocktail napkins. They externalize thought and thereby promote thought. Taking ideas that are in the mind out of the mind and putting them into the world in front of our eyes helps our own thinking and that of others. Putting thought into the world is key to collaboration, to working together, to the joint action that is core to human society, and to survival.

Both gesture and graphics abstract. They abbreviate, truncate, schematize, generalize. Gestures don't capture entire actions, only thumbnails of them. Much like the words for action. *Lift* doesn't say how an object is lifted, with a finger or a hand or two hands or eight hands. Or a machine, a fork lift. Whether you *lift* a crumb from the floor or a piano, it's the same word. Gestures can actually be more specific, showing, if useful, how something is lifted. A sketch map schematizes a route; there's so much missing from sketch maps, and what's there gets simplified and distorted.

Gestures, in common with diagrams and other graphics, abstract thought in other ways. Gestures can create overall schemas in space. They set a stage for ideas. Here's one that's frequent because it's so very useful: compare and contrast. One hand puts one set of imaginary things on one side of the body, the other hand places another set of imaginary things on the other side. On the one hand, on the other. Columns and rows on a page, imaginary ones in the air. Then point back and forth as you go through the comparison. Each place now represents a separate set of ideas. You show it; you don't have to say it. Here's another: set up an order, along a horizontal line. Could be a sequence of events in time, could be a sequence of preferences for movies, restaurants, or baseball teams. Now a circle, showing events that repeat. Now a vertical line, going upward. Could be temperature or achievements or power or mood. Forms again. Am I describing diagrams on a page or gestures in the air? Both. Both gestures and graphics put thought in the world, arrange thought, and abstract thought. Both gestures and graphics put checkers on a checkerboard to play in a game of thought, ideas on a stage to perform in a theater of thought.

All those patterns and forms we've collected. The ones our feet create moving in the world: points and paths and boxes and networks and trees and circles. The ones our hands create in designing the world: boxes and lines and circles again, rows and columns and symmetries and repetitions and one-to-one correspondences. We put those on a page to use them to represent many kinds of ideas and many kinds of relations between ideas. They become maps and tables and charts and diagrams. They organize the thoughts in our mind, show them to others, and help us generate more thoughts. There are so many more forms and patterns in math, in physics, in biology, in chemistry, in engineering, in art. Patterns in space, forms in space that are the foundation for each of them. They get formed and transformed, rotated, translated, taken apart and put together. Arches and crystals and Bucky balls and Mobius strips.

THE DESIGNED WORLD SPEAKS A SPATIAL LANGUAGE

So much information emanates from the spatial forms and patterns that we create and that surround us. They are informative in and of themselves. They tell us what they are and how to interact with them. They also express abstractions, the kind that go into logic or math or computer science: linear orders in bookshelves and assembly lines, categories and hierarchies of categories in kitchen cabinets and drawers of clothing and supermarket shelves, one-to-one correspondences in table settings, symmetries and repetitions in buildings. Rooms are organized by themes: stuff for cooking in the kitchen, stuff for personal care in the bathrooms, stuff for socializing and relaxing in the living room. Those organizations were not created by nature; they were created by and for human actions, by conscious minds. They were created for a purpose. The rows and columns of shelves and windows and buildings form regular patterns that are good gestalts. They're tables and graphs. They bring the eye, inviting a search for their meanings, for the reasons the arrangements were created. Typically, we can figure them out. As can children, each person in the family gets a plate and silverware—and a treat, the plates stacked in categories on shelves, beds and pillows in the bedroom, towels and bathtubs in the bathroom. We use the same organizations in our minds, in our homes, and on the streets.

There's another layer on the streets. The streets are organized the ways our homes and supermarkets are, in boxes, lines, rows, columns, orders, and more. But the streets go further; they are marked and labeled, sometimes, like diagrams, with words, but so often not. The whole world has become like a string of basketball courts, golf courses, soccer fields, and baseball diamonds. Lines of various colors and styles indicate pedestrian crossing lanes, bus lanes, bike lanes, car lanes, one-way streets, turning lanes, parking places for cars, motorcycles, bikes. The different functions are clearly marked: crossing lanes are zebra-striped, bike lanes are green, parking places are pairs of diagonal or parallel lines, slots to fit your car into. Car-sized boxes. There are arrows drawn on lanes that tell you you cannot turn or you must turn. There are bicycles painted on the ground to tell you to keep your car or feet out of the bike lanes. Dare not drive across a double yellow line. Those lines, for parking and turning and crossing and no crossing, have legal status. The laws are inscribed lines on the streets. Laws also appear in signs of different shapes and colors, hexagon for stop and triangle for yield, no U-turn with an icon and one-way streets with an arrow. Stop lights, red on top to halt, green on the bottom to go. Curious, laws that are not in words but in lines on the streets and signs along them.

The world is diagrammed. We've fastened our collective minds onto the world. The diagram in the world is information; it tells you where you are and what kinds of things are around you. It tells you where and when you can go, and where and when you cannot go. What you can do and what you cannot do. It controls, directs, and enables the ways you move and act in the world. Enter here, exit there. That way, people won't bump into each other. Cross at the zebra stripes or when the light is green; put recyclables in the green trash can, a slit for paper, a circle for cans. It's labeled, just like the fruit you buy in the supermarket, placed in lines and bins of appropriate shapes that are adorned with colors and symbols that are instructions for actions. The designed world is a diagram that reveals its meanings through place and marks in space and guides our action. The view from above is a map. The view from within tells us where people can walk, where cars and buses and bikes can go, when to stop and when to go, where to park, where to enter, and where to exit. The patterns on our bookshelves and in cabinets and table settings and on building facades express abstract ideas: categories, hierarchies, repetitions, one-to-one correspondences, linear orders. We organize the world the way we organize our minds and our lives.

The patterns created by our actions, lines and rows and columns and stacks, are not random, not like the leaves strewn on the ground or the sand rolling in the dunes or the trees scattered in the forests. They are regular and tidy, parallel and perpendicular, symmetric and repetitive. They enclose and separate; they are scaffolds for the things in the world. They didn't happen by chance, they must have been put there for a reason. We can read the reasons, sometimes without trying, and use that information to guide our thoughts and our actions.

The forms and patterns on the ground are made by actions of our feet. Places and paths and circles and more. The forms and patterns on buildings and on tables and on computer screens are made by actions of our hands. Rows and columns and stacks and orders and embeddings and symmetries and more. The forms and patterns are good gestalts that attract the eye and inform the mind. We detach the actions and the patterns from whatever made them and use them to represent something else, so many things, they're extraordinarily useful actions and patterns. On a page or in the air. In the world. The gestures we draw with our hands in the air abstract the actions that created the forms and patterns. They turn real actions on real objects into schematic actions on imaginary objects, ideas. They become actions on thought, any kind of thought. The diagrams we draw with our hands on the page abstract the patterns that we use to arrange objects in the world. We use them to arrange thoughts on a page, creating tools for thought that benefit thought. For everyone. And it all begins with our action in space. A spiral going ever upward. *Spraction: actions* in *space* create *abstractions*.

The Nine Laws of Cognition

First Law of Cognition: There are no benefits without costs.

Second Law of Cognition: Action molds perception.

Third Law of Cognition: Feeling comes first.

Fourth Law of Cognition: The mind can override perception.

Fifth Law of Cognition: Cognition mirrors perception.

Sixth Law of Cognition: Spatial thinking is the foundation of abstract thought.

Seventh Law of Cognition: The mind fills in missing information.

Eighth Law of Cognition: When thought overflows the mind, the mind puts it into the world.

Ninth Law of Cognition: We organize the stuff in the world the way we organize the stuff in the mind.

Figure Credits

Figure 1.1. *Source:* OpenStax College, *Anatomy & Physiology*. OpenStax CNX. July 30, 2014. Retrieved from http://cnx.org/contents/14fb4ad7 -39a1-4eee-ab6e-3ef2482e3e22@6.27

Figure 3.1. *Source:* Tversky, B., & Hard, B. M. (2009). Embodied and disembodied cognition: Spatial perspective-taking. *Cognition, 110*(1), 124–129.

Figure 4.3. *Source:* Adapted from Kosslyn, S. M. (1980). *Image and mind*. Cambridge, MA: Harvard University Press.

Figure 4.4. *Source:* From Novick, L. R., & Tversky, B. (1987). Cognitive constraints on ordering operations: The case of geometric analogies. *Journal of Experimental Psychology: General, 116*(1), 50–67.

Figure 4.5. *Source:* Wai, J., Lubinski, D., & Benbow, C. P. (2009). Spatial ability for STEM domains: Aligning over 50 years of cumulative psychological knowledge solidifies its importance. *Journal of Educational Psychology, 101*(4), 817.

Figure 5.1. *Source:* Guidonian hand from a manuscript from Mantua, last quarter of fifteenth century (Oxford University MS Canon. Liturgy 216. f.168 recto) (Bodleian Library, University of Oxford).

Figure 8.1. *Source:* Photo by Scott Catron. May 14, 2006. Retrieved from https://commons.wikimedia.org/wiki/File:HuntSceneNMC.JPG

Figure 8.2. Courtesy of Professor Pilar Utrilla. Utrilla, P., Mazo, C., Sopena, M. C., Martínez-Bea, M., & Domingo, R. (2009). A paleolithic map from 13,660 calBP: Engraved stone blocks from the Late Magdalenian in Abauntz Cave (Navarra, Spain). *Journal of Human Evolution, 57*(2), 99–111.

Figure 8.3. *Source:* British Museum, Department of British and Mediaeval Antiquities and Ethnography, *Handbook to the Ethnographical Collections* (Oxford, England: Trustees, British Museum, 1910), 170. https://www .flickr.com/photos/internetarchivebookimages/14783361945/

Figure 8.4. *Source:* "Map" in *Encyclopaedia Britannica* (11th ed., Vol. XVII, p. 638). Retrieved from https://commons.wikimedia.org/wiki/File:EB_1911 _Map_Fig_10.png

Figure 8.5. *Source:* Snow, J. (1855). *On the mode of communication of cholera* (2nd ed.). London, England: John Churchill. Retrieved from http://matrix. msu.edu/~johnsnow/images/online_companion/chapter_images/fig12-5.jpg

Figure 8.6. *Source:* Intitut Royal des Sciences naturelles de Belgique, Bruxelles.

Figure 8.8. Courtesy of Mark Wexler (1993).

Figure 8.9. *Source:* Swetz, F. (2012). *Mathematical expeditions: Exploring word problems across the ages.* Baltimore, MD: Johns Hopkins Press. Photograph by Jon Bodsworth between 2001 and 2011.

Figure 8.11. *Source:* Agrawala, M., Phan, D., Heiser, J., Haymaker, J., Klingner, J., Hanrahan, P., & Tversky, B. (2003, July). Designing effective step-by-step assembly instructions. *ACM Transactions on Graphics (TOG), 22*(3), 828–837.

Figure 8.12. *Source:* Diderot's *L'Encyclopédie* (1762). Retrieved from https:// commons.wikimedia.org/wiki/File:Defehrt_epinglier_pl2.jpg

Figure 8.13. *Source:* Tversky, B., & Lee, P. (1999). Pictorial and verbal tools for conveying routes. In C. Freksa & D. M. Mark (Eds.), *Spatial information theory. Cognitive and computational foundations of geographic information science. Lecture Notes in Computer Science* (Vol. 1661). Berlin, Germany: Springer, Berlin, Heidelberg.

Figure 8.14. *Source:* Fibonacci. Retrieved from https://en.wikipedia.org/wiki /Illusory_contours#/media/File:Kanizsa_triangle.svg

Figure 8.15. *Source:* Zacks, J., & Tversky, B. (1999). Bars and lines: A study of graphic communication. *Memory & Cognition, 27*(6), 1073–1079.

Figure 8.17. *Source:* Heiser, J., & Tversky, B. (2006). Arrows in comprehending and producing mechanical diagrams. *Cognitive Science, 30*(3), 581–592.

Figure 8.18. Visual notes courtesy of Yoon Bahk. Photo courtesy of Andrea Kantrowitz.

Figure 8.19. Courtesy of *Chicago Tribune* and estate of Frank O. King. Retrieved from http://www.mascontext.com/issues/20-narrative-winter-13 /comics-and-architecture-comics-in-architecture-a-not-so-short-recount-of-the-interactions-between-architecture-and-graphic-narrative-1/

Figure 8.20. *Source:* McCay, W. (c. 1913). Seite des Comicstrips Little Nemo in Slumberland. Retrieved from https://commons.wikimedia.org/wiki/File :Little_nemo_the_walking_bed.jpg

Figure 8.21. *Source:* McCay, W. (1905, September 24). *Little Sammy Sneeze* comic strip. Retrieved from https://commons.wikimedia.org/w/index .php?curid=30363015

Figure 8.22. *Source:* Carlin, J., Karasik, P., & Walker, B. (Eds.). (2005). *Masters of American comics*. Los Angeles, CA: Hammer Museum and the Museum of Contemporary Art, Los Angeles, in association with Yale University Press.

Figure 9.1. *Source:* Bobek, E., & Tversky, B. (2016). Creating visual explanations improves learning. *Cognitive Research: Principles and Implications, 1*(1), 27.

Figure 9.2. *Source:* Bobek, E., & Tversky, B. (2016). Creating visual explanations improves learning. *Cognitive Research: Principles and Implications, 1*(1), 27.

Figure 9.3. *Source:* Suwa, M., & Tversky, B. (1997). What do architects and students perceive in their design sketches? A protocol analysis. *Design Studies, 18*(4), 385–403.

Figure 9.4. *Source:* Suwa, M., & Tversky, B. (2003). Constructive perception: A metacognitive skill for coordinating perception and conception. *Proceedings of the Annual Meeting of the Cognitive Science Society, 25*(25).

All photos in Chapter Ten are courtesy of the author.

Bibliographic Notes

CHAPTER ONE: THE SPACE OF THE BODY: SPACE IS FOR ACTION

Cortical regions selectively activated by objects, faces, and bodies

Grill-Spector, K., & Weiner, K. S. (2014). The functional architecture of the ventral temporal cortex and its role in categorization. *Nature Reviews Neuroscience, 15*(8), 536–548.

Kanwisher, N. (2010). Functional specificity in the human brain: A window into the functional architecture of the mind. *Proceedings of the National Academy of Sciences, 107*(25), 11163–11170.

Weiner, K. S., & Grill-Spector, K. (2013). Neural representations of faces and limbs neighbor in human high-level visual cortex: Evidence for a new organization principle. *Psychological Research, 77*(1), 74–97.

Best views of objects

Palmer, S., Rosch, E., & Chase, P. (1981). Canonical perspective and the perception of objects. In J. B. Long & A. D. Baddeley (Eds.), *Attention and performance*, IX. Hillsdale, NJ: Erlbaum.

Tversky, B., & Hemenway, K. (1984). Objects, parts, and categories. *Journal of Experimental Psychology: General, 113*(2), 169.

Homunculus

Azevedo, F. A., Carvalho, L. R., Grinberg, L. T., Farfel, J. M., Ferretti, R. E., Leite, R. E., & Herculano Houzel, S. (2009). Equal numbers of neuronal and nonneuronal cells make the human brain an isometrically scaled-up primate brain. *Journal of Comparative Neurology, 513*(5), 532–541.

Specialized individual neurons

Perrett, D. I., Harries, M. H., Bevan, R., Thomas, S., Benson, P. J., Mistlin, A. J. . . . . Ortega, J. E. (1989). Frameworks of analysis for the neural representation of animate objects and actions. *Journal of Experimental Biology, 146*(1), 87–113.

Names more abstract than depictions

Morrison, J. B., & Tversky, B. (2005). Bodies and their parts. *Memory & Cognition, 33*, 696–709.

Figurative uses of parts of object

Lakoff, G., & Johnson, M. (2008). *Metaphors we live by*. Chicago: University of Chicago Press.

Tversky, B., & Hemenway, K. (1984). Objects, parts, and categories. *Journal of Experimental Psychology: General, 113*(2), 169.

Development of babies' brains

Bremner, A. J., Lewkowicz, D. J., & Spence, C. (2012). *Multisensory development*. Oxford, England: Oxford University Press.

Eliot, L. (1999). *What's going on in there? How the brain and mind develop in the first five years of life*. New York, NY: Bantam Books.

Posner, M. I., & Rothbart, M. K. (2007). *Educating the human brain*. Washington, DC: American Psychological Association.

Distorting lenses

Mack, A., & Rock, I. (1968). A re-examination of the Stratton effect: Egocentric adaptation to a rotated visual image. *Perception & Psychophysics, 4*(1), 57–62.

Stratton, G. M. (1897). Vision without inversion of the retinal image. *Psychological Review, 4*, 341–360, 463–481.

Tool use enlarges body schema

Maravita, A., & Iriki, A. (2004). Tools for the body (schema). *Trends in Cognitive Sciences, 8*(2), 79–86.

Martel, M., Cardinali, L., Roy, A. C., & Farnè, A. (2016). Tool-use: An open window into body representation and its plasticity. *Cognitive Neuropsychology, 33*(1–2), 82–101.

Quallo, M. M., Price, C. J., Ueno, K., Asamizuya, T., Cheng, K., Lemon, R. N., & Iriki, A. (2009). Gray and white matter changes associated with tool-use learning in macaque monkeys. *Proceedings of the National Academy of Sciences, 106*(43), 18379–18384.

Ownership of rubber hands

Beauchamp, M. S. (2005). See me, hear me, touch me: Multisensory integration in lateral occipital-temporal cortex. *Current Opinion in Neurobiology, 15*(2), 145–153.

Botvinick, M., & Cohen, J. (1998). Rubber hands "feel" touch that eyes see. *Nature, 391*(6669), 756.

Ehrsson, H. H., Wiech, K., Weiskopf, N., Dolan, R. J., & Passingham, R. E. (2007). Threatening a rubber hand that you feel is yours elicits a cortical anxiety response. *Proceedings of the National Academy of Sciences, 104*(23), 9828–9833.

Babies' understanding of goal-directed behavior

Falck-Ytter, T., Gredebäck, G., & von Hofsten, C. (2006). Infants predict other people's action goals. *Nature Neuroscience, 9*(7), 878–879.

Sommerville, J. A., & Woodward, A. L. (2005). Pulling out the intentional structure of action: The relation between action processing and action production in infancy. *Cognition, 95*(1), 1–30.

Sommerville, J. A., Woodward, A. L., & Needham, A. (2005). Action experience alters 3-month-old infants' perception of others' actions. *Cognition, 96*(1), B1–B11.

Mirror neurons

Rizzolatti, G. (2005). The mirror neuron system and imitation. *Perspectives on Imitation: Mechanisms of Imitation and Imitation in Animals, 1,* 55.

Rizzolatti, G., Fadiga, L., Gallese, V., & Fogassi, L. (1996). Premotor cortex and the recognition of motor actions. *Cognitive Brain Research, 3*(2), 131–141.

Motor resonance

Fadiga, L., Craighero, L., & Olivier, E. (2005). Human motor cortex excitability during the perception of others' action. *Current Opinion in Neurobiology, 15*(2), 213–218.

Iacoboni, M. (2009). Imitation, empathy, and mirror neurons. *Annual Review of Psychology, 60,* 653–670.

Iacoboni, M. (2009). *Mirroring people: The science of empathy and how we connect with others.* New York, NY: Picador.

Mirror neurons in humans

Mukamel, R., Ekstrom, A. D., Kaplan, J., Iacoboni, M., & Fried, I. (2010). Single-neuron responses in humans during execution and observation of actions. *Current Biology, 20,* 750–756.

Children detect animacy from motion paths

Gelman, R., Durgin, F., & Kaufman, L. (1996). Distinguishing between animates and inanimates: Not by motion alone. In D. Sperber, D. Premack, & A. J. Premack (Eds.), *Causal Cognition: A Multidisciplinary Debate* (pp. 150–184). Oxford, England: Clarendon Press.

Brains of experts more reactive to viewed action

Calvo-Merino, B., Glaser, D. E., Grezes, J., Passingham, R. E., & Haggard, P. (2005). Action observation and acquired motor skills: An FMRI study with expert dancers. *Cerebral Cortex, 15*(8), 1243–1249.

Players better than coaches at predicting free throw success

Aglioti, S. M., Cesari, P., Romani, M., & Urgesi, C. (2008). Action anticipation and motor resonance in elite basketball players. *Nature Neuroscience, 11*(9), 1109–1116.

Knoblich, G., Butterfill, S., & Sebanz, N. (2011). Psychological research on joint action: Theory and data. *Psychology of Learning and Motivation, 54,* 59–101.

Understanding action from lights on moving joints

Johansson, G. (1973). Visual perception of biological motion and a model for its analysis. *Perception & Psychophysics, 14*(2), 201–211.

Kozlowski, L. T., & Cutting, J. E. (1977). Recognizing the sex of a walker from a dynamic point-light display. *Perception & Psychophysics, 21*(6), 575–580.

Recognition of self from viewed action better than recognition of others

Loula, F., Prasad, S., Harber, K., & Shiffrar, M. (2005). Recognizing people from their movement. *Journal of Experimental Psychology: Human Perception and Performance, 31,* 210.

Synchronizing action with others

Neda, Z., Ravasz, E., Brechte, Y., Vicsek, T., & Barabasi, A.-L. (2000). The sound of many hands clapping. *Nature, 403,* 849–850.

van Ulzen, N. R., Lamoth, C. J., Daffertshofer, A., Semin, G. R., & Beek, P. J. (2008). Characteristics of instructed and uninstructed interpersonal coordination while walking side-by-side. *Neuroscience Letters, 432*(2), 88–93.

Cooperation across species

Daura-Jorge, F. G., Cantor, M., Ingram, S. N., Lusseau, D., & Simões-Lopes, P. C. (2012). The structure of a bottlenose dolphin society is coupled to a unique foraging cooperation with artisanal fishermen. *Biology Letters*, rsbl20120174.

Hare, B., & Woods, V. (2013). *The genius of dogs*. London, England: Oneworld Publications.

Plotnik, J. M., Lair, R., Suphachoksahakun, W., & De Waal, F. B. (2011). Elephants know when they need a helping trunk in a cooperative task. *Proceedings of the National Academy of Sciences, 108*(12), 5116–5121.

Tomasello, M. (2009). *Why we cooperate*. Cambridge, MA: MIT Press.

Tomasello, M., & Vaish, A. (2013). Origins of human cooperation and morality. *Annual Review of Psychology, 64*, 231–255.

Visco-Comandini, F., Ferrari-Toniolo, S., Satta, E., Papazachariadis, O., Gupta, R., Nalbant, L. E., & Battaglia-Mayer, A. (2015). Do non-human primates cooperate? Evidences of motor coordination during a joint action task in macaque monkeys. *Cortex, 70*, 115–127.

Coordinating joint action

Knoblich, G., Butterfill, S., & Sebanz, N. (2011). Psychological research on joint action: Theory and data. *Psychology of Learning and Motivation, 54*, 59–101.

Knoblich, G., & Sebanz, N. (2008). Evolving intentions for social interaction: From entrainment to joint action. *Philosophical Transactions of the Royal Society of London B: Biological Sciences, 363*(1499), 2021–2031.

Sebanz, N., Bekkering, H., & Knoblich, G. (2006). Joint action: Bodies and minds moving together. *Trends in Cognitive Sciences, 10*(2), 70–76.

Sebanz, N., Knoblich, G., & Prinz, W. (2005). How two share a task: Corepresenting stimulus-response mappings. *Journal of Experimental Psychology: Human Perception and Performance, 31*(6), 1234.

Zacks, J. M., Tversky, B., & Iyer, G. (2001). Perceiving, remembering, and communicating structure in events. *Journal of Experimental Psychology: General, 130*(1), 29.

Coupled brains

Frith, U., & Frith, C. (2010). The social brain: Allowing humans to boldly go where no other species has been. *Philosophical Transactions of the Royal Society B: Biological Sciences, 365*(1537), 165–176.

Hasson, U., Ghazanfar, A. A., Galantucci, B., Garrod, S., & Keysers, C. (2012). Brain-to-brain coupling: A mechanism for creating and sharing a social world. *Trends in Cognitive Sciences, 16*(2), 114–121.

Hommel, B. (2011). The Simon effect as tool and heuristic. *Acta Psychologica, 136*(2), 189–202.

Hommel, B., Colzato, L. S., & Van Den Wildenberg, W. P. (2009). How social are task representations? *Psychological Science, 20*(7), 794–798.

Sebanz, N., Knoblich, G., Prinz, W., & Wascher, E. (2006). Twin peaks: An ERP study of action planning and control in coacting individuals. *Journal of Cognitive Neuroscience, 18*(5), 859–870.

Collaborating to create meaning in conversation

Clark, H. H. (1996). *Using language.* Cambridge, England: Cambridge University Press.

Imitation increases liking

Chartrand, T. L., & Van Baaren, R. (2009). Human mimicry. *Advances in Experimental Social Psychology, 41,* 219–274.

Van Baaren, R., Janssen, L., Chartrand, T. L., & Dijksterhuis, A. (2009). Where is the love? The social aspects of mimicry. *Philosophical Transactions of the Royal Society of London B: Biological Sciences, 364*(1528), 2381–2389.

CHAPTER TWO: THE BUBBLE AROUND THE BODY: PEOPLE, PLACES, AND THINGS

Fast judgments of people, places, and things

Biederman, I. (1972). Perceiving real-world scenes. *Science, 177,* 77–80.

Fei-Fei, L., Iyer, A., Koch, C., & Perona, P. (2007). What do we perceive in a glance of a real-world scene? *Journal of Vision, 7*(1), 10–10.

Greene, M. R., & Fei-Fei, L. (2014). Visual categorization is automatic and obligatory: Evidence from Stroop-like paradigm. *Journal of Vision, 14*(1), 14–14.

Greene, M. R., & Oliva, A. (2009). The briefest of glances: The time course of natural scene understanding. *Psychological Science, 20,* 464–472. doi:10.1111/j.1467-9280.2009.02316.x

Hafri, A., Papafragou, A., & Trueswell, J. C. (2013). Getting the gist of events: Recognition of two-participant actions from brief displays. *Journal of Experimental Psychology: General, 142*(3), 880.

Kahneman, D. (2011). *Thinking fast and slow.* New York, NY: Farrar, Straus and Giroux.

Kraus, M. W., Park, J. W., & Tan, J. J. (2017). Signs of social class: The experience of economic inequality in everyday life. *Perspectives on Psychological Science, 12*(3), 422–435.

Potter, M. C., & Levy, E. I. (1969). Recognition memory for a rapid sequence of pictures. *Journal of Experimental Psychology, 81,* 10–15.

Recovered vision deficits

Sinha, P. (2013). Once blind and now they see. *Scientific American, 309*(1), 48–55.

Von Senden, M. (1960). *Space and sight: The perception of space and shape in the congenitally blind before and after operation*. London, England: Metheun.

Brain regions specialized for people, places, things

Downing, P. E., Jiang, Y., Shuman, M., & Kanwisher, N. (2001). A cortical area selective for visual processing of the human body. *Science, 293*(5539), 2470–2473.

Grill-Spector, K., & Weiner, K. S. (2014). The functional architecture of the ventral temporal cortex and its role in categorization. *Nature Reviews Neuroscience, 15*(8), 536–548.

Kanwisher, N. (2010). Functional specificity in the human brain: A window into the functional architecture of the mind. *Proceedings of the National Academy of Sciences, 107*(25), 11163–11170.

Weiner, K. S., & Grill-Spector, K. (2013). Neural representations of faces and limbs neighbor in human high-level visual cortex: Evidence for a new organization principle. *Psychological Research, 77*(1), 74–97.

Extraordinary memory for dates

LePort, A. K., Mattfeld, A. T., Dickinson-Anson, H., Fallon, J. H., Stark, C. E., Kruggel, F., . . . McGaugh, J. L. (2012). Behavioral and neuroanatomical investigation of highly superior autobiographical memory (HSAM). *Neurobiology of Learning and Memory, 98*(1), 78–92.

Categories of things

Borges, J. L. (1966). *Other inquisitions 1937–1952*. New York, NY: Washington Square Press.

Brown, R. (1958). How shall a thing be called? *Psychological Review, 65*(1), 14.

Rosch, E. (1978). Principles of categorization. In E. Rosch & B. B. Lloyd (Eds.), *Cognition and categorization* (pp. 27–48). Hillsdale, NJ: Erlbaum. [I took the lovely Borges quote from Eleanor Rosch's influential paper summarizing her work on categorization.]

Rapid pace of word learning in toddlers

Miller, G. A., & Gildea, P. M. (1987). How children learn words. *Scientific American, 257*(3), 94–99. http://dx.doi.org/10.1038/scientificamerican0987

Basic level

Brown, R. (1958). How shall a thing be called? *Psychological Review, 65*(1), 14.

Markman, E. M. (1989). *Categorization and naming in children: Problems of induction.* Cambridge, MA: MIT Press.

Rosch, E. (1978). Principles of categorization. In E. Rosch & B. Lloyd (Eds.), *Cognition and categorization* (pp. 27–48). Hillsdale, NJ: Erlbaum.

Parts unite the basic level

Brown, R. (1958). How shall a thing be called? *Psychological Review, 65*(1), 14.

Rosch, E. (1978). Principles of categorization. In E. Rosch & B. Lloyd (Eds.), *Cognition and categorization* (pp. 27–48). Hillsdale, NJ: Erlbaum.

Tversky, B., & Hemenway, K. (1984). Objects, parts, and categories. *Journal of Experimental Psychology: General, 113*(2), 169.

Faces are special

Diamond, R., & Carey, S. (1986). Why faces are and are not special: An effect of expertise. *Journal of Experimental Psychology: General, 115*(2), 107.

Liu, J., Harris, A., & Kanwisher, N. (2010). Perception of face parts and face configurations: An fMRI study. *Journal of Cognitive Neuroscience, 22*(1), 203–211.

Tanaka, J. W., & Farah, M. J. (2003). The holistic representation of faces. In M. A. Peterson & G. Rhodes (Eds.), *Perception of faces, objects, and scenes: Analytic and holistic processes* (pp. 53–74). Oxford, England: Oxford University Press.

Face recognition ability

Wilmer, J. B. (2017). Individual differences in face recognition: A decade of discovery. *Current Directions in Psychological Science, 26,* 225–230. Summarized in Einstein, G., & May, C. (2018). Variations in face recognition ability: Stable, specific, and substantial. *APS Observer, 31,* 38–39.

Prosopagnosia

Calder, A. J., & Young, A. W. (2005). Understanding the recognition of facial identity and facial expression. *Nature Reviews Neuroscience, 6*(8), 641–651.

Duchaine, B. C., Parker, H., & Nakayama, K. (2003). Normal recognition of emotion in a prosopagnosic. *Perception, 32*(7), 827–838.

Rosenthal, G., Tanzer, M., Simony, E., Hasson, U., Behrmann, M., & Avidan, G. (2017). Altered topology of neural circuits in congenital prosopagnosia. *bioRxiv,* 100479.

Sacks, O. (2009). *The man who mistook his wife for a hat.* London, England: Picador.

Emotion and cooperation

Harari, Y. N. (2014). *Sapiens: A brief history of humankind*. New York, NY: Random House.

Feeling comes first

Frijda, N. H. (2000). The psychologists' point of view. In M. Lewis, J. M. Haviland-Jones, & L. F. Barrett (Eds.), *Handbook of emotions* (pp. 59–74). New York, NY: Guilford Press.

Frischen, A., Eastwood, J. D., & Smilek, D. (2008). Visual search for faces with emotional expressions. *Psychological Bulletin, 134*(5), 662–676.

Roberts, N. A., Levenson, R. W., & Gross, J. J. (2008). Cardiovascular costs of emotion suppression cross ethnic lines. *International Journal of Psychophysiology, 70*(1), 82–87.

Zajonc, R. B. (1984). On the primacy of affect. *American Psychologist, 39*(2), 117–123.

Empathy

Chartrand, T. L., & Bargh, J. A. (1999). The chameleon effect: The perception–behavior link and social interaction. *Journal of Personality and Social Psychology, 76*(6), 893.

Hatfield, E., & Rapson, R. L. (2010). Emotional contagion. In I. B. Weiner & W. E. Craighead (Eds.), *Encyclopedia of psychology*, 4th ed. Hoboken, NJ: Wiley.

Madsen, E. A., & Persson, T. (2013). Contagious yawning in domestic dog puppies (*Canis lupus familiaris*): The effect of ontogeny and emotional closeness on low-level imitation in dogs. *Animal Cognition, 16*(2), 233–240.

Romero, T., Konno, A., & Hasegawa, T. (2013). Familiarity bias and physiological responses in contagious yawning by dogs support link to empathy. *PLoS One, 8*(8), e71365.

Saxe, R., & Kanwisher, N. (2003). People thinking about thinking people: The role of the temporo-parietal junction in "theory of mind." *Neuroimage, 19*(4), 1835–1842.

Waters, S. F., West, T. V., & Mendes, W. B. (2014). Stress contagion: Physiological covariation between mothers and infants. *Psychological Science, 25*(4), 934–942.

Yong, M. H., & Ruffman, T. (2014). Emotional contagion: Dogs and humans show a similar physiological response to human infant crying. *Behavioural Processes, 108*, 155–165.

Recognizing emotions in faces

Ekman, P., & Friesen, W. V. (2003). *Unmasking the face: A guide to recognizing emotions from facial clues*. Los Altos, CA: Malor Books.

Oatley, K., Keltner, D., & Jenkins, J. M. (2006). *Understanding emotions*. Malden, MA: Blackwell.

Tracy, J. L., & Robins, R. W. (2008). The automaticity of emotion recognition. *Emotion, 8*(1), 81.

Nuances of emotions and emotion recognition

Barrett, L. F. (2006). Are emotions natural kinds? *Perspectives on Psychological Science, 1*(1), 28–58.

de Gelder, B., Meeren, H. K., Righart, R., Van den Stock, J., van de Riet, W. A., & Tamietto, M. (2006). Beyond the face: Exploring rapid influences of context on face processing. *Progress in Brain Research, 155*, 37–48.

Lewis, M., Haviland-Jones, J. M., & Barrett, L. F. (Eds.). (2010). *Handbook of emotions*. New York, NY: Guilford Press.

Russell, J. A. (1994). Is there universal recognition of emotion from facial expressions? A review of the cross-cultural studies. *Psychological bulletin, 115*(1), 102.

Russell, J. A., & Barrett, L. F. (1999). Core affect, prototypical emotional episodes, and other things called emotion: Dissecting the elephant. *Journal of Personality and Social Psychology, 76*(5), 805.

Taste recognition is nuanced

How does our sense of taste work? (2016, August 17). Retrieved from https://www.ncbi.nlm.nih.gov/pubmedhealth/PMH0072592/

Colors, basic and crayons

Berlin, B., & Kay, P. (1991). *Basic color terms: Their universality and evolution*. Berkeley: University of California Press.

Brown, R. W., & Lenneberg, E. H. (1954). A study in language and cognition. *Journal of Abnormal and Social Psychology, 49*, 454–462.

Crayola. (n.d.). Explore colors. Retrieved from http://www.crayola.com/explore-colors/

Rosch, E. H. (1973). Natural categories. *Cognitive psychology, 4*, 328–350.

Emotion appraisal depends on context and culture

Adolphs, R. (2002). Recognizing emotion from facial expressions: Psychological and neurological mechanisms. *Behavioral and Cognitive Neuroscience Reviews, 1*, 21–62.

Barrett, L. F. (2017). *How emotions are made: The secret life of the brain*. New York, NY: Houghton Mifflin Harcourt.

Barrett, L. F., Mesquita, B., & Gendron, M. (2011). Context in emotion perception. *Current Directions in Psychological Science, 20*, 286–290.

Mauss, I. B., Levenson, R. W., McCarter, L., Wilhelm, F. H., & Gross, J. J. (2005). The tie that binds? Coherence among emotion, experience, behavior, and physiology. *Emotion, 5,* 175–190.

Niedenthal, P. M. (2007). Embodying emotion. *Science, 316*(5827), 1002–1005.

Kuleshov effect

Baranowski, A. M., & Hecht, H. (2016). The auditory Kuleshov effect: Multisensory integration in movie editing. *Perception,* 0301006616682754.

Barratt, D., Rédei, A. C., Innes-Ker, Å., & Van de Weijer, J. (2016). Does the Kuleshov effect really exist? Revisiting a classic film experiment on facial expressions and emotional contexts. *Perception, 45*(8), 847–874.

Calbi, M., Heimann, K. Barratt, D. Siri, F., Umiltà Maria A., & Gallese, V. (2017). How context influences our perception of emotional faces: A behavioral study on the Kuleshov effect. *Frontiers in Psychology, 8,* 1684.

Mobbs, D., Weiskopf, N., Lau, H. C., Featherstone, E., Dolan, R. J., & Frith, C. D. (2006). The Kuleshov effect: The influence of contextual framing on emotional attributions. *Social Cognitive and Affective Neuroscience, 1*(2), 95–106.

Mind in the eye

Baron-Cohen, S., Wheelwright, S., Hill, J., Raste, Y., & Plumb, I. (2001). The "Reading the Mind in the Eyes" test revised version: A study with normal adults, and adults with Asperger syndrome or high-functioning autism. *Journal of Child Psychology and Psychiatry, 42*(2), 241–251.

Michaels, T. M., Horan, W. P., Ginger, E. J., Martinovich, Z., Pinkham, A. E., & Smith, M. J. (2014). Cognitive empathy contributes to poor social functioning in schizophrenia: Evidence from a new self-report measure of cognitive and affective empathy. *Psychiatry Research, 220,* 803–810.

New York Times. (2013, October 3). Can you read people's emotions [blog post]. Retrieved from https://well.blogs.nytimes.com/2013/10/03/well-quiz-the-mind-behind-the-eyes/

Warrier, V., Grasby, K. L., Uzefovsky, F., Toro, R., Smith, P., Chakrabarti, B., . . . Baron-Cohen, S. (2018). Genome-wide meta-analysis of cognitive empathy: Heritability, and correlates with sex, neuropsychiatric conditions and cognition. *Molecular Psychiatry, 23*(6), 1402–1409. doi:10.1038/mp.2017.122

Eyes dominate mouths in interpreting emotion

Lee, D. H., & Anderson, A. K. (2017). Reading what the mind thinks from what the eye sees. *Psychological Science, 28*(4) 494–503. doi:10.1177/0956797616687364

Rapid judgments of trust in faces predict elections outcomes

Ballew, C. C., & Todorov, A. (2007). Predicting political elections from rapid and unreflective face judgments. *Proceedings of the National Academy of Sciences, 104*(46), 17948–17953.

Olivola, C. Y., & Todorov, A. (2010). Elected in 100 milliseconds: Appearance-based trait inferences and voting. *Journal of Nonverbal Behavior, 34*(2), 83–110.

Todorov, A. (2017). *Face value.* Princeton, NJ: Princeton University Press.

Todorov, A., Olivola, C. Y., Dotsch, R., & Mende-Siedlecki, P. (2015). Social attributions from faces: Determinants, consequences, accuracy, and functional significance. *Annual Review of Psychology, 66,* 519–545.

Todorov, A., Said, C. P., Engell, A. D., & Oosterhof, N. N. (2008). Understanding evaluation of faces on social dimensions. *Trends in Cognitive Sciences, 12*(12), 455–460.

Emotion inferred from bodies

Aviezer, H., Bentin, S., Dudarev, V. & Hassin, R. R. (2011). The automaticity of emotional face-context integration. *Emotion, 11,* 1406–1414.

Aviezer, H., Trope, Y. & Todorov, A. (2012). Body cues, not facial expressions, discriminate between intense positive and negative emotions. *Science, 338,* 1225–1229.

Aviezer, H., Trope, Y., & Todorov, A. (2012). Holistic person processing: Faces with bodies tell the whole story. *Journal of Personality and Social Psychology, 103*(1), 20.

Coulson, M. (2004). Attributing emotion to static body postures: Recognition accuracy, confusions, and viewpoint dependence. *Journal of Nonverbal Behavior, 28*(2), 117–139.

De Gelder, B. (2009). Why bodies? Twelve reasons for including bodily expressions in affective neuroscience. *Philosophical Transactions of the Royal Society of London B: Biological Sciences, 364*(1535), 3475–3484.

Recognizing action from bodies

Downing, P. E., Jiang, Y., Shuman, M., & Kanwisher, N. (2001). A cortical area selective for visual processing of the human body. *Science, 293*(5539), 2470–2473.

Kourtzi, Z., & Kanwisher, N. (2000). Activation in human MT/MST by static images with implied motion. *Journal of Cognitive Neuroscience, 12*(1), 48–55.

Liu, J., Harris, A., & Kanwisher, N. (2010). Perception of face parts and face configurations: An fMRI study. *Journal of Cognitive Neuroscience, 22*(1), 203–211.

Schwarzlose, R. F., Baker, C. I., & Kanwisher, N. (2005). Separate face and body selectivity on the fusiform gyrus. *Journal of Neuroscience, 25*(47), 11055–11059.

Recognizing intention from gaze

Sartori, L., Becchio, C., & Castiello, U. (2011). Cues to intention: The role of movement information. *Cognition, 119*(2), 242–252.

Eye gaze in event understanding

Hard, B. M., Recchia, G., & Tversky, B. (2011). The shape of action. *Journal of Experimental Psychology: General, 140*(4), 586.

Mennie, N., Hayhoe, M., & Sullivan, B. (2007). Look-ahead fixations: Anticipatory eye movements in natural tasks. *Experimental Brain Research, 179,* 427–442. doi:10.1007/s00221-006-0804-0

Pierno, A. C., Becchio, C., Wall, M. B., Smith, A. T., Turella, L., & Castiello, U. (2006). When gaze turns into grasp. *Journal of Cognitive Neuroscience, 18,* 2130–2137. doi:10.1162/jocn.2006.18.12.2130

Sebanz, N., & Frith, C. (2004). Beyond simulation? Neural mechanisms for predicting the actions of others. *Nature Neuroscience, 7*(1), 5–6.

Understanding intention by infants

Brooks, R., & Meltzoff, A. N. (2005). The development of gaze following and its relation to language. *Developmental Science, 8*(6), 535–543.

D'Entremont, B., Hains, S. M. J., & Muir, D. W. (1997). A demonstration of gaze following in 3- to 6-month-olds. *Infant Behavior and Development, 20*(4), 569–572.

Sommerville, J. A., & Woodward, A. L. (2005). Pulling out the intentional structure of action: The relation between action processing and action production in infancy. *Cognition, 95*(1), 1–30.

Sommerville, J. A., Woodward, A. L., & Needham, A. (2005). Action experience alters 3-month-old infants' perception of others' actions. *Cognition, 96*(1), B1–B11.

Places of places in the brain

Epstein, R. A. (2008). Parahippocampal and retrosplenial contributions to human spatial navigation. *Trends in Cognitive Sciences, 12*(10), 388–396.

Epstein, R., & Kanwisher, N. (1998). A cortical representation of the local visual environment. *Nature, 392*(6676), 598–601.

Categories of scenes

Tversky, B., & Hemenway, K. (1983). Categories of environmental scenes. *Cognitive Psychology, 15*(1), 121–149.

Scene recognition is excellent

Biederman, I. (1972). Perceiving real-world scenes. *Science, 177*, 77–80.

Epstein, R. A., & Higgins, J. S. (2007). Differential parahippocampal and retrosplenial involvement in three types of visual scene recognition. *Cerebral Cortex, 17*, 1680–1693.

Greene, M. R., & Fei-Fei, L. (2014). Visual categorization is automatic and obligatory: Evidence from Stroop-like paradigm. *Journal of Vision, 14*(1), 14.

Madigan, S. (2014). Picture memory. In J. C. Yuille (Ed.), *Imagery, memory and cognition* (pp. 65–89). New York, NY: Psychology Press.

Potter, M. C., & Levy, E. I. (1969). Recognition memory for a rapid sequence of pictures. *Journal of Experimental Psychology, 81*, 10–15.

Shepard, R. N. (1967). Recognition memory for words, sentences, and pictures. *Journal of Verbal Learning and Verbal Behavior, 6*(1), 156–163.

Standing, L. (1973). Learning 10000 pictures. *Quarterly Journal of Experimental Psychology, 25*(2), 207–222.

Walther, D. B., Chai, B., Caddigan, E., Beck, D. M., & Fei-Fei, L. (2011). Simple line drawings suffice for functional MRI decoding of natural scene categories. *Proceedings of the National Academy of Sciences, 108*(23), 9661–9666.

Zhou, B., Lapedriza, A., Xiao, J., Torralba, A., & Oliva, A. (2014). Learning deep features for scene recognition using places database. *Advances in Neural Information Processing Systems, 27*, 487–495.

Change blindness

Simons, D. J., & Rensink, R. A. (2005). Change blindness: Past, present and future. *Trends in Cognitive Science, 9*, 16–20.

Categories and features

Malt, B. C., & Smith, E. E. (1984). Correlated properties in natural categories. *Journal of Memory and Language, 23*(2), 250.

Tversky, A. (1977). Features of similarity. *Psychological Review, 84*(4), 327.

Biological evolution

Pagel, M. (1999). Inferring the historical patterns of biological evolution. *Nature, 401*(6756), 877.

Correcting misconceptions in knowledge about the world

Rosling, H., Rönnlund, A. R., & Rosling, O. (2018). *Factfulness: Ten reasons we're wrong about the world—and why things are better than you think*. New York, NY: Flatiron Books.

Scenes, actions, and events

Hannigan, S. L., & Tippens Reinitz, M. (2001). A demonstration and comparison of two types of inference-based memory errors. *Journal of Experimental Psychology: Learning, Memory, and Cognition, 27*(4), 931.

Intraub, H. (1997). The representation of visual scenes. *Trends in Cognitive Sciences, 1*(6), 217–222.

Lampinen, J. M., Copeland, S. M., & Neuschatz, J. S. (2001). Recollections of things schematic: Room schemas revisited. *Journal of Experimental Psychology: Learning, Memory, and Cognition, 27*(5), 1211.

Owens, J., Bower, G. H., & Black, J. B. (1979). The "soap opera" effect in story recall. *Memory & Cognition, 7*(3), 185–191.

Tversky, B., & Marsh, E. J. (2000). Biased retellings of events yield biased memories. *Cognitive Psychology, 40*(1), 1–38.

Hypotheses override perception

Bruner, J. S., & Potter, M. C. (1964). Interference in visual recognition. *Science, 144*(3617), 424–425.

Biased perception

Hastorf, A. H., & Cantril, H. (1954). They saw a game; a case study. *Journal of Abnormal and Social Psychology, 49*(1), 129.

Confirmation bias

Ross, L. (1977). The intuitive psychologist and his shortcomings: Distortions in the attribution process. *Advances in Experimental Social Psychology, 10*, 173–220.

Nisbett, R. E., & Ross, L. (1980). *Human inference: Strategies and shortcomings of social judgement.* Englewood Cliffs, NJ: Prentice Hall.

Wason, P. C, & Johnson-Laird, P. N. (1972). *Psychology of reasoning: Structure and content.* Cambridge, MA: Harvard University Press.

Confirmation bias quote

Nickerson, R. S. (1998). Confirmation bias: A ubiquitous phenomenon in many guises. *Review of General Psychology, 2*(2), 211.

What is true for perception is true for all thought

Kahneman, D., & Tversky, A. (1996). On the reality of cognitive illusions. *Psychological Review, 103*, 582–591. http://dx.doi.org/10.1037/0033-295X.103.3.582

Feynman on visual thinking

Feynman, R. (1988). *"What do you care what other people think?": Further adventures of a curious character.* New York, NY: W. W. Norton.

CHAPTER THREE: HERE AND NOW AND THERE AND THEN: THE SPACES AROUND US

Spatial Frameworks

Franklin, N., & Tversky, B. (1990). Searching imagined environments. *Journal of Experimental Psychology: General, 119*(1), 63.

Imagining others' perspectives

Bryant, D. J., & Tversky, B. (1999). Mental representations of perspective and spatial relations from diagrams and models. *Journal of Experimental Psychology: Learning, Memory, and Cognition, 25*(1), 137.

Bryant, D. J., Tversky, B., & Franklin, N. (1992). Internal and external spatial frameworks for representing described scenes. *Journal of Memory and Language, 31*(1), 74–98.

Franklin, N., Tversky, B., & Coon, V. (1992). Switching points of view in spatial mental models. *Memory & Cognition, 20*(5), 507–518.

Tversky, B. (1991). Spatial mental models. *Psychology of Learning and Motivation, 27*, 109–145.

Tversky, B., Kim, J., & Cohen, A. (1999). Mental models of spatial relations and transformations from language. *Advances in Psychology, 128*, 239–258.

Remembering instead of looking

Bryant, D. J., Tversky, B., & Lanca, M. (2001). Retrieving spatial relations from observation and memory. In E. van der Zee & U. Nikanne (Eds.), *Conceptual structure and its interfaces with other modules of representation* (pp. 116–139). Oxford, England: Oxford University Press.

When taking another's perspective is easier than taking one's own

Cavallo, A., Ansuini, C., Capozzi, F., Tversky, B., & Becchio, C. (2017). When far becomes near: Perspective taking induces social remapping of spatial relations. *Psychological Science, 28*(1), 69–79. doi:10.1177/0956797616672464

Tversky, B., & Hard, B. M. (2009). Embodied and disembodied cognition: Spatial perspective-taking. *Cognition, 110*(1), 124–129.

Oldest map (so far)

Clarke, K. C. (2013). What is the world's oldest map? *Cartographic Journal, 50*(2), 136–143.

Utrilla, P., Mazo, C., Sopena, M. C., Martínez-Bea, M., & Domingo, R. (2009). A paleolithic map from 13,660 calBP: engraved stone blocks from the Late Magdalenian in Abauntz Cave (Navarra, Spain). *Journal of Human Evolution, 57*(2), 99–111.

Place and grid cells

Fyhn, M., Molden, S., Witter, M. P., Moser, E. I., & Moser, M. B. (2004). Spatial representation in the entorhinal cortex. *Science, 305*, 1258–1264.

Moser, E. I., Kropff, E., & Moser, M. B. (2008). Place cells, grid cells, and the brain's spatial representation system. *Annual Review of Neuroscience, 31.*

O'Keefe, J. (1976). Place units in the hippocampus of the freely moving rat. *Experimental Neurology, 51*, 78–109.

O'Keefe, J., & Nadel, L. (1978). *The hippocampus as a cognitive map.* Oxford, England: Clarendon Press.

Allocentric coding of space (even in babies)

Burgess, N. (2006). Spatial memory: How egocentric and allocentric combine. *Trends in Cognitive Science, 10*(12), 551–557.

Doeller, C. F., Barry, C., & Burgess, N. (2010). Evidence for grid cells in a human memory network. *Nature, 463*(7281), 657–661.

Ekstrom A., Kahana M. J., Caplan, J. B., Fields, T. A., Isham, E. A., Newman, E. L., & Fried, I. (2003). Cellular networks underlying human spatial navigation. *Nature, 425*, 184–188.

Jacobs, J., Weidemann, C. T., Miller, J. F., Solway, A., Burke, J. F., Wei, X. X., Suthana, N., . . . Kahan, M. J. (2013). Direct recordings of grid-like neuronal activity in human spatial navigation. *Nature Neuroscience, 16*, 1188–1190.

Kaufman, J., & Needham, A. (1999). Objective spatial coding by 6.5-month-old infants in a visual dishabituation task. *Developmental Science, 2*(4), 432–441.

Brain substrates for navigation

Epstein, R. A., Patai, E. Z., Julian, J. B., & Spiers, H. J. (2017). The cognitive map in humans: Spatial navigation and beyond. *Nature Neuroscience, 20*(11), 1504.

Marchette, S. A., Ryan, J., & Epstein, R. A. (2017). Schematic representations of local environmental space guide goal-directed navigation. *Cognition, 158*, 68–80.

Test for London taxi drivers

Knowledge Taxi. (n.d.). London knowledge. Retrieved from https://www.the-knowledgetaxi.co.uk/

Hippocampi of London taxi cab drivers grow larger

Maguire, E. A., Gadian, D. G., Johnsrude, I. S., Good, C. D., Ashburner, J., Frackowiak, R. S., & Frith, C. D. (2000). Navigation-related structural change in the hippocampi of taxi drivers. *Proceedings of the National Academy of Sciences, 97*(8), 4398–4403.

Neural reuse

Anderson, M. L. (2010). Neural reuse: A fundamental organizational principle of the brain. *Behavioral and Brain Sciences, 33*(4), 245–266.

Hippocampus for episodic memory

Eichenbaum, H., & Cohen, N. J. (2014). Can we reconcile the declarative memory and spatial navigation views on hippocampal function? *Neuron, 83*(4), 764–770.

Poppenk, J., Evensmoen, H. R., Moscovitch, M., & Nadel, L. (2013). Long-axis specialization of the human hippocampus. *Trends in Cognitive Sciences, 17*(5), 230–240.

H.M.

Corkin, S. (2002). What's new with the amnesic patient HM? *Nature Reviews Neuroscience, 3*(2), 153.

Milner, B., Corkin, S., & Teuber, H. L. (1968). Further analysis of the hippocampal amnesic syndrome: 14-year follow-up study of HM. *Neuropsychologia, 6*(3), 215–234.

Scoville, W. B., & Milner, B. (1957). Loss of recent memory after bilateral hippocampal lesions. *Journal of Neurology, Neurosurgery, and Psychiatry, 20*(1), 11.

Hippocampus plans future events

Addis, D. R., & Schacter, D. (2012). The hippocampus and imagining the future: Where do we stand? *Frontiers in Human Neuroscience, 5*, 173.

Bellmund, J. L., Deuker, L., Schröder, T. N., & Doeller, C. F. (2016). Grid-cell representations in mental simulation. *Elife, 5*, e17089.

Benoit, R. G., & Schacter, D. L. (2015). Specifying the core network supporting episodic simulation and episodic memory by activation likelihood estimation. *Neuropsychologia, 75*, 450–457.

Hassabis, D., Kumaran, D., & Maguire, E. A. (2007). Using imagination to understand the neural basis of episodic memory. *Journal of Neuroscience, 27*(52), 14365–14374.

Hassabis, D., & Maguire, E. A. (2007). Deconstructing episodic memory with construction. *Trends in Cognitive Sciences, 11*(7), 299–306.

Mullally, S. L., & Maguire, E. A. (2014). Memory, imagination, and predicting the future: A common brain mechanism? *Neuroscientist, 20*(3), 220–234.

Schacter, D. L. (2012). Adaptive constructive processes and the future of memory. *American Psychologist, 67*(8), 603.

Schacter, D. L., Benoit, R. G., & Szpunar, K. K. (2017). Episodic future thinking: Mechanisms and functions. *Current Opinion in Behavioral Sciences, 17*, 41–50.

Grid cells map space, time, and abstract relations

Gratitude to friends who are experts and who have helped me over the years to understand the many roles of hippocampal-entorhinal cortex and to find these references, especially Lynn Nadel, Morris Moscovitch, Dan Schacter, and Anthony Wagner. In previous years, John O'Keefe, Russell Epstein, Randy Gallistel, and Eleanor Maguire. They are in no way responsible for my oversimplification, and I hope it won't make them cringe.

Collin, S. H., Milivojevic, B., & Doeller, C. F. (2017). Hippocampal hierarchical networks for space, time, and memory. *Current Opinion in Behavioral Sciences, 17,* 71–76.

Constantinescu, A. O., O'Reilly, J. X., & Behrens, T. E. (2016). Organizing conceptual knowledge in humans with a gridlike code. *Science, 352*(6292), 1464–1468.

Deuker, L., Bellmund, J. L., Schröder, T. N., & Doeller, C. F. (2016). An event map of memory space in the hippocampus. *Elife, 5,* e16534.

Epstein, R. A., Patai, E. Z., Julian, J. B., & Spiers, H. J. (2017). The cognitive map in humans: Spatial navigation and beyond. *Nature Neuroscience, 20*(11), 1504.

Garvert, M. M., Dolan, R. J., & Behrens, T. E. (2017). A map of abstract relational knowledge in the human hippocampal-entorhinal cortex. *Elife, 6,* e17086.

Howard, M. W., & Eichenbaum, H. (2015). Time and space in the hippocampus. *Brain Research, 1621,* 345–354.

Stachenfeld, K. L., Botvinick, M. M., & Gershman, S. J. (2017). The hippocampus as a predictive map. *Nature Neuroscience, 20*(11), 1643.

Tavares, R. M., Mendelsohn, A., Grossman, Y., Williams, C. H., Shapiro, M., Trope, Y., & Schiller, D. (2015). A map for social navigation in the human brain. *Neuron, 87*(1), 231–243.

Spatial schemas in abstract thought

Gattis, M. (Ed.). (2003). *Spatial schemas and abstract thought.* Cambridge, MA: MIT Press.

Schubert, T. W., & Maass, A. (Eds.). (2011). *Spatial dimensions of social thought.* Berlin, Germany: Walter de Gruyter.

Systematic distortions in cognitive maps

Byrne, R. W. (1979). Memory for urban geography. *Quarterly Journal of Experimental Psychology, 31,* 147–154.

Hirtle, S. C., & Jonides, J. (1985). Evidence of hierarchies in cognitive maps. *Memory & Cognition, 13*(3), 208–217.

Hirtle, S. C., & Mascolo, M. F. (1986). The effect of semantic clustering on the memory of spatial locations. *Journal of Experimental Psychology: Learning, Memory and Cognition, 12*, 181–189.

Holyoak, K. J., & Mah, W. A. (1982). Cognitive reference points in judgments of symbolic magnitude. *Cognitive Psychology, 14*(3), 328–352.

Maki, R. H. (1981). Categorization and distance effects with spatial linear orders. *Journal of Experimental Psychology: Human Learning and Memory, 7*, 15–32.

McNamara, T. P., & Diwadkar, V. A. (1997). Symmetry and asymmetry of human spatial memory. *Cognitive Psychology, 34*(2), 160–190.

Milgram, S. (1976). Psychological maps of Paris. In H. M. Proshansky, W. Ittelson, & L. Rivlin (Eds.), *Environmental psychology: People and their physical settings* (pp. 104–124). New York, NY: Holt, Rinehart & Winston.

Portugali, Y. (1993). *Implicate relations: Society and space in the Israeli-Palestinian conflict.* The Netherlands: Kluwer.

Sadalla, E. K., Burroughs, W. J., & Staplin, L.J. (1980). Reference points in spatial cognition. *Journal of Experimental Psychology: Human Learning and Memory, 6*(5), 516.

Stevens, A., & Coupe, P. (1978). Distortions in judged spatial relations. *Cognitive Psychology, 10*(4), 422–437.

Tversky, B. (1981). Distortions in memory for maps. *Cognitive Psychology, 13*(3), 407–433.

Tversky, B. (1993). Cognitive maps, cognitive collages, and spatial mental models. In A. U. Frank & I. Compari (Eds.), *Conference on spatial information theory* (pp. 14–24). Berlin, Germany: Springer.

Tversky, B. (2000). Levels and structure of spatial knowledge. In R. Kitchin & S. Freundschuh (Eds.), *Cognitive mapping: Past, present and future* (pp. 24–43). New York, NY: Psychology Press.

Tversky, B. (2005). Functional significance of visuospatial representations. In P. Shah & A. Miyake (Eds.), *Cambridge Handbook of visuospatial thinking* (pp. 1–34). New York, NY: Cambridge University Press.

Tversky, B. (2018). Spatial biases in thought and judgment. In T. Hubbard (Ed.), *Spatial biases in perception and cognition.* Cambridge, England: Cambridge University Press.

Wilton, R. N. (1979). Knowledge of spatial relations: The specification of information used in making inferences. *Quarterly Journal of Experimental Psychology, 31*, 133–146.

Partonomies

Miller, G. A., & Johnson-Laird, P. N. (1976). *Language and perception.* Cambridge, MA: Belknap Press.

Tversky, B., & Hemenway, K. (1984). Objects, parts, and categories. *Journal of Experimental Psychology: General, 113*(2), 169.

Parallel distortions in social thought

Jones, E. E., Wood, G. C., & Quattrone, G. A. (1981). Perceived variability of personal characteristics in in-groups and out-groups: The role of knowledge and evaluation. *Personality and Social Psychology Bulletin, 7*(3), 523–528.

Park, B., & Rothbart, M. (1982). Perception of out-group homogeneity and levels of social categorization: Memory for the subordinate attributes of in-group and out-group members. *Journal of Personality and Social Psychology, 42*(6), 1051.

Quattrone, G. A. (1986). On the perception of a group's variability. In S. Worchel & W. Austin (Eds.), *The psychology of intergroup relations* (pp. 25–48). New York, NY: Nelson-Hall.

Rosch, E., Mervis, C. B., Gray, W. D., Johnson, D. M., & Boyes-Braem, P. (1978). Basic objects in natural categories. *Cognitive Psychology, 8*, 382–439.

Trope, Y., & Liberman, N. (2010). Construal-level theory of psychological distance. *Psychological Review, 117*, 440–463.

Asymmetric similarity

Rosch, E. (1975). Cognitive reference points. *Cognitive Psychology, 7*(4), 532–547.

Tversky, A. (1977). Features of similarity. *Psychological Review, 84*(4), 327.

Cognitive maps

Baird, J. C. (1979). Studies of the cognitive representation of spatial relations: I. Overview. *Journal of Experimental Psychology: General, 108*, 90–91.

Landau, B., Spelke, E., & Gleitman, H. (1984). Spatial knowledge in a young blind child. *Cognition, 16*, 225–260.

Tolman, E. C. (1948). Cognitive maps in rats and men. *Psychological Review, 55*, 189–208.

World can resolve ambiguities

Tversky, B. (2002). Navigating by mind and by body. In C. Freksa, W. Brauer, C. Habel, & K. F. Wender (Eds.), *Spatial cognition III* [Lecture Notes in Computer Science] (Vol. 2685). Berlin, Germany: Springer. https://doi.org/10.1007/3-540-45004-1_1

CHAPTER FOUR: TRANSFORMING THOUGHT

Mental rotation of objects

Shepard, R. N., & Cooper, L. A. (1986). *Mental images and their transformations*. Cambridge, MA: MIT Press.

Shepard, R. N., & Metzler, J. (1971). Mental rotation of three-dimensional objects. *Science, 171,* 701–703.

Part-by-part mental rotation

Just, M. A., & Carpenter, P. A. (1985). Cognitive coordinate systems: Accounts of mental rotation and individual differences in spatial ability. *Psychological Review, 92*(2), 137.

Mental rotation spatial ability test

Vandenberg, S. G., & Kuse, A. R. (1978). Mental rotations, a group test of three-dimensional spatial visualization. *Perceptual and Motor Skills, 47*(2), 599–604.

Rotating hands helps mental rotation

Chu, M., & Kita, S. (2008). Spontaneous gestures during mental rotation tasks: Insights into the microdevelopment of the motor strategy. *Journal of Experimental Psychology: General, 137*(4), 706.

Wexler, M., Kosslyn, S. M., & Berthoz, A. (1998). Motor processes in mental rotation. *Cognition, 68*(1), 77–94.

Mental rotation activates motor cortex

Zacks, J. M. (2008). Neuroimaging studies of mental rotation: A meta-analysis and review. *Journal of Cognitive Neuroscience, 20*(1), 1–19.

Mental rotation of one's body

Parsons, L. M. (1987). Imagined spatial transformation of one's body. *Journal of Experimental Psychology: General, 116*(2), 172.

Parsons, L. M. (1987). Imagined spatial transformations of one's hands and feet. *Cognitive Psychology, 19*(2), 178–241.

Zacks, J. M., Ollinger, J. M., Sheridan, M. A., & Tversky, B. (2002). A parametric study of mental spatial transformations of bodies. *Neuroimage, 16*(4), 857–872.

Zacks, J., Rypma, B., Gabrieli, J. D. E., Tversky, B., & Glover, G. H. (1999). Imagined transformations of bodies: An fMRI investigation. *Neuropsychologia, 37*(9), 1029–1040.

Zacks, J. M., & Tversky, B. (2005). Multiple systems for spatial imagery: Transformations of objects and bodies. *Spatial Cognition and Computation, 5*(4), 271–306.

Losing an arm slows mental rotation of hand

Nico, D., Daprati, E., Rigal, F., Parsons, L., & Sirigu, A. (2004). Left and right hand recognition in upper limb amputees. *Brain, 127*(1), 120–132.

Actually turning the body facilitates imagined turning

Klatzky, R. L., Loomis, J. M., Beall, A. C., Chance, S. S., & Golledge, R. G. (1998). Spatial updating of self-position and orientation during real, imagined, and virtual locomotion. *Psychological Science, 9*(4), 293–298.

No facilitation from actual translations for imagined translations

Rieser, J. J. (1989). Access to knowledge of spatial structure at novel points of observation. *Journal of Experimental Psychology: Learning, Memory, and Cognition, 15*(6), 1157.

More mental transformations: Mental scanning, mental shape comparison, mental transformations of size

Bundesen, C., Larsen, A., & Farrell, J. E. (1981). Mental transformations of size and orientation. *Attention and Performance, 9*, 279–294.

Denis, M., & Kosslyn, S. M. (1999). Scanning visual mental images: A window on the mind. *Cahiers de Psychologie Cognitive/Current Psychology of Cognition, 18*, 409–465.

Shepard, R. N., & Chipman, S. (1970). Second-order isomorphism of internal representations: Shapes of states. *Cognitive Psychology, 1*(1), 1–17.

Constructing mental images in parts

Finke, R. A., Pinker, S., & Farah, M. J. (1989). Reinterpreting visual patterns in mental imagery. *Cognitive Science, 13*(1), 51–78.

Kosslyn, S. M. (1980). *Image and mind*. Cambridge, MA: Harvard University Press.

Mental drawing underlies creating mental images

Novick, L. R., & Tversky, B. (1987). Cognitive constraints on ordering operations: The case of geometric analogies. *Journal of Experimental Psychology: General, 116*(1), 50–67.

Failures of imagining speed of motion: Pedestrian casualties

Guo, H., Wang, W., Guo, W., Jiang, X., & Bubb, H. (2012). Reliability analysis of pedestrian safety crossing in urban traffic environment. *Safety Science, 50*(4), 968–973.

Wierwille, W. W., Hanowski, R. J., Hankey, J. M., Kieliszewski, C. A., Lee, S. E., Medina, A., . . Dingus, T. A. (2002). *Identification and evaluation of driver errors: Overview and recommendations* (No. FHWA-RD-02-003). Washington, DC: National Academies of Sciences, Engineering, and Medicine.

People and dogs use heuristics to catch balls and Frisbees

McBeath, M. K., Shaffer, D. M., & Kaiser, M. K. (1995). How baseball outfielders determine where to run to catch fly balls. *Science, 268*(5210), 569.

Shaffer, D. M., Krauchunas, S. M., Eddy, M., & McBeath, M. K. (2004). How dogs navigate to catch Frisbees. *Psychological Science, 15*(7), 437–441.

Shaffer, D. M., & McBeath, M. K. (2005). Naive beliefs in baseball: Systematic distortion in perceived time of apex for fly balls. *Journal of Experimental Psychology: Learning, Memory, and Cognition, 31*(6), 1492.

Mental animation is step-by-step, not continuous

Hegarty, M. (1992). Mental animation: Inferring motion from static displays of mechanical systems. *Journal of Experimental Psychology: Learning, Memory, and Cognition, 18*(5), 1084.

Hegarty, M., & Sims, V. K. (1994). Individual differences in mental animation during mechanical reasoning. *Memory & Cognition, 22*(4), 411–430.

Spatial ability is multifaceted

Hegarty, M., & Waller, D. (2005). Individual differences in spatial abilities. In P. Shah & A. Miyake (Eds.), *The Cambridge handbook of visuospatial thinking* (pp. 121–169). New York, NY: Cambridge University Press.

Both genes and environment contribute to spatial ability

Tosto, M. G., Hanscombe, K. B., Haworth, C. M. A., Davis, O. S. P., Petrill, S. A., Dale, P. S., . . . Kovas, Y. (2014). Why do spatial abilities predict mathematical performance? *Developmental Science, 17,* 462–470. doi:10.1111/desc.12138

Genes for athletics

Epstein, D. (2014). *The sports gene: Inside the science of extraordinary athletic performance.* New York, NY: Penguin.

Several tests of spatial ability

Wai, J., Lubinski, D., & Benbow, C. P. (2009). Spatial ability for STEM domains: Aligning over 50 years of cumulative psychological knowledge solidifies its importance. *Journal of Educational Psychology, 101*(4), 817.

Gender and mental rotation

Halpern, D. F. (2013). *Sex differences in cognitive abilities.* New York, NY: Psychology Press.

Linn, M. C., & Petersen, A. C. (1985). Emergence and characterization of sex differences in spatial ability: A meta-analysis. *Child Development, 56*(6), 1479–1498.

Voyer, D. (2011). Time limits and gender differences on paper-and-pencil tests of mental rotation: A meta-analysis. *Psychonomic Bulletin and Review, 18*(2), 267–277.

Voyer, D., Voyer, S., & Bryden, M. P. (1995). Magnitude of sex differences in spatial abilities: A meta-analysis and consideration of critical variables. *Psychological Bulletin, 117,* 250–270.

Gender and object recognition

Herlitz, A., & Lovén, J. (2013). Sex differences and the own-gender bias in face recognition: A meta-analytic review. *Visual Cognition, 21*(9–10), 1306–1336.

Lewin, C., & Herlitz, A. (2002). Sex differences in face recognition—women's faces make the difference. *Brain and Cognition, 50*(1), 121–128.

McClure, E. B. (2000). A meta-analytic review of sex differences in facial expression processing and their development in infants, children, and adolescents. *Psychological Bulletin, 126*(3), 424–453.

Voyer, D., Postma, A., Brake, B., & Imperato-McGinley, J. (2007). Gender differences in object location memory: A meta-analysis. *Psychonomic Bulletin & Review, 14*(1), 23–38.

Spatial ability is important for STEM professions

Tosto, M. G., Hanscombe, K. B., Haworth, C. M. A., Davis, O. S. P., Petrill, S. A., Dale, P. S., . . . Kovas, Y. (2014). Why do spatial abilities predict mathematical performance? *Developmental Science, 17,* 462–470.

Wai, J., Lubinski, D., & Benbow, C. P. (2009). Spatial ability for STEM domains: Aligning over 50 years of cumulative psychological knowledge solidifies its importance. *Journal of Educational Psychology, 101*(4), 817.

Brain underpinnings for spatial and math skills overlap

Dehaene, S., Bossini, S., & Giraux, P. (1993). The mental representation of parity and number magnitude. *Journal of Experimental Psychology: General, 122,* 371–396.

Spatial skills important for explaining STEM concepts

Bobek, E., & Tversky, B. (2016). Creating visual explanations improves learning. *Cognitive Research: Principles and Implications, 1*(1), 27.

Daniel, M. P., & Tversky, B. (2012). How to put things together. *Cognitive Processing, 13*(4), 303–319.

Hegarty, M. (2004). Mechanical reasoning by mental simulation. *Trends in Cognitive Sciences, 8*(6), 280–285.

Hegarty, M., & Kozhevnikov, M. (1999). Types of visual-spatial representations and mathematical problem solving. *Journal of Educational Psychology, 91*(4), 684.

Tversky, B., Heiser, J., & Morrison, J. (2013). Space, time, and story. In B. H. Ross (Ed.), *The psychology of learning and motivation* (pp. 47–76). San Diego, CA: Elsevier Academic Press. https://doi.org/10.1016/B978-0-12-407237-4.12001-8

Spatial skills vary across professions

Blazhenkova, O., & Kozhevnikov, M. (2009). The new object-spatial-verbal cognitive style model: Theory and measurement. *Applied Cognitive Psychology, 23*(5), 638–663.

Blajenkova, O., Kozhevnikov, M., & Motes, M. A. (2006). Object-spatial imagery: A new self-report imagery questionnaire. *Applied Cognitive Psychology, 20*(2), 239–263.

Kozhevnikov, M., Kosslyn, S., & Shephard, J. (2005). Spatial versus object visualizers: A new characterization of visual cognitive style. *Memory & Cognition, 33*(4), 710–726.

Specific spatial skills underlie navigation

Hegarty, M., Richardson, A. E., Montello, D. R., Lovelace, K., & Subbiah, I. (2002). Development of a self-report measure of environmental spatial ability. *Intelligence, 30*(5), 425–447.

Gender and navigation

Dabbs, J. M., Chang, E. L., Strong, R. A., & Milun, R. (1998). Spatial ability, navigation strategy, and geographic knowledge among men and women. *Evolution and Human Behavior, 19*(2), 89–98.

Lawton, C. A. (1994). Gender differences in way-finding strategies: Relationship to spatial ability and spatial anxiety. *Sex Roles, 30*(11–12), 765–779.

The National Academy of Sciences recommends teaching spatial skills

Committee on Support for Thinking Spatially. (2006). *Learning to think spatially*. Washington, DC: National Academies Press.

Many activities build spatial skills

Dye, M. W., Green, C. S., & Bavelier, D. (2009). The development of attention skills in action video game players. *Neuropsychologia, 47*(8), 1780–1789.

Dye, M. W. G., Green, C. S., & Bavelier, D. (2009). Increasing speed of processing with action video games. *Current Directions in Psychological Science, 18*(6), 321–326.

Wrestling builds spatial skills

Moreau, D., Clerc, J., Mansy-Dannay, A., & Guerrien, A. (2012). Enhancing spatial ability through sport practice. *Journal of Individual Differences, 33,* 83–88.

Athletics and spatial skills

Voyer, D., & Jansen, P. (2017). Motor expertise and performance in spatial tasks: A meta-analysis. *Human Movement Science, 54,* 110–124.

Building spatial skills in children (and adults)

Ehrlich, S. B., Levine, S. C., & Goldin-Meadow, S. (2006). The importance of gesture in children's spatial reasoning. *Developmental Psychology, 42(6),* 1259–1268.

Ferrara, K., Golinkoff, R., Hirsh-Pasek, K., Lam, W., & Newcombe, N. (2011). Block talk: Spatial language during block play. *Mind, Brain and Education, 5(3),* 143–151.

Frick, A., & Wang, S. H. (2014). Mental spatial transformations in 14- and 16-month-old infants: Effects of action and observational experience. *Child Development, 85(1),* 278–293.

Joh, A. S., Jaswal, V. K., & Keen, R. (2011). Imagining a way out of the gravity bias: Preschoolers can visualize the solution to a spatial problem. *Child Development, 82(3),* 744–745.

Kastens, K. A., & Liben, L. S. (2007). Eliciting self-explanations improves children's performance on a field-based map skills task. *Cognition and Instruction, 25,* 45–74.

Levine, S. C., Ratliff, K. R., Huttenlocher, J., & Cannon, J. (2011). Early puzzle play: A predictor of preschoolers' spatial transformation skill. *Developmental Psychology, 48,* 530–542.

Liben, L. S., & Downs, R. M. (1989). Understanding maps as symbols: The development of map concepts in children. In H. W. Reese (Ed.), *Advances in child development and behavior* (Vol. 22, pp. 145–201). New York, NY: Academic Press.

Newcombe, N. S. (2010). Picture this: Increasing math and science learning by improving spatial thinking. *American Educator, 34(2),* 29.

Newcombe, N. S., & Fricke, A. (2010). Early education for spatial intelligence: Why, what, and how. *Mind, Brain, and Education, 4(3),* 102–111.

Newman, S. D., Mitchell Hansen, T., & Gutierrez, A. (2016). An fMRI study of the impact of block building and board games on spatial ability. *Frontiers in Psychology, 7,* 1278. doi:10.3389/fpsyg.2016.01278

Training spatial skills works

Uttal, D. H., Meadow, N. G., Tipton, E., Hand, L. L., Alden, A. R., Warren, C., & Newcombe, N. S. (2013). The malleability of spatial skills: A meta-analysis of training studies. *Psychological Bulletin, 139,* 352–402. doi:10.1037/a0028446

CHAPTER FIVE: THE BODY SPEAKS A DIFFERENT LANGUAGE

Gesture the foundation for language

Rizzolatti, G., & Arbib, M. A. (1998). Language within our grasp. *Trends in Neurosciences, 21*(5), 188–194.

Gestures in apes

Genty, E., & Zuberbühler, K. (2014). Spatial reference in a bonobo gesture. *Current Biology, 24*(14), 1601–1605.

Genty, E., & Zuberbühler, K. (2015). Iconic gesturing in bonobos. *Communicative & Integrative Biology, 8*(1), e992742.

Graham, K. E., Furuichi, T., & Byrne, R. W. (2017). The gestural repertoire of the wild bonobo (*Pan paniscus*): A mutually understood communication system. *Animal Cognition, 20*(2), 171–177.

Hobaiter, C., & Byrne, R. W. (2014). The meanings of chimpanzee gestures. *Current Biology, 24*(14), 1596–1600.

Moore, R. (2014). Ape gestures: Interpreting chimpanzee and bonobo minds. *Current Biology, 24*(14), R645–R647.

Pika, S., Liebal, K., & Tomasello, M. (2005). Gestural communication in subadult bonobos (*Pan paniscus*): Repertoire and use. *American Journal of Primatology, 65*(1), 39–61.

Cultural transmission in apes

Horner, V., Whiten, A., Flynn, E., & de Waal, F. B. (2006). Faithful replication of foraging techniques along cultural transmission chains by chimpanzees and children. *Proceedings of the National Academy of Sciences, 103*(37), 13878–13883.

Tomasello, M. (1994). Cultural transmission in the tool use and communicatory signaling of chimpanzees? In S. T. Parker & K. R. Gibson (Eds.), *"Language" and intelligence in monkeys and apes: Comparative developmental perspectives* (pp. 274–311). New York, NY: Cambridge University Press. http://dx.doi.org/10.1017/CBO9780511665486.012

Whiten, A., Horner, V., & De Waal, F. B. (2005). Conformity to cultural norms of tool use in chimpanzees. *Nature, 437*(7059), 737.

Entrainment

Brennan, S. E., & Clark, H. H. (1996). Conceptual pacts and lexical choice in conversation. *Journal of Experimental Psychology: Learning, Memory, and Cognition, 22*(6), 1482.

Holler, J., & Wilkin, K. (2011). Co-speech gesture mimicry in the process of collaborative referring during face-to-face dialogue. *Journal of Nonverbal Behavior, 35*(2), 133–153.

Mimicry is social glue

Chartrand, T. L., & Lakin, J. L. (2013). The antecedents and consequences of human behavioral mimicry. *Annual Review of Psychology, 64,* 285–308.

Chartrand, T. L., & Van Baaren, R. (2009). Human mimicry. *Advances in Experimental Social Psychology, 41,* 219–274

Emotion perception, imitation, and contagion

Decety, J., & Jackson, P. L. (2004). The functional architecture of human empathy. *Behavioral and Cognitive Neuroscience Reviews, 3*(2), 71–100.

Gallese, V., Keysers, C., & Rizzolatti, G. (2004). A unifying view of the basis of social cognition. *Trends in Cognitive Sciences, 8,* 396–403.

Gergely, G., & Watson, J. S. (1999). Early socio-emotional development: Contingency perception and the social-biofeedback model. *Early Social Cognition: Understanding Others in the First Months of Life, 60,* 101–136.

Hatfield, E., & Rapson, R. L. (2010). Emotional contagion. In I. B. Weiner & W. E. Craighead (Eds.), *Encyclopedia of psychology* (4th ed.). Hoboken, NJ: Wiley.

Meltzoff, A. N., & Moore, M. K. (1992). Early imitation within a functional framework: The importance of person identity, movement, and development. *Infant Behavior and Development, 15*(4), 479–505.

Oatley, K., Keltner, D., & Jenkins, J. M. (2006). *Understanding emotions.* Hoboken, NJ: Blackwell.

Early gesture predicts early speech

Iverson, J. M., & Goldin-Meadow, S. (2005). Gesture paves the way for language development. *Psychological Science, 16*(5), 367–371.

Özçalışkan, Ş., & Goldin-Meadow, S. (2005). Gesture is at the cutting edge of early language development. *Cognition, 96*(3), B101–B113.

The blind gesture

Goldin-Meadow, S. (2018, December 18). Harper lecture with Susan Goldin-Meadow: Hearing gesture: How our hands help us think [YouTube video]. Retrieved from https://www.youtube.com/watch?v=LXaQAtGybFc

Iverson, J. M., & Goldin-Meadow, S. (1997). What's communication got to do with it? Gesture in children blind from birth. *Developmental Psychology, 33*(3), 453.

Iverson, J. M., & Goldin-Meadow, S. (1998). Why people gesture when they speak. *Nature, 396*(6708), 228–228.

Iverson, J. M., & Goldin-Meadow, S. (2001). The resilience of gesture in talk: Gesture in blind speakers and listeners. *Developmental Science, 4*(4), 416–422.

Why gesture?

Cartmill, E. A., Goldin-Meadow, S., & Beilock, S. L. (2012). A word in the hand: Human gesture links representations to actions. *Philosophical Transactions of the Royal Society, 367*(1585), 129–143.

Goldin-Meadow, S., & Alibali, M. W. (2013). Gesture's role in speaking, learning, and creating language. *Annual Review of Psychology, 64,* 257.

Hostetter, A. B., & Alibali, M. W. (2008). Visible embodiment: Gestures as simulated action. *Psychonomic Bulletin & Review, 15*(3), 495–514.

Kinds of gestures

Goldin-Meadow, S. (2005). *Hearing gesture: How our hands help us think.* Cambridge, MA: Harvard University Press.

Kendon, A. (2004). *Gesture: Visible action as utterance.* Cambridge, England: Cambridge University Press.

McNeill, D. (1992). *Hand and mind: What gestures reveal about thought.* Chicago, IL: University of Chicago Press.

McNeill, D. (2006). Gesture: A psycholinguistic approach. In K. Brown (Ed.), *The encyclopedia of language and linguistics* (2nd ed., pp. 58–66). New York, NY: Elsevier Science.

Deixis

Fillmore, C. J. (1982). Towards a descriptive framework for spatial deixis. In R. J. Jarvella & W. Klein (Eds.), *Speech, place and action: Studies in deixis and related topics* (pp. 31–59). London, England: Wiley.

Depicting as communication

Clark, H. H. (2016). Depicting as a method of communication. *Psychological Review, 123*(3), 324–347.

Metaphors

Lakoff, G., & Johnson, M. (2008). *Metaphors we live by.* Chicago, IL: University of Chicago Press.

Gesture in explanations often precedes words developmentally

Alibali, M.W., & Goldin-Meadow, S. (1993). Gesture-speech mismatch and mechanisms of learning: What the hands reveal about a child's state of mind. *Cognitive Psychology, 25,* 468–523.

Goldin-Meadow, S., Alibali, M. W., & Church, R. B. (1993). Transitions in concept acquisition: Using the hand to read the mind. *Psychological Review, 100*(2), 279.

Gestures signal readiness to learn to teachers

Goldin-Meadow, S., & Sandhofer, C. M. (1999). Gesture conveys substantive information about a child's thoughts to ordinary listeners. *Developmental Science, 2*, 67–74.

Goldin-Meadow, S., & Singer, M. A. (2003). From children's hands to adults' ears: Gesture's role in the learning process. *Developmental Psychology, 39*, 509–520.

Gestures show strategies not conveyed in speech

Broaders, S. C., Cook, S. W., Mitchell, Z., & Goldin-Meadow, S. (2007). Making children gesture brings out implicit knowledge and leads to learning. *Journal of Experimental Psychology: General, 136*, 539–550.

Emotion

LeDoux, J. (1998). *The emotional brain: The mysterious underpinnings of emotional life.* New York, NY: Simon & Schuster.

Lewis, M., Haviland-Jones, J. M., & Barrett, L. F. (Eds.). (2010). *Handbook of emotions.* New York, NY: Guilford Press.

Oatley, K., Keltner, D., & Jenkins, J. M. (2006). *Understanding emotions.* Hoboken, NJ: Blackwell Publishing.

Mirroring emotion

Gallese, V., Keysers, C., & Rizzolatti, G. (2004). A unifying view of the basis of social cognition. *Trends in Cognitive Science, 8*(9), 396–403.

Using space to describe space

Emmorey, K., Tversky, B., & Taylor, H. A. (2000). Using space to describe space: Perspective in speech, sign, and gesture. *Spatial Cognition and Computation, 2*(3), 157–180.

Using space to order time

Bender, A., & Beller, S. (2014) Mapping spatial frames of reference onto time: A review of theoretical accounts and empirical findings. *Cognition, 132*, 342–382.

Boroditsky, L., Fuhrman, O., & McCormick, K. (2011). Do English and Mandarin speakers think about time differently? *Cognition, 118*(1), 123–129.

Marghetis, T., & Núñez, R. (2013). The motion behind the symbols: A vital role for dynamism in the conceptualization of limits and continuity in expert mathematics. *Topics in Cognitive Science, 5*(2), 299–316.

Núñez, R., & Cooperrider, K. (2013). The tangle of space and time in human cognition. *Trends in Cognitive Sciences, 17*(5), 220–229.

Tversky, B., Kugelmass, S., & Winter, A. (1991). Cross-cultural and developmental trends in graphic productions. *Cognitive Psychology, 23*(4), 515–557.

Gestures help explain action and causality

Engle, R. A. (1998). Not channels but composite signals: Speech, gesture, diagrams and object demonstrations are integrated in multimodal explanations. In *Proceedings of the Twentieth Annual Conference of the Cognitive Science Society* (pp. 321–326). New York, NY: Psychology Press.

Kang, S., Tversky, B., & Black, J. B. (2015). Coordinating gesture, word, and diagram: Explanations for experts and novices. *Spatial Cognition & Computation, 15*(1), 1–26.

Sitting on hands disrupts speaking

Krauss, R. M. (1998). Why do we gesture when we speak? *Current Directions in Psychological Science, 7*(2), 54–60.

Krauss, R. M., Chen, Y., & Gottesman, R. F. (2000). Lexical gestures and lexical access: A process model. *Language and Gesture, 2*, 261.

Gestures help thinking

Carlson, R. A., Avraamides, M. N., Cary, M., & Strasberg, S. (2007). What do the hands externalize in simple arithmetic? *Journal of Experimental Psychology: Learning, Memory, and Cognition, 33*(4), 747.

Chu, M., & Kita, S. (2008). Spontaneous gestures during mental rotation tasks: Insights into the microdevelopment of the motor strategy. *Journal of Experimental Psychology: General, 137*(4), 706.

Schwartz, D. L. (1999). Physical imagery: Kinematic versus dynamic models. *Cognitive Psychology, 38*(3), 433–464.

Schwartz, D. L., & Black, J. B. (1996). Shuttling between depictive models and abstract rules: Induction and fallback. *Cognitive Science, 20*(4), 457–497.

Gestures for self help solve spatial problems

Jamalian, A., Giardino, V., & Tversky, B. (2013). Gestures for thinking. *Proceedings of the Annual Meeting of the Cognitive Science Society, 35*. Retrieved from https://escholarship.org/uc/item/0zk7z5h9

Tversky, B., & Kessell, A. (2014). Thinking in action. *Pragmatics & Cognition, 22*(2), 206–223.

Gestures lighten cognitive load

Cook, S.W., Yip, T., & Goldin-Meadow, S. (2012). Gestures, but not meaningless movements, lighten working memory load when explaining math. *Language and Cognitive Processing, 27,* 594–610.

Goldin-Meadow, S., Nusbaum, H., Kelly, S. D., & Wagner, S. M. (2001). Explaining math: Gesturing lightens the load. *Psychological Science, 12,* 516–522.

Ping, R., & Goldin-Meadow, S. (2010). Gesturing saves cognitive resources when talking about nonpresent objects. *Cognitive Science, 34,* 602–619.

Gesture helps mechanical problem solving

Schwartz, D. L., & Black, J. B. (1996). Shuttling between depictive models and abstract rules: Induction and fallback. *Cognitive Science, 20*(4), 457–497.

Gestures better than imagery for dynamic problem solving

Schwartz, D. L. (1999). Physical imagery: Kinematic versus dynamic models. *Cognitive Psychology, 38*(3), 433–464.

Gesture helps mental rotation

Chu, M., & Kita, S. (2008). Spontaneous gestures during mental rotation tasks: Insights into the microdevelopment of the motor strategy. *Journal of Experimental Psychology: General, 137*(4), 706.

Wexler, M., Kosslyn, S. M., & Berthoz, A. (1998). Motor processes in mental rotation. *Cognition, 68*(1), 77–94.

Gesture for self helps comprehension and memory of complex systems

Liu, Y., Bradley, M., & Tversky, B. (2018). Gestures for self help learning complex systems. *Proceedings of Embodied and Situated Language Processing.*

Gesture for self helps (or hinders) spatial problem solving

Tversky, B., & Kessell, A. (2014). Thinking in action. *Pragmatics & Cognition, 22*(2), 206–223.

Learned gestures help math

Goldin-Meadow, S., Cook, S. W., & Mitchell, Z. A. (2009). Gesturing gives children new ideas about math. *Psychological Science, 20,* 267–272. doi:10.1111/j.1467-9280.2009.02297.x

Congruent touchpad gestures help math problem solving

Segal, A., Tversky, B., & Black, J. (2014). Conceptually congruent actions can promote thought. *Journal of Applied Research in Memory and Cognition, 3*(3), 124–130.

Babies benefit from gesture

Acredolo, L. P., & Goodwyn, S. W. (2002). *Baby signs: How to talk with your baby before your baby can talk*. New York, NY: McGraw-Hill.

Gestures help children understand set and cardinality

Alibali, M. W., & DiRusso, A. A. (1999). The function of gesture in learning to count: More than keeping track. *Cognitive Development, 14*(1), 37–56.

Gelman, R., & Gallistel, C. R. (1986). *The child's understanding of number*. Cambridge, MA: Harvard University Press.

Jamalian, A. (2014). *Grouping gestures promote children's effective counting strategies by adding a layer of meaning through action* (unpublished doctoral dissertation). Columbia University, New York, NY.

People make larger gestures for others than for self

Bavelas, J. B., Chovil, N., Coates, L., & Roe, L. (1995). Gestures specialized for dialogue. *Personality and Social Psychology Bulletin, 21*(4), 394–405.

Goldin-Meadow, S. (2005). *Hearing gesture: How our hands help us think*. Cambridge, MA: Harvard University Press.

McNeill, D. (1992). *Hand and mind: What gestures reveal about thought*. Chicago, IL: University of Chicago Press.

Learning action of complex systems is harder than learning structure

Hmelo-Silver, C. E., & Pfeffer, M. G. (2004). Comparing expert and novice understanding of a complex system from the perspective of structures, behaviors, and functions. *Cognitive Science, 28*(1), 127–138.

Tversky, B., Heiser, J., & Morrison, J. (2013). Space, time, and story. In B. H. Ross (Ed.), *The psychology of learning and motivation* (pp. 47–76). San Diego, CA: Elsevier Academic Press. https://doi.org/10.1016/B978-0-12-407237-4.12001-8

Teachers' action gestures give students deep understanding of actions of complex systems

Kang, S., & Tversky, B. (2016). From hands to minds: Gestures promote understanding. *Cognitive Research: Principles and Implications, 1*(1), 4.

Diagrams help understanding of simultaneity

Glenberg, A. M., & Langston, W. E. (1992). Comprehension of illustrated text: Pictures help to build mental models. *Journal of Memory and Language, 31*, 129–151.

Gestures alter thinking about time: Simultaneity, cyclicity, and perspective

Jamalian, A., & Tversky, B. (2012). Gestures alter thinking about time. In N. Miyake, D. Peebles, & R. P. Cooper (Eds.), *Proceedings of the 34th annual conference of the Cognitive Science Society* (pp. 551–557). Austin, TX: Cognitive Science Society.

History of math notation

Ifrah, G., (2000). *The universal history of computing: From the abacus to quantum computing.* Translated by E. F. Harding, D. Bellos, & S. Wood. New York, NY: Wiley.

Gestures help coordinate conversation

Clark, H. H. (1992). *Arenas of language use.* Chicago, IL: University of Chicago Press.

Clark, H. H. (1996). *Using language.* Cambridge, England: Cambridge University Press.

Garrod, S., & Pickering, M. J. (2009). Joint action, interactive alignment and dialogue. *Topics in Cognitive Science, 1*(2), 292–304.

Goodwin, C. (1981). *Conversational organization: Interaction between speakers and hearers.* New York, NY: Academic Press.

McNeill, D. (1992). *Hand and mind: What gestures reveal about thought.* Chicago, IL: University of Chicago Press.

Gesture and diagram working together

Engle, R. A. (1998). Not channels but composite signals: Speech, gesture, diagrams and object demonstrations are integrated in multimodal explanations. In *Proceedings of the Twentieth Annual Conference of the Cognitive Science Society* (pp. 321–326). New York, NY: Psychology Press.

Heiser, J., Tversky, B., & Silverman, M. (2004). Sketches for and from collaboration. *Visual and Spatial Reasoning in Design III, 3,* 69–78.

Gestures explode when designers get new ideas

Edelman, J. A. (2011). *Understanding radical breaks: Media and behavior in small teams engaged in redesign scenarios* (Unpublished doctoral dissertation). Stanford University, Stanford, CA.

Edelman, J., Agarwal, A., Paterson, C., Mark, S., & Leifer, L. (2012). Understanding radical breaks. In H. Plattner, C. Meinel, & L. Leifer (Eds.), *Design Thinking Research* (pp. 31–51). Berlin, Germany: Springer, Berlin, Heidelberg.

Edelman, J. A., & Leifer, L. (2012). Qualitative methods and metrics for assessing wayfinding and navigation in engineering design. In H. Plattner, C. Meinel, & L. Leifer (Eds.), *Design Thinking Research* (pp. 151–181). Berlin, Germany: Springer, Berlin, Heidelberg.

Gestures sketch dance

Kirsh, D. (2010). *Thinking with the body*. Paper presented at the 32nd Annual Conference of the Cognitive Science Society, Austin, TX.

Kirsh, D. (2011). How marking in dance constitutes thinking with the body. *Versus: Quaderni di Studi Semiotici*, 113–115, 179–210.

Conducting music

Kumar, A. B., & Morrison, S. J. (2016). The conductor as visual guide: Gesture and perception of musical content. *Frontiers in Psychology*, 7, 1049.

Visual more important than auditory in judgment of music

Tsay, C. J. (2013). Sight over sound in the judgment of music performance. *Proceedings of the National Academy of Sciences*, 110(36), 14580–14585.

Creative feats of spatial thinking

Biello, D. (2006, December 8). Fact or fiction?: Archimedes coined the term "Eureka!" in the bath. *Scientific American*. Retrieved from https://www.scientificamerican.com/article/fact-or-fiction-archimede/

Shepard, R. N. (1978). Externalization of mental images and the act of creation. *Visual Learning, Thinking, and Communication*, 133–189.

CHAPTER SIX: POINTS, LINES, AND PERSPECTIVE: SPACE IN TALK AND THOUGHT

Lao Tzu quote

Le but n'est pas seulement le but, mais le chemin qui y conduit. (n.d.). Paul Andreu. Retrieved from http://www.paul-andreu.com/ [Note: This quote has been attributed to Lao-Tzu but may be from Confucius. In French, it is beautiful partly because of the multiple meanings of *but*: end, goal, destination.]

Structure of route descriptions

Denis, M. (1997). The description of routes: A cognitive approach to the production of spatial discourse. *Cahiers de psychologie cognitive*, 16(4), 409–458.

Levelt, W. J. M. (1989). *Speaking: From intention to articulation.* Cambridge, MA: MIT Press.

Structure of route maps

Tversky, B., & Lee, P. (1999). Pictorial and verbal tools for conveying routes. In C. Freksa & D. M. Mark (Eds.), *Spatial information theory. Cognitive and computational foundations of geographic information science. Lecture Notes in Computer Science* (Vol. 1661). Berlin, Germany: Springer, Berlin, Heidelberg.

Preferring others' perspectives

Mainwaring, S. D., Tversky, B., Ohgishi, M., & Schiano, D. J. (2003). Descriptions of simple spatial scenes in English and Japanese. *Spatial Cognition and Computation, 3*(1), 3–42.

Schober, M. F. (1993). Spatial perspective-taking in conversation. *Cognition, 47*(1), 1–24.

Odd specification of address succeeds

Abed, F. (2017, August 11). Delivering a package in a city short on street names. *New York Times.*

People spontaneously mix perspectives

Taylor, H. A., & Tversky, B. (1992). Descriptions and depictions of environments. *Memory & Cognition, 20*(5), 483–496.

Mixing perspectives slows understanding, but only briefly

Lee, P. U., & Tversky, B. (2005). Interplay between visual and spatial: The effect of landmark descriptions on comprehension of route/survey spatial descriptions. *Spatial Cognition & Computation, 5*(2–3), 163–185.

People mix perspectives when describing environments

Taylor, H. A., & Tversky, B. (1992). Descriptions and depictions of environments. *Memory and Cognition, 20*(5), 483–496.

People understand descriptions that mix perspectives

Lee, P. U., & Tversky, B. (2005). Interplay between visual and spatial: The effect of landmark descriptions on comprehension of route/survey spatial descriptions. *Spatial Cognition & Computation, 5*(2–3), 163–185.

Taylor, H. A., & Tversky, B. (1992). Spatial mental models derived from survey and route descriptions. *Journal of Memory and Language, 31*(2), 261–292.

Different languages describe space differently

Levinson, S. C. (2003). *Space in language and cognition: Explorations in cognitive diversity* (Vol. 5). Cambridge, England: Cambridge University Press.

New Guinea sketch maps

Harley, J. B. and Woodward, D. (Eds.). (1992). *The history of cartography. Vol. 2. Book One: Cartography in the traditional Islamic and South Asian societies.* Chicago, IL: University of Chicago Press.

Survey sketch maps are networks

Fontaine, S., Edwards, G., Tversky, B., & Denis, M. (2005). Expert and non-expert knowledge of loosely structured environments. In D. Mark & T. Cohn (Eds.), *Spatial information theory: Cognitive and computational foundations.* Berlin, Germany: Springer.

CHAPTER SEVEN: BOXES, LINES, AND TREES: TALK AND THOUGHT ABOUT ALMOST EVERYTHING ELSE

Susan Sontag on center and middle

Cott, J. (2013). *Susan Sontag: The complete* Rolling Stone *interview*. New Haven, CT: Yale University Press.

How language describes space

Talmy, L. (1983). How language structures space. In H. L. Pick & L. P. Acredolo (Eds.), *Spatial orientation* (pp. 225–282). Boston, MA: Springer.

Forms in art and architecture

Arnheim, R. (1969). *Visual thinking*. Berkeley: University of California Press.
Arnheim, R. (1982). *The Power of the center: A study of composition in the visual arts*. Berkeley: University of California Press.
Kandinsky, W. (1947). *Point and line to plane*. New York, NY: Guggenheim Foundation.
Klee, P. (1953). *Pedagogical Notebook*. New York, NY: Praeger.

Trees are ancient representations of knowledge

Eco, U. (1984). Metaphor, dictionary, and encyclopedia. *New Literary History, 15*(2), 255–271.
Gontier, N. (2011). Depicting the Tree of Life: The philosophical and historical roots of evolutionary tree diagrams. *Evolution: Education and Outreach, 4*(3), 515–538.
Lima, M. (2014). *The book of trees: Visualizing branches of knowledge*. Princeton, NJ: Princeton Architectural Press.

Branching in neurons

Cajal, S. R. (1995). *Histology of the nervous system of man and vertebrates* (Vol. 1). Translated by N. Swanson & L. Swanson. New York, NY: Oxford University Press.

Galbis-Reig, D. (2004). Sigmund Freud, MD: Forgotten contributions to neurology, neuropathology, and anesthesia. *Internet Journal of Neurology, 3*, (1).

Triarhou, L. C. (2009). Exploring the mind with a microscope: Freud's beginnings in neurobiology. *Hellenic Journal of Psychology, 6*, 1–13.

Trees as visualizations

Lima, M. (2014). *The book of trees: Visualizing branches of knowledge*. Princeton, NJ: Princeton Architectural Press.

Six degrees of separation

Dodds, P. S., Muhamad, R., & Watts, D. J. (2003). An experimental study of search in global social networks. *Science, 301*(5634), 827–829.

Travers, J., & Milgram, S. (1967). The small world problem. *Psychology Today, 1*(1), 61–67.

Social networks

Henderson, M. D., Fujita, K., Trope, Y., & Liberman, N. (2006). Transcending the "here": The effect of spatial distance on social judgment. *Journal of Personality and Social Psychology, 91*(5), 845.

Yu, L., Nickerson, J. V., & Tversky, B. (2010, August 9–11). Discovering perceptions of personal social networks through diagrams. In A. K. Goel, M. Jamnik, & N. H. Narayanan (Eds.), *Diagrammatic representation and inference: 6th International Conference, Diagrams 2010, Portland, OR, USA, August 9-11, 2010, Proceedings* (pp. 352–354). Berlin, Germany: Springer-Verlag Berlin Heidelberg. doi:10.1007/978-3-642-14600-8

Creating tree visualizations

Munzner, T. (2014). *Visualization analysis and design*. Boca Raton, FL: CRC Press.

Shneiderman, B. (1992). Tree visualization with tree-maps: 2-d space-filling approach. *ACM Transactions on Graphics (TOG), 11*(1), 92–99.

Ancient depictions of time on a line

Hassig, R. (2001). *Time, history, and belief in Aztec and colonial Mexico*. Austin: University of Texas Press.

Sharer, R. J., & Traxler, L. P. (2006). *The ancient Maya*. Stanford, CA: Stanford University Press.

Smith, W. S., & Simpson, W. K. (1998). *The art and architecture of ancient Egypt*. New Haven, CT: Yale University Press.

Mixed time metaphors

New York Times. (2017, November 26). Weekend briefing newsletter.

Ego-moving or time-moving metaphors

Boroditsky, L. (2000). Metaphoric structuring: Understanding time through spatial metaphors. *Cognition, 75*(1), 1–28.

Clark, H. H. (1973). Time, space, semantics, and the child. In T. E. Moore (Ed.), *Cognitive development and the acquisition of language* (pp. 27–63). New York, NY: Academic Press.

McGlone, M. S., & Harding, J. L. (1998). Back (or forward?) to the future: The role of perspective in temporal language comprehension. *Journal of Experimental Psychology: Learning, Memory, and Cognition, 24,* 1211–1223.

Space structures time (not vice versa)

Boroditsky, L. (2000). Metaphoric structuring: Understanding time through spatial metaphors. *Cognition, 75*(1), 1–28.

Language and space

Clark, H. H. (1973). Space, time, semantics, and the child. In T. E. Moore (Ed.), *Cognitive development and the acquisition of language* (pp. 27–63). New York, NY: Academic Press.

Talmy, L. (1983). How language structures space. In H. L. Pick Jr. & L. P. Acredolo (Eds.), *Spatial orientation: Theory, research and application* (pp. 225–282). New York, NY: Plenum.

Gestures alter thinking about time

Jamalian, A., & Tversky, B. (2012). Gestures alter thinking about time. In N. Miyake, D. Peebles, & R. P. Cooper (Eds.), *Proceedings of the Cognitive Science Society, 34,* 551–557.

Distortions in memory for events in time

Huttenlocher, J., Hedges, L. V., & Prohaska, V. (1988). Hierarchical organization in ordered domains: Estimating the dates of events. *Psychological Review, 95,* 471–484.

Loftus, E. F., & Marburger, W. (1983). Since the eruption of Mt. St. Helens, has anyone beaten you up? Improving the accuracy of retrospective reports with landmark events. *Memory and Cognition, 11,* 114–120.

Homeostasis

Bernard, C. (1927). *An introduction to the study of experimental medicine.* Translated by H. C. Greene. New York, NY: Macmillan. (Original work published 1865)

Cannon, W. B. (1963). *The wisdom of the body.* New York, NY: Norton Library. (Original work published 1932)

Feedback in computers

Wiener, N. (1961). *Cybernetics or control and communication in the animal and the machine* (Vol. 25). Cambridge, MA: MIT Press.

Past is in front in Aymara language

Núñez, R., & Cooperrider, K. (2013). The tangle of space and time in human cognition. *Trends in Cognitive Sciences, 17*(5), 220–229.

Núñez, R. E., & Sweetser, E. (2006). With the future behind them: Convergent evidence from Aymara language and gesture in the crosslinguistic comparison of spatial construals of time. *Cognitive Science, 30*(3), 401–450.

Future is sometimes down in Mandarin (and calendars)

Boroditsky, L. (2001). Does language shape thought? Mandarin and English speakers' conceptions of time. *Cognitive Psychology, 43*(1), 1–22.

Fuhrman, O., McCormick, K., Chen, E., Jiang, H., Shu, D., Mao, S., & Boroditsky, L. (2011). How linguistic and cultural forces shape conceptions of time: English and Mandarin time in 3D. *Cognitive Science, 35*(7), 1305–1328.

Direction of time is direction of writing

Tversky, B., Kugelmass, S., & Winter, A. (1991). Cross-cultural and developmental trends in graphic productions. *Cognitive Psychology, 23*(4), 515–557.

Time gestured left-to-right

Santiago, J., Lupáñez, J., Pérez, E., & Funes, M. J. (2007). Time (also) flies from left to right. *Psychonomic Bulletin & Review, 14*(3), 512–516.

Perspective in signed and spoken languages

Emmorey, K., Tversky, B., & Taylor, H. A. (2000). Using space to describe space: Perspective in speech, sign, and gesture. *Spatial Cognition and Computation, 2*(3), 157–180.

Symbolic distance

Banks, W. P., & Flora, J. (1977). Semantic and perceptual processes in symbolic comparisons. *Journal of Experimental Psychology: Human Perception and Performance, 3,* 278–290.

Holyoak, K. J., & Mah, W. A. (1981). Semantic congruity in symbolic comparisons: Evidence against an expectancy hypothesis. *Memory and Cognition, 9,* 197–204.

Moyer, R. S. (1973). Comparing objects in memory: Evidence suggesting an internal psychophysics. *Perception and Psychophysics, 1,* 180–184.

Paivio, A. (1978). Mental comparisons involving abstract attributes. *Memory and Cognition, 6,* 199–208.

Symbolic distance in other species

D'Amato, M. R., & Colombo, M. (1990). The symbolic distance effect in monkeys (*Cebus paella*). *Animal Learning & Behavior, 18,* 133–140.

Gelman, R., & Gallistel, C. R. (2004). Language and the origin of numerical concepts. *Science, 306*(5695), 441–443.

Transitive inference in other species

Bond, A. B, Kamil, A. C, & Balda, R. P. (2003). Social complexity and transitive inference in corvids. *Animal Behavior, 65,* 479–487.

Byrne, R. W., & Bates, L. A. (2007). Sociality, evolution and cognition. *Current Biology, 17,* 714–723.

Byrne, R. W. & Whiten, A. (1988). *Machiavellian intelligence: Social expertise and the evolution of intellect in monkeys, apes, and humans.* Oxford, England: Clarendon Press.

Davis, H. (1992). Transitive inference in rats (*Rattus norvegicus*). *Journal of Comparative Psychology, 106,* 342–349.

Grosenick, L., Clement, T. S., & Fernald, R. D. (2007). Fish can infer social rank by observation alone. *Nature, 445,* 429–432.

MacLean, E. L., Merritt, D. J., & Brannon, E. M. (2008). Social complexity predicts transitive reasoning in Prosimian primates. *Animal Behavior, 76,* 479–486.

Von Fersen, L., Wynee, C. D. L., Delius, J. D., & Staddon, J. E. R. (1991). Transitive inference formation in pigeons. *Journal of Experimental Psychology: Animal Behavior Processes, 17,* 334–341.

Approximate number system in children and other species

Brannon, E. M., & Terrace, H. S. (1998). Ordering of the numerosities 1 to 9 by monkeys. *Science, 282*(5389), 746–749.

Brannon, E. M., Wusthoff, C. J., Gallistel, C. R., & Gibbon, J. (2001). Numerical subtraction in the pigeon: Evidence for a linear subjective number scale. *Psychological Science, 12*(3), 238–243.

Cantlon, J. F., Platt, M. L., & Brannon, E. M. (2009). Beyond the number domain. *Trends in Cognitive Sciences, 13*(2), 83–91.

Gallistel, C. R., Gelman, R., & Cordes, S. (2006). The cultural and evolutionary history of the real numbers. *Evolution and Culture, 247.*

Henik, A., Leibovich, T., Naparstek, S., Diesendruck, L., & Rubinsten, O. (2012). Quantities, amounts, and the numerical core system. *Frontiers in Human Neuroscience, 5,* 186.

McCrink, K., & Spelke, E. S. (2010). Core multiplication in childhood. *Cognition, 116*(2), 204–216.

McCrink, K., & Spelke, E. S. (2016). Non-symbolic division in childhood. *Journal of Experimental Child Psychology, 142,* 66–82.

McCrink, K., Spelke, E. S., Dehaene, S., & Pica, P. (2013). Non-symbolic halving in an Amazonian indigene group. *Developmental Science, 16*(3), 451–462.

Scarf, D., Hayne, H., & Colombo, M. (2011). Pigeons on par with primates in numerical competence. *Science, 334*(6063), 1664–1664.

Brain substrates for approximate and exact number systems

Cohen Kadosh, R., Henik, A., Rubinsten, O., Mohr, H., Dori, H., van de ven, V., . . . Linden, D. E. J. (2005). Are numbers special? The comparison systems of the human brain investigated by fMRI. *Neuropsychologia, 43,* 1238–1248.

Spatial-numerical associations of response (SNARC)

Dehaene, S., Bossini, S., & Giraux, P. (1993). The mental representation of parity and number magnitude. *Journal of Experimental Psychology: General, 122*(3), 371–396.

Tversky, B., Kugelmass, S., & Winter, A. (1991). Cross-cultural and developmental trends in graphic productions. *Cognitive Psychology, 23*(4), 515–557.

Greater sensitivity to smaller values (Weber-Fechner effect)

Cantlon, J. F., Platt, M. L., & Brannon, E. M. (2009). Beyond the number domain. *Trends in Cognitive Sciences, 13*(2), 83–91.

Greater sensitivity to smaller values in language

Talmy, L. (1983). How language structures space. In *Spatial orientation* (pp. 225–282). Boston, MA: Springer.

Numerical reasoning in cultures lacking names for numbers greater than three

Frank, M. C., Everett, D. L., Fedorenko, E., & Gibson, E. (2008). Number as a cognitive technology: Evidence from Pirahã language and cognition. *Cognition, 108*(3), 819–824.

Gordon, P. (2004). Numerical cognition without words: Evidence from Amazonia. *Science, 306*(5695), 496–499.

Pica, P., Lemer, C., Izard, V., & Dehaene, S. (2004). Exact and approximate arithmetic in an Amazonian indigene group. *Science, 306*(5695), 499–503.

Brain damage can selectively disrupt exact and approximate number systems

Dehaene, S. (2011). *The number sense: How the mind creates mathematics.* New York, NY: Oxford University Press.

Lemer, C., Dehaene, S., Spelke, E., & Cohen, L. (2003). Approximate quantities and exact number words: Dissociable systems. *Neuropsychologia, 41*(14), 1942–1958.

Exact and approximate number systems interact in intact brains

Gallistel, C. R., & Gelman, R. (1992). Preverbal and verbal counting and computation. *Cognition, 44,* 43–74.

Holloway, I. D., & Ansari, D. (2009). Mapping numerical magnitudes onto symbols: The numerical distance effect and individual differences in children's mathematics achievement. *Journal of Experimental Child Psychology, 103*(1), 17–29.

Lonnemann, J., Linkersdörfer, J., Hasselhorn, M., & Lindberg, S. (2011). Symbolic and non-symbolic distance effects in children and their connection with arithmetic skills. *Journal of Neurolinguistics, 24*(5), 583–591.

Mazzocco, M. M., Feigenson, L., & Halberda, J. (2011). Preschoolers' precision of the approximate number system predicts later school mathematics performance. *PLoS One, 6*(9), e23749.

Training approximate number system helps exact number system

Libertus, M. E., Feigenson, L., & Halberda, J. (2013). Is approximate number precision a stable predictor of math ability? *Learning and Individual Differences, 25,* 126–133.

Lyons, I. M., & Beilock, S. L. (2011). Numerical ordering ability mediates the relation between number-sense and arithmetic competence. *Cognition, 121*(2), 256–261.

Park, J., Bermudez, V., Roberts, R. C., & Brannon, E. M. (2016). Non-symbolic approximate arithmetic training improves math performance in preschoolers. *Journal of Experimental Child Psychology, 152,* 278–293.

Wang, J. J., Odic, D., Halberda, J., & Feigenson, L. (2016). Changing the precision of preschoolers' approximate number system representations changes their symbolic math performance. *Journal of Experimental Child Psychology, 147,* 82–99.

History of number notation

Aczel, A. D. (2016) *Finding zero*. New York, NY: St. Martin's Griffin.

Cajori, F. (1928). *A history of mathematical notations. Vol. I, Notations in elementary mathematics*. North Chelmsford, MA: Courier Corporation.

Cajori, F. (1928). *A history of mathematical notations. Vol. II, Notations mainly in higher mathematics*. Chicago, IL: Open Court Publishing.

Ifrah, G. (2000). *The universal history of numbers: From prehistory to the invention of the computer*. Translated by D. Vellos, E. F. Harding, S. Wood, & I. Monk. Toronto, Canada: Wiley.

Mazur, J. (2014). *Enlightening symbols: A short history of mathematical notation and its hidden powers*. Princeton, NJ: Princeton University Press.

Notation and writing began with accounting in the West

Schmandt-Besserat, D. (1992). *Before writing, Vol. I: From counting to cuneiform*. Austin: University of Texas Press.

Space is crucial to math notation

Dehaene, S. (2011). *The number sense: How the mind creates mathematics*. New York, NY: Oxford University Press.

Gelman, R., & Gallistel, C. R. (1978). *The child's understanding of number*. Cambridge, MA: Harvard University Press.

Lakoff, G., & Núñez, R. (2000). *Where mathematics comes from: How the embodied mind brings mathematics into being*. New York, NY: Basic Books.

Eye movements track absent places

Kahneman, D. (1973). *Attention and effort*. Englewood Cliffs, NJ: Prentice Hall.

Imagined spatial distance affects reading times

Bar-Anan, Y., Liberman, N., Trope, Y., & Algom, D. (2007). Automatic processing of psychological distance: Evidence from a Stroop task. *Journal of Experimental Psychology: General, 136*(4), 610.

Imagined spatial distance affects personality judgments

Liberman, N., Trope, Y., & Stephan, E. (2007). Psychological distance. In A. W. Kruglanski & E. T. Higgins (Eds.), *Social psychology: Handbook of basic principles* (2nd ed., pp. 353–383). New York, NY: Guilford Press.

Ross, L. (1977). The intuitive psychologist and his shortcomings: Distortions in the attribution process. In L. Berkowitz (Ed.), *Advances in experimental social psychology* (Vol. 10, pp. 173–220). New York, NY: Academic Press.

Trope, Y., & Liberman, N. (2010). Construal-level theory of psychological distance. *Psychological Review, 117*(2), 440.

Greater distance evokes more abstract language and more abstract thought

Förster, J., Friedman, R. S., & Liberman, N. (2004). Temporal construal effects on abstract and concrete thinking: consequences for insight and creative cognition. *Journal of Personality and Social Psychology, 87*(2), 177.

Jia, L., Hirt, E. R., & Karpen, S. C. (2009). Lessons from a faraway land: The effect of spatial distance on creative cognition. *Journal of Experimental Social Psychology, 45*(5), 1127–1131.

Liberman, N., Polack, O., Hameiri, B., & Blumenfeld, M. (2012). Priming of spatial distance enhances children's creative performance. *Journal of Experimental Child Psychology, 111*(4), 663–670.

Semin, G. R., & Smith, E. R. (1999). Revisiting the past and back to the future: Memory systems and the linguistic representation of social events. *Journal of Personality and Social Psychology, 76*(6), 877.

Cognitive reference points expand close distances and shrink far ones (Weber-Fechner)

Holyoak, K. J., & Mah, W. A. (1982). Cognitive reference points in judgements of symbolic magnitude. *Cognitive Psychology, 14,* 328–352.

Social perspectives: Within or above

Keltner, D., Gruenfeld, D. H., & Anderson, C. (2003). Power, approach, and inhibition. *Psychological Review, 110*(2), 265.

Keltner, D., Van Kleef, G. A., Chen, S., & Kraus, M. W. (2008). A reciprocal influence model of social power: Emerging principles and lines of inquiry. *Advances in Experimental Social Psychology, 40,* 151–192.

Van Kleef, G. A., Oveis, C., Van Der Löwe, I., Luo Kogan, A., Goetz, J., & Keltner, D. (2008). Power, distress, and compassion: Turning a blind eye to the suffering of others. *Psychological Science, 19*(12), 1315–1322.

Language points to percepts

Arnheim, R. (1974). *Art and visual perception.* Berkeley: University of California Press.

Spatial language in a child who is blind

Landau, B., Gleitman, L. R., & Landau, B. (2009). *Language and experience: Evidence from the blind child* (Vol. 8). Cambridge, MA: Harvard University Press.

Landau, B., Spelke, E., & Gleitman, H. (1984). Spatial knowledge in a young blind child. *Cognition, 16*(3), 225–260.

Claiming propositions as minimal units of thought

Anderson, J. R. (2013). *The architecture of cognition*. New York, NY: Psychology Press.

Pylyshyn, Z. W. (1973). What the mind's eye tells the mind's brain: A critique of mental imagery. *Psychological Bulletin, 80*(1), 1.

Spatial thinking as foundation for language

Fauconnier, G. (1994). *Mental spaces: Aspects of meaning construction in natural language*. Cambridge, England: Cambridge University Press.

Fauconnier, G., & Sweetser, E. (Eds.). (1996). *Spaces, worlds, and grammar*. Chicago, IL: University of Chicago Press.

Lakoff, G., & Johnson, M. (2008). *Metaphors we live by*. Chicago, IL: University of Chicago Press.

Talmy, L. (1983). How language structures space. In H. L. Pick & L. P. Acredolo (Eds.), *Spatial orientation* (pp. 225–282). Boston, MA: Springer.

CHAPTER EIGHT: SPACES WE CREATE:
MAPS, DIAGRAMS, SKETCHES, EXPLANATIONS, COMICS

Paraphrased Pessoa quote

Art proves that life is not enough. (n.d.). AZ Quotes. Retrieved from https://www.azquotes.com/author/11564-Fernando_Pessoa?p=3

Neanderthal cave paintings in Spain

Hoffmann, D. L., Standish, C. D., García-Diez, M., Pettitt, P. B., Milton, J. A., Zilhão, J., . . . Lorblanchet, M. (2018). U-Th dating of carbonate crusts reveals Neanderthal origin of Iberian cave art. *Science, 359*(6378), 912–915.

Cognitive design principles

Adapted from Tversky, B., Morrison, J. B., & Betrancourt, M. (2002). Animation: Can it facilitate? *International Journal of Human-Computer Studies, 57*(4), 247–262.

Also see Norman, D. (2013). *The design of everyday things: Revised and expanded edition*. New York, NY: Basic Books.

History of writing

Gelb, I. J. (1952). *A study of writing*. Chicago, IL: University of Chicago Press.

Oldest map (so far)

Utrilla, P., Mazo, C., Sopena, M. C., Martínez-Bea, M., & Domingo, R. (2009). A Paleolithic map from 13,660 calBP: Engraved stone blocks from the Late

Magdalenian in Abauntz Cave (Navarra, Spain). *Journal of Human Evolution, 57*(2), 99–111.

History of calendars

Boorstin, D. J. (1985). *The discoverers: A history of man's search to know his world and himself.* New York, NY: Vintage.

Maps of constellations in ancient caves

Rappenglück, M. (1997). The Pleiades in the "Salle des Taureaux," grotte de Lascaux. Does a rock picture in the cave of Lascaux show the open star cluster of the Pleiades at the Magdalénien era (ca 15.300 BC)? In C. Jaschek & F. Atrio Barendela (Eds.), *Proceedings of the IVth SEAC Meeting "Astronomy and Culture"* (pp. 217–225). Salamanca, Spain: University of Salamanca.

Wikipedia. (n.d.). Star chart. Retrieved from https://en.wikipedia.org/wiki/Star_chart

Native American hand maps, annotated with gestures

Finney, B. (1998). Nautical cartography and traditional navigation in Oceania. In D. Woodward & G. M. Lewis (Eds.), *The history of cartography. Vol. 2, Book Three: Cartography in the traditional African, American, Arctic, Australian, and Pacific societies* (pp. 443–492). Chicago, IL: University of Chicago Press.

Lewis, G. M. (1998). Maps, mapmaking, and map use by native North Americans. In D. Woodward & G. M. Lewis (Eds.), *The history of cartography. Vol. 2, Book Three: Cartography in the traditional African, American, Arctic, Australian, and Pacific societies* (pp. 51–182). Chicago, IL: University of Chicago Press.

Smethurst, G. (1905). *A narrative of an extraordinary escape out of the hands of the Indians, in the gulph of St. Lawrence.* Edited by W. F. Ganong. Whitefish, MT: Kessinger Publishing. (Original work published London, 1774).

Depictive maps in Aztec codices

Boone, E. H. (2010). *Stories in red and black: Pictorial histories of the Aztecs and Mixtecs.* Austin: University of Texas Press.

Syntax and semantics of sketch maps

Denis, M. (1997). The description of routes: A cognitive approach to the production of spatial discourse. *Cahiers de Psychologie, 16,* 409–458.

Tversky, B., & Lee, P. U. (1998). How space structures language. In C. Freksa, W. Brauer, C. Habel, & K. F. Wender (Eds.), *Spatial cognition III* [Lecture

Notes in Computer Science] (Vol. 1404, pp. 157–175). Berlin, Germany: Springer, Berlin, Heidelberg.

Tversky, B., & Lee, P. U. (1999). Pictorial and verbal tools for conveying routes. In *International Conference on Spatial Information Theory* (pp. 51–64). Berlin, Germany: Springer, Berlin, Heidelberg.

Empirically establishing cognitive guidelines for map design

Agrawala, M., & Stolte, C. (2001, August). Rendering effective route maps: Improving usability through generalization. *Proceedings of the 28th Annual Conference on Computer Graphics and Interactive Techniques,* 241–249.

Tversky, B., Agrawala, M., Heiser, J., Lee, P., Hanrahan, P., Phan, D., . . . Daniel, M.-P. (2006). Cognitive design principles for automated generation of visualizations. In G. L. Allen (Ed.), *Applied spatial cognition: From research to cognitive technology* (pp. 53–75). New York, NY: Psychology Press.

Three Ps (production, preference, and performance) for designing designs

Kessell, A., & Tversky, B. (2011). Visualizing space, time, and agents: Production, performance, and preference. *Cognitive Processing, 12*(1), 43–52.

Interpreting the Ishango rod

Pletser, V., & Huylebrouck, D. (1999). The Ishango artefact: The missing base 12 link. *FORMA-TOKYO, 14*(4), 339–346.

Pletser, V., & Huylebrouck, D. (2008, January). An interpretation of the Ishango rods. In *Proceedings of the Conference Ishango, 22000 and 50 Years Later: The Cradle of Mathematics* (pp. 139–170). Brussels, Belgium: Royal Flemish Academy of Belgium, KVAB.

Development of understanding of number

Gelman, R., & Gallistel, C. R. (1986). *The child's understanding of number.* Cambridge, MA: Harvard University Press.

Formal notations are diagrams

Landy, D., & Goldstone, R. L. (2007). Formal notations are diagrams: Evidence from a production task. *Memory & Cognition, 35*(8), 2033–2040.

People use space to solve math problems; proofs are stories

Landy, D., & Goldstone, R. L. (2007). How abstract is symbolic thought? *Journal of Experimental Psychology: Learning, Memory, and Cognition, 33*(4), 720.

Eastern environments more complex than Western in eyes of both

Miyamoto, Y., Nisbett, R. E., & Masuda, T. (2006). Culture and the physical environment: Holistic versus analytic perceptual affordances. *Psychological Science, 17*(2), 113–119.

Chinese arithmetic diagrams rated more complex than US

Wang, E. (2011). *Culture and math visualization: Comparing American and Chinese math images* (Unpublished master's thesis). Columbia Teachers College, New York, NY.

Zheng, F. (2015). *Math visualizations across cultures: Comparing Chinese and American math images.* (Unpublished master's thesis). Columbia Teachers College, New York, NY.

Measurement and calculation can reduce some biases and error

Kahneman, D., & Tversky, A. (2013). Choices, values, and frames. In W. Ziemba & L. C. MacLean (Eds.), *Handbook of the fundamentals of financial decision making: Part I* (pp. 269–278). Hackensack, NJ: World Scientific Publishing Co.

Tversky, A., & Kahneman, D. (1974). Judgment under uncertainty: Heuristics and biases. *Science, 185*(4157), 1124–1131.

Tversky, A., & Kahneman, D. (1981). The framing of decisions and the psychology of choice. *Science, 211*(4481), 453–458.

Tversky, A., & Kahneman, D. (1983). Extensional versus intuitive reasoning: The conjunction fallacy in probability judgment. *Psychological Review, 90*(4), 293.

In ancient geometry, the language annotated the diagrams, not vice versa

Netz, R. (2003). *The shaping of deduction in Greek mathematics: A study in cognitive history* (Vol. 51). Cambridge, England: Cambridge University Press.

Spatial mental models

Johnson-Laird, P. N. (1980). Mental models in cognitive science. *Cognitive Science, 4*(1), 71–115.

Tversky, B. (1991). Spatial mental models. *Psychology of Learning and Motivation, 27,* 109–145. https://doi.org/10.1016/S0079-7421(08)60122-X

Euler diagrams in reasoning

Chapman, P., Stapleton, G., Rodgers, P., Micallef, L., & Blake, A. (2014). Visualizing sets: An empirical comparison of diagram types. In T. Dwyer, H. Purchase, & A. Delaney (Eds.), *Diagrammatic representation and inference. Diagrams 2014, Lecture Notes in Computer Science* (Vol. 8578, pp. 146–160). Berlin, Germany: Springer, Berlin, Heidelberg.

Sato, Y., Mineshima, K., & Takemura, R. (2010). The efficacy of Euler and Venn diagrams in deductive reasoning: Empirical findings. In A. K. Goel, M. Jamnik, & N. H. Narayanan (Eds.), *Diagrammatic representation and inference: 6th International Conference, Diagrams 2010, Portland, OR, USA, August 9–11, 2010, Proceedings* (pp. 6–22). Berlin, Germany: Springer-Verlag Berlin Heidelberg. doi:10.1007/978-3-642-14600-8

Syllogistic reasoning with diagrams

Barwise, J., & Etchemendy, J. (1994). *Hyperproof: For Macintosh*. Center for the Study of Language and Inf.

Giardino, V. (2017). Diagrammatic reasoning in mathematics. In L. Magnani & T. Bertolotti (Eds.), *Springer handbook of model-based science* (pp. 499–522). New York, NY: Springer.

Green, T. R. G., & Petre, M. (1996). Usability analysis of visual programming environments: A "cognitive dimensions" framework. *Journal of Visual Languages & Computing, 7*(2), 131–174.

Shin, S. J. (1994). *The logical status of diagrams*. Cambridge, England: Cambridge University Press.

Stenning, K., & Lemon, O. (2001). Aligning logical and psychological perspectives on diagrammatic reasoning. *Artificial Intelligence Review, 15*(1–2), 29–62.

Wexler, M. (1993). Matrix models on large graphs. *Nuclear Physics, B410*, 377–394.

Music notation

Wikipedia. (n.d.). Musical notation. Retrieved from https://en.wikipedia.org /wiki/Musical_notation

Dance notation

Encyclopaedia Britannica. (n.d.). Dance notation. Retrieved from https://www .britannica.com/art/dance-notation

History of devices for time

Bruxton, E. (1979). *The history of clocks and watches*. New York, NY: Crescent.

Ancient Chinese calendars

Calendars Through the Ages. (n.d.). The Chinese calendar. Retrieved from http://www.webexhibits.org/calendars/calendar-chinese.html

Petroglyph of supernova

Sule, A., Bandey, A., Vahia, M., Iqbal, N., & Tabasum, M. (2011). Indian record for Kepler's supernova: Evidence from Kashmir Valley. *Astronomische Nachrichten, 332*(6), 655—657.

Depictions of events in classical art

Small, J. P. (1999). Time in space: Narrative in classical art. *Art Bulletin, 81*(4), 562–575.

Small, J. P. (2003). *Wax tablets of the mind: Cognitive studies of memory and literacy in classical antiquity*. New York, NY: Routledge.

Event perception and cognition

Daniel, M. P., & Tversky, B. (2012). How to put things together. *Cognitive Processing, 13*(4), 303–319.

Hard, B. M., Recchia, G., & Tversky, B. (2011). The shape of action. *Journal of Experimental Psychology: General, 140*(4), 586.

Tversky, B., & Zacks, J. M. (2013). Event perception. In D. Riesberg (Ed.), *Oxford handbook of cognitive psychology* (pp. 83–94). Oxford, England: Oxford University Press.

Zacks, J. M., & Radvansky, G. A. (2014). *Event cognition*. Oxford, England: Oxford University Press.

Zacks, J. M., & Swallow, K. M. (2007). Event segmentation. *Current Directions in Psychological Science, 16*(2), 80–84.

Zacks, J. M., & Tversky, B. (2001). Event structure in perception and conception. *Psychological Bulletin, 127*(1), 3.

Empirically establishing cognitive design principles for sequence of actions

Agrawala, M., Phan, D., Heiser, J., Haymaker, J., Klingner, J., Hanrahan, P., & Tversky, B. (2003, July). Designing effective step-by-step assembly instructions. *ACM Transactions on Graphics (TOG), 22*(3), 828–837.

Daniel, M. P., & Tversky, B. (2012). How to put things together. *Cognitive Processing, 13*(4), 303–319.

Tversky, B., Agrawala, M., Heiser, J., Lee, P., Hanrahan, P., Phan, D., . . . Daniel, M. P. (2006). Cognitive design principles for automated generation of visualizations. In G. L. Allen (Ed.), *Applied spatial cognition: From research to cognitive technology* (pp. 53–75). Mahwah, NJ: Erlbaum.

Robots using IKEA instructions to assemble chair

Suárez-Ruiz, F., Zhou, X., & Pham, Q. C. (2018). Can robots assemble an IKEA chair? *Science Robotics, 3*(17), eaat6385.

Warren, M. (2018, April 18). Can this robot build an IKEA chair faster than you? *Science*. Retrieved from http://www.sciencemag.org/news/2018/04/can-robot-build-ikea-chair-faster-you

Classic work on info graphics

Bertin, J. (1983). *Semiology of graphics: Diagrams, networks, maps*. Madison: University of Wisconsin.

Card, S. K., Mackinlay, J. D., & Shneiderman, B. (1999). *Readings in information visualization: Using vision to think*. San Francisco, CA: Morgan Kaufman.

Enlightenment values

Pinker, S. (2018). *Enlightenment now: The case for reason, science, humanism, and progress*. New York, NY: Penguin.

History of diagrams and diagrammatology

Bender, J., & Marrinan, M. (2010). *The culture of diagram*. Stanford, CA: Stanford University Press.

Stjernfelt, F. (2007). *Diagrammatology: An investigation on the borderlines of phenomenology, ontology, and semiotics* (Vol. 336). New York, NY: Springer Science & Business Media.

Spontaneous use of space to convey time, quantity, and preference by children and adults across cultures

Tversky, B., Kugelmass, S., & Winter, A. (1991). Cross-cultural and developmental trends in graphic productions. *Cognitive Psychology, 23*(4), 515–557.

Up-down used metaphorically in language

Clark, H. H. (1973). Space, time, semantics, and the child. In T. E. Moore (Ed.), *Cognitive development and acquisition of language* (pp. 27–63). New York, NY: Academic Press.

Lakoff, G., & Johnson, M. (2008). *Metaphors we live by*. Chicago, IL: University of Chicago Press.

Talmy, L. (2000). *Toward a cognitive semantics*. Cambridge, MA: MIT Press.

You are the center of your social network

Yu, L., Nickerson, J. V., & Tversky, B. (2010). Discovering perceptions of personal social networks through diagrams. In A. K. Goel, M. Jamnik, & N. H. Narayanan (Eds.), *Diagrammatic representation and inference: 6th International Conference, Diagrams 2010, Portland, OR, USA, August 9-11, 2010, Proceedings* (pp. 352–354). Berlin, Germany: Springer-Verlag Berlin Heidelberg. doi:10.1007/978-3-642-14600-8

Seeing lines where there are none: Kanizsa figures

Kanizsa, G. (1976). Subjective contours. *Scientific American, 234*(4), 48–53.

Obsessed by lines

Tversky, B. (2011). Obsessed by lines. In A. Kantrowitz, A. Brew, & M. Fava (Eds.), *Thinking through Drawing: Practice into Knowledge: Proceedings of an Interdisciplinary Symposium on Drawing, Cognition and Education* (p. 15). New York, NY: Teachers College Columbia University Art and Art Education.

Tversky, B. (2013). Lines of thought. In H. D. Christensen, T. Kristensen, & A. Michelsen (Eds.), *Transvisuality: The cultural dimension of visuality: Vol. 1: Boundaries and creative openings* (pp. 142–156). Liverpool, England: Liverpool University Press.

Tversky, B. (2016). Lines: Orderly and messy. In Y. Portugali & E. Stolk (Eds.), *Complexity, cognition, urban planning and design* (pp. 237–250). Dordrecht, the Netherlands: Springer.

Klee: A line is a dot that went for a walk

Klee, P. (n.d.). A line is a dot that went for a walk. Paul Klee: Paintings, Biography and Quotes. Retrieved from http://www.paulklee.net/paul-klee-quotes .jsp

Points, lines, planes

Kandinsky, W. (1947). *Point and line to plane.* Translated by H. Dearstyne & H. Rebay. New York, NY: Guggenheim. (Original work published 1926)

Klee, P., & Moholy-Nagy, S. (1953). *Pedagogical sketchbook.* New York, NY: Praeger.

Interpreting and producing line and bar graphs

Zacks, J., & Tversky, B. (1999). Bars and lines: A study of graphic communication. *Memory & Cognition, 27*(6), 1073–1079.

Different inferences from different formats for data visualization

Kessell, A., & Tversky, B. (2011). Visualizing space, time, and agents: Production, performance, and preference. *Cognitive Processing, 12*(1), 43–52.

Nickerson, J. V., Corter, J. E., Tversky, B., Rho, Y. J., Zahner, D., & Yu, L. (2013). Cognitive tools shape thought: Diagrams in design. *Cognitive Processing, 14*(3), 255–272.

Nickerson, J. V., Tversky, B., Corter, J. E., Yu, L., Rho, Y. J., & Mason, D. (2010). Thinking with networks. In *Proceedings of the Annual Meeting of the Cognitive Science Society, 32*(32).

Tversky, B. (2011). Visualizing thought. *Topics in Cognitive Science, 3*(3), 499–535.

Tversky, B., Corter, J. E., Yu, L., Mason, D. L., & Nickerson, J. V. (2012, July). Representing category and continuum: Visualizing thought. In *International Conference on Theory and Application of Diagrams* (pp. 23–34). Berlin, Germany: Springer, Berlin, Heidelberg.

Tversky, B., Gao, J., Corter, J. E., Tanaka, Y., & Nickerson, J. V. (2016). People, place, and time: Inferences from diagrams. In M. Jamnik, Y. Uesaka, & S. Elzer Schwartz (Eds.), *Diagrammatic representation and inference. Dia-*

grams 2016. Lecture Notes in Computer Science (Vol. 9781, pp. 258–264). Switzerland: Springer, Cham.

Arrows

Denis, M. (2018). Arrow in diagrammatic and navigational spaces. In J. M. Zacks & H. A. Taylor (Eds.), *Representations in mind and world: Essays inspired by Barbara Tversky* (pp. 63–84). New York, NY: Routledge.

Heiser, J., & Tversky, B. (2006). Arrows in comprehending and producing mechanical diagrams. *Cognitive Science, 30*(3), 581–592.

Horn, R. E. (1998). Visual language. Bainbridge Island, WA: Macrovu.

MacKenzie, R. (n.d.). *Diagrammatic narratives: Telling scientific stories effectively with diagrams* (Honors thesis in psychology). Stanford University, Stanford, CA.

Mayon, C. (2010). *A child's conception of the multiple meanings of arrow.* (Unpublished master's thesis). Columbia Teachers College, New York, NY.

Tversky, B., Heiser, J., MacKenzie, R., Lozano, S., & Morrison, J. B. (2007). Enriching animations. In R. Lowe & W. Schnotz (Eds.), *Learning with animation: Research implications for design* (pp. 263–285). New York, NY: Cambridge University Press.

Tversky, B., Zacks, J., Lee, P., & Heiser, J. (2000). Lines, blobs, crosses and arrows: Diagrammatic communication with schematic figures. In M. Anderson, P. Cheng, & V. Haarslev (Eds.), *Theory and application of diagrams. Diagrams 2000. Lecture notes in computer science* (Vol. 1889, pp. 221–230). Berlin, Germany: Springer, Berlin, Heidelberg.

Animated visualizations

Mayer, R. E., & Anderson, R. B. (1991). Animations need narrations: An experimental test of a dual-coding hypothesis. *Journal of Educational Psychology, 83*(4), 484.

Mayer, R. E., & Moreno, R. (2002). Animation as an aid to multimedia learning. *Educational Psychology Review, 14*(1), 87–99.

Tversky, B., Heiser, J., Mackenzie, R., Lozano, S., & Morrison, J. (2008). Enriching animations. In R. Lowe & W. Schnotz (Eds.), *Learning with animation: Research implications for design* (pp. 263–285). New York, NY: Cambridge University Press.

Tversky, B., Heiser, J., & Morrison, J. (2013). Space, time, and story. In B. H. Ross (Ed.), *The psychology of learning and motivation* (pp. 47–76). San Diego, CA: Elsevier Academic Press. https://doi.org/10.1016/B978-0-12-407237-4.12001-8.

Tversky, B., Morrison, J. B., & Betrancourt, M. (2002). Animation: Can it facilitate? *International Journal of Human-Computer Studies, 57*(4), 247–262.

Zacks, J. M., & Tversky, B. (2003). Structuring information interfaces for procedural learning. *Journal of Experimental Psychology: Applied, 9*(2), 88.

Congruent touchpad gestures help thinking and computation

Segal, A., Tversky, B., & Black, J. (2014). Conceptually congruent actions can promote thought. *Journal of Applied Research in Memory and Cognition, 3*(3), 124–130.

Isotypes and universal picture language

Neurath, O. (1936). *International Picture Language. The first rules of Isotype.* London, England: Kegan Paul.

Neurath, O., & Ogden, C. K. (1937). *BASIC by Isotype.* London, England: K. Paul, Trench, Trubner.

Graphic facilitator

Horn, R. E. (1999). Information design: Emergence of a new profession. In R. E. Jacobson (Ed.), *Information design* (pp. 15–33). Cambridge, MA: MIT Press.

Diagrams help learning

Carney, R. N., & Levin, J. R. (2002). Pictorial illustrations still improve students' learning from text. *Educational Psychology Review, 14*(1), 5–26.

Levie, W. H., & Lentz, R. (1982). Effects of text illustrations: A review of research. *ECTJ, 30*(4), 195–232.

Mayer, R. E. (2002). Multimedia learning. In B. H. Ross (Ed.), *The Psychology of learning and motivation* (Vol. 41, pp. 85–139). New York, NY: Academic Press.

Mayer, R. E., & Gallini, J. K. (1990). When is an illustration worth ten thousand words? *Journal of Educational Psychology, 82*(4), 715.

Tversky, B., Heiser, J., & Morrison, J. (2013). Space, time, and story. In B. H. Ross (Ed.), *The psychology of learning and motivation* (pp. 47–76). San Diego, CA: Elsevier Academic Press. https://doi.org/10.1016/B978-0-12-407237-4.12001-8.

Simple diagram that convinced Bill Gates to devote his foundation to promoting global health

I am indebted to Eleanor Fox for this example.

Duenes, S. (2008, February 25). Talk to the newsroom: Graphics director Steve Duenes. *New York Times.* Retrieved from https://www.nytimes.com/2008/02/25/business/media/25asktheeditors.html

Kristof, N. D. (1997, January 9). For third world, water is still a deadly drink. *New York Times.* Retrieved from http://www.nytimes.com/1997/01/09/world/for-third-world-water-is-still-a-deadly-drink.html

Storytelling

This is a tiny portion of the many thoughtful expositions of forms of discourse, especially stories.

Bordwell, D. (1985). *Narration in the fiction film*. Madison: University of Wisconsin Press.

Bordwell, D., & Thompson, K. (2003). *Film art: An introduction*. New York, NY: McGraw-Hill.

Branigan, E. (1992). *Narrative comprehension and film*. New York, NY: Routledge.

Bruner, J. (1987). *Actual minds, possible worlds*. Cambridge, MA: Harvard University Press.

Bruner, J. (2004). Life as narrative. *Social Research, 71*, 691–710.

Gee, J. P. (2014). *An introduction to discourse analysis: Theory and method*. New York, NY: Routledge.

Lupton, E. (2017). *Design is story-telling*. New York, NY: Cooper Hewitt Design Museum.

McPhee, J. (2013, January 14). Structure. *The New Yorker*, pp. 46–55.

McPhee, J. (2015, September 14). Omission. *The New Yorker*.

Prince, G. (2003). *A dictionary of narratology* (Rev. ed.). Lincoln: University of Nebraska Press.

Rumelhart, D. E. (1975). Notes on a schema for stories. In D. G. Bobrow & A. Collins (Eds.), *Representation and understanding: Studies in cognitive science* (pp. 211–237). New York, NY: Academic Press.

Schiffrin, D., Tannen, D., & Hamilton, H. E. (Eds.). (2008). *The handbook of discourse analysis*. New York, NY: Wiley.

Tversky, B. (2018). Story-telling in the wild: Implications for data storytelling. In S. Carpendale, N. Diakopoulos, N. Henri-Riche, & C. Hurter (Eds.), *Data-driven storytelling*. New York, NY: CRC Press.

Tversky, B., Heiser, J., & Morrison, J. (2013). Space, time, and story. In B. H. Ross (Ed.), *The psychology of learning and motivation* (pp. 47–76). San Diego, CA: Elsevier Academic Press. https://doi.org/10.1016/B978-0-12-407237-4.12001-8

Comics can be effective for learning

Aleixo, P. A., & Sumner, K. (2017). Memory for biopsychology material presented in comic book format. *Journal of Graphic Novels and Comics, 8*(1), 79–88.

Caldwell, J. (2012, October). Information comics: An overview. *2012 IEEE International Professional Communication Conference* (pp. 1–7). doi:10.1109/IPCC.2012.6408645

Short, J. C., Randolph-Seng, B., & McKenny, A. F. (2013). Graphic presentation: An empirical examination of the graphic novel approach to communicate business concepts. *Business Communication Quarterly, 76*(3), 273–303.

Theories and analyses of the comics medium

I am deeply indebted to Jon Bresman's generous collaboration on this project. He has an encyclopedic memory for comics and a scholar's understanding of them. Every time I asked, Is there a comic that does *X*? he came up with not only several examples but also more subtle phenomena I hadn't yet thought about. He taught me how rich and funny and clever and beautiful the medium is.

Cartoon guides: Larry Gonick: http://www.larrygonick.com

Comics for kids: Toon Books: http://www.toon-books.com

Journalism: Archcomix: http://www.archcomix.com; Palestine (comics) in Wikipedia: https://en.wikipedia.org/wiki/Palestine_(comics); *The Influencing Machine: Brooke Gladstone on the Media:* https://en.wikipedia.org /wiki/Influencing_Machine_(book)

Compendium of excellent examples of comics art: Carlin, J., Karasik, P., & Walker, B. (2005). *Masters of American comics.* Los Angeles, CA: Hammer Museum and the Museum of Contemporary Art, Los Angeles, in association with Yale University Press.

Some lovely visual poetry expressing some of these ideas can be found in Nick Sousanis's (2015). *Unflattening.* Cambridge, MA: Harvard University Press. Before he crafted the book, I had the pleasure of having Sousanis as a student in my course, where I taught many of the ideas on these pages and more.

Cohn, N. (2013). *The visual language of comics.* London, England: Bloomsbury.

Eisner, W. (2008). *Graphic storytelling and visual narrative.* New York, NY: W. W. Norton.

Eisner, W. (2008). *Comics and sequential art: Principles and practices from the legendary cartoonist.* New York, NY: W. W. Norton.

Groensteen, T. (2007). *The system of comics.* Translated by B. Beaty & N. Nguyen. Jackson: University Press of Mississippi.

McCloud, S. (1993). *Understanding comics.* New York, NY: William Morrow Paperbacks.

Spiegelman, A. (2011). *MetaMaus.* New York, NY: Pantheon.

Spiegelman, A. (2013). *Co-Mix: A retrospective of comics, graphics, and scraps.* Montreal, Canada: Drawn and Quarterly.

Picture remembered better than words

Paivio, A. (1991). Dual coding theory: Retrospect and current status. *Canadian Journal of Psychology/Revue canadienne de psychologie, 45*(3), 255.

Explosion of emojis and GIFs

I am indebted to Oren Tversky for this example.

Clarke, T. (2018, October 5). 24+ Instagram statistics that matter to marketers in 2019. Hootsuite. Retrieved from https://blog.hootsuite.com/instagram-statistics/

Dua, T. (2015). Emojis by the numbers: A Digiday data dump. Retrieved from https://digiday.com/marketing/digiday-guide-things-emoji/

Konrad, A. (2016). Giphy passes 100 million daily users who send 1 billion GIFs each day, reveals GV as investor. *Forbes*. Retrieved from https://www.forbes.com/sites/alexkonrad/2016/10/26/giphy-passes-100-million-users-reveals-gv-as-investor/#2273a37f4d64

Freytag-Aristotelian narrative arc

Freytag, G. (1863). *Die Technik des Dramas.*

Structure of boxes and speech balloons in comics

Groensteen, T. (2007). *The system of comics*. Translated by B. Beaty & N. Nguyen. Jackson: University Press of Mississippi.

Adding information to words and images

Clark, H. H. (1975). Bridging. In *Proceedings of the 1975 Workshop on Theoretical Issues in Natural Language Processing* (pp. 169–174). Cambridge, MA: Association for Computational Linguistics.

Intraub, H., Bender, R. S., & Mangels, J. A. (1992). Looking at pictures but remembering scenes. *Journal of Experimental Psychology: Learning, Memory, and Cognition, 18*(1), 180.

Segmenting events and stories

McCloud, S. (1993). *Understanding comics*. New York, NY: William Morrow Paperbacks.

Tversky, B. and Zacks, J. M. (2013). Event perception. In D. Riesberg (Ed.), *Oxford handbook of cognitive psychology* (pp. 83–94). Oxford, England: Oxford University Press.

Zacks, J. M. (2014). *Flicker: Your brain on movies*. New York, NY: Oxford University Press.

Culture and language affect creation of comics

Tversky, B. & Chow, T. (2017). Language and culture in visual narratives. *Cognitive Semiotics, 10*(2), 77–89.

CHAPTER NINE: CONVERSATIONS WITH A PAGE: DESIGN, SCIENCE, AND ART

Picasso and Braque quotes

Georges Braque. (n.d.). Retrieved from https://en.wikiquote.org/wiki/Georges_Braque

Interview with Gaston Diehl. (1945). Les Problèmes de la Peinture. Paris, France.

Picasso, P., & Fraisse, G. (1999). *Conversations with Picasso*. Chicago, IL: University of Chicago Press.

Da Vinci's life and oeuvre

Kemp, M. (2005). *Leonardo*. Oxford, England: Oxford University Press.

Advantages of ambiguity

Tversky, B. (2015). On abstraction and ambiguity. In J. Gero (Ed.), *Studying visual and spatial reasoning for design* (pp. 215–223). New York, NY: Springer.

Da Vinci's designs

Gopnik, A. (2005, January 17). Renaissance man: The life of Leonardo. *The New Yorker*.

Isaacson, W. (2017). *Leonardo da Vinci*. New York, NY: Simon & Schuster.

Kemp, M. (2005). *Leonardo*. Oxford, England: Oxford University Press.

Kemp, M. (2006). *Seen/unseen: Art, science, and intuition from Leonardo to the Hubble telescope*. Oxford, England: Oxford University Press.

Rosand, D. (2002). *Drawing acts: Studies in graphic expression and representation*. Cambridge, England: Cambridge University Press.

Wikipedia. (n.d.). Vebjørn Sand Da Vinci Project. Retrieved from https://en.wikipedia.org/wiki/Vebj%C3%B8rn_Sand_Da_Vinci_Project

Gemma Anderson's collaborations with scientists

Anderson, G. (2017). *Drawing as a way of knowing in art and science*. Bristol, England: Intellect Limited.

Creating visual explanations improves STEM understanding

Bobek, E., & Tversky, B. (2016). Creating visual explanations improves learning. *Cognitive Research: Principles and Implications, 1*(1), 27.

Diagramming in active STEM laboratories

Burnston, D. C., Sheredos, B., Abrahamsen, A., & Bechtel, W. (2014). Scientists' use of diagrams in developing mechanistic explanations: A case study from chronobiology. *Pragmatics & Cognition, 22*(2), 224–243.

WORGODS: WORking Group on Diagrams in Science. (n.d.). Diagrams in science. Retrieved from http://mechanism.ucsd.edu/WORGODS/index.html

Architects make discoveries in their own sketches

Goldschmidt, G. (1991). The dialectics of sketching. *Creativity Research Journal, 4*(2), 123–143.

Goldschmidt, G. (2014). *Linkography: Unfolding the design process.* Cambridge, MA: MIT Press.

Schön, D. A. (1987). *Educating the reflective practitioner: Toward a new design for teaching and learning in the professions.* San Francisco, CA: Jossey-Bass.

Suwa, M., & Tversky, B. (1997). What do architects and students perceive in their design sketches? A protocol analysis. *Design Studies, 18*(4), 385–403.

Expertise in finding new ideas from sketches

Ericsson, K. A., Hoffman, R. R., Kozbelt, A., & Williams, A. M. (Eds.). (2018). *The Cambridge handbook of expertise and expert performance.* Cambridge, England: Cambridge University Press.

Ericsson, K. A., & Smith, J. (Eds.). (1991). *Toward a general theory of expertise: Prospects and limits.* Cambridge, England: Cambridge University Press.

Suwa, M., & Tversky, B. (1997). What do architects and students perceive in their design sketches? A protocol analysis. *Design Studies, 18*(4), 385–403.

How designers and ordinary people find new ideas in sketches

Suwa, M., & Tversky, B. (1996). What architects see in their sketches: Implications for design tools. *Conference Companion on Human Factors in Computing Systems* (pp. 191–192). Vancouver, BC, Canada: ACM. doi:10.1145/257089.257255

Suwa, M., & Tversky, B. (1997). What do architects and students perceive in their sketches? A protocol analysis. *Design Studies, 18*(4), 385–403.

Suwa, M., & Tversky, B. (2002). How do designers shift their focus of attention in their own sketches? In M. Anderson, B. Meyer, & P. Olivier (Eds.), *Diagrammatic representation and reasoning* (pp. 241–254). London, England: Springer.

Tversky, B., & Suwa, M. (2009). Thinking with sketches. In A. B. Markman & K. L. Wood (Eds.), *Tools for innovation: The science behind the practical methods that drive new ideas.* New York, NY: Oxford University Press.

Effective strategy: Reorganizing parts

Suwa, M., Tversky, B., Gero, J., & Purcell, T. (2001). Seeing into sketches: Regrouping parts encourages new interpretations. In J. S. Gero, B. Tversky, & T. Purcell (Eds.), *Visual and spatial reasoning in design* (pp. 207–219). Sydney, Australia: Key Centre of Design Computing and Cognition.

Constructive perception

Suwa, M., & Tversky, B. (2003). Constructive perception: A metacognitive skill for coordinating perception and conception. *Proceedings of the Annual Meeting of the Cognitive Science Society, 25*(25).

Tversky, B., & Suwa, M. (2009). Thinking with sketches. In A. B. Markman & K. L. Wood (Eds.), *Tools for innovation: The science behind the practical methods that drive new ideas*. New York, NY: Oxford University Press.

Creativity: Finding new ideas

Chou, J. Y., & Tversky, B. (n.d.). *Top-down strategies outperform bottom-up strategies for finding new interpretations*. Unpublished manuscript.

Tversky, B. (2015). On abstraction and ambiguity. In J. Gero (Ed.), *Studying Visual and Spatial Reasoning for Design Creativity* (pp. 215–223). Dordrecht, the Netherlands: Springer.

Tversky, B., & Chou, J. Y. (2011). Creativity: Depth and breadth. In T. Taura & Y. Nagai (Eds.), *Design Creativity 2010* (pp. 209–214). London, England: Springer.

Zahner, D., Nickerson, J. V., Tversky, B., Corter, J. E., & Ma, J. (2010). A fix for fixation? Rerepresenting and abstracting as creative processes in the design of information systems. *AI EDAM, 24*(2), 231–244.

Mind wandering

Baird, B., Smallwood, J., Mrazek, M. D., Kam, J. W., Franklin, M. S., & Schooler, J. W. (2012). Inspired by distraction: Mind wandering facilitates creative incubation. *Psychological Science, 23*(10), 1117–1122.

Christoff, K., Gordon, A. M., Smallwood, J., Smith, R., & Schooler, J. W. (2009). Experience sampling during fMRI reveals default network and executive system contributions to mind wandering. *Proceedings of the National Academy of Sciences, 106*(21), 8719–8724.

Mrazek, M. D., Smallwood, J., & Schooler, J. W. (2012). Mindfulness and mind-wandering: Finding convergence through opposing constructs. *Emotion, 12*(3), 442.

Architects as pastry chefs

A new school of pastry chefs got its start in architecture. (2018, January 24). *New York Times*. Retrieved from https://www.nytimes.com/2018/01/23/dining/pastry-chefs-architecture.html

Paradigm shifts

Kuhn, T. S. (2012). *The structure of scientific revolutions*. Chicago, IL: University of Chicago Press.

Shifting perspective leads to discoveries

Mukherjee, S. (2017, September 11). Cancer's invasion equation. *The New Yorker*. Retrieved from https://www.newyorker.com/magazine/2017/09/11/cancers-invasion-equation

Shifting perspective improves forecasting

Mellers, B., Stone, E., Murray, T., Minster, A., Rohrbaugh, N., Bishop, M., . . . Ungar, L. (2015). Identifying and cultivating superforecasters as a method of improving probabilistic predictions. *Perspectives on Psychological Science, 10*(3), 267–281.

Tetlock, P. E. (2017). *Expert political judgment: How good is it? How can we know?* Princeton, NJ: Princeton University Press.

Tetlock, P. E., & Gardner, D. (2016). *Superforecasting: The art and science of prediction*. New York, NY: Random House.

Improving predictions

Schwartz, T. (2018, May 9). What it takes to think deeply about complex problems. *Harvard Business Review*. Retrieved from https://hbr.org/2018/05/what-it-takes-to-think-deeply-about-complex-problems

How experienced artists create

Kantrowitz, A. (2018). What artists do (and say) when they draw. In J. M. Zacks & H. A. Taylor (Eds.), *Representations in mind and world: Essays inspired by Barbara Tversky* (pp. 209–220). New York, NY: Routledge.

CHAPTER TEN: THE WORLD IS A DIAGRAM

Moving farther in space enables moving up economically

Rosling, H., Rönnlund, A. R., & Rosling, O. (2018). *Factfulness: Ten reasons we're wrong about the world—and why things are better than you think*. New York, NY: Flatiron Books.

Cultural transmission in apes is by imitation, not by teaching

Whiten, A., Horner, V., & De Waal, F. B. (2005). Conformity to cultural norms of tool use in chimpanzees. *Nature, 437*(7059), 737.

Gesture important in human cultural transmission

Legare, C. H. (2017). Cumulative cultural learning: Development and diversity. *Proceedings of the National Academy of Sciences, 114*(30), 7877–7883.

Little, E. E., Carver, L. J., & Legare, C. H. (2016). Cultural variation in triadic infant–caregiver object exploration. *Child Development, 87*(4), 1130–1145.

Laws (norms) on the streets

Moroni, S., & Lorini, G. (2017). Graphic rules in planning: A critical exploration of normative drawings starting from zoning maps and form-based codes. *Planning Theory, 16*(3), 318–338.

Index

absolute reference frame, 151
abstract geometric ideas, 156–157
abstract thought, 14, 36, 57, 59,
    71–74, 79, 87, 115, 118, 119,
    121, 122, 125, 128, 130, 142,
    153, 156, 157, 160, 163, 165,
    172–175, 180, 181, 185, 187,
    195, 203, 207–210, 220, 224,
    227, 250, 258, 263, 274, 277,
    284–288
abstraction
    created by actions in space, 277
    creative thinking, 263
    diagrams, 288
    forced by drawing, 258
    gestures, 115, 130, 284–285, 288
    graphics and, 284–285
    ordering and, 163, 175
    possibilities left open by, 258
    spatial forms and patterns, 286

spraction, 277, 288
tallies as, 203
trunk and branches, 160
words and, 142
action(s)
    abstractions created by, 277, 288
    bodies and, 48–49
    brain affected by, 17–18
    in comics, 246
    continuum from perception to
        action, 105–106
    dynamics and, 132–133
    enhancements of, 282
    events distinguished from, 216
    as foundation for language, 111
    gestures, 111, 115–116, 130
    on ideas, 86, 88
    intentions of, 48–49
    joint, 27–29
    perception and, 16–19, 21–23

action(s) *(continued)*
  perspective taking and, 66
  sensation and, 16–19, 30
  in space, 115–116, 130, 277, 288
  words for, 184–185, 284–285
addresses, 149, 151–152
alignment, 76–77
allocentric, 66, 69, 143, 146–149,
    151, 153, 165–166, 183–184
alphabetic languages, 194
ambiguity, 83, 137, 142, 148, 150,
    164–166, 199, 232, 263, 264–
    265, 267
anaphors, 245
animals, transitive inferences by,
    173–174
animation, mental, 97–98
animations, educational, 235–236
approximate number system (ANS),
    174–175, 176, 177, 178, 208
architecture, reliance on drawing,
    262–264
arithmetic operations, 206, 207
arrows, 180, 232–235, 233 (fig.),
    234 (fig.)
art, gestures in, 140
artists, exploration and, 274–275
aspect-to-aspect transitions, 245
assembly instructions, 217–220,
    218 (fig.), 219 (fig.)
asymmetric relationships, 232
axes, 62–63

babies, 15, 27, 31, 34, 36, 42, 132,
    164, 174, 214, 279, 281
  actions, intentions, and goals,
    19–21
  gestures and communication, 112–
    114, 117, 131
  integrating action and sensation, 16
bar graphs, 230–231, 230 (fig.)
baseball, catching fly balls, 97–98

basic-level categories of scenes, 49
basic-level categories of things,
    36–39
beat gesture, 117, 133
biases
  approximate number system and,
    176–177
  confirmation, 56–57, 273
  impeding perception and discovery,
    169
  judgments and, 46–47, 73
  linear, 168–169
  perception influenced by, 55–57
  perspective taking to overcome, 273
  time and, 166, 168–169
biomimicry, 270
blindness, 34, 61, 113, 114, 124, 126
bodies
  action and, 48–49
  axes of, 62–63
  in comics, 241
  coordinated actions of, 109
  coordination with others, 26–30
  emotion and, 43, 47–48
  integrating action and sensation,
    16–19
  internal perspective, 10–11
  parts and, 10–16
  people, places, and things
    surrounding, 33–58
  understanding others', 19–20
  words describing, 185
body-centered framework, 66–67
body language, 109–140
body orientation, perspectives of,
    92–94, 92 (fig.)
body parts
  figurative extensions, 14–15
  significance versus size, 13–14
body schema, 18–19
body-to-body communication,
    111–112

borders, 179–180
Borges, Jorge, 35
bottom-up perceptual strategy,
    266–267
boundary, 179–180
boxes, 52, 58, 86, 101, 130, 155–159,
    184, 193, 215, 220, 222, 223,
    226, 227, 231, 236, 238, 241,
    244, 247, 250, 252–254, 278,
    279, 283, 285, 286, 287
    in comics, 244, 252–254
    as containers for stuff and ideas,
        155–159
    in designed world, 286–287
    labels for, 158
    organization of kinds, 158–159
    in the world and in the mind,
        158–159
brain
    action effect on, 17–18
    face recognition, 40–41
    linear conceptualizations of, 169
    maps in, 68–71
    maturation of, 34
    pruning of synapses, 15
    regions for recognizing who, what,
        and where, 34–35
    scene recognition and
        understanding, 49
    structure of, 11–13

calculation, 177–179, 192, 205–207
calendar perspective, 166
calendars, 213
cardinal directions, 74–75, 147, 151
cardinality, 131, 205
cartoons. *See* comics
categorical thinking, 52, 53–54, 224
categories, 43–44
    design of our world, 278–280, 286
    dimensions versus, 51–54, 58
    efficiency of, 77–78

grouping and, 77
hierarchies, 286
kinds and boxes, 158–159
spatial, 77–78
themes and, 159
for things, 35–39
usefulness of, 52
causality
    connection of event units, 216
    dynamics and, 132
    explanations, 239
    gestures and, 123
    ordering events in time, 172
    time and, 212, 214
cave paintings, 192
center, 156, 226
certainty, words denoting, 181
change, words describing, 185
change blindness, 50–51
chemical bonding, 260,
    260 (fig.)–261 (fig.)
children
    animacy, understanding of, 23
    connection of action and
        sensation, 16
    counting by, 131
    gesturing by, 112–114
    goal-directed behavior, 20
    intentions of the actions of others,
        understanding, 21
    recognition by, 34
    thinking by, 19–20
    training joint action, 27
    vocabulary acquisition and
        gestures, 131
    word acquisition, 36
cholera (1854), map of, 200–201
circles, 131, 134, 167–169, 209, 227
cities, layouts of, 72–73
cocktail napkins, 262
cognitive behavior therapy, 273
cognitive collage, 83

cognitive design principles, 193–194,
    199, 201
Cognitive Laws, 289
    First, 15–16, 39, 51, 150, 157,
        169, 194, 240, 274
    Second, 18
    Third, 42
    Fourth, 13, 36, 55, 64
    Fifth, 57, 73, 81
    Corollary of Fifth, 60
    Sixth, 72, 142, 165
    Seventh, 78, 244
    Eighth, 190
    Ninth, 280
cognitive load, 127, 146
cognitive maps, 72, 82–83
cognitive reference points, 81
coherence, check for, 261
collaboration, 29, 136–137, 284
color, 44
comics, 240–255
    advantages of, 241–243
    beginning of, 243
    connections in, 245
    contrasting word and picture,
        249–250
    disconnection in, 245–246
    effectiveness, 241
    end of, 246
    figures of depiction, 250–253,
        251 (fig.)–253 (fig.)
    meaning created by, 247–255
    middle of, 243–246
    motion expressed in, 246
    multiple meanings expressed by,
        252–255
    multiple views in, 247–249,
        248 (fig.)
    rule breaking by, 242
    scrutiny encouraged and rewarded
        by, 242–243
    segmentation, 243–245
    splash pages, 243

visual anaphors to establish
        continuity, 245
    written language in, 249
common fate, 74–75
communication, redundancy in,
        47–48
competence judgments, 46
completeness, check for, 261
complex systems, 132
conceptual maps, 71–72, 201
conducting, gestures and, 138–139
confirmation bias, 56–57, 273
congruent mapping, 94, 129,
        134–135, 208
construction, mental, 95–97, 95 (fig.)
constructive perception, 266
containers, 230
context, map use in, 199
continuity, 245–246
continuous data, 230–231
continuous gestures, 236
conversation, 29–30, 136, 240
cooperation, 27, 41, 282–283
coordination with others, 26–30
correspondence, principle of,
        193–194, 201, 208, 210, 235
counting
    by children, 131
    exact number system (ENS), 177
    gestures and, 124, 134
    notation systems for, 177
    taboos against, 205
    tallies, 203–205, 204 (fig.), 208
    as tool of thought, 206
creating, drawing and, 262–267
creative thinking, 263
creativity, 267–271
cultural differences in math
        diagrams, 207–208
cycle/cyclicity, 134, 167

da Vinci, Leonardo, 140, 257–259,
        261, 270

dance, 138, 211–212
data stories, 240
deictic center, 143–144, 164, 170
deictic gestures, 117
depictions
  of events, people, places, and
    things, 214–216
  figures of, 250–253,
    251 (fig.)–253 (fig.)
descriptions, 72, 126, 127–128, 143,
    144–145, 146, 148, 149–150,
    152, 227, 233–234, 239
design
  empathetic, 269
  gestures and, 137–138
  reliance on drawing, 262–267
  spatial language of the designed
    world, 286–288
designed world as diagrams,
    287–288
designing the world, 277–280,
    277 (fig.)–280 (fig.)
diagrams
  abstraction, 288
  advantage over text, 238
  animations compared to static
    graphics, 235–236
  arrows in, 232–235, 234 (fig.)
  benefits, 261
  comics as, 241
  contrasting to a natural scene,
    222
  creating effective, 238–239
  discourse forms, 239–240
  effectiveness of, 237
  Euler, 209, 209 (fig.)
  Feynman, 210–211, 210 (fig.)
  in *L'Encyclopédie*, 221, 221 (fig.)
  math, 207–208
  memorability, 236–237
  reasoning from, 209–211,
    209 (fig.)–210 (fig.)
  semantics of, 220

tree, 222
world as diagrammed, 287–288
Diderot, Denis, 220–222, 221 (fig.),
    226
differences, sensitivity to, 176
dimensional thinking, 224
dimensions, 51–54, 58
  of dots, lines, and enclosures, 226
  neutral, 223, 225
  value-laden, 223, 225
direct mapping, 148, 208, 238, 261
direction judgments, 78
directionality, 170–171
directions
  arrows and, 232
  egocentric perspective and,
    143–144
  frame of reference and, 146–147
  route, 144–145, 146, 182
  sketch maps, 145
discourse, forms of, 239–240
discrete data, 230–231
discrete gestures, 236
distance
  quality or value as symbolic, 173
  symbolic, 173, 175
distance judgments
  distortion related to perspective,
    81–82
  reference points as proxy for, 80–81
  spatial categories as proxies for,
    78–79
distant perspective, 181
distortion
  of approximate number system,
    176
  on maps, 199, 201
  in time, 166–167
divergent thinking, 266, 269
dots, 157–158, 163
drawing
  artists, 274–275
  to create, 262–267

drawing *(continued)*
  as empirical method, 258–259
  in the mind, 94–97
  new interpretations, discovering,
    264–267, 265 (fig.)
  to see and discover, 257–259
  to understand and learn, 259–261
  unintended discoveries, 264
  See also sketches
dynamics, 132–133

edges, 157
ego, moving, 164–165
egocentric body-centered framework,
    66–67, 149, 150–151
egocentric perspective, 65–66,
    142–146, 153, 183
egocentric reference frame, 151
Einstein, Albert, 140, 163
embedded figures, 266
embedded perspectives, 274
emblems, 116
embodiment, 23
emojis, 242
emotional mirroring, 112
emotions
  appraisal of, 44
  cooperation and, 41
  eyes and, 45–46
  faces and, 41–45
  gestures and, 121–122
  judgments of, 43
  positive and negative, 42
  valence, 42, 47
empathetic design, 269
empathetic perspective, 269–270
empathy, 42
  emotional mirroring, 112
  lack of, 184
  perspective taking, 273
empirical research, drawing as form
    of, 258–259
empirical semantics, 227

enclosures, 226–227
entorhinal cortex, 68–71, 147, 156
entrainment, 29–30, 111, 137
environment
  gestures and descriptions of, 126
  spatial perspective in new, 64
epidemiology, 201
error, 17, 29, 39, 47, 75–80, 83,
    86, 89, 91, 94, 97, 133, 148,
    174–175, 181, 192, 208
estimates, 174–175, 182, 208
Euler diagram, 209, 209 (fig.)
events
  actions distinguished from, 216
  background, 247
  cyclical, 167–169
  depictions of, 214–216
  distortions in time, 166–167
  ordering in time, 170–172
  segmentation, 243
evolution, 70, 110–111
exact number system (ENS), 174,
    177–179, 208
expertise, 263, 265–266
explanations, 35, 102, 103, 123, 127,
    133, 144, 168, 182, 190, 193,
    201, 216–221, 235, 239
  knowledge and understanding
    increased by creating, 260
  verbal, 259–261
  visual, 259–261, 260 (fig.)–261 (fig.)
exploration, 274–275
eyes, 20, 29, 39, 40, 45–46, 48–49,
    59, 62–63, 90, 118, 122, 180,
    222, 262, 284

face blindness, 41
face-to-face communication,
    242–243
faces
  emotion and, 41–45
  eyes, 45–46
  memory for, 41

recognizing, 40–41
traits and, 46–47
far, perspective and, 181
feet, enhancements of, 281
Feynman, Richard, 58, 253–254
Feynman diagram, 210–211,
210 (fig.)
figures of depiction, 250–253,
251 (fig.)–253 (fig.)
First General Fact Worth
Remembering, 14
fixation, release from, 266, 268
forecasters, 271–273
forms, 156–157
in designed world, 288
ideas and, 284–286
qualities of, 156
in space, 285–286
frame of reference, 74, 143,
146–147
language differences and, 150–151
mixed when talking, 149
frames, 247
Freud, Sigmund, 160–161
future, planning for, 71, 190–191

games, cooperation and, 282–283
Gasoline Alley (comic strip), 247,
248 (fig.)
gender differences, 101, 103
General Cognitive Design Principles,
193–194, 199
geography, 72–83
geometric analogies, 95–97, 95 (fig.)
geometry, 156–157, 209
gestures, 48, 109–140
abstraction, 115, 130, 284–285,
288
as actions in space, 115–116, 130
as actions on invisible objects
(ideas), 284
by babies, 112–114
beats, 117, 133

benefits, 148
cardinality understanding helped
by, 131
circular, 106, 131, 134, 168
continuous, 236
deictic, 117–118
directionality, in describing events,
171
discrete, 236
emblems, 116
entrainment, 111, 137
environmental descriptions, 126
explicit nature of, 137
graphics compared to, 114–115
how representational gestures
work, 130
iconic, 118
to locate things when face-to-face,
148
metaphoric, 118–119
mismatches with words, 120–121
one-to-one, 120, 130
points, 117–118
in primates, 110–111
reasons for using, 113–114
role in guiding and teaching, 283
as social glue, 136–140
space, time, and causality
represented by, 121–123
spatial communication, 104
as spatial-motor, 126, 128
talking aided by, 124
thinking aided by, 124–130
thought revealed by, 119–121,
125, 130–131
thoughts of others changed by,
131–134
truncated action, 111
types, 116–119
words compared to, 110
glyphs, 220, 226–227
goal-directed behavior, 20
grammar, 110, 114, 116

graphics, 284–285
  gestures compared to, 114–115
  See also diagrams
graphs, 223
  bar, 230–231, 230 (fig.)
  lines, 230–232, 230 (fig.)
gravity, 1, 63, 187, 223
grid cells, 69–72
grouping, 74, 75–77
Guidonian hand, 135–136, 135 (fig.)
gutter, 244

habituation of looking, 20
handedness, 63
handprints, 192
hands, 284
  enhancement of actions of, 282
  Guidonian, 135–136, 135 (fig.)
  pointing by, 232
  use in math or counting, 134–135,
    178, 179
hierarchical organization
  kinds, 159
  partonomies, 77–78, 159
  spatial, 77–79
  trees, 159–161
hippocampus, 68–71, 147, 156
homeostasis, 169, 271
homunculus, 11–13, 12 (fig.)
horizontal direction as neutral,
    223–224
horizontal plane, 170–172
hypotheses, perception overridden
    by, 55–57

iconic gestures, 118
icons, 220, 236
ideas
  actions on, 86
  arrays of, 156
  brain structure and, 156
  forms and, 284–286
  gestures and, 284–285

metaphoric gestures depictions of,
    118–119
  new, 85
  nodes for, 155
  points and lines in, 157
  thinking and, 284
images
  animating, 97–98
  creating, 94–97
imitation, 22, 30, 31, 283
improvisation, 267
inference, 55, 57, 72
  categories and, 77
  gesturing and, 126
  from line graphs, 230–232
  order and, 173–174, 175, 176
  from tables, 231–232
  transitive, 172, 173–174, 176
innovation, 267–268
inside perspective, 182, 273
insider knowledge, 23–24
instructions, 216–220, 218 (fig.),
    219 (fig.)
intentions, 21, 48–49
Ishango bone, 204, 204 (fig.)

joint action, 27–29
judgments, 46–47, 72–73, 79, 82

Kandinsky, Wassily, 229–230, 249
Kanizsa figures, 229, 229 (fig.)
kinds, 158–159
Klee, Paul, 229–230, 232, 259
knowledge, dissemination and
    accumulation of, 190
Krazy Kat (Herriman), 250, 253 (fig.)

labels, 36–39, 158
landmarks, 80–81, 147–148, 152, 228
language
  allocentric perspective and, 147
  alphabetic, 194
  anaphors, 245

in comics, 249
describing space and action in
    space, 184–187
development of, 186
discourse forms, 239
evolution of, 110–111
gestures and graphics compared
    to, 115
logographic, 194
manner of motion, expressions of,
    246
ordering and, 175
perspectives and, 150–151
points and lines in, 157
semantic congruity, 175–176
spatial of the designed world,
    286–288
thought and, 90, 186
time and, 164, 170–171
writing, 192, 194
Last Supper (da Vinci), 140
laws in the world, 287
laws of cognition. *See* Cognitive Laws
L'Encyclopédie (Diderot and
    d'Alembert), 221, 221 (fig.)
line graphs, 230–231, 230 (fig.)
linear bias, 168–169
lines, 229–230
    aliases of, 156
    asymmetric, 180
    as basic building blocks, 157
    boundaries and, 179–180
    in designed world, 286–287
    directionality, 170–171
    edges, 157
    illusory, 229 (fig.)
    inferences from, 230–232
    inside perspectives, 182
    in Kanizsa figures, 229, 229 (fig.)
    meanings of, 238
    in the mind and in the world, 163
    movement and, 228–230
    order and, 163, 171–172, 175, 180

as polysemous, 227
on sketch maps, 228
time on, 163–165
ubiquity of, 229
links
    in networks, 161
    nodes (boxes) connected by,
        155–156
    patterns of, 156
Little Nemo (McCay), 250, 251 (fig.)
Little Sammy Sneeze (McCay), 250,
    252 (fig.)
logic, Euler diagrams, 209, 209 (fig.)
logographic writing, 194
London tube map, 198–199
looking, habituation of, 20

mapping
    abstract concepts to space, 224
    congruent, 134–135
    direct, 148, 208, 238, 261
    reading/writing order and,
        223–225
maps, 194–203, 283
    as allocentric, 183–184
    ancient and historic, 94–199,
        195 (fig.)–197 (fig.), 200 (fig.)
    in the brain, 68–71
    conceptual, 71–72, 201
    effect on the world, 192
    flattened spatial framework, 67
    history of, 67–68
    London tube, 198–199
    math notation compared, 207–208
    in minds as cognitive collages,
        72–73
    perspective, 146–148
    pitch, 211
    representations, 87
    rotation and alignment errors in
        fictional maps, 74–77
    route, 227–228, 228 (fig.)
    rules of thumb for design, 201–203

maps *(continued)*
    sketch, 145, 227–228, 228 (fig.), 285
    spatial, 71–72
    of stars, 195
    stories and, 68
    as surveys, 182–183
    use in context, 199
    uses for, 199–201
marking, 138
marks in space, 220, 226–227
Marshall Islanders, 196, 196 (fig.), 198
math notation, 192, 206, 207–208
mathematics, 203–208
    diagrams and culture, 207–208
    number systems, 174–179
    skills, spatial skills and, 102
    space in, 208
    tallies, 203–205, 204 (fig.)
    use of hand in, 134–135
meaning
    elements of, 238
    expression of multiple, 252–255
mechanical system, 97, 101, 102
memorability, 236–237, 239
memory, 34
    brain structures involved in, 70–71
    for faces, 41
    perception overridden by, 64
    of places, 70
    retrospective and prospective, 71
    for scenes, 50
mental actions, 86, 88, 91–94, 187, 284
mental animation, 97–98
mental construction, 95–97, 95 (fig.)
mental imagery, 61
mental rotation, 88–94, 88 (fig.)
    connection between mental actions and physical ones, 91–94
    gender differences, 101
    gesturing and, 127
    as measure of spatial ability, 90, 99
    visual-spatial transformation, 89
mental spatial framework. *See* spatial framework
metaphor, 187, 220
metaphoric gestures, 118–119
mimicry, social, 111–112
mind
    creativity and, 267–269
    enhancements, 282–283
mind wandering, 268–269
Mind in the Eyes test, 45
mirror neurons, 21–23, 111
mirroring, 21–23, 30–31, 66, 112
moment-to-moment transitions, 245
motion
    in comics, 246
    lines and, 228–230
    reading/writing order and, 225
    in space, 1–2, 283
    time as, 164
motor resonance, 22, 23–25
motor simulation, 23–24
moving ego, 164–165
moving time, 164–165
music, 135–136, 135 (fig.), 211

names for things, 36–39
naming game, 36, 283
narration in comics, 249
narrative arc, 243, 246
narrative voice, in stories, 239
nature, world designed by, 278 (fig.)
navigation, 72
    abilities, 102–103
    gender differences, 103
    neural underpinnings of, 68–71
near, perspective and, 181
networks, 283
    organization of, 156
    outside perspectives, 92, 141, 182
    partonomies, 159
    places and paths, 152–153

representations, 161
  social, 162
  trees, 222, 283
  as trees, 161
neurons, 15
  connections between, 156, 157
  mirror, 21–23, 111
  sensory, 11–13
  single-cell recordings from, 68
  trees and, 160–161
nodes, as boxes, 155
north, on maps, 197–198
notation
  logic and physics, 209–211,
    209 (fig.)–210 (fig.)
  music and dance, 211–212
notation systems, 178–179, 206,
  207–208
notes, visual, 237, 237 (fig.)
number line estimation, 129–130
number systems, 174–175
  approximate, 174–175, 176, 177,
    178, 208
  exact, 175, 177–179, 208
numbers
  notation systems, 178–179
  symbols, 206
  tallies, 203–205, 204 (fig.)

objects, segmentation, 243
one-to-one correspondences, 120,
  130–131, 134–135, 177, 179,
  205, 208, 279, 285–287
order/ordering
  by amount, 174
  direction of, 224–225
  implications of, 175–177
  by non-human animals, 173–174
  number systems, 174–179
  by quality, preference of value,
    173
  space and, 165
  time and, 165, 170–172
  transitive inference, 176
  ubiquity of ordering, 172–174
ordered lines, 180
organizations, perspectives in,
  183–184
outside perspective, 182
overview
  in organizations, 183–184
  perspective, 147, 148, 273–274
  provided by maps, 182–183

page, putting thought on, 67, 97, 123,
  126, 130, 132, 147, 148, 167,
  168, 170–171, 181, 190, 191,
  201, 206–208, 211, 224, 229,
  241–244, 247, 253, 257–275
Paleolithic map, 194–195, 195 (fig.)
paragraphs, prose segmented by, 244
parity rule, 127
partonomies, 77, 78, 159, 160
parts, words describing, 185
past, referring to, 190–191
paths
  asymmetric arrows and, 232
  on maps, 202, 228
  networks, 152–153
  in route descriptions, 144–145
  through time, 165
patterns, 2, 156–157, 185, 277, 279,
  284–288
people, 39–49
  describing, 40
  eyes, 45–46
  faces and emotion, 41–45
  recognition of faces, 40–41
perception
  action and, 16–19, 21–23, 24
  animacy, 23
  biases and, 55–57
  constructive, 266
  continuum from perception to
    action, 105–106
  embodiment, 23

perception *(continued)*
  enhancements of, 282
  impeded by biases, 169
  inference versus, 55
  linked to meaning by segments,
    216
  memory override of, 64
  mind override of, 55–57
  number systems, 174–175
  representations from, 87–88
perceptual regrouping, 264–267
performance, map design and, 203
periphery, 156, 226
perspective, 180–184
  absolute, 147
  allocentric, 143, 146–148, 149,
    153, 165–166, 183–184
  bird's-eye, 147
  on body orientation, 92–94, 92 (fig.)
  calendar, 166
  choosing between yours and mine,
    145–146
  distant spatial, 181
  egocentric, 65–66, 142–146, 153,
    183–184
  embedded, 274
  frames and, 247, 249
  insider, 10, 92–94, 141, 182, 273
  language differences and, 150–151
  maps and, 195, 197–198
  mixing, 149–150
  near and far, 181
  in organizations, 183–184
  outsider, 92, 141, 182
  overview, 147, 148, 273–274
  route, 144
  shared, 142, 143
  spatial reasoning, 81–83
  survey, 147, 148, 166
  switching, 153, 270–271
  taking other, 60, 63–66, 65 (fig.)
  talk and thought about space,
    142–153
  on time, 165–166
  ways to find new, 273–274
perspective taking, 268, 270–271
  and creativity, 270–271
  empathetic, 269
  increasing accuracy of prediction,
    271–273
petroglyph, 189 (fig.), 214–215
physics
  Feynman, 210–211, 210 (fig.)
  gestures and, 127, 129
pictograms, 194, 236
pictures
  associations to, 14
  remembered better than words,
    242
  words contrasting with,
    249–250
places
  brain cells associated to, 68–72
  memory and organization of, 70
  networks, 152–153
  parts and, 159
  recognition, categorization, and
    understanding of, 49–51
  in route descriptions, 145
point-light videos, experiments with,
  24–25
points/pointing, 36, 112, 113,
  117–118, 120, 122, 124, 126,
  129, 131, 136, 137, 144, 145,
  151, 179, 180, 184, 196, 229,
  230, 243, 283, 284, 285
  aliases of, 156
  as basic building blocks, 157
  on diagrams, 156, 157, 191, 230,
    236
  on maps, 199, 202, 227, 228
  as stationary, 228
power, mapping of, 226
practice
  mental rotation improvement with,
    91

spaced versus massed, 266
spatial ability, 99, 103–105
prediction, 271–273
preferences, 173
    map design and, 203
    ordering and, 224–225
prepositions, with spatial meaning, 226
primates, imitation in, 283
Principle of Correspondence, 193–194, 201, 208, 210, 235
Principle of Use, 193–194, 201, 208, 210, 235
prismatic glasses, experiments with, 16–17
problem-solving strategies, gestures and, 121, 125, 127–130
process, idea of, 271
production, map design and, 203
production, preference, performance (Three Ps), 203, 231, 239
propositions, 186, 210
prosopagnosia, 41
proximity, 1, 75–76, 187

qualities, as ordering principle, 173
quantity, as ordering/organizing principle, 175–176, 224–225

rats, navigation experiments with, 68–69
reading/writing direction, mapping and, 223–225
reasoning, from diagrams, 209–211, 209 (fig.)–210 (fig.)
reference frames. *See* frame of reference
reference points, 80–81
regrouping, 264–267
relationships, words describing, 185
representations
    described, 87–88
    formats and properties of, 87–88

perceptions and, 87–88
    sources of, 87
    worldly expressions of thought, 193
rhythm, 26, 29, 31
role-playing, as perspective taking, 273
Rosling, Hans, 53–54, 280
rotation, 74–75
rotation, mental, 88–94, 88 (fig.)
route
    as egocentric, 183–184
    perspective, 144, 145, 146, 152, 165, 166, 182, 183
    as sets of directions, 51, 79, 92, 94, 113, 114, 144, 145, 148, 152, 182, 183, 202, 203, 228, 232, 285
route descriptions, 144–145, 146
route maps
    cognitive design guidelines for, 202–203
    elements of, 227–228
    production, preference, performance, 203
rubber arm, experiments with, 18–19
Rubin, Gideon, 4
Rules of Thumb
    for assembly instructions, 219–220
    for map design, 201–203

scenes, 49–50
    change blindness, 50–51
    splitting, 247
schematic maps, 199
scripts, 85–86
scrutiny, comics and, 242–243
Second General Fact Worth Remembering, 123
seeing, words of, 184
segmentation, 216, 243–245
self-regulation, 169
semantic congruity, 175–176

semantics
  of arrows, 233
  of diagrams, 220–237
  empirical, 227
sensation, action and, 16–19, 30
sensory input, 11–13, 15
shape
  for recognizing and categorizing
    things, 35
  words describing, 185
similarity
  cognitive reference points and, 81
  as distance in conceptual space, 79
size, words describing, 185
sketch maps, 145, 227–228, 228 (fig.),
    285
sketches
  architects, designers, 262–266
  cocktail napkins, 262
  dance sequences, 138
  new interpretations of, 264–267,
    265 (fig.)
smiling, 42–43
social glue, gestures as, 136–140
social judgments, 73, 79, 82
social mimicry, 111–112
social networks, 162
space
  actions in, 115–116, 130, 277, 288
  around us, 59–83
  of the body, 9–31
  forms in, 285–286
  gestures and, 122
  language and, 184–187
  mapping abstract concepts to, 224
  marks in, 220, 226–227
  in math, 208
  moving in, 283
  order and, 165
  place in, 223
  talk and thought about, 142–153,
    155–156

time and, 163–165
spatial ability, 98–106
  acquiring spatial skills, 103–105
  assembly ability, 217–218
  gender differences, 101
  genetic and environmental
    influences on, 99
  improvement with practice, 99
  measuring, 99–101, 100 (fig.)
  mental rotation and, 90, 99
  scope of, 105–106
  uses of, 99, 102–103
spatial alignment, 76–77
spatial descriptions, shared
    perspective and, 143
spatial framework, 73
  body-centered, 60, 66–67
  flattening, 66–68
  new environments, 64
  taking a different spatial
    perspective, 60, 63–66
spatial hierarchies, 77–79
spatial language of the designed
    world, 286–288
spatial maps, 71–72
spatial-motor reasoning, 93, 126,
    128, 210
spatial-numerical association of
    response (SNARC) effect, 176
spatial position, use for calculations,
    206
spatial reasoning, 76–77
  alignment, 76–77
  common fate, 74–75
  grouping, 74, 75–77
  hierarchical organization, 77–79
  rotation, 74–75
  straightening, 80
spatial schemas, 72–73
spatial thinking, 57
  abstract thought and, 71–74
  directionality and, 62–63

speech balloons, in comics, 249
spiral, 106, 156, 169, 185, 191, 240, 277, 280, 288
splash pages, 243
spontaneous graphing, 223–226
sports, spatial abilities and, 104
spraction, 277, 288
stars, mapping of, 195
stories, 239–255
    comics, 240–255
    as discourse form, 239–240
    facts overridden by, 240
straightening, and spatial reasoning, 80
Stratton, George, 17
structure, 2–3, 132–133
subordinate categories of things, 37
superforecasters, 271–273
superordinate categories, 36–37, 49
surveys, 152, 182, 183–184
symbolic distance, 175
symbolic thought, 190
symbols
    for arithmetic operations, 206
    for numbers, 179, 206, 208
    for position in space, 206
    words as, 141
synecdoche, 220
system
    action, 12, 24
    address, 73
    causal, 123
    cognitive, 205
    complex, 132
    computer, 169, 283
    diagrammatic, 221
    dynamic, 132, 233–234
    geometry, 209
    mechanical, 97, 98, 101, 102, 123, 128, 223, 233–234
    mirror, 21, 23, 25, 30, 31, 66
    motion, 24

navigation, 103, 152
nervous, 18, 169, 176
notation, 178–179, 206, 208, 211, 212
number, 174–175, 176–179, 182, 205, 208
self-regulatory, 169
sensory, 11, 15
STEM, 102, 160, 233–234
transport, 198
visual, 35

T-O map, 197, 197 (fig.)
tables, inferences from, 231–232
talking
    about space, 142–153, 155–156
    about time, 170–172
    from an allocentric perspective, 147
    gestures and, 124
    linear nature of, 152
    mixed perspectives and reference frames, 149
    thought and, 141–142
tally, 203–205, 204 (fig.), 208
taste, categories of, 43
taxonomy, 77, 159–160
teaching, 121, 129, 190, 237, 241, 260, 282–283
technology, 270, 281–282
themes, as organizing principle, 159, 279, 286
thermostat, 169, 271
things
    hierarchical organization, 36–39
    names/labels for, 36–39
    recognition, categorization, and understanding of, 35–39
    words describing, 185
thinking/thought, 283–286
    as actions on ideas, mental actions, 86, 88, 91, 92, 94, 187, 284

thinking/thought *(continued)*
  categorical, 224
  creative, 263
  dimensional, 224
  divergent, 266, 269
  gestures as aid to, 124–139, 284
  graphics, externalized and
    promoted by, 284–285
  language and, 90
  minimal unit of, 186
  putting into the world, 189–193
  revealed by gestures, 119–121,
    125, 130–131
  symbolic, 190
  talk and, 141–142
  worldly expressions of, 191–193
Three Ps (production, preference,
  performance), 203, 231, 239
time
  allocentric perspective on,
    165–166
  calendar perspective, 122, 164,
    166, 170, 171, 182
  causality, 212, 214
  circular, 167–169
  directionality, 170, 213, 223–225
  distortions and biases, 166–167
  gestures and, 122–123, 133–134,
    171
  language and, 164, 170–171
  on lines, 163–165
  measurement, 212–214
  as movement, 164–165
  moving ego, 164–165
  moving time, 164–165
  music notation, 211
  order and, 165, 170–173
  space and, 163–165
  unidirectional, 167
toddler, 36, 131, 194, 241
tool use, 17–18
top-down cognitive strategy,
  266–267

trade-offs, 15, 39
transactions, between mind and
    world, 206–207
transformation order, 96–97
transformations
  geometric analogies, 95–97,
    95 (fig.)
  mental as internalized actions, 88
  mental rotation, 88–94
  of thought, 85–106
transitions in comics, 244–245
transitive inference, 172, 173–174,
    176
trees, 159–161, 222, 283
turns, in route maps, 202, 227

unintended discoveries, 264
use, principle of, 193–194, 201, 208,
    210, 235

valence, 42, 47
value, as ordering principle, 173
verbal ability, 99
vertical direction, value carried by,
    223, 225
vertical plane, 170–172
visual explanations, 260–261,
    260 (fig.)–261 (fig.)
visual-spatial reasoning, 127
visual-spatial transformation, 88–97,
    98–99, 99–101, 105–106
voice, emotion and, 47–48

wall paintings, in Egyptian tombs,
    215, 215 (fig.), 216
when, brain's processing of, 34–35
where, sense of, 59–60
Whorf-Sapir hypothesis, 151
words, 184–186
  abstraction, 142
  acquisition by children, 36
  for action, 184–185, 284–285
  arbitrary nature of, 113

in comics, 249
denoting certainty versus
uncertainty, 181
describing actions, objects,
locations, or relationships,
184–185
gestures compared to, 110
literal and abstract usage, 185
mismatches with gestures,
120–121
pictures contrasting with,
249–250

pictures remembered better than,
242
remote associations among, 266
of seeing, 184
as symbols, 141
world, designing of the, 277–280,
277 (fig.)–280 (fig.)
writing, 192, 194

yawns, contagious nature of, 42

zero, 178–179

BARBARA TVERSKY is an emerita professor of psychology at Stanford University and a professor of psychology at Teachers College at Columbia University. She is also the president of the Association for Psychological Science. Tversky has published over two hundred scholarly articles about memory, spatial thinking, design, and creativity and regularly speaks about embodied cognition at interdisciplinary conferences and workshops around the world. She has had the joy and privilege of collaborating not only with psychologists but also with linguists, scientists, philosophers, computer scientists, designers, artists, and more. She lives in New York.